CHANGING ROLES OF WOMEN WITHIN THE CHRISTIAN CHURCH IN CANADA

Canadian religious history has been written with relatively little reference to the role of women. Throughout the years, the church itself has intensified this problem by restricting the options of women – excluding them from valued roles and senior positions. In the past, Christian women were obliged to find alternative avenues for the expression of their faith and, as a result, their experience has been unusually rich and varied. This pioneering anthology traces the history of Canadian women in the Roman Catholic, Anglican, and Protestant traditions from the early days through the 1960s.

Seventeen Canadian scholars tell the stories of individuals who have worked in traditional and nontraditional roles, alone and as members of groups, both within and outside church structures. All of the articles present new or little-known material, relating the faith, determination, and inventiveness of women whose experience has so far been overlooked. The volume includes an introductory overview of women's church work as well as a comprehensive bibliography of papers and books published about women in the Christian church in Canada, both in English and in French.

The incorporation of feminist analysis and an emphasis on gender issues set this collection apart from all other studies of Canadian church history. A unique and valuable book, it not only fills a void in the chronicles of religion, it adds an important new dimension to Canadian history.

ELIZABETH GILLAN MUIR is a lecturer in Canadian Studies, University of Waterloo, and is on the national executive staff of the United Church of Canada.

MARILYN FÄRDIG WHITELEY is an independent scholar affiliated with the Centre for the Study of Religion in Canada, Emmanuel College, University of Toronto

EDITED BY
ELIZABETH GILLAN MUIR AND
MARILYN FÄRDIG WHITELEY

Changing Roles of Women within the Christian Church in Canada

UNIVERSITY OF TORONTO PRESS
Toronto Buffalo London

© University of Toronto Press Incorporated 1995
Toronto Buffalo London
Printed in Canada

ISBN 0-8020-0669-8 (cloth)
ISBN 0-8020-7623-8 (paper)

Printed on acid-free paper

Canadian Cataloguing in Publication Data

Main entry under title:

Changing roles of women within the Christian church in Canada

Includes bibliographical references and index.
ISBN 0-8020-0669-8 (bound) ISBN 0-8020-7623-8 (pbk.)

1. Women in christianity – Canada – History.
2. Women in church work – Canada – History.
I. Muir, Elizabeth Gillan, 1934–   . II. Whiteley,
Marilyn Färdig.

BV639.W7C53 1995   270'.082   C94-932514-7

University of Toronto Press acknowledges the financial assistance to its
publishing program of the Canada Council and the Ontario Arts Council.

This book has been published with the help of a grant from the Canadian
Federation for the Humanities, using funds provided by the Social Sciences and
Humanities Research Council of Canada.

To the memory of Elizabeth Dart,
and L.H. Dimsdale,
and that great host of Canadian women,
known and unknown,
who have done what they could.

Contents

Preface

In November 1990 twenty-six scholars from across Canada gathered in Toronto to share their research on the contribution of women to the Christian tradition in Canada and to determine the best process for producing a collective history of these women. Modern technology brought into the discussions two others who were unable to attend. The meeting, under the auspices of the Centre for the Study of Religion in Canada at Emmanuel College, had been convened by Elizabeth Gillan Muir and Marilyn Färdig Whiteley, the editors of this volume.

Drawing upon the model of feminist scholarship, it was agreed that the methodology for this anthology should be collegial. The editors had already solicited abstracts of proposed contributions from the participants and had circulated these prior to this first collaboration. Because of access before the meeting to each other's analysis and theses, the participants were able to suggest how their own contribution fit into the whole and to offer constructive criticism concerning the theories others posited. The women and men determined a structure for the volume and went away committed to the methodology and the project. In some cases theories were modified. In every instance work was enriched as discoveries were made about how a particular piece of research threw light upon another. Some researchers discovered that churchwomen they had been studying appeared in another person's research. One participant noted that in all his years of contributing to scholarly projects, never previously had he been invited to have such major input into another scholar's work.

Working in a collaborative fashion is a slow process. For several months the editors and writers consulted and shared manuscripts, modified, and revised. The editors themselves found co-writing to be a challenge. Yet we believe that the result is worth the struggle. The anthology is more than just a collection of isolated works: Each chapter bears the stamp of the thinking of the whole body.

The history of women in the Christian church in Canada, however, is still far from complete. There are major gaps, such as the contributions of women in the Society of Friends (the Quaker tradition) and the Salvation Army, and the role of Native women. In some instances the timing was inopportune for historians working in this arena to participate in this project. In many areas of women's work in the church the surface has barely been scratched. There is still much to be done before a definitive study of women in the Christian church in Canada can be realized. But the contributors to this project believe that the ground has been broken; this work may inspire and encourage others to press forward with new study and insights.

A number of people have supported this project, offering their wisdom and encouragement. Phyllis Airhart and Roger Hutchinson of the Centre for the Study of Religion in Canada have been helpful in a variety of ways, and Phyllis Airhart assisted by reading some of the manuscripts and making editorial suggestions. Alison Prentice of the Ontario Institute for Studies in Education gave welcome direction. And a number of scholars who were themselves unable to participate, demonstrated their support in a very useful way: they let us know of others who were working in the field. Laura Macleod and Gerald Hallowell guided us through the publishing process at the University of Toronto Press. To all of these we are grateful. We are also indebted to the Canadian Federation for the Humanities for its support.

Unfortunately, not all of those participating in the initial colloquium are represented in this work. Space constraints have resulted in the inclusion of only a selection of the manuscripts produced. But working together with other scholars from across the country has enriched the chapters that follow.

The editors are well aware that, with some exceptions, reference to the extensive contribution to religion made by women in French Canada is missing. It was felt that such a large subject needed to be dealt with separately in another volume. French works have been included in the bibliography, however, and we are indebted to Micheline d'Allaire of the University of Ottawa for her assistance in editing an early version of these entries.

Contributors

Marilyn Barber teaches history at Carleton University in Ottawa, specializing in Canadian immigration and women's history. She is currently writing a book on the Fellowship of the Maple Leaf.

Sharon Anne Cook is an associate professor in the Faculty of Education, University of Ottawa. She has recently written *Through Sunshine and Shadow: The Woman's Christian Temperance Union, Evangelicalism and Social Reform in Ontario, 1874–1930*.

Marlene Epp is a doctoral candidate in Canadian history at the University of Toronto. She has published articles on Mennonite women and is the author of *Mennonites in Ontario: An Introduction*.

Rosemary R. Gagan is an adjunct professor in the Department of History, University of Winnipeg, where she teaches women's history. She is the author of *A Sensitive Independence: Canadian Methodist Women Missionaries in Canada and the Orient, 1881–1925*.

John Webster Grant is Professor Emeritus at Emmanuel College of Victoria University, Toronto. Among his many books is *Moon of Wintertime*, an account of the interaction of Christian missionaries with Canada's Native peoples.

Helen G. Hobbs has taught for a number of years at Vancouver School of Theology and is the author of *The Prophets Speak*. She is currently the minister at Ashcroft United Church in Ashcroft, British Columbia.

Mary Anne MacFarlane, a diaconal minister, works as editor and resource consultant in adult education for the United Church of Canada. She has published several articles on the history of religious education in Canada.

Katherine M.J. McKenna is an assistant professor in the Institute of Women's Studies at Queen's University, Kingston. Her most recent publication is *A Life of Propriety: Anne Murray Powell and Her Family, 1755–1849.*

Elizabeth Gillan Muir teaches Canadian studies at the University of Waterloo and is on the national staff of the United Church of Canada. She is the author of *Petticoats in the Pulpit: The Story of Early Nineteenth-Century Methodist Women Preachers in Upper Canada*

Jan Noel teaches Canadian history at Erindale College, University of Toronto. She has published articles on women in early French Canada and is the author of *Canada Dry: Temperance Crusades before Confederation.*

Diana Pedersen is an assistant professor of history at Concordia University, Montreal, where she teaches Canadian history and women's history. She has published several articles on the Young Women's Christian Association.

H. Miriam Ross teaches in the Faculty of Theology, Acadia University, Nova Scotia. She has published several articles about Maritime Baptist women missionaries (1867–1929) and is currently researching the life of Hannah Maria Norris Armstrong.

Elizabeth Smyth is a faculty member with the Ontario Institute for Studies in Education, Northwestern Centre, Thunder Bay. She is engaged in a multiyear historical study of communities of teaching sisters in English Canada.

Laurie C.C. Stanley, an associate professor in the Department of History at St Francis Xavier University, Nova Scotia, is the author of *The Well-Watered Garden: The Presbyterian Church in Cape Breton, 1798–1860.*

Randi R. Warne is currently Director of Women's Studies and an assistant professor of Religious Studies at the University of Wisconsin. Her recent publications include *Literature as Pulpit: The Christian Social Activism of Nellie McClung.*

Margaret Whitehead teaches Canadian women's history at Camosun College, Victoria. She is the author of books and articles on First Nations and Christian churches' contact history, including *They Call Me Father: Memories of Father Nicholas Coccola.*

Marilyn Färdig Whiteley, an independent scholar in church history and women's history, is the author of numerous articles and papers on women in Canadian methodism, and editor of the papers of the missionary and teacher Annie Leake Tuttle.

A PSALM FOR EVERYWOMAN

M.T. Winter

Who will retrieve our stories
from the void of the unremembered?

Who will believe we were who we are
and did all the things we do?

I have seen women breaking bread
and taking the cup of salvation.

I have heard women preaching the word
and teaching theology.

I have met women in mission abroad,
restructuring church and society.

I have met women here at home
doing much the same.

I have sung songs that women have written,
but seldom in church on Sunday.

I have even prayed to my Mother God,
but not in the sacred rites.

Where are the books to record the deeds
of the prophets of the present?

Where are the ones who will keep and preserve
the truth of women's ways?

Who will take the time we have taken
to find the lost lives of our sisters?

Who will seek us and find us?
Who will remember our names?

WOMANWORD: A Feminist Lectionary and Psalter by Miriam Therese Winter. Copyright © 1990 by Medical Mission Sisters. Reprinted by permission of the Crossroad Publishing Company

CHANGING ROLES OF WOMEN WITHIN THE
CHRISTIAN CHURCH IN CANADA

Introduction:
Putting Together the Puzzle
of Canadian Women's Christian Work

ELIZABETH GILLAN MUIR and

MARILYN FÄRDIG WHITELEY

At the 1920 jubilee celebrations of the Maritime Baptist Woman's Mission-ary Union, the guest speaker, Mrs Peabody, unwittingly illustrated wom-en's place throughout the history of the Christian church in Canada. Claiming that 'God intended women to be homemakers, to be teachers, especially of little children, and to take care of sick people,' Peabody rein-forced the idea that permeated both society and the church at that time: Women were expected to fulfil the traditional roles of nurturer and care-giver (see H. Miriam Ross, in this volume). Yet Mrs Peabody's presence on the platform belied her words. The accepted mythology of woman's place was contradicted by the reality of a woman assuming leadership in a public forum, addressing a group of women who that year had raised and admin-istered almost eighty-four thousand dollars.

This tension between mythology and reality can be found in every decade and in almost every branch of the Christian church in Canada over at least the past two centuries. What women were actually doing differed substantially from what official records describe. Traditional histories are accounts of institutions, their breakups and mergers, their conflicts or accommodation with government. They tell the stories of men who held power in the structure and developed theologies that were taught in class-rooms and argued in councils not open to women. Most reports have ignored the presence and activity of women within religious institutions. In those few instances when women are mentioned, their work is generally downplayed, especially if it falls outside society's traditional expectations for women. Women's activity was often named as helping, their initiative and their skilled labour erased from memory.

Recently some scholars have been attempting to redress this deficiency. In Canada, Wendy Mitchinson did pioneering work in her 1977 dissertation 'Aspects of Reform: Four Women's Organizations in Nineteenth Century Canada,' and in articles describing portions of her findings. Research in the 1980s has led to full-length studies including those by Marta Danylewycz and Ruth Compton Brouwer. Other books and scattered articles have been giving attention to women's church work. The chapters included in this volume greatly extend the picture of the work of religiously motivated women in Canada. Yet the picture they paint is still preliminary. Not only are there many important areas awaiting research; there are also difficulties facing researchers in the field.

In her study of women and social welfare work in the Montreal region, Jan Noel (in this volume) has compared her problem to 'putting together a jigsaw puzzle that has many lost or warped pieces.' This is true for the story of all Canadian women and their Christian work. Much of their activity is lost because it was not recorded: It simply seemed so ordinary. Other parts are lost because, although they were documented, those records were not valued and preserved. Then there are warped pieces of information that are difficult to interpret outside their original context. Those who would understand the story of how Canadian women have lived out their Christian faith must often be creative both in their search for source materials and in their approach to what they have found.

The traditional records of the churches can yield new information when they are read afresh. Minute books and ledgers of local congregations document the work of women in their home churches, and denominational reports and journals make it possible to trace the change in women's status in the national bodies. In some parts of the church, a tradition of record-keeping encouraged the maintenance and preservation of records of women's work. For example, the faithful annalists of Roman Catholic sisterhoods produced documents that are now invaluable for our understanding of these religious communities and their activities. The members of some other women's associations, such as missionary societies, the Woman's Christian Temperance Union (WCTU) and the Young Women's Christian Association (YWCA), attended regularly to the minute books and ledgers that now await study. Church periodicals frequently published a rich mix of material, including prescriptive literature, reports on women's work, and writing by women; at times they even offered space for a voice of dissent.

Women's writing about their religious beliefs and activities, however, includes not only the brief letters and articles found in church papers, but longer works as well. For example, Eva Hasell wrote books about the caravan mission in western Canada that she founded in 1920, and Nellie

McClung presented in both fiction and non-fiction the views that made her an important Christian social reformer. Other women wrote not for publication, but for themselves, their families, and their friends. Where these diaries, autobiographies, and letters survive, they add immeasurably to our understanding. But many women do not leave such personal writings. The traces of their lives may be found only in public records, in the membership roles of churches, the registers of schools, and the reception books of convents. Yet some historians of women have learned that when these records are analysed, even they can serve as valuable resources for piecing together some aspects of women's history. Other researchers are collecting oral history so that they may study the recent past and ensure that those recollections will serve as a record for the future.

Patient and creative workers have begun to seek out and use documentation that lets us start to put together the puzzle. Although the picture is incomplete, we can see something of the enormous amount of labour that women undertook; the variety of leadership positions they held; the pressures that society, the church hierarchy, and peers brought to bear upon these women leaders; and the significance that faith and denominational heritage held in women's everyday lives. The research of the writers included in this volume allows us to identify in a preliminary way the outstanding contours of that picture: the discrepancy between the myth of women's work and its reality, and the energy and creativity with which women sought to find and claim those territories that were open to them.

CONSTRAINTS

Throughout the history of the Christian church, women as well as men have expressed their spirituality in a variety of ways. Feminist historians have uncovered periods when women held professional and administrative positions in religious institutions or had other opportunities to serve on an equal basis with their male peers. Yet, by and large, the most highly valued offices in the churches have been open mainly or even exclusively to men and closed to women. Excluded from such traditional avenues, women have developed their own methods of expressing their Christian faith.

The factors that motivated women to preach, enter religious communities, or engage in Christian service, however, were often the same as those that motivated men. Many felt that God had called them to this work, and they could not disobey. For some, this was a calling to preach or to evangelize within their own communities. For others, saving 'heathen souls' was a primary motivation for missionary work that might be done abroad, among the Native peoples in Canada, or within the crowded areas of Canada's growing cities. Christian women, like Christian men, also frequently sought to give creative expression to their faith not simply through preaching, but through serving those whose temporal needs they recognized or through attempting to reform society. Often their work cannot be placed neatly in one category or another, for their labours were creative mixtures. The categories of evangelism and social action are more nuanced than it may sometimes appear.

While women's motivation for religious activity may have been similar to that of men, nevertheless a number of factors in the church and in society placed severe constraints on women's work. Women were forced to be both determined and inventive in finding ways to live out the gospel beyond the walls of their home.

Ever since the Industrial Revolution effectively separated the workplace from the home, woman's work was increasingly restricted to that of mother and housewife. Religion, too, became a function of the private sphere, and the religious education of children the preserve of women. Instructing young children in Christian precepts was an important function, women were assured, for the future of the world rested upon the family. Destined to be the guardians of children's moral and spiritual upbringing and the keepers of the nations's religious and ethical values, women were sheltered from the seamier side of life. Not for them was the dirty public world of commerce, politics, finance, or the professions. By the Victorian age, this 'cult of true womanhood' was in full flower, protecting the gentler sex from dangerous activity for which it was thought to be ill-suited. When Mrs Peabody spoke at the 1920 Jubilee celebrations of the Woman's Missionary Union, she was simply articulating beliefs about women's capabilities and purpose in life that were still very much in vogue at that time – unaware that she, herself, had stepped part way outside this mould.

Biblical passages informed, supported, and sanctified this mythology about women. A woman was considered to be both temptress and virgin, both feared as Eve, and worshipped as Mary. As temptress, she was responsible for the fall of humanity: She had encouraged Adam to disobey God in the Garden of Eden. Her punishment for this first sin was to be assigned a role subordinate to man. As virgin, however, she was a saintly being; Like Mary, the mother of Jesus, she was placed upon a pedestal and adored. In either case, society believed that limits needed to be placed around a woman's activity. As a saint, she must be kept from defilement; as a siren she must be kept from defiling man. A literal interpretation of

Pauline letters in the New Testament reinforced the thinking that women's position in the church should be severely restricted. The early Christian missionary Paul had written that women were to be silent in the church, and wives were to defer to their husbands.

This pattern of interpretation supported the myth of the self-denying Christian woman: either the saint for whom service is natural, or the siren for whom it is redemptive. New Testament injunctions to serve the 'brethren' made no distinction according to gender. All were required to serve. Yet the common interpretations of Paul's writing about women and of the creation of Eve as a helpmeet and her responsibility for the fall of humanity combined to give weight to the view that self-sacrificial Christian service was the special duty of Christian women.

These were the myths that placed constraints on women's work. Given this climate of thought, it is surprising that women contributed so much to Canadian religious and social institutions. Indeed a great deal of what they achieved was accomplished within boundaries imposed by predominantly male church hierarchies and social conventions. This was true for women throughout Canadian church history, although women were able to exercise more freedom at certain times and within certain denominations.

Some of the women living in religious communities achieved a measure of independence unavailable to many of their peers, but they were circumscribed by a set of rigid rules that effectively separated them from that part of church and society designated as a male preserve. Generally, as well, women in communities were contained by dress regulations designed to eliminate any hint of sexuality, thus reducing the possibility of leading their brothers into temptation. Possibly it was easier to exercise control on women in religious communities set apart from mainstream society; yet all women in church and society were effectively set apart and carried an unequal burden. Higher ethical standards were demanded of them than of men.

Marriage and childbearing, considered to be the destiny of women, either prevented women from professional involvement in the church or added extra responsibilities if they were allowed to work in their profession once they married. Many women opted to remain single and continue in careers where they could. But because marriage was considered to be women's ultimate fulfilment, women who did not marry suffered social stigma and emotional turmoil. Only single women in Roman Catholic communities were in a somewhat different position. As 'brides of Christ,' they were in one sense married. Their choice gave them status within their community of faith.

Canadian women's lives were shaped not only by these ideologies, but by the myth of women's physical weakness as well. Even women who toiled in the mission field, who scrubbed and baked and raised several children, fell heir to the stereotype of the sweet-faced and delicate angel of mercy. Of course some of the women did find mission work too gruelling and either left or succumbed to illness – as did some men – but most of the women who worked as church professionals gave the lie to the myth of female weakness. These women were no hothouse flowers, and the conspicuous strength and initiative of some is echoed in quieter ways in the activities of a host of others.

Although the realities of many women contradicted the stereotypes, mythologies acted as deterrents to women entering the workforce. The concepts of female weakness, of woman's destiny as wife, mother, and spiritual nurturer in the home, and of the family as the backbone of society were so much a part of the social fabric that it was difficult for most women to imagine an alternative. Education for young women also reinforced this image. Girls who attended church-sponsored schools were given the mixed message that all professions should be open to them, yet at the same time the home should receive the greater part of their attention.

Those women who resisted stereotyping and tried to find their fulfilment in what were considered to be traditional male roles met opposition from male hierarchies and male decision-makers whose attitudes had also been shaped by the gender ideals of the day. Men often ignored or disregarded the women, and they rarely sought out their opinions on issues that affected them.

The hostility of men to women's work is easy to identify. Yet other, less obvious, attitudes were also damaging to women. Many experienced the paternalism of men who wished to protect them by removing from weak female shoulders the heavy burden of responsibility. Men protected women by encouraging them to live in religious communities, or by imposing on them higher ethical standards than men required of other men. Generally, whenever and wherever women felt called to Christian ministry outside the home in roles considered to be beyond their natural destiny as caregivers and nurturers, they met persistent male opposition, either undisguised or cloaked as paternalistic protection.

Women also found that the work they did was ignored, devalued, and trivialized. While this can most commonly be inferred by omissions from official records, sometimes it does become visible there, as when Sisters who successfully carried out extremely demanding work were praised only for their good housekeeping, and when dedicated and innovative women attending an international YWCA conference were commended because they 'had found something to do' (see Laurie C.C. Stanley and Diana Pedersen, both in this volume).

OPPORTUNITIES

Operating within the constraints under which they were forced to work, women displayed resourcefulness, adaptability, and skill in working around these obstacles or even using them to their own advantage. Those who faced opponents quoting biblical injunctions learned to use the Bible themselves, reinterpreting passages to support their own or other women's activity. Limited by what they were allowed to do in traditional church programs, some women developed projects of their own that proved to be both effective and popular, and gave women an expanded role in the ministry of the church. In mission fields, many women found that the restrictions imposed on them to labour only with women and children could in fact work in their favour. They seized the opportunity to work in arenas denied to men, and in the process gained considerable leadership and administrative experience.

What was politically and socially acceptable, however, did shift over the centuries, and women were allowed greater liberty during some decades than in others. Surprisingly, in the earlier years of the history of Canada and of the Church in Canada, women had greater freedom and more access to positions of authority and power than they did in the later nineteenth century, although by the latter period women became much more demanding of a number of their rights and more radical in their understanding of what these rights were.

In the earlier periods women appear to have been reasonably content to operate within the boundaries established by society. Although some did chafe against the strictures placed upon them, most of the women active in the church at that time devoted their energies to bringing Christianity to an irreligious society or to people devoid of spiritual opportunities. Women also expressed their religious faith in active concern for the destitute, the sick, and the orphaned, but this was viewed as an extension of their mothering role and not as an attempt to subvert social structures. By the early twentieth century, however, women were becoming vocal in their criticism of church and society, demanding radical change and equal opportunity for all.

Even in periods of limited opportunity for women in the Canadian church, some women were more advantaged than others. Women in religious denominations such as the Methodist Church reaped the benefits of church polity, doctrine, and traditions that were more receptive to women in leadership positions. Because of a charismatic emphasis, male and female followers often accepted women's assertions that they had been called by the Holy Spirit to preach and to lead. It was difficult to quench this flame. The early Methodist use of small groups made up exclusively of women or of men resulted in the need for, and subsequent development of skills among scores of women leaders.

Other women had the advantage of being able to work in areas where men were either unable or unwilling to go. In western Canada some women laboured when men were temporarily absent or unavailable to fill all positions. And in foreign missions, not only did women work more easily with other women, but the customs of many countries dictated that only female missionaries were allowed close contact with women and girls. Often, too, women gained opportunities because they were willing to work under difficult conditions that would not be tolerated by men.

Sometimes it was a question of being in the right place at the right time, and enterprising women might seize opportunities. Women's activities flourished when old norms were broken and old patterns shattered. During social crises, rules were changed; iconoclastic situations allowed women to act differently. The shifting frontier and wartime provided new, though often temporary, possibilities for women.

Certain women had built-in advantages because of birth, education, or marriage, and some benefited from men's support of the women's career aspirations. Women who had the resources to obtain higher education also had access to career options not open to their less-educated sisters.

Women benefited from role models, too. The Roman Catholic Church offered a strong heritage of religious careers for women, and from the early days of Canada's history, Catholic sisters had been important contributors to Canadian society. Protestants reached into their own histories to develop patterns of religious careers for women, such as in mission and deaconess work. Eventually, of course, networks of Canadian women supported one another. This was especially true in mission work, where the numerous women's missionary societies across both Canada and the United States shared their expertise and their encouragement.

Canadian women benefited from contact with an international network of feminists. Especially important for some was the role-modelling of women who worked and lived in the United States. Born out of revolution and democratic ideals, the United States encouraged a tradition of individ-

ual rights much more than did Canada, a country in which governments
had spent a large part of the nineteenth century trying to prevent rebellion.
Women were more active in leadership in the churches in the United States,
and Canadian women gained new ideas and insights for their own institutions by reading American works, inviting speakers from the United States,
and travelling themselves to American cities.

Yet even with the opportunities of time, place, denomination, or status,
and the support of like-minded men and women, it was usually the determined, even aggressive, woman who was most likely to succeed in her bid
for a church career. As one can well imagine, however, assertive women
were not always welcomed and tolerated. The same traits that gave success
might inspire strong resistance.

COMMONALITIES

Women worked in the Christian churches in Canada as missionaries, both
at home and abroad, as professional church workers, as members of religious communities, and as social activists. Commonalities can be found in
all these areas of labour, both in working style and in type of activity, that
set women's work apart from that of men. Although many instances of
women working across gender lines can be documented, generally women
were marginalized, in that they were restricted to working with other
women and young children. Women tended to respond to practical needs,
and they brought to their work humane and caring touches.

Because a number of traditional church jobs were closed to them,
women often found themselves working as volunteers. This was an especially common role for married women who were active in benevolence
and social reform, both administering projects and taking to the streets
when necessary. If much of the story written so far of Christian, and especially of Protestant, women in the last centuries is the story of middle class
women, it is partly because these were the women who had the leisure for
such work and had been educated and trained in the necessary skills. The
unpaid work of these women was significantly connected with women's
full-time paid labour in the church: It was, for example, the female volunteer who administered and supported the work of the female missionary
overseas. In the same way, volunteers enabled women to be employed
within Canada in home missions and in Christian institutions.

Women's work was frequently subordinate and carried on behind the
scenes. One can read records of national church bodies and local parishes

and find no recognition of the ministry of women. Yet they were there, raising funds and teaching Sunday school, educating for mission, and aiding the marginalized. Often it was assumed that women would work under the direction of male leaders. Often, too, their activities were devalued or valued only for what society saw as acceptable, resulting in opportunities on the fringes of the churches' labour force, and lower salaries. The cost for women, however, was not just economic: They also paid a price emotionally for working outside socially accepted roles.

Perhaps because of their marginalization in the workforce or their socially conditioned maternalism, women church workers tended to function in a shared leadership or collegial working style and cultivated valuable networks of support. Yet it is certainly not true that men had a monopoly on hierarchical leadership or attitudes. In church organization, convent, or mission field, women sometimes developed their own hierarchies. They could also buy into an existing hierarchy of race or class, for example, and attempt to consolidate and capitalize on the status that gave them.

Two other considerations that surface again and again in the women's stories are the need for women to express themselves in writing and the value they placed on higher education. Long-distance communication before the invention of the telephone was, of course, primarily by letter. But isolated in their work or their homes, and denied adult companionship to a degree not felt by men, women seem to have relied much more heavily on letters and diaries for companionship, information, and solace. Denied access to opportunities for expressing their spirituality orally – in the pulpit – many women turned to writing down their religious thoughts and witnessing to their faith on the printed page.

Missionaries, too, wrote letters. Some of these were published and served to forge bonds between them and the women who gave them financial as well as emotional support. The value of missionary reports worked both ways: They educated and increased the enthusiasm of women at home, while providing a lifeline of information for women in the field. Many other women's groups also began journals or newspapers and used them to support one another. For those working in new and developing organizations such shared information was invaluable.

The emphasis on education, of course, was closely related to that on writing. Many of the women themselves saw education as a key to both spiritual and social advancement. Thus, it became a major thrust of the work of women as they organized schools and Christian education for children and for marginalized adults.

DIFFERENCES

While women's church work had much in common across denominations, it is natural that there were also differences. Each branch of Christianity had distinctive traditions that helped to shape the patterns of women's work. Women in Methodist, Baptist, Quaker, and related denominations such as the Gospel Workers Church were accepted more readily as leaders than those in other Christian traditions such as the Anglican or Roman Catholic Churches. There were precedents in the former churches for women in preaching or other prominent leadership roles because of church polity and doctrine. In other denominations, where sacramental theology and a strongly hierarchical structure appeared to justify an exclusively male leadership, women worked in more subordinate positions. Yet Roman Catholicism offered a history of female religious communities that allowed women to claim their own space within the larger church, and Anglicans had a strong volunteer tradition. Historically the Presbyterians were a diverse group, but they consistently valued education and put great energy into missions, and it was in mission work that many Presbyterian women were able to find their places. As time passed, however, denominations underwent changes, and in some groups a move to a more conservative stance in the twentieth century reduced the number of professional opportunities open to women.

Not all women moved by Christian experience and ideals worked within the churches. Some worked independently, outside church structures, while remaining clearly committed to the development of Christian goals within the social context of their day. Other women acted out of their Christian faith in groups that cut across denominational boundaries. Organizations such as the YWCA and the WCTU were founded by women with strong Christian principles. Those who worked as volunteers or in paid positions in these groups were operating outside the structures of the institutionalized church; therefore, they were subject only to their individual consciences and beliefs and not to the hierarchies of the denominations to which they personally belonged. On the whole, women in these institutions had greater opportunities for leadership training, administrative experience, and skill development than those within church structures.

Like men, women were rarely able to distance themselves from their social, geographic, and economic context; acculturation to a large degree dictated women's attitudes and work style. Women normally reflected the viewpoints of their race and class. Early preachers and missionaries were products of their age, and they acted out of a strong belief in the efficacy of

Christianity and therefore the need of all for conversion; many women as well as men worked hard to convert men and women to their own particular version of Christianity. Women who had lived in the United States, or had contact with Americans, tended to emphasize their own individual rights over their traditional role in Canadian society.

Many women involved themselves in social action, but their approaches differed greatly from one generation to the next, as they both shaped and were shaped by the prevailing views. In the early nineteenth century benevolence was the accepted mode of social amelioration; over the years some Christians were motivated by the hope of reforming individuals. Later, Social Gospellers were convinced that the answer to society's ills was nothing short of the subversion of the basic structures of society itself.

Women's work was also strongly influenced by their marital status. Only single women were accepted into some careers, such as deaconess work. Even when there was no such requirement, few women with families and housework were able to pursue a professional church career, and those who did carried a double burden. For the most part, married women or single women still supported by their families engaged in unpaid labour within the church structures or in secular society in organizations inspired by Christian principles.

Not only did women work differently, but the reception given their work was varied. Women met with both encouragement and hostility; they were honoured by men for the changes they brought about in society and relieved of their responsibilities because they assumed too much independence. Some were taken advantage of or deliberately misconstrued. Women in positions where they excelled might find themselves lacking newly established professional qualifications, a move that effectively excluded them. Professionalization in ministry and also in health care and in social work diminished the role of those who were perceived as being situated in the lower echelons of a hierarchy of expertise.

Some hostility undoubtedly masked fear. While such fears generally remained hidden, one form was sometimes expressed: fear of the feminization of the church. Those who saw power as limited in quantity feared losing some of it to women. If women gained positions of power, what would become of the men?

BENEFITS

But in spite of frustrations and disappointments, and at times enormous sacrifices, women undoubtedly benefited from the opportunities available in the Christian church in Canada. In secular society prior to the twentieth century, women had few options for permanent careers, and women who were engaged as paid workers were in the minority. Paid careers in the church, then, would seem attractive. Those who served on mission fields in Canada and abroad found an exhilarating freedom and an opportunity for innovation not open to the average Canadian woman confined to the hearth and nursery. In addition these women enjoyed the satisfaction of knowing that they had made a difference in the lives of many men, women, and children. Other women who were allowed to preach or serve as pastors had a unique opportunity to express their spirituality and respond to what they experienced as God's call.

For many women Christian work opened the door to new opportunities for training and education. Women who worked to express their Christian faith – whether in volunteer organizations, in paid positions within the church, or in unwaged labour there – gained self-confidence and either learned new administrative and interpersonal skills or honed those that they already had. While there were those who in anger or bitterness either left their denomination or abandoned the church entirely, for many women these career and volunteer outlets may well have meant the difference between emotional and mental well-being and loneliness and depression; church work brought companionship and intellectual and peer stimuli to many women who otherwise would have been isolated in their homes.

While women received much from these opportunities, the church gained even more from women's involvement. Because women served as volunteers or as poorly paid workers, the church was able to tap a vast body of unpaid and underpaid labour. Conditioned by church and society not to expect more, the women were willing to provide flexible help during times of emergencies and changing needs. Many in this labour pool were either formally well educated or possessed skills acquired through their volunteer work. Social pressures dictated that most women serve as educators, caregivers, and nurturers, skills traditionally underdeveloped in male church professionals and therefore much needed in the church institutions. And because women were forced to seek non-traditional ways of serving their church and expressing their spirituality, the church became the beneficiary of many innovative and imaginative programs initiated by the women themselves. These projects often gave care to women and children – a boon to churches because women consistently made up more than half the regular adult membership in all denominations, and the church's future vitality depended upon the faithfulness of its children.

Society, too, became the recipient of women's labours. Whether accomplished by benevolent ladies-bountiful or by social activists, paid workers, or volunteers, much social welfare and social change were the direct result of women's concerns and practical action. Women who took the gospel mandate seriously believed they had no option but to attempt to effect change through their writings, their preaching, or their physical work.

Society defined a role for women, and the leaders of the church defined a role for Christian women. Yet these women were often unconfined by these roles and the constraints which society and the church would place upon them. Women redefined their roles, not theoretically but pragmatically, through their actions. They used varied resources, worked in varied ways, and met varied responses. Yet, however much some contemporaries opposed them and many historians ignored them, one thing is clear: The women worked. Claimed by their religious faith, they claimed space to act according to that faith. The Christianity that limited their roles also offered them opportunities or, perhaps more accurately, they made opportunities within it. Thus, the religious history of Canadian women is the history of the creative, practical expressions of faith that here we can only begin to recount.

Women in Religious Communities:
Claiming Space within Institutions

1

'So Many Crosses to Bear': The Religious Hospitallers of St Joseph and the Tracadie Leper Hospital, 1868–1910

LAURIE C.C. STANLEY

Sisters of the Religious Hospitallers of St Joseph founded a religious community in Tracadie, New Brunswick, to care for lepers, who were among the most marginalized of all human beings. These cloistered women used their considerable administrative skills, their adaptability, and their hard physical labour to run the lazaretto. Yet their independence was circumscribed by the interference of bureaucrats and the paternalism of ecclesiastical officials, and over time the community's authority was curtailed. Although many lauded the labour of the sisters, these commentators directed their praise towards an idealized view of the women's activity, activity that was deemed appropriate for Christian women. The sisters' devout and sacrificial service was exalted, their resourceful and resolute hard work not fully appreciated.

But hark! the silence breaks at last
A tinkling sleigh is hurrying past
In sombre weeds, two maidens clad
And hooded, with pale faces sad,
It beareth nuns whose lives are spent
In Lazaretted settlement.

Union Advocate, 9 December 1869

In September 1868 six sisters from the Montreal Motherhouse of the Religious Hospitallers of St Joseph arrived in Tracadie, New Brunswick. They came to Tracadie on a special mission: to assume direction of the provincially funded Tracadie lazaretto and its leper patients.[1] The sisters' approach to the small coastal village in northeastern New Brunswick was signalled by a tolling bell, waving flags, and the discharge of muskets. The sisters could hardly dismount from their carriage because of the rush of onlookers. Some of the throng knelt before the Hospitallers as 'to saints,' convinced that they would bring liberation from the 'scourge of leprosy.'[2]

Almost immediately the sisters' humility found pious expression in the austerity of their circumstances and in their personal attendance upon the lazaretto patients. The experience, however, was not as uplifting as they had hoped. It was marked by an inexorable circle of frustrations that tested their Christian fortitude. These crises in turn became the crosses that the sisters had to bear. Mère Marie Pagé, the first Mother Superior at Tracadie, intimated as much, when she nicknamed the new foundation 'la Tracasserie.'[3]

Convoluted negotiations, involving the government of New Brunswick, church officials, and the Tracadie Board of Health, brought the sisters from

Montreal to Tracadie. It was, however, the Caraquet priest, Father Joseph-Marie Paquet, who made the initial arrangements in January 1868, inviting the order, commonly known in lay circles as the Hôtel-Dieu, to establish a religious foundation in Tracadie. The order, not to be confused with the sisters of St Joseph (discussed in the chapter by Elizabeth Smyth), was founded in France during the seventeenth century and had illustrious roots in New France, dating back to 1659. During the mid-nineteenth-century flowering of religious communities in Quebec, the order was poised to extend its field of activity.

Although the sisters at the Montreal convent responded enthusiastically to Father Paquet's offer, there were economic practicalities to be considered. The Mother Superior studied the invitation cautiously. Her apprehensions were echoed by the Bishop of Montreal, who feared that the sisters would arrive in Tracadie homeless and penniless, alighting 'comme l'oiseau sur la branche.'[4] In her correspondence the Mother Superior sought further assurances from Paquet and reminded him that the sisters, according to the rules of their institute, were not 'des religieuses missionaires, mais des religieuses fondatrices.'[5] As such, they would undertake to found a permanent religious community, but not a mission station in Tracadie. Moreover, she explained that they were cloistered nuns and that each community of the Religious Hospitallers of St Joseph was autonomous, each responsible for its own finances and noviciates. For this reason the sisters required some tangible guarantees that their tenure at Tracadie would be permanent. They would need lands and income to produce sufficient funds to meet their expenses. A small annual subsidy of £200 sterling for the sisters (in addition to operating funds for the lazaretto), she suggested, would suffice as surety.[6]

Although no fixed guarantees were forthcoming, the Mother Superior despatched two sisters in May 1868 to assess the situation firsthand in Tracadie. When they returned their graphic narratives about the lepers excited pity and spurred the sisters to begin their preparations. The promptings of the Spirit were irresistible. Practical considerations were increasingly crowded out by zealous faith, even though the New Brunswick government had not yet voted funds for the sisters.

Paquet's overtures and the prospect of caring for those stricken with leprosy had a mystical attraction for this expanding order. It held out to the sisters the opportunity to reaffirm their apostolic commitment to the poor and sick. After all, the ministry of healing had always been regarded as a special function of the church. But caring for lepers, a service historically connected with the church, had an even more magnetic appeal. It was hoped that the experience would be a source of spiritual renewal, rekindling the 'primitive fervour' of their original founders.[7] The *Annales* of the order expressed these sentiments in euphoric tones:

Voici une mission nouvelle, qui élève à un suprême degré notre vocation d'Hospitalières, déjà si belle! Appelé à faire revivre, après plus de sept siècles, le dévouement sublime des chevaliers de Saint-Lazare, qui se consacraient autrefois au service et au soulagement des pauvres lépreux, notre Institut se sent grandir et voit naître en son sein le même courage et le même dévouement que l'Église entière admire en ces héros du moyen âge.[8]

According to tradition, all the sisters at the Montreal Hôtel-Dieu eagerly embraced this errand of mercy. The Mother Superior, therefore, hand-picked only the 'most talented and holy' to go.[9] Among the successful six candidates was Amanda Viger, better known as Sister St Jean de Goto, daughter of Bonaventure Viger, a leading Patriote during the Lower Canadian rebellion. He protested against her chosen vocation among the lepers, but she silenced her father's objections with a sharp rebuttal, alluding to his own gold-seeking adventures in California:

Hé quoi! père chéri, vous n'avez pas craint de vous exiler pour aller chercher de l'or et vous me refuseriez votre consentement pour aller me sacrifier dans un pays où j'espère trouver les moyens d'une plus grande sanctification! ... De grâce, laissez-moi partir![10]

Those selected considered themselves an elect group, 'les plus dignes' chosen for 'un si beau sacrifice' to consecrate their lives to the most dispossessed and disenfranchised of humankind.[11] The Religious Hospitallers of St Joseph came to Tracadie with the deliberate resolve to dedicate themselves to the unfortunate sufferers of leprosy.

Another set-back presented itself when the sisters finally arrived in New Brunswick, at the port town of Chatham, fifty miles from Tracadie. Here they were greeted by Bishop James Rogers, their new diocesan, and his pronouncement that their plans to go to Tracadie should be aborted. The provincial government had not yet formally committed itself to provide the sisters with an annual subsidy, and his diocese was too impoverished to support them at the lazaretto. Realizing that the sisters would be an adornment to Chatham, his episcopal seat, Rogers offered them his protection and hospitality and urged them to consider establishing a house in Chatham instead. The sisters were saddened by this untoward disruption of their plans, but Paquet, Rogers's vicar-general, intervened with a timely solution. He suggested that the sisters go to Tracadie for a year on a trial basis, during which time he would support them. Rogers tried to wheedle another compromise. Could not two sisters remain in Chatham and the balance go to Tracadie? The sisters mustered an unequivocal, 'No.' They had set their sights and hearts on going to the Tracadie lazaretto. No one would divert them from their chosen path to sanctity.

Finally, on 29 September 1868, the Feast of St Michael, the six sisters set out for Tracadie, 'cette chère terre promise!'[12] They did not have long to savour their triumphal arrival in the village. Their installation ceremony was an unostentatious affair, made all the more barren by the bishop's absence. Fully convinced that the sisters' sojourn in Tracadie would be short-lived, he preferred that they should withdraw discreetly without 'éclat' and return to Chatham.[13] In a sense, then, their labours began without Rogers's official blessing. However, the sisters' mission was not as problematical as he had imagined. Government funding materialized within the year, as did a generous donation of farmland from the village priest, Father Ferdinand-Edmond Gauvreau. Besides, local residents came forth with gifts of firewood, livestock, and food. The sisters' work among the lepers was now on a more solid footing, and their future in Tracadie seemed firmly anchored.

During the early years at the lazaretto the sisters demonstrated a maximum of adaptation and fortitude. They directed their energies to a variety of needs, such as stitching mattresses by hand, guiding visitors through the wards, maintaining the lazaretto register, binding sores, edifying patients with catechisms and spiritual readings, supervising a well-stocked dispensary, planting gardens, and washing cadavers and wrapping them in shrouds. After 1880 the sisters also prepared the lepers' meals, assisted by a hired servant. They tended to virtually all the lepers' needs except washing and scrubbing, which was the dubious privilege of the washerwoman until 1906, when the sisters were obliged to incorporate this chore into their repertoire of tasks. Additionally, during the early years the sisters did much of the sewing for the churches in the neighbouring missions, and they prepared the altar bread for eleven charges in the diocese.[14] By all accounts it was strenuous work bending over the large blazing hearth and wielding the heavy, ungainly moulds.

The sisters' arrival in Tracadie marked a watershed in the institutional treatment of the lepers at the lazaretto. From a medical, sociological, and humanistic point of view, they introduced measures that were more benevolent than any previously effected. The sisters firmly imbedded their faith in the scenes of their labours. Religious rule became a dominant motif, as the sisters implemented reforms that reflected the premium they placed on obedience, regularity, and respect. Visitors were always impressed to discover that the hospital was run like an efficient household, its routine unfolding at a clocklike tempo.

Although cleanliness, routine, and sexual segregation were the foundation of administrative policy, these precepts did not preclude the sisters' efforts to humanize the lazaretto. They strove to dispel the institutional gloom by making the lepers' apartments as cheerful and homelike as possible. By 1871 the high wall that had enclosed the hospital was replaced with a board fence. The residents were permitted to amuse themselves, bathing, boating, sailing, and fishing outside the precincts of the leper hospital. The beds were not conventional hospital cots, but iron beds covered with blue counterpanes and fitted with white curtains to afford privacy. Furthermore, flowers were often placed in the female dormitory during the summer months. In 1905 the Mother Superior recommended that the roof and verandahs be painted 'to take away the sombre, *prison-like* appearance of the building.'[15] In accenting the lazaretto's homely qualities, however, the sisters did not mute its ecclesiastical character. Plaster statues and religious pictures were much in evidence throughout the leper wards. Each bed was dedicated to a saint whose name was inscribed on a little plate fastened to the curtain frame.

The administrative routine at Tracadie was infused with efficiency and apostolic fervour, as the sisters laboured with an enlightened sense of purpose. Life, however, was far from heavenly or halcyon, even if the bishop referred to the sisters as the 'happy and holy Community of Spouses of Christ.'[16] The sisters' first days at Tracadie marked only the beginning of 'leurs misères et leurs mortifications.'[17] Upon their arrival, the leper hospital presented a tableau of horrors: stench, filth, and scantily clad lepers. Even after a marathon of scrubbing, and the eviction of vermin and nesting hens from the wards, the work still remained arduous and stressful.

Certainly, the sisters' accommodations were hardly conducive to comfort. The original convent was spartan, draughty, and drab. Because the board of health had failed to insulate the small monastery, frost bristled on the refectory and kitchen floors, and even the benches, during the first winter season. One of the sisters was compelled to put cinders in her shoes while tending to her cooking chores. By 1874 these conditions had progressively worsened. The institution was leaky and dilapidated; its foundations sagged, the cellar was often flooded, and rats overran the adjoining outhouses.[18] For thirteen years the sisters shifted without a morgue or isolation room for the patients. Any periodic renovations were of a provisional nature, so that by 1887 the convent and lazaretto resembled a rambling 'roughly-built barn.'[19] By the 1890s the sisters were lobbying desperately to acquire new accommodations and to vacate a building that had become 'old, cold, and a pile of decaying wood,' 'an unfit place for human beings.'[20] Several of the sisters turned their talents to devising plans and specifications for a new building. Their determination was so intense that one sister vowed, 's'il n'y a pas assez d'hommes pour nous aider, nous porterons nous-mêmes les pierres dans nos tabliers.'[21] They would willingly scrimp and save and 'se contenter de manger de vieilles patates et de la mélasse.'[22]

Even the new three-storey lazaretto finished in 1896 was not free from discomforts for the sisters. Admittedly, with high-ceilinged and brightly lit wards, a warm exterior of brownish-grey stone and ample verandahs, it was an improvement over its predecessor. But by 1908 rain seeped into the attic rooms, plaster tumbled from the walls, and the sheet metal roof, corroded by the salt sea air, clattered with every gust of wind.[23] During the winter the sleeping quarters in the mansard storey were barely habitable. Furthermore, despite its many modern amenities, the institution still lacked a steam laundry and wringer as late as 1908. The sisters, therefore, had to clean the lepers' dirty clothes and bedlinens almost entirely by hand on a washboard, a practice that they found 'exceedingly unpleasant, as well as ... dangerous.'[24] During inclement weather they were forced to hang these wet garments throughout the building.

Superadded to the hardships of leper work were the burdens of physical isolation. The Religious Hospitallers who came from Montreal to the remote Tracadie lazaretto felt a profound sense of exile. Sister St Jean de Goto dubbed Tracadie her 'solitude des solitudes.'[25] It was almost with worldly glee that she informed the sisters at the Montreal Hôtel-Dieu in June 1872 that the telegraph had finally been hooked up to Tracadie. Many of the early sisters continued to think of the Montreal Hôtel-Dieu as 'chez nous' and eagerly awaited news of their old convent.[26] With a whimsical turn of phrase, Sister St Jean de Goto assured her former Mother Superior that correspondence from the Montreal convent always boosted their spirits: 'Qu'en les lisant nous sommes toutes aussi émoustillées qu'une pochée de souris.'[27]

The actual care of the leper patients brought its own heavy burden. The lepers often arrived in the most foul condition. One sister later recalled spending two hours bandaging a recent arrival who was a mass of ulcers. The sisters resorted to a rotation schedule, for the putrid air in the wards was intolerable for extended periods. The poorly ventilated rooms were especially foul and stifling during the winter months, when the dormer windows were nailed shut, and the stoves were blazing. Three-month stints marked the limit of endurance for those nurses assigned to change old dressings.[28] The sisters also played an active part in other aspects of their patients' therapeutic regimen. They routinely dispensed arsenic, quinine, mercury, strong tea, and cough mixtures from their dispensary.

Not all the patients surrendered to their diseased condition with cheerful submissiveness. Some chafed against the constraints of their almost monastic existence and bitterly construed their confinement as captivity and punishment. Under such circumstances, the sisters sometimes became a target for verbal abuse, tantrums, and surliness. Chronic despondency permeated the wards on a daily basis, but during the winter months of ward-bound inactivity, depression sometimes searched for more turbulent forms of expression. The rebelliousness of one hospital inmate verged on the homicidal, as he resorted to brute force to intimidate the sisters. He hurled rocks through the windows of the women's ward, overturned trays of dishes in the refectory, ransacked the armoire in the pharmacy, and threatened the lazaretto physician with a poker and a gun.[29] Clearly, the reality of caring for lepers was devoid of glamour. The sisters tackled 'disgusting work which previously no one could be found to do.'[30] Only in the popular imagination did they appear enveloped in a penumbra of spiritual euphoria and sacrificial love.

But if leper care was so fraught with trials, what was its attraction? Why did the sisters refer so tenderly, even possessively to their patients as 'nos chers lépreux,' as 'le trésor de la communauté'?[31] What inspired one sister to rejoice in her vocation, 'Je me glorifié et suis heureuse'?[32] Why was the binding of the sores of the lepers 'un grand privilège' reserved for the professed sisters and denied to the novices?[33]

Perhaps the motivations of the sisters can never be fully fathomed. But one must consider their attitudes towards the leper in the wider matrix of Roman Catholic thought. In most clerical circles, the leper enjoyed a half-mystical glamour and was esteemed as an edifying emblem of suffering and unquestioning conformity to God's will.[34] More importantly, however, the leper, as the most lowly and despised, was seen to have a particular intimacy with God. By extension, then, those individuals consecrating their lives to the care of lepers would reap a bounty of spiritual rewards. The leper became the means to test Christian virtues, to affirm heroism, and to realize holiness: to become living symbols of the gospel message, 'Whatever you have done unto one of these, the least of my brethren, you have done it unto me.'

The sisters' fervent interest in leprosy also mirrored a wider nineteenth-century popular phenomenon. During this period leprosy was invested with a unique mystique. As one newspaper journalist observed, it had an 'inspiring picturesqueness, ... remote genealogy, and Biblical dignity' that put it in a class by itself.[35] Its fatal nature appealed to the Victorian appetite for the morbid, repelling and attracting simultaneously, creating a singular compound of fear and fascination.

Two specific events shaped public perceptions at this time: the discovery in 1874 of the *Mycobacterium leprae* by the Norwegian scientist, G.H. Armauer Hansen, and the death in 1889 of Father Joseph Damien, the celebrated Belgian priest who contracted leprosy while caring for his leprous flock in Molokai, Hawaii. These events firmly established leprosy as bacterial and contagious, yet its causation and means of transmission were still undetermined. This murkiness contributed in no small way to the leprosy scare that rippled through Europe and North America during the 1880s and 1890s.

It was in this period that leprosy work became synonymous with Christian service and sacrifice. The disease provided missionaries with an extraordinary sphere of activity, for it promised, more than all charitable acts, the 'reproduction of the Christ-life.'[36] In short, it was the ideal instrument for modern-day martyrdom. Throughout the late nineteenth and early twentieth centuries, the Church, as it had in medieval times, clearly staked out leprosy as its peculiar responsibility. A vast network of villages, homes, and asylums for lepers sprang up as Christians of various denominations vied for the opportunity to minister to the lepers. Men and women alike were caught up in this 'passion of pity' and nourished their sense of purpose on the inspiration of Christ's ministry and the idolized death of Father Damien.[37]

In the public mind the care of lepers was closely linked with women. Lepers, it was argued, were the natural charges of the 'devout female sex.'[38] This rationalization flowed from several assumptions. First, leprosy in the nineteenth century was widely regarded as an incurable disease. For this reason it was designated a custodial problem, rather than a medical one: It demanded 'caring' rather than 'curing.' Since the more prestigious function of 'curing' was largely a male preserve, and 'caring' was thought to be a female vocation, ministrations to lepers tended to be relegated to women.[39] Second, leper care was regarded as woman's true sphere of action because it embodied the virtues of womanhood, namely self-denial, charity, and compassion – domains in which that gender was alleged supreme. To perform this 'most loathsome work in the world'[40] was a most perfect act of

'Christian womanhood.'[41] Third, the image of a female ministering to lepers had a symbolic appeal, expressed so eloquently in the hagiographical imagery of the medieval saint embracing the leper. Woman, sanctified, innocent, and pure, and the leper, reviled, immoral, and impure, provided a compelling juxtaposition. Visitors to the Tracadie lazaretto were frequently struck by this partnership of polarities. Journalists were moved to comment on the edifying irony of female religious in the 'very flower of perfect womanhood' toiling among diseased and deformed lepers.[42]

The image of women performing Christlike labours had appeal, particularly during the latter part of the nineteenth century, as North American Catholic and Protestant orthodoxy underwent 'feminization.'[43] The most salient feature of this phenomenon was the recasting of Christ as an 'exemplar of meekness and humility, the sacrificial victim.'[44] Such conceptions could be comfortably integrated with traditional secular perceptions of leprosy and expectations about the role of women. Within such a context the religious sister was the *beau idéal* of Christian womanhood.[45] And the Tracadie Religious Hospitaller, who was selfless and pure, who busied herself with scrub-brush and broom making a 'home' for her leper charges, was the quintessential caregiver and caretaker.

From both religious and secular perspectives, the sisters at Tracadie were seen as ideally suited to their task. Public reports, private correspondence, and newspaper articles usually depicted them as ministering angels, 'sunny,' 'benign,' 'sweet-faced' women, almost waxlike abstractions.[46] The significance of the fact that they were cloistered did not go unappreciated. There was symmetry to this situation. Cloistered nun and incarcerated leper, both in a state of enforced seclusion, seemed logical co-tenants in the so-called 'living tomb.' It is hardly accidental that during the nineteenth century convents and leper colonies shared the same gothic, sepulchral vocabulary.

Clearly, however, the sisters' lives did not conform to society's blueprint of expectations. Nor did their existence mirror the fantasy-peddling of journalists. The task of running a lazaretto was more grimy than grandiose, but this fact alone did not deter the sisters at Tracadie. What took its emotional toll and eroded their morale was an overwhelming sense of precariousness. For this reason the history of the Tracadie foundation was marked by the quest for stability and security.

A number of factors coalesced to create this unstable situation. The first was chronic poverty. But this predicament was not insurmountable, for the sisters regulated their material needs 'au rythme de ventes de charité, de bazars et d'autres expédients.'[47] A second, more decisive factor was the sisters' peculiar status as employees in a government institution; they resided on government property and subsisted on government funding. Robbing them of a sense of autonomy and permanence, this arrangement left them feeling that they were more the servants of the state than of God. It also left them uncertain as to their fate were the government to close the lazaretto. Third, the sisters were distressed by the spectre of their own impending obsolescence. The declining leper population in New Brunswick, which so gladdened government officials, filled the sisters with dread. It raised a dilemma about their continued role in Tracadie and further heightened their sense of defencelessness. What would be their fate when the lepers were gone? This fear prompted the sisters to expand and diversify their activities as a means to lessen their dependence on their leper patients and mitigate the uncertainties surrounding their foundation. To consolidate their foothold for the future, the Tracadie sisters established a school (1873), an orphanage (1888), and a general hospital (1898).[48]

Although the creation of these ancillary institutions may have alleviated the sisters' insecurities, the Tracadie sisters still had to fend off the demoralizing sense of being subordinated to politicians, chaplains, bishops, bureaucrats, and physicians. In the first decade of their history, the sisters were forced to endure the meddlesome politics of the local board of health, which refused to relinquish its hold over the lazaretto. Some of the board members were so intrusive that they spied on the sisters in the wards at night through the windows. Board officials refused to surrender control of the cooking department to the sisters, thereby keeping the board's foot in the lazaretto door. In 1880 the board was dissolved, completely discredited by a government inquiry that had revealed that certain board members – many of them merchants – had exploited the lazaretto as a source of profit and patronage and had treated the sisters and the leper patients as little more than hostages to their partisanship and opportunism.

Politicians also threw up obstacles when the sisters attempted to protect themselves. In March 1869 the sisters petitioned the government for the civil incorporation of their religious community. The final legislation fell far short of their objectives: it vested in the government residual power to suspend 'such bye laws, rules, and regulations' relating to the Tracadie corporation 'when it shall appear expedient and necessary.'[49] For the sisters such words were hardly worth the paper on which they were printed. As a precautionary measure, they decided that all future deeds of property and grants should be made out to individual sisters rather than the Tracadie foundation.

Even after the government turned the administration of the lazaretto over completely to the sisters in 1880, their aspirations for autonomy continued to be hampered. They found themselves at odds with bureaucrats, who routinely deflected their entreaties for additional funding and renovations. They found themselves in competition with the lazaretto physician, who challenged the prominence of religious imperatives and the sisters' 'sole charge' of the lazaretto.[50] To federal authorities, the physician confided the view that the sisters' exclusive control over the lazaretto 'would not be in the interest of those for whom the institution is supposed to exist.'[51] He was concerned that the order's goals of sanctification and salvation were overshadowing those of rehabilitation. In 1898 a government commission recommended that the leper hospital be placed on a more professional level of management; the physician was promoted to the rank of general superintendent. He prevailed over the institution, supervising the lepers' well-being, their diets, their hygiene, and their prescriptions. Given a permanent office on the hospital premises and unrestricted access to the lepers, he no longer required the sisters, bearing the keys, to escort him through the wards. Henceforth, the lazaretto was governed from a 'scientific and practical viewpoint,' and the role of the sisters was a supportive one.[52] They were the doctor's helpmates and handmaidens. Government officials tactfully explained to the sisters that the new policy would minimize their accountability and insulate them from abusive patients. But, in effect, these new measures greatly reduced the sisters' status in the leper wards.

The sisters also found themselves colliding with ecclesiastical authorities. The heavy-handed paternalism of Bishop Rogers often balked their quest for permanence. Although the sisters referred to him as 'leur bienfaiteur,' his actions occasionally injured the morale of their community. Had he not deliberately absented himself from their installation ceremony and plainly displayed his preference for the non-cloistered Grey Nuns as more suitable candidates to administer the Tracadie lazaretto? In later years it disheartened the sisters when Rogers stalled their plans to borrow funds for the construction of an orphanage with his rigid practicality, stipulating 'there must be no debt, we should pay as we go!'[53] It must have rankled, too, when the bishop, who had collected offerings from religious houses in France for the lepers of New Brunswick, asked the financially starved Tracadie foundation to surrender these donations to his own diocesan projects. And it must have also smarted when the bishop sometimes treated them as adjuncts to a second foundation of the Religious Hospitallers of St Joseph established in 1869 at Chatham, dragging his heels in granting the Tracadie sisters permission to open their own noviciate.

The sisters also found their authority undermined by Father Joseph-Auguste Babineau, who performed the varied roles of parish priest, lazaretto chaplain, and confessor to the sisters. Babineau not only saw himself as the sisters' personal protector but as an indispensable member of the lazaretto staff. Throughout the 1880s and 1890s he became the self-appointed liaison between the federal government and the sisters and arrogated to himself responsibility for the business affairs of the lazaretto. He supervised the contracts and manual work at the establishment, drafted letters to the government, and signed virtually all the accounts sent to the Department of Public Works. It was Babineau who stormed the offices of politicians and civil servants and helped secure for the sisters their new lazaretto. He also kept before government officials the sacrifices and needs of the sisters, periodically reminding federal bureaucrats that 'the work done by them [the sisters] could not be got for the hire of men.' [54]

By the early 1900s Babineau's activities became more intrusive and meddlesome. He increasingly infringed on the internal workings of the convent. Even the elections of the Mother Superior attracted his interference. And with the lazaretto and convent barely a three-minute walk from the presbytery, he seemed omnipresent, coming and going freely.

It is difficult to decipher Babineau's motivations. Perhaps he was driven by a grandiose personal vision inspired by the celebrated martyrdom of Father Damien. Perhaps the elevated importance of the lazaretto physician as general superintendent intensified Babineau's need to reassert his privileged place in the institution. In any case, by the summer of 1901 his excessively proprietorial attitude towards the sisters and the lazaretto brought him into conflict with the Mother Superior, and resulted in the convent being split into two camps. This struggle reached its climax when he summoned the Tracadie sisters, recited before this assembly his grievances against the superior, and commanded her to kneel forthwith to be pardoned. The Mother Superior felt deeply the indignity and humiliation. It did not help matters when the bishop responded sluggishly to her requests in December 1901 for corrective measures to forestall 'la ruine totale vers laquelle la Communauté semble marcher rapidement.' [55] Nor did the situation improve when he arrived and delivered a sermon on respect and submission. The morale and the equilibrium of the lazaretto and convent were seriously compromised. The conflict continued to fester until June 1902, when Apostolic Delegate Diomede Falconio (the senior papal representative in Canada) took matters in hand and commanded the dismissal of Babineau as chaplain and confessor to the lazaretto and convent. [56] Eight months later the Tracadie priest was reassigned to another parish.

After Babineau's departure the sisters tried to reclaim the authority lost through the chaplain's encroachments. The Mother Superior crisply informed the government that henceforth she should be considered the 'seule administratice' of the lazaretto.[57] She would no longer conduct its affairs through an intermediary.

What was at the root of these conflicts at the Tracadie lazaretto and convent? Hierarchical struggles were endemic at most nineteenth-century leper institutions. Conflicts usually erupted between the advocates of science and the defenders of religious tradition, as the former insisted that the priorities of science should be paramount, while the latter upheld the Church's traditional monopoly over victims of leprosy. Each group felt acutely the impact of the other's encroachments. The occupation of caring for lepers also seemed to encourage an inordinate possessiveness among its workers as they competed for heavenly prizes and a special intimacy with God.

Also at the root of the struggle at Tracadie was the tradition of the cloister. The primary function of the cloister was the enforcement of monastic seclusion, a mechanism by which sisters in religious orders could be safeguarded from physical harm, moral contagion, and the lures of society. More importantly, the cloister also discouraged female apostolic activism, enforcing obedience to male ecclesiastics, and strictly regulating communal life. In short, the cloister represented the imposition of a vow of powerlessness. The claustral rule embodied certain restrictions. For example, no female religious could venture outside the convent walls without the bishop's permission. Moreover, there were clearly demarcated areas within the convent from which laity were barred. The central fixture in every cloistered community was the grille, a latticed screen in the parlour, which minimized contact between the sisters and their visitors.

The clergy's attitude also reflected society's tendency, despite all the florid tributes heaped on the sisters, to devalue their work among the lepers. Government administrators and physicians regarded them as little more than biblical Marthas, and acclaimed their housekeeping skills: the lazaretto's model neatness, the marblelike luminosity of its waxed floors, and the snow-white attire of the leper patients. Clerical commentators admired the selfless devotion of those celebrated as heroines of charity, 'glorious victim[s] of the love of Christ.'[58] The sisters' acts of oblation and their imputed sacrificial meekness were touted as their highest virtue. Even in the lay press self-sacrifice was a much-esteemed feminine attribute. Newspapers such as the *Miramichi Advance* expatiated on the 'martyrs to the truest cause' who surrendered 'their lives on this altar of sacrifice.'[59]

Writers were especially attracted to the Tracadie lazaretto, exploring its tragic limits and festooning plain fact with literary embellishment. They harlequinized the sisters' lives with such mawkish phrases as 'the gloomy abode of misery,' 'the everlasting sobbing on the bleak shore,' and 'the muffled convent bell.'[60]

Although writers concocted doleful romantic tales, few individuals appreciated the stoicism and stamina required to perform the sisters' grim labours. Even fewer acknowledged their managerial efficiency, business acumen, nursing abilities, and capable superintendence of the lazaretto dispensary. And although Sister St Jean de Goto's comely appearance usually attracted praise, her proficiency in pharmacology was treated as quite incidental.[61] The sisters' skills as nurses were only dimly perceived. One local board of health administrator characterized them as 'night watchers,' while the staff physician identified their primary medical contribution as 'smoothing' the lepers' 'passage to the tomb.'[62] It was a rare tribute indeed when the deputy minister of agriculture complimented sister Delphine Brault in October 1881 on her aptitude 'comme financière accomplie.'[63] Much more typical were the views of the bureaucrat, who wrote: 'The sisters, all of them, down at the Tracadie lazaretto, have a pretty easy time of it.'[64]

The lives of the sisters at Tracadie contradicted the ideal of leper work. Their existence was fraught with inconsistencies. The often conflicting priorities of service and the cloister caused a tension at the heart of their community. But the contradictions were more than organizational. The sisters, who were supposed to be the 'glorious victim[s] of the love of Christ,' were also the inglorious victims of prelates, politicians, and preconceptions. At the same time they were virtually apotheosized, their contributions were measured by society in terms of obedience and sacrifice. The fact is, the sisters' activities at the Tracadie lazaretto were not the stuff of romance, whatever the public alleged. Nor were they the meek heroines of popular invention. Had they been so, they would never have struggled against and withstood the repeated incursions of both politicians and clergy. Nor would they have survived the privations and tentativeness of their early years at the lazaretto. Admittedly, their struggles for security, self-preservation, and stability denied leper work some of its spiritual pleasure; their road to sanctity was an arduous one. But the sisters took comfort from the fact that their own crises and crosses had enlarged their hearts and souls and deepened their affection for the lepers and the Tracadie lazaretto. The sisters' survival at Tracadie during these years was a testament to their strength, faith, and resourcefulness.

ACKNOWLEDGMENT

Research for this article was made possible by doctoral fellowship funding
from the Social Sciences and Humanities Research Council of Canada and
a UCR grant from St Francis Xavier University.

NOTES

1 For a discussion of the origins of leprosy in New Brunswick see Laurie C.C.
  Stanley, *Unclean! Unclean! Leprosy in New Brunswick, 1844–1880* (Moncton:
  Les Editions d'Acadie, 1982); Laurie Stanley-Blackwell, 'Leprosy in New
  Brunswick, 1844–1910: A Reconsideration' (PhD dissertation, Queen's University, 1988). Although the label 'Hansen's disease' is now considered less stigma-
  laden, this expression was not part of the popular or medical vocabulary of the
  nineteenth century; for the sake of historical authenticity, the words 'leper' and
  'leprosy' are employed throughout this chapter.
2 Amy Pope, 'At Tracadie New Brunswick,' *Catholic World*, 36 (Mar. 1883): 744.
  See also *Annales* 1868–1881, 282, Archives of the Religious Hospitallers of Saint
  Joseph (ARHSJ), Tracadie.
3 Rogers to Sr St-Jean de Goto, 30 June 1895, Tracadie Correspondence, 4/155,
  Archives of the Diocese of Bathurst (ADB). See also Reel F-7687, Public
  Archives of New Brunswick (PANB). Tracasserie translates as vexation or
  worry.
4 Antoine Bernard, *Les Hospitalières de Saint-Joseph et Leur Oeuvre en Acadie*
  (Montreal: Ateliers des Sourds-Muets, 1958), 82.
5 Ibid., 91.
6 Barry to Rogers, 23 June 1868, Rogers Papers, Reel F-7652, PANB. See also
  Bernard, 85.
7 Sr Sproule's typescript translation of Félix-M. Lajat, *Le Lazaret de Tracadie et
  la Communauté des religieuses hospitalières de Saint-Joseph* (Montreal:
  L'Action Paroissiale, 1938), 79, ARHSJ (Amherstview).
8 Bernard, 78.
9 Toronto *Globe*, 24 Aug. 1885; *Moniteur Acadien*, 10 Sept. 1885.
10 Sr Corinne LaPlante, 'Soeur Amanda Viger; La Fille d'un Patriote de 1837,
  véritable fondatrice de l'H.D. de Tracadie,' *La Revue d'histoire de la Société
  historique Nicolas-Denys* 12 (Jan.–May 1984), 8.
11 'Recueil de recettes pour faire les remèdes apportés de Montréal en 1868,' Reel
  F-611, PANB. In later years young women were still drawn to the Tracadie
  convent by the irresistible urge to devote their lives to the care of leper patients.

Marie-Anne Doucet of Bathurst, for example, abandoned the management of her brother's household and a brief career in teaching and appeared at the Tracadie noviciate in 1877 to 'work for the lepers' (Sproule translation of Lajat, 106, ARHSJ [Amherstview]).

12 *Annales 1868–1881*, 274, ARHSJ (Tracadie).
13 Ibid., 278.
14 *Moniteur Acadien*, 6 Aug. 1874. This issue has a copy of Sr St-Jean de Goto's letter to 'Ma très honorée Mère et mes chères soeurs,' 10 Nov. 1868 (not 1862 as printed).
15 Smith to Montizambert, 4 Mar. 1905, RG 29, vol. 5, file 937015, 1/2 pt. 4, National Archives of Canada (NAC).
16 Rogers to Pagé, 2 Oct. 1868, ARHSJ (Tracadie).
17 *Moniteur Acadien*, 10 Sept. 1885.
18 Babineau to Minister of Agriculture, 10 Dec. 1891, RG 11, vol. 874, file 128173, NAC.
19 *Globe*, 25 Aug. 1885.
20 Babineau to Minister of Agriculture, 26 Jan. 1893, reel F-140, PANB; Babineau to Gobeil, 1 Feb. 1894, RG 11, B 2 (a), vol. 950, NAC.
21 Lajat, 301.
22 Ibid.
23 Smith to Montizambert, 16 Jan. 1908, RG 29, vol. 5, file 937015, 1/2 pt. 5, NAC.
24 Smith to Montizambert, 10 Feb. 1904, 30, Smith papers, letterbook 105–6, Le Centre de Documentation de la Société Historique Nicolas-Denys (CD-SHND).
25 LaPlante, 'Soeur Amanda Viger,' 29.
26 St-Jean de Goto to 'Ma très honorée Mère et mes chères Soeurs,' 26 Nov. 1874, printed in 'La Picote à Caraquet et Pokemouche: Deux lettres de Sr St-Jean,' *La Revue d'histoire de la Société historique Nicolas-Denys* 12 (Jan.–May, 1984): 53.
27 LaPlante, 22.
28 Sormany to Smith, n.d., Smith papers, 105-3-7, CD-SHND.
29 Young to Tweedie, 21 Nov. 1904, RG 29, vol. 4, file 937015, pt. 4, NAC; Smith to Montizambert, 15 May 1905, Smith papers, box 105–2, scrapbook, CD-SHND.
30 Anglin to Scott, 22 Mar. 1875, RG 17, A.1.1., vol. 129, NAC.
31 'Mission de Tracadie' extract of letter, 10 Feb. 1868, *Annales de la Propagation de la Foi pour le Diocèse de Montréal* 29 (1 June 1874): 83. See also L.-C. Cousineau, 'M. l'abbé François-Xavier Lafrance,' *La Revue Canadienne*, n.s. 16 (July–Dec., 1915), 488.
32 'Mission de Tracadie,' 83.
33 *Courrier des Provinces Maritimes*, 27 Feb. 1890.

34 Stanley-Blackwell, 610–82.

35 *Union Advocate*, 5 Sept. 1906.

36 John Jackson, *Lepers, Thirty-One Years' Work among Them* (London: Marshall, 1906), 4.

37 J.C. Furnas, *Voyage to Windward: The Life of Robert Louis Stevenson* (New York: William Sloane, 1951), 336. See also Zachary Gussow and George S. Tracy, 'Stigma and the Leprosy Phenomenon: The Social History of a Disease in the Nineteenth and Twentieth Centuries,' *Bulletin of the History of Medicine* 44 (Sept.–Oct. 1970), 425–49.

38 Morell Mackenzie, 'The Dreadful Revival of Leprosy,' *Wood's Medical and Surgical Monographs*, vol. 5 (New York: William Wood, 1890), 626.

39 The gender-dictated dichotomy between 'curing' and 'caring' is explored in Judi Coburn, '"I See and am Silent": A Short History of Nursing in Ontario,' in *Women at Work, 1650–1930*, Janice Acton et al., eds. (Toronto: Canadian Women's Educational Press, 1974), 127–63.

40 Lynch to Minister of Agriculture, 31 Aug. 1885, Lynch papers, box 3A, Archives of the Archdiocese of Toronto (AAT).

41 Samuel J. Thomas, 'Catholic Journalists and the Ideal Woman in Late Victorian America,' *International Journal of Women's Studies* 4 (Jan./Feb. 1981), 94. This was clearly expressed by Kate Marsden, a British nurse who ventured to Siberia to serve 'Christ's lepers.' Beckoning to 'all members of my sex' to follow her example, she exclaimed, 'This leprosy work is essentially woman's work' (Kate Marsden, *On Sledge and Horseback to Outcast Siberian Lepers* [London: Record Press, 1893], 14).

42 Undated clipping 'Spread of Leprosy,' 13; undated clipping 'The Leper Settlement at Tracadie,' 90, Smith papers, Album 105–8, CD-SHND.

43 Barbara Welter, 'The Feminization of American Religion, 1800–1860,' in *Clio's Consciousness Raised: New Perspectives on the History of Women*, Mary S. Hartman and Lois Banner, eds. (New York: Harper and Row, 1974), 141.

44 Ibid.

45 Thomas, 94.

46 Herman Hayd, 'A Visit to the New Brunswick Lazaretto,' *The Medical Record* 32 (1 Oct. 1887), 450; *Miramichi Advance*, 11 May 1890. See also Canada, *Sessional Papers (CSP)* vol. 5, 1889, appendix 40, Smith's Annual Report on the Lazaretto, Tracadie, NB, 31 Dec. 1888, 153; *CSP*, vol. 6, 1898, appendix 13, Smith's Annual Report, 31 Oct. 1897, 50. See also Mary Ewens, *The Role of the Nun in Nineteenth-Century America* (Salem: Ayer, 1984 – reprint of 'The Role of the Nun in Nineteenth-Century America: Variation on the International Theme,' PhD thesis, University of Minnesota, 1971), 299–304.

47 Sr Corinne LaPlante and Sr Georgette Desjardins, 'Oeuvres des Religieuses

Hospitalières de Saint-Joseph du Nouveau-Brunswick (1868–1986),' *Revue de la société historique du Madawaska*, 14 (Jan.–June 1986), 6.

48 Shortly after they came to Tracadie, the sisters established a dispensary, which served not only the lazaretto, but the local area. The sisters did not have a separate, distinct general hospital until its construction was completed in 1898.

49 New Brunswick, *Journal of the House of Assembly*, 15 Apr. 1869, 151; *Union Advocate*, 22 Apr. 1869.

50 Smith to Scarth, 25 Apr. 1898, Smith papers, 105-5-4, CD-SHND.

51 Ibid., 105-2-2, Smith to Montizambert, 12 Apr. 1902.

52 Excerpt from the LaChapelle Report, Nov. 1898, RG 29, vol. 2355, 'Tracadie Lazaretto c. 1880–1901, Notes, Excerpts of Letters, Reports,' NAC.

53 Rogers to Sr St-Jean de Goto, 30 June 1895, Tracadie Correspondence, 4/155, ADB. See also Reel F-7687, PANB.

54 Babineau to Fisher, 6 June 1899, RG 17, A.I.1., vol. 297, NAC.

55 Doucet to Rogers, 17 Dec. 1901, Tracadie Correspondence, 4/157; Doucet to Rogers, 21 Apr. 1901, Tracadie Correspondence, 4/158, ADB. See also Reel F-7687, PANB.

56 A sketchy account of this conflict is given in Roberto Perin, *Rome in Canada* (Toronto: University of Toronto Press, 1990), 202–3.

57 Doucet to Montizambert, 29 July 1901, RG 29, vol. 5, file 937025, 1/2 pt. 4, NAC.

58 Lynch to Macdonald, 22 Aug. 1885, Sweeney Correspondence, no. 1384 (copy), Diocesan Archives of Saint John (DASJ).

59 *Miramichi Advance*, 22 May 1890.

60 *Free Press*, 22 Apr. 1892 (clipping entitled 'Tracadie Lazaretto'); *Toronto Mail*, 21 July 1880, 747(b), Smith papers, album 105-7, CD-SHND.

61 Sr St-Jean de Goto was renowned for her nursing skills, and people flocked to her dispensary at the Tracadie lazaretto for medical advice and treatment. Between August 1869 and February 1870 she recorded no fewer than 1,659 clients. Furthermore, she experimented in her pharmacy with various compounds in an attempt to find a specific for leprosy, despite the fact that most physicians at this time had cast lepers aside as incurable. See LaPlante, 10–1.

62 *CSP*, vol. 5, 1895, appendix 14, Smith's Annual Report on the Lazaretto, 31 Oct. 1894, 31; ibid., vol. 10, 1887, appendix 13, Smith's Annual Report on the Lazaretto, 31 Dec. 1886, 180; ibid., vol. 7, 1886, appendix 37, Smith's Annual Report on the Lazaretto, 31 Dec. 1885, 156.

63 Taché to Sr Superior, 25 Oct. 1881, file A(I), ARHSJ (Vallée Lourdes, Bathurst).

64 Fisher to Laurier, 24 Mar. 1898, Laurier papers, MG 26, G, General Correspondence, 21984, NAC.

2

Christian Perfection and Service to Neighbours: The Congregation of the Sisters of St Joseph, Toronto, 1851–1920

ELIZABETH SMYTH

The work of the Toronto community of the Congregation of the Sisters of St Joseph lacked the singular focus of the Sisters of the Religious Hospitallers of St Joseph at the Tracadie lazaretto. Nevertheless, this uncloistered community allowed Roman Catholic women to claim space for themselves within their church. When postulants, dressed as 'brides of Christ,' were formally received into the congregation, they made a choice that gave them a status within their community of faith not often available to single Protestant women. Within the congregation, the sisters found room to exercise their varied skills. The work of the Sisters of St Joseph was defined as 'service of neighbour,' but the definition of this service shifted over the decades, as the women responded to ever-changing but urgent community needs.

We Superiors and Sisters of St Joseph of the Sisters of St Joseph Toronto assembled in Chapter, having examined or caused to be examined *JANE MCCARTHY* born in *CORK, IRELAND* and aged *19* have admitted her to receive our holy habit which by the permission of our Superior has been given her with the name *SISTER MARY FRANCIS*, the *15* day of the month of *DECEMBER* in the year of our Lord *1851*. In testimony of which we have subscribed this present act.[1]

Affixing her signature to this act of reception, Jane McCarthy became Sister Mary Francis de Sales, the first of the 655 women who, between 1851 and 1920, entered the Sisters of St Joseph in Toronto. Jane McCarthy's reception into the newly established Toronto community marked both a new chapter in the history of the Sisters of St Joseph and the continuation of a tradition that was over two hundred years old. The Congregation of the Sisters of St Joseph was established at Le Puy, France, in the mid-seventeenth century as an uncloistered and decentralized community of women religious oriented towards meeting community-based needs. The sisters staffed schools for children, academies for girls and young women, orphanages, and hospitals. The sisters also engaged in other charitable activities including prison visitations, ministering to the ill and infirm, and aiding abandoned women and their children. By the year 1836 the order had enough human and financial resources to undertake mission activities, and it made its initial North American foundation in the Diocese of St Louis, Missouri.

In 1851 four Sisters of St Joseph arrived in Toronto from the United States. They came in response to the invitation issued by Bishop Armand de Charbonnel for the order to staff an orphanage. The sisters began their work in Toronto's Catholic elementary schools in 1852. By 1854 the sisters were operating a boarding-school for young women. With Jane McCarthy's entry into the order, the small community had its first postulant, and its modest abode had become a noviciate.

The ceremony by which Jane McCarthy was received into the Congregation of the Sisters of St Joseph had embedded within it both tangible and intangible links to the community's recent American and only slightly more distant European past. Mother Delphine Fontbonne was the Toronto Superior who, on behalf of the community, signed the documents receiving Jane McCarthy into the order. Mother Delphine was the niece of Mother St John Fontbonne, the woman responsible for the 'second foundation' of the order. Mother St John Fontbonne had gathered about her the remnant of the community that had been shattered by the French Revolution and rebuilt the order. She also sent her community to the mission fields of North America. Mother Delphine Fontbonne was part of the first group of the sisters who volunteered to leave the motherhouse at Lyons and go to the United States. From Carondelet, Missouri, Mother Delphine joined the mission to Philadelphia, where she met Bishop de Charbonnel of Toronto, a compatriot Frenchman whose uncle had supported Mother St John Fontbonne in the re-establishment of the order. From Philadelphia Mother Delphine and three companions travelled to Toronto to begin the order's missions in education and social service in British North America.

The activities of the Toronto community grew rapidly. As the numbers expanded, so did the enterprises in which the sisters engaged. As well as the work in the Toronto separate schools and in the orphanage, the order established St Joseph's Academy (1854), a private school for girls and young women; the House of Providence (1856), a combination orphanage, health care facility, and old people's home; St Nicholas' Home for Boys (1869), where the sisters also taught in a night school; Notre Dame des Anges (1871), a boarding-house for female workers; St Mary's (1873), a convent and select school; and St Michael's Hospital (1892). In addition, during the period 1851 to 1911 the Toronto community established missions dedicated to education and social services in centres throughout Ontario: Hamilton (1852), St Catharines (1856), Niagara (1857), Oshawa (1858), Barrie (1858), Thorold (1866), London (1868), Port Arthur (1881), and Orillia (1903).

The Sisters of St Joseph began their Canadian existence as a diocesan community. In the course of the nineteenth century, with the growth in population, it became necessary to redraw the diocesan boundaries of Ontario. As new dioceses were created, the local convents applied to the Bishop of Toronto to become independent of the Toronto motherhouse and elected their own superiors.[2] Thus, three independent communities of the Sisters of St Joseph were established: the Sisters of St Joseph of Hamilton (1856), the Sisters of St Joseph of London (1871), and the Sisters of St Joseph of Peterborough (1890). In the twentieth century two new dioceses were created out of the Diocese of Peterborough, and two additional communities became independent of the Peterborough foundation: the Sisters of St Joseph of Pembroke (1921) and the Sisters of St Joseph of Sault Ste Marie (1936). In 1966 the six English-language groups came together to establish the Federation of the Sisters of St Joseph in Canada.

The history of the Congregation of the Sisters of St Joseph in the Archdiocese of Toronto illustrates the diversity of roles for women that were open to members of religious communities. It also documents how both a traditional and a non-traditional view of the role of women in society could coexist within the same institution – in this case, the Roman Catholic Church.

I

This case study of one community of women religious in English Canada is set within the context of recent works in Canadian women's history and the history of the Roman Catholic Church in English Canada. The works of historiographical analysis in women's history point out both how far the field has grown and how much further it has yet to grow. The works on English Canadian Roman Catholic history point out the extent to which the history of women religious is underrepresented and document the need for further research.

In her review of the study of Canadian women's history, Gail Cuthbert Brandt writes that 'the recognition of the important diversity in women's experience underlines the considerable distances we have moved from a monolithic and static interpretation of gender and suggests pathways that require further exploration.'[3] One of these pathways is the world of women and religion. Ruth Compton Brouwer has observed that historians of Canadian women 'have appeared uninterested in or uneasy with the topic of religion' and, thus, 'there has been a striking reluctance in feminist historiography in English-speaking Canada to make women's experience in the realm of religion the central focus of scholarly study.'[4] While this observation is valid for all Christian denominations, it is perhaps most dramatically observable when examining the history of women religious within the Roman Catholic Church in English-speaking Canada. Even within works on the church, the absence of significant focus on the roles that communities of women religious played in the field of social service, health care, and education is most striking.

In his introduction to the 1993 collection *Creed and Culture: The Place of English-speaking Catholics in Canadian Society*, Terrence Murphy comments that until recently 'the study of Catholicism in English Canada ... has suffered most from parochialism and lack of imagination.' Murphy contrasts this with the historiography of Catholicism in French Canada, which he describes as 'vital and creative ... a rapidly growing body of outstanding works, many employing innovative methodologies.' He suggests that whereas the essays in the collection document the development of Catholicism in English Canada from an 'almost sectarian' status to one of 'integration into the mainstream,' they also demonstrate the need for further research. Murphy identifies Catholic education and social Catholicism as potential foci.[5]

Using these same arguments and observations, Murphy could have called for research on women religious in English Canada. What characterizes a significant body of the 'vital and creative' French-Canadian scholarship on Catholicism is the study of women religious, especially teaching sisters. Yet, in the pages of recent works on the history of education and teachers, and even in research represented in *Creed and Culture*, the role of women religious in general and teaching sisters specifically is remarkably absent, minimally represented, or identified as an area for much-needed research. Brian Clarke's essay, 'The Parish and the Hearth: Women's Confraternities and the Devotional Revolution among the Irish Catholics of Toronto, 1850–85,' which appears in *Creed and Culture*, and his longer study, *Piety and Nationalism*, point out the need for analysis of the roles played by women religious in the shaping of the devotional life of Catholic women.[6] Such analysis could be achieved through an exploration of the overt and hidden curriculum implicit in the records and recollections of members of communities of women religious who taught. To further address Murphy's challenge, the analysis of women religious and their endeavours in health care and social services could greatly add to an understanding of social Catholicism.

Two of the seventeen essays contained in the Mark McGowan and Brian Clarke sesquicentennial collection deal specifically with communities of women religious and their work in education and social service within the Archdiocese of Toronto. Barbara Cooper's essay analyses the early years of the Institute of the Blessed Virgin Mary, and Sister Mary Alban Bouchard's piece describes the social services undertaken by the Sisters of St Joseph.[7] Both of the latter essays point out the need for further research and analysis on women religious in education and health care.

One may suggest several reasons for the lack of scholarly focus on women religious. As Brouwer has pointed out, rather than exploring religious issues that are problematic, some historians have chosen to ignore them. Exploring the world of women religious is a challenge. It is an examination of women in a community who have chosen to set themselves apart – physically, theologically, and spiritually. Women religious see their lives as a vocation. They have responded to a personal call from their God to dedicate their lives in service. Spirituality defies much academic analysis. The vows of poverty, chastity, and obedience that women religious take, and the lifestyle they lead are likewise viewed by some as problematic. They are seen as methods used by the church – a male-dominated institution – to keep women in a subservient role. Second, contemporary secular Western society has trivialized the role of women religious, portraying them in the media as childlike 'singing nuns,' overseen by mother inferiors. Third, until recently, many communities of women religious, such as the one studied here, tended not to focus on their historical significance. They perceived their roles to be in the background – supportive and ever vigilant and quietly going about their chosen endeavours. True, they documented their works; however, the documentation is housed in private archives where the researcher is the guest of the order, and access is strictly controlled. Many communities are now actively engaged in telling their story. Some are cooperating with historians in allowing access. They realize that their membership is declining; their histories need to be recorded, their contributions analysed.

This chapter provides an analysis of the contribution of one Toronto-based community of women religious in English Canada: the Congregation of the Sisters of St Joseph in the Archdiocese of Toronto, between the years 1851 and 1920. It focuses on the demographics of the order and the roles undertaken by the community in education, health care, and social service, for it was in these three fields that the order moulded its works to meet the needs of the people it served.

II

Within the first fifty years of its Canadian existence, the Congregation of the Sisters of St Joseph expanded its endeavours. The phrase 'Christian perfection and ... service of their neighbour'[8] is both the simplest and most complex description of the congregation's work. The sisters' prime objective was personal sanctity – the attainment of 'Christian perfection' – which would be achieved through spiritual development and temporal works of mercy – 'service of neighbour.' In the course of the nineteenth century, 'service of neighbour' expanded from the initial charge of running an orphanage to work in schools and hospitals.

The 1855 act that incorporated the Sisters of St Joseph in the Diocese of Toronto described the order as 'an Association of Religious Ladies ... who have formed an institution for the reception and instruction of orphans, and the relief of the poor, the sick and other necessitous.'[9] The act of incorporation did not identify education as a work of the order, in spite of the fact that since 1852 sisters had been teaching in the Toronto separate schools and since 1854 in St Joseph's Academy – a school which would grow to become St Joseph's College affiliated through St Michael's College with the University of Toronto. In the early twentieth century, when the order revised its constitution, the sisters described their works in broader terms: 'The end of the Institute is the instruction and Christian education of youth and the direction of charitable works such as orphanages, hospitals and homes for the poor and aged.'[10] How the order actualized its charism or mission came to be refined by the members of the order, the leadership team, and the bishops of the diocese.

Initially, in English Canada, the Sisters of St Joseph was organized along diocesan lines into diocesan communities and under the authority of the local bishop.[11] It was essentially a network of independent communities governed by a common constitution – a set of rules governed by Canon Law and a more or less similar set of customs – interpretations of the constitutions and instructions for daily, monthly, and annual ceremonies and celebrations. Each diocesan community was under the direction of a locally elected Mother Superior and a series of elected officers who oversaw the temporal and spiritual administration of the motherhouse and the other local houses, called missions. Each community accepted potential members into the order for an orientation period called a postulancy. Utilizing the data drawn from the order's *Reception Book*, a demographic analysis of the women who entered the Sisters of St Joseph of Toronto between the years 1851 and 1920 illustrates how powerful an appeal that 'service to neighbour' as a member of this community had to women from the Diocese of Toronto and beyond.

To become a member of the congregation, a young woman was first interviewed by the Mother Superior. The constitutions of the community directed the Mother Superior to evaluate the woman's potential as a sister by questioning her motivation for seeking membership and by identifying what skills and training she would bring to the community. The candidate had to be a Roman Catholic, although there is evidence that not all candidates were raised in Catholic families.[12] The candidate was required to present a recommendation from the priest who had been acting as her spiritual director – the priest who had been assisting her in the spiritual preparation to follow her vocation. If the candidate was accepted as a postulant, she would live within the motherhouse for a minimum of three months. There was no habit for the postulants. They wore secular dress. At the end of this period the postulant's suitability for membership was again assessed by the Mother Superior, and her candidacy was voted upon by the professed sisters. If she was acceptable, she would receive the habit and become a novice. If she was unacceptable, the superior was directed to quickly and politely have her withdraw from the motherhouse. Of the 655 women who presented themselves as potential members of the sisters of St Joseph on Toronto before 1920, some 5 per cent left before receiving the habit.

It is significant to note the age at which women presented themselves as potential sisters. Contrary to popular mythology, the majority of women did not present themselves in their teens. Between 1851 and 1920 71.1 per cent of women who came forth to enter the order were in their twenties. Also noteworthy is the fact that only 4.4 per cent of the women who entered the order were graduates of the boarding-school that shared the building with the motherhouse.[13] This contradicts the common assumption that the order was using the boarding-school as their primary source of new members.

The reception of the habit marked the formal entry of a woman into religious life. For most of the period under study this ceremony was open to the public. The bishop or his designate oversaw the ceremony. The potential sisters proceeded into the church dressed in wedding gowns to symbolize the beginning of their lives as brides of Christ. They proceeded into the church preceded by 'flower girls' who carried the habits in baskets. In the course of the ceremony, the 'brides' left the church and returned dressed in the habit of the order. They were given their names in religion – the name of a saint – and became novices within the order.

The habit had both practical and symbolic value. Not only was it the outward sign of unity with the other members in a life of community, but it also denoted the status of the woman within the order: a choir sister or a lay sister. This internal stratification was common among the majority of communities of women religious in the period under study. Choir sisters could be viewed as the professional women within the order. According to the congregation's constitution, choir sisters were 'chiefly employed in teaching or in the works of charity,' whereas lay sisters were primarily 'employed in the domestic duties of the house.'[14] Although both classes of sisters took similar vows, the subtlety in difference in dress was not the only difference between them. Choir sisters exercised the real power in the order: They were eligible to stand for election to the community's offices and to meet in chapter – the central decision-making body of the congregation.

Whether a woman was received as a choir sister or a lay sister was determined by the Mother Superior and her council. This decision was based upon the academic potential and the skills that a candidate possessed: Would she be able to meet the standards set to become qualified as a teacher or other professional? Or was she, in the opinion of the council, better suited for tasks in and around the motherhouse and the other enterprises of the order. The presence of lay sisters indicates that the growth of the order and the commitment of its members to a variety of educational and social service duties within the diocese necessitated the designation of sisters who would take responsibility specifically for domestic tasks. The lay sisters' work in the daily operations of the motherhouse, and in other locations, enabled the choir sisters to devote their time and energies to the broadly defined mission of the congregation within the Diocese of Toronto. Yet lay sisters never had a large presence within the Toronto community. For the period under study, lay sisters represented 6.4 per cent of the total membership in the order. No women were received as lay sisters after 1910, and with the revisions in the constitutions in the following years, the classification of lay sister was removed. While the order continued to direct its members to carry out their mandate of 'service to neighbour' in different ways, including domestic service, there was no longer the difference in voice in community: All sisters participated in chapter.

The women who became novices within the congregation had to bring with them a dowry – although the amount is not specified, nor have financial records survived. The constitutions directed that this money was not to be spent while the sister was alive. If at any stage in her religious life she left the congregation, her dowry was returned to her as a means of facilitating her return to secular life.

The overwhelming majority of women who entered the sisters of St Joseph in Toronto, 75.9 per cent, were Canadian-born and of these, 92.4 per cent were born in Ontario. Even though only 15.4 per cent of the sisters were born in Ireland, there was a strong Irish influence in the order throughout this period. The evidence presented in the *Annals* of the community, which record the many celebrations of Irish culture, and the obituary notices of the sisters, which indicate their Irish roots, document that a significant percentage of the sisters were first- or second-generation Irish-Canadian.

This overview of the demographics of the community enables conclusions to be drawn about the composition of the Congregation of the Sisters of St Joseph in the Archdiocese of Toronto between 1851 and 1920. From a modest beginning with four members, the community grew to be the largest order of women religious in the Archdiocese of Toronto by the end of the period under study. As the order expanded its works into the fields of education (especially secondary and post-secondary education), health care, and social service, it became increasingly aware of the professional potential of women who presented themselves as candidates. As a result one can observe an increase in the age at which women were accepted into the order in the first fifty years of its existence. Women came from throughout the province to join the Toronto community. They were drawn to become members of the Congregation of the Sisters of St Joseph by the example that its members set in its diverse enterprises.

III

In her study *From Nuns to Sisters: An Expanding Vocation*, Marie Augusta Neal argues that 'the institutional form the vowed life takes in each historical era rises out of the major social structural strains of that era. This, accordingly, engenders resistance to the new form of the vowed life within the church, linked as it is to the society at large and caught within these strains.'[15] Neal identifies three periods within the history of the vowed life: from the Early Christian Period up to 1600, from 1600 to 1950, from 1950 to the present. The Congregation of the Sisters of St Joseph had its origins in this second period, a period that saw the rise of communities of women religious who believed it was their mission not to live as nuns in cloister and constant prayer, but to engage with the secular world in works of mercy. Marta Danylewycz describes religious life in the subtitle of her analysis of Quebec's Congregation de Notre Dame and the Misercordia sisters as an alternative to 'marriage and motherhood.'[16] In the array of communities of women religious and the great variety in their chosen missions, religious life offered Catholic women many choices.

Within the period under study, no fewer than nine communities of women religious had established foundations within the Archdiocese of Toronto.[17] There were communities of both nuns and sisters. Nuns lived in total cloister, generating revenue from making altar breads and spending their days in prayer and perpetual adoration (Religious of the Precious

Blood). There was a community of sisters dedicated to working with exploited women (Sisters of Charity of Refuge). Women who presented themselves as candidates for the Sisters of St Joseph sought a life of service in teaching children and youth or in caring for orphans, the elderly, and the infirm. The Sisters of St Joseph broadly defined the mission of their order and in the course of the nineteenth century developed enterprises in education, health care, and social service.

It was the practical need to care for those children who were orphaned by the epidemics of typhus, cholera, and typhoid that swept Toronto in the mid-nineteenth century that brought the Sisters of St Joseph to Toronto. An orphanage was their first charge. Neal explains this as an extension of the vow of chastity whose purpose she explains is 'to assure the presence of some loving people to all who need to be loved and cared for. The vow of chastity lived assures people that altruism is alive in the church and that the world is not fundamentally selfish, even though individuals may act selfishly sometimes.'[18] The orphanage of the Toronto community moved several times. It was housed within the motherhouse until the new House of Providence building was completed in 1857. It occupied a wing of that building until it moved to its own separate building – the Sacred Heart orphanage at Sunnyside in 1876.

The House of Providence was constructed because the sisters and their bishop readily identified another suffering group – the elderly and the infirm. The sisters' efforts met with some public resistance. On 11 August 1857 an attempt was made to blow up the House of Providence. The proclamation issued by Toronto Mayor John Hutchinson offering a reward of £100 describes the event as 'placing a Jar or crook of gunpowder in the building, and firing it off, by which means injury was done to the said building.'[19]

Financing these charitable enterprises was not easy. Most of the orphans and elderly were destitute, and the charity of others was the source of revenue for their upkeep. The sisters engaged in activities such as 'begging campaigns' to support their work. In pairs they would go to parishes in Toronto and beyond to collect money. The sisters, supported by laymen and laywomen, also staged benefit concerts to generate revenues. These featured visiting artists, local entertainers, and sometimes, as in Hamilton, the orphans themselves.

The congregation's second major endeavour was education. Within a year of their arrival, the sisters were asked by Bishop de Charbonnel to teach in the Toronto separate schools, thereby becoming the second order of women religious engaged in this task – the Institute of the Blessed Virgin Mary (the Loretto Sisters) were the first. The four pioneering Sisters of St

Joseph all had teaching experience in the schools of St Louis and Philadelphia, and by 1854 they established in their motherhouse a 'convent academy' for girls and young women. By 1892 the Sisters of St Joseph represented over 80 per cent of the teaching sisters in the Toronto separate schools.[20] By 1939 the six branches of Sisters of St Joseph had an educational presence across Canada in 187 elementary and secondary schools, a college for women within the University of Toronto, and a college for bilingual teacher education in the Diocese of Pembroke.

The Sisters of St Joseph became the backbone of the Ontario separate school system. They staffed elementary and secondary schools. As a community, they responded to the changing regulations of the provincial department of education and by ensuring that they as teachers and their school curricula met department regulations, they enabled their graduates to become certified as Ontario teachers and to teach as secular women and men in Ontario's schools.

As teaching sisters, the Sisters of St Joseph contributed to the building of a English-Canadian Catholic culture. They played a direct role in the spiritual formation of their pupils. The sisters assisted in the popularization of devotional forms of worship and aided in the formation of lay organizations. Among the graduates of St Joseph's Academy Toronto one finds women who played a formative role in the establishment of the Catholic Women's League – an organization still active in 1994. Graduates of the academy played key roles in the International Federation and the Canadian Federation of Convent Alumnae, associations that numbered among their goals to provide scholarships for the higher education of women religious and to build libraries in convent academies. Alumnae associations such as the one established through St Joseph's Academy Toronto provided a forum for the further intellectual development of the convent academy graduates through sponsored lectures and literary magazines (like *Saint Joseph Lilies*, which survived for almost fifty years). The associations also cemented bonds between secular women and the religious who operated the academies. These examples are drawn from one convent academy housed in the Toronto motherhouse. Parallels can be found in the other convent academies administered by the Sisters of St Joseph and other orders of women religious across Canada.

Like other communities of teaching sisters, the Sisters of St Joseph assisted in the building of the parish infrastructure within the Catholic Church in English Canada. Separate schools are tied to church parishes. The teaching sisters took an active role in parish life. By preparing children to receive the sacraments (particularly First Communion and Confirmation), the teaching sisters played a key role in the parish celebrations. They orchestrated public events such as the May Crowning ceremonies, Corpus Christi processions, and devotions. They trained choirs for both secular and religious celebrations.

A third major endeavour of the Sisters of St Joseph was health care. This mission, too, began with the community's arrival within Toronto. The involvement of women religious with the sick in response to the epidemics that raced through North America in the nineteenth and twentieth centuries is well known. So, too, is the fact that many sisters themselves became victims of the epidemics. Mother Delphine Fontbonne, the first superior of the Sisters of St Joseph in Toronto, died of typhus in 1856.

Although the Toronto community did not formally begin its hospital work until 1890, commencing with their arrival the sisters nursed the sick among their own members, the clergy, the inhabitants of the House of Providence, and the orphanage. One of the books that the community brought with them from France was a prescription book.[21] This collection of treatments for ailments such as rheumatism, headaches, and influenza indicates that the sisters had both access to and familiarity with potentially dangerous ingredients. A prescription 'For the spine' recommends a mixture of twenty-five drops each of opium, chloroform, and olive oil be applied to the spine with flannel.[22] For treating cholera the following mixture is set out:

To 1 pint of the best brandy add one ounce of the compound spirits of lavender, —— ounces of tincture of caienne [sic] pepper, 3 ounces of maregorie [sic], an ounce of peppermint, mix it well together and take 3–4 tablespoonfuls together in a hot toddy on the first appearance of the diarrhoea or cramps. If the pain does not subside, repeat the dose.[23]

The caring for those afflicted with disease and the preparation of healing medicines was a tradition in the order which could be traced back to its foundation. Ontario's first St Joseph's Hospital was established by the Sisters of St Joseph of Hamilton in Guelph in 1861.[24] Elsewhere in the province, including Toronto, the Sisters of St Joseph commenced their work in hospital administration in the 1890s. In conjunction with their hospitals, the order also provided nursing education through a network of schools of nursing throughout Ontario and across Canada. In their hospital work, the Sisters of St Joseph laboured collaboratively with the laity and the secular authorities to ensure that the needs of 'the least of My brethren' would be met.[25]

In the course of the nineteenth and twentieth centuries, the Sisters of St Joseph in the Archdiocese of Toronto expanded their definition of 'service to neighbour' to include activity in the fields of social service, education, and health care. With this three-pronged mission, the community attracted women who were interested in serving God as women religious in a variety of fields of activities.

IV

The roles played by communities of women religious, such as the Sisters of St Joseph, within the Catholic Church in English Canada were highly significant. Being a woman religious presented an option to Catholic women to engage in a variety of endeavours and professional pursuits – all in the service of God and neighbour. Women who entered communities of religious dedicated their lives to God through the professions of teaching, nursing, and social service. These occupations were not intermediary steps between schooling and marriage; they were a lifelong commitment. Entering these professions as women religious was not a means of gaining economic stability or advantage; it was a commitment to a life in community where the community, not the individual, gained the financial remuneration. Teaching, nursing, and social work were not jobs. They were means of living out a vocation in a life of service to God and neighbour. Being a woman religious offered Catholic women the opportunity to live in community with women dedicated to the same goals. Living within such a community gave new members access to mentors in the persons of more experienced members of the community. Convents and motherhouses represented institutes of lifelong learning as women scattered along a continuum of age and experience and bonded by a vowed life of service to God shared with each other personal and practical knowledge.

More research on the history of women religious in English Canada needs to be undertaken. In addition to the issues identified in this chapter, there are several other foci of research. The roles played by women religious in education, social service, and health care need to be systematically explored. Far too little attention has been paid to these topics. The opportunities that religious orders afforded women to hold leadership positions within the schools, hospitals, and social service institutions must be researched. The relationships that existed among women religious and laity; among women religious of various orders; among women religious and clerical and secular authorities and institutions; and among women religious and other Christian women's organizations should be examined.

There is much research to undertake. The time is right to break the stereotypes of the 'singing nuns' and the 'mother inferiors' and to analyse just
what is the rightful place of women religious in the history of the Christian
Church in Canada.

ACKNOWLEDGMENTS

This paper is part of an ongoing historical study of communities of women
religious in English Canada. The author acknowledges the support of the
Ontario Institute for Studies in Education and the Social Sciences and
Humanities Research Council of Canada in the data collection. The author
wishes to thank the Sister Archivists of the six communities of the Sisters of
St Joseph, especially Sister Mary Jane Trimble, Archivist for the Congregation of the Sisters of St Joseph in the Archdiocese of Toronto, for their
assistance.

NOTES

1 'Act of Reception 1853–1883,' box 49, Archives of the Sisters of St Joseph,
   Toronto (hereafter ASSJ) [names supplied].
2 A typical response to this request was that of Archbishop Lynch to the members of the London house. In 1878 they requested the 'transfer of obedience' to
   the Bishop of London. Archbishop Lynch replied, 'We fully appreciate your
   motives and reason for changing your missionary condition into a regularly
   constituted House of your Order.' Congregation of the Sisters of St Joseph of
   the Archdiocese of Toronto, *Community Annals Sisters of St Joseph of Toronto,*
   10 Dec. 1878, 26. (hereafter *Annals*), ASSJ.
3 Gail Cuthbert Brandt, 'Postmodern Patchwork: Some Recent Trends in the
   Writing of Women's History in Canada,' *Canadian Historical Review* 72, 4
   (Dec. 1991), 441–70.
4 Ruth Compton Brouwer, 'Transcending the "Unacknowledged Quarantine":
   Putting Religion into English-Canadian Women's History,' paper presented
   before the Joint Meeting of the Canadian Society for Church History and the
   Canadian Historical Association, Kingston, Ontario, June, 1991.
5 Terrence Murphy, *Creed and Culture: The Place of English-speaking Catholics
   in Canadian Society,* Terrence Murphy and Gerald Stortz, eds. (Montreal:
   McGill-Queen's University Press, 1993), xvii.
6 Brian Clarke, 'The Parish and the Hearth: Women's Confraternities and the

Devotional Revolution among the Irish Catholics of Toronto 1850–85' in *Creed and Culture*, Murphy and Stortz, eds. 185–203; Brian Clarke, *Piety and Nationalism: Lay Voluntary Associations and the Creation of an Irish-Catholic Community in Toronto 1850–95* (Montreal: McGill-Queen's University Press, 1993).

7 Barbara J. Cooper, 'A Re-examination of the Early Years of the Institute of the Blessed Virgin Mary (Loretto Sisters) in Toronto,' 89–104; Mary Alban Bouchard CSJ, 'Pioneers Forever: The Community of St Joseph in Toronto and Their Ventures in Social Welfare and Health Care,' 105–18, in *Catholics at the 'Gathering Place': Historical Essays in the Archdiocese of Toronto 1841–1991*, Mark McGowan and Brian Clarke, eds. (Hamilton: Dundurn Press, 1993).

8 Congregation of the Sisters of St Joseph of the Archdiocese of Toronto, *Constitution and Rules of the Congregation of the Sisters of St Joseph in the Archdiocese of Toronto* (Toronto: 1881), 11 (hereafter *Constitution of 1881*).

9 Upper Canada. An Act to Incorporate the Sisters of St Joseph for the Diocese of Toronto. 18 Victoria 1855. CAP CCXXV, 969–70.

10 Sisters of St Joseph of Toronto, *Constitutions of the Sisters of St Joseph, Toronto, Canada* (Toronto: Sisters of St Joseph, 1914[?]).

11 A diocese can be defined as the area presided over by a bishop. In 1920 the Sisters of St Joseph of Toronto became a Pontifical Institute, under the direction of a Mother General. This change in canonical status means that the local bishops have less authority over the sisters – especially over the internal governance of the order. For further details see Michel Theriault, *The Institutes of Consecrated Life in Canada* (Ottawa: National Library of Canada, 1980).

12 The *Annals* record the death of a sister who was 'a convert' and expressed the relief of the community that the sister's family left the funeral 'with very kindly feelings.' Implicit in these remarks is the fact that the sister's family was not completely supportive of her decision to become a Roman Catholic sister. *Annals*, 25 Nov. 1902, 325.

13 'Reception Book,' ASSJ.

14 *Constitution of 1881*, 16.

15 Marie Augusta Neal SNDDN, *From Nuns to Sisters: An Expanding Vocation* (Mystic, Conn.: Twenty-third Publications, 1990).

16 Marta Danylewycz, *Taking the Veil: An Alternative to Marriage, Motherhood, and Spinsterhood* (Toronto: McClelland and Stewart, 1986).

17 Institute of the Blessed Virgin Mary, Sisters of St Joseph, Sister Adorers of the Precious Blood, Sisters of Charity of St Vincent de Paul, Sisters of Our Lady of Charity of Refuge, Sisters of the Holy Cross, Carmelite Sisters of the Divine Heart of Jesus, Congregation of the Sisters of St Martha, Misericorde Sisters.

18 Neal, *Nuns to Sisters*, 78.

19 *Toronto Colonist*, 14 Aug. 1857, ASSJ.

20 John Read Teefy CSB, *Archdiocese of Toronto: Jubilee Volume* (Toronto: Dixon, 1892). Teefy reports that there were 13 separate schools staffed by 56 teaching sisters: 45 were Sisters of St Joseph, 11 were Loretto Sisters (269).

21 'Prescription Book,' ASSJ.

22 Ibid., 54.

23 Ibid., 43–4.

24 Sisters of St Joseph of Hamilton, *A Centennial Memorial of Rev Mother St John Fontbonne 1843–1943* (Hamilton: Sisters of St Joseph, 1943), Archives of the Sisters of St Joseph of Hamilton.

25 Irene MacDonald CSJ took this gospel phrase for her 1992 Centenary History of St Michael's Hospital, Toronto. Irene MacDonald CSJ, *For the Least of My Brethren* (Hamilton: Dundurn Press, 1992).

3

Nonconformity and Nonresistance: What Did It Mean to Mennonite Women?

MARLENE EPP

Women and men of the Mennonite Conference of Ontario have lived in religious communities not by virtue of withdrawing into convents, but by choosing to live in a way that set them apart from their neighbours. Although in theory both men and women upheld nonconformity and nonresistance, in practice they were affected in different ways. Decisions vitally affecting women were often in the hands of men. In the late nineteenth and early twentieth centuries a growing conservatism affected the Mennonites, making it increasingly important to them to witness to their distinctive values. It was women who were expected to carry the burden of faithfulness for their denomination as standards of plain dress were applied more rigorously to them than to their brothers and husbands. For men the paths of nonresistance were well recognized; women had to deal with the effects of the men's actions and also to develop their own ways to express their pacifist beliefs.

Throughout its two-hundred year sojourn in Canada the Mennonite community has been identifiable by a number of distinct characteristics. At various times and places Mennonites were easily recognizable by the clothes they wore, clothing that sometimes approached a uniform. Today the Old Order Mennonites of southern Ontario, with dark and sober nineteenth-century style costume, best exemplify this. During both world wars of the twentieth century, Mennonites stood out because of their conscientious objection to military service. Both of these examples are manifestations of distinct principles of faith based on the literal reading of the Bible characteristic of the Mennonite tradition and shaped by historical experience. Mennonites have often described their desire to live differently from surrounding society, sometimes displayed in distinct costume, as nonconformity. Their objection to war and military involvement, most commonly called pacifism, has traditionally been known as nonresistance.

Because both principles were forcefully put to the test as the Mennonites found themselves absorbed into Canadian society, particularly during the twentieth century, the doctrines of nonconformity and nonresistance became highly significant for Mennonites. Yet the recorded history and the oral mythology that have described these traditions have failed to recognize that women may well have experienced the implementation of these beliefs in dissimilar ways from men, and women may also have found unique forms of expressing them. The impulse towards nonconformity, expressed in church warnings and official pronouncements against such aspects of women's culture as family allowances, fashionable dress, make-up, and jewellery, were more frequent than admonitions against items associated with men – handsome automobiles, modern farm machinery, or membership in agricultural associations. The doctrine of nonresistance, so central to the Mennonite witness in the world, was historically defined primarily in terms of exemption of young men from military service during wartime. Whereas living out nonconformity sometimes created a glaring double standard, living out a narrowly defined nonresistance could leave women out entirely.

Mennonites in Canada historically represent two cultural or ethnic streams based on different migratory paths. The Russian Mennonites came to Canada from the Russian Empire and the Soviet Union in several waves of immigration beginning in the 1870s. The Swiss Mennonites, so-called because of their European origins, first arrived in Canada from Pennsylvania in the late 1700s. Furthermore, across the Swiss and Russian categorization are no less than twenty-five separate Mennonite groups. These many subgroups, some only a single congregation, are frequently placed along a continuum of progressive to conservative, depending on their degree of modernization or assimilation to secular society.[1] While the issues of nonconformity and nonresistance have asserted themselves to a degree for each subgroup of Mennonites, the discussion that follows will focus primarily on Mennonites of Swiss origin living in Ontario, and, even more specifically, on those who today would be classified as progressive in the sense that they have for the most part adopted a modern lifestyle akin to that of their non-Mennonite neighbours. Their umbrella church organization was called the Mennonite Conference of Ontario (MCO) until the 1980s.[2]

The concept of nonconformity has held varying levels of prominence throughout Mennonite history and has been expressed in different ways by each group of Mennonites. Generally speaking, Mennonites believed that they should follow a lifestyle that was nonconformed to the rest of the world, based on their reading of Romans 12:2. A popular descriptive phrase for this stance was 'separation from the world,' a position deemed necessary for a truly holy and Christian life. This view manifested itself, for example, in abstinence from voting in political elections or refusal to swear an oath in a court of law, in establishing separate schools, in insisting upon the maintenance of the German language, in disallowing marriage with non-Mennonites, and in objections to the use of musical instruments, electricity, and motorized transportation. The language of nonconformity was most prevalent among the Mennonites of Swiss background, living in southern Ontario and parts of Alberta and Saskatchewan. Here the influences of revivalism and denominationalism during the late nineteenth century and of American fundamentalism during the early twentieth century represented a threat to separateness; Mennonites were attracted to both movements. Yet these influences, particularly fundamentalism, were a reinforcement of the biblical literalism that justified nonconformist measures.[3]

The most discussed issue of non-conformity and that which had unique implications for Mennonite women was the subject of dress. Even beyond objections to the trends and wiles of modern fashion and consistent calls for modest dress common to many evangelical Protestant sects, around the turn of the century Swiss Mennonites developed a uniform dress code that became the focus of much debate over the next half-century.[4] The application of this dress code was more stringent in the United States, but because Canadian Swiss Mennonites maintained strong institutional and familial ties with their American co-religionists, they too were caught up in the 'dress question.'[5] During the first few decades of the twentieth century, dress forms were encoded in conference statutes and constitutions, and to a widely varying degree they were made a test of membership in the church. Dress regulations also caused considerable conflict in some congregations when local ministers or groups of individuals, seeing no justifiable grounds for such rigidity, chose to defy them. Resistance to plain dress was particularly acute when it was apparent that standards were applied more rigorously to women than to men. Not only were women required to be more nonconformist than men in spurning the fashions of the day, but the dictates about appropriate dress were accompanied by an unequivocal message regarding a woman's place in church, home, and society.

The prescribed Mennonite uniform was composed of several items of clothing that were either outmoded fashions or long-established customs that took on doctrinal significance. For women, the head covering, bonnet, and cape dress constituted plain dress, while for men, only the plain coat signified 'Mennonite dress.'

The wearing of a head covering, known also as a devotional covering, veiling, and prayer cap, came to be officially established and described as a church ordinance during the late nineteenth century; this became the primary symbol of a woman's membership in the Mennonite Conference of Ontario.[6] In an earlier time throughout society women had customarily worn a white cap on their heads. Mennonite leaders came to interpret this practice in the context of I Corinthians 11, where the apostle Paul commands that women have their heads covered during worship in recognition of their subordinate place in the universal order. Before long the scriptural injunction was construed to mean that a woman must have her head covered at all times as a sign of constant prayer and as a reminder of her subjection to God and man. Wearing their prayer veilings, Mennonite women were sometimes called 'brides of Christ' not unlike the Catholic Sisters of St Joseph described by Elizabeth Smyth.

The theme of headship – of man's authority over woman – was a constant in the many discussions on the covering that occurred over the years in the Mennonite community. Sociologists have emphasized the covering's function in preserving ethnic identity and thwarting assimilation, and distinctive dress did indeed serve the purpose of setting Mennonites apart from their non-Mennonite neighbours. The tracts, treatises, and defences of the practice, however, stress the covering's symbolic role of reminding women of their place in the church and in society, rather than presenting it only as a mechanism of nonconformity.[7] An American church leader, generally considered a moderate among Mennonites, offered one of the most orthodox justifications for the head covering: 'The entire question is not one of moral or religious nature, but social. The covering of the head is not a necessity to make God hear the woman's prayers, or to recognize as valid her contribution to the religious life of the community – it is a necessity to preserve the divinely ordained social order from disruption and to enforce the lesson of woman's submission to man.'[8]

One Canadian minister argued that the devotional head covering was a sign to the angels that a woman was serving in her proper spiritual sphere, which was different from that of man. A woman required the 'power of angels,' he said, first of all for physical reasons, because of her responsibility in procreation. Second, she needed extra power spiritually because she was more easily led astray, as epitomized in Eve's transgression in the Garden of Eden. As a result of this 'spiritual peculiarity,' women must clearly be disqualified from filling positions of authority within the church.[9] According to this minister's perspective, there was a clear relationship between the wearing of the head covering and the proper place for women in the community. Another minister, Ontario Bishop Oscar Burkholder, argued that any woman who refused to wear the head covering was 'usurping man's position and power' and 'scorning her God-given position of motherhood.' In his opinion, the 'greatest meaning' implicit in the covering was in defining woman's relationship to man.[10]

Closely related to the head covering was the bonnet which, because it did not carry the same doctrinal significance, became the focus of most of the friction surrounding the dress issue. The rationale most often put forward for the wearing of the plain bonnet rested on the belief that it was more appropriate to wear with a covering than the hats worn by modern women. If the bonnet were discarded in favour of the hat, then the covering would be the next to go. Like the head covering, the outmoded plain bonnet identified the Mennonite woman as different and thus served as a testimonial to her beliefs and adherence to a simple lifestyle. To the extent that it was related to the head covering, the bonnet also reinforced the lesson of female subordination.

A third article of women's clothing that became part of the Mennonite 'uniform' was the cape dress, which was essentially a dress with a v-shaped or square piece of material covering the bodice. The cape dress received less rigorous attention than the bonnet and, though it was highly favoured, did not become a regulation to the same extent as did the prescribed forms of headgear. In fact, in many congregations, only the wives of ministers and deacons wore the cape dress. Arguments in favour of the cape dress emphasized scriptural simplicity and uniformity in light of drastically changing secular fashion. Modesty was also a consideration, because the cape functioned to hide or at least de-emphasize the female form.

The primary feature of plain dress for men was the 'plain coat' – a suit coat fastened to the neck and without lapels. For the most part, plain coats were worn consistently only by ordained men – bishops, ministers, and deacons – though MCO regulations officially made no distinction between laity and clergy.

Towards the end of the nineteenth century, after evangelistic meetings became popular in Canada, the topic of dress was prominent on the agendas of Mennonite conferences in both the United States and Canada. Gradually dress became the subject of official pronouncements. At its 1901 annual meeting (a meeting at which only men were delegates), the MCO resolved, 'That we stand united in the common practice of our sisters, in the matter of head dress,' and furthermore, 'That we use our influence to bring about more simplicity and unity in the church in the matter of dress.'[11] At its semiannual meeting in 1905 the conference stated its unanimous disapproval of 'the wearing of hats by the sisters of our church.'[12] At this time the wearing of bonnets was strongly endorsed but was not yet a test of church membership. In 1913 the conference delegates discussed the question of disallowing communion to those who were not acting in obedience to the 'order of the Church in regard to attire.' Although it stopped short of delivering an ultimatum, the leadership moved that 'we regret the attitude of some of our brethren and sisters who have disregarded the regulations and practices of the Church with regard to their attire, and urgently request their consistent compliance.'[13] Once again, in 1918, the MCO passed a resolution declaring itself in favour of the wearing of the bonnet by women and the regulation plain coat by men.[14] In the years to come, however, only the bonnet was tied to church membership.

During the decade of the twenties, when fundamentalist-style theology and language found an increasingly sympathetic base among Mennonites, the mood was right for a further entrenchment of dress regulations.[15] Much of the prevailing sentiment was clearly a reaction against changing fashions. One article reprinted in a Canadian Mennonite periodical blamed women for what was considered an evil in female fashion trends: 'It would seem that the woman is still bent on dragging man down; she was the one who first tempted man, and she is still at the same old game.'[16] In the context of a discussion on the head covering, Bishop Oscar Burkholder decried the 'physical freedom' offered by the fashion of the 1920s which was at cross-purposes with woman's recognition of her subordinate relationship to man.[17]

In Ontario the reactionary spirit of the times was manifest in conflicts over conference dress regulations particularly at the Toronto Mission and at First Mennonite Church in Kitchener. At the Toronto Mission, established in 1907, superintendent Nelson Martin resigned in 1923, ostensibly over his unwillingness to enforce dress regulations on new female converts who 'were constantly subjected to criticism and misunderstanding' when wearing bonnets.[18] At First Mennonite Church problems arose when the minister in charge, Urias K. Weber, also refused to enforce the bonnet regulation in his urban congregation. An investigating committee appointed to look into the problems at First Church was told by one woman that too great a distinction was made between men and women.[19] The unwillingness of Weber and of like-minded men and women to bow to pressure from the conference resulted in the departure of almost half the membership who, in 1924, formed a new congregation called Stirling Avenue Mennonite Church.

These two situations were not isolated events but simply extreme examples of conflicts that were occurring at other mission stations and in many Ontario Mennonite congregations. The resistance to official church standards and the further entrenchment of regulations continued well into the 1950s. In 1942 the Amish Mennonite Conference passed concurrent resolutions on apparel and 'women's sphere,' making clear the link between a woman's dress and her place in the church and society. In 1943 the MCO placed the bonnet in its official 'Constitution and Discipline' for the first time, stating that it favoured 'the wearing of a plain bonnet as the approved headdress of our sisters, and insist[ed] on a faithful compliance of the same as the continued practice of the church.'[20]

Although the wearing of the cape dress and the bonnet began to decline rapidly during the 1950s despite ongoing admonitions from conference officials and minority conservative groups within the Ontario Mennonite constituency, the demise of the head covering did not begin until the 1960s. At that point the issue was dealt with in local congregations more often than within the larger conference body. Some congregations chose to make the wearing of a covering a matter of individual conscience. In others, dress standards simply faded into history with little discussion.

The decline of plain dress is related to the gradual secularization of Ontario Mennonites after the Second World War. However, the steps that women took in replacing their bonnets with hats, removing the capes from their dresses, and unobtrusively discarding their head coverings did more to cause the demise of plain dress than any active change of position on the part of church officials. Even when plain dress was introduced at the turn of the century, there is evidence that the actual behaviour of women did not always reflect the ideal practice as expressed in prescriptive literature and the official record. There was substantial resentment among women over the double standard that prevailed. As one woman stated succinctly, 'They [the men] could wear the ordinary things and we had to wear the plain things.'[21] Clearly Mennonite women were identified more visibly than men, and this caused no small amount of bitterness: 'I always thought there was a differentiation that wasn't quite fair. The men ... could have the best kind of cloth in their suits and be very well-dressed. But the women were supposed to abide by a pattern, a very plain pattern of dress. And of course a headdress that matched. A Mennonite woman was very easily recognized as a Mennonite.'[22] Certainly the men were able to interact more inconspicuously with non-Mennonites as a result. The most extreme consequence of this double standard was that men began dating non-Mennonite women and marrying out of the church, leaving behind the 'plain' Mennonite females.[23] Women were expected to carry the 'nonconformity banner' for the entire church.[24]

Women experienced discomfort over the wearing of plain dress more often than men. As early as 1895 Malinda Bricker wrote, 'I made a cap for myself and I want to go to Berlin [Kitchener] tomorrow if I can to get a bonnet. If I would live to please men or even myself I would never join the Mennonite Church as you well know.'[25] One Elmira, Ontario, woman recalled embarrassment about her bonnet and even feelings of persecution when girls at her high school would try on her bonnet in fun.[26] A Waterloo minister's wife said that she 'just hated that old bonnet,' and when she went to high school chose to wear a hat instead, even if it meant being put out of the church.[27] The bonnet created especial resentment because it simply did not have a clear biblical basis as did the head covering. For those in their teen years, the age many Mennonites were baptized, the bonnet was the source of both inner and outer rebellion. As one woman of Amish background recalled: 'I had one made pretty much against my will. We just went to the bonnetmaker's and she measured me. I wasn't asked whether I wanted one or not. I didn't care to wear anything on my head.'[28] This same woman was 'shocked and surprised' when she finally discovered that this particular form of plain dress had not always been part of Mennonite teaching. Her reaction illustrates the difficulty in enforcing the dress code when women could easily refute arguments about custom and tradition by pointing to the attire of their mothers and grandmothers, which in the nineteenth century did not differ to any great extent from the rest of society.

Women who felt that simplicity and modesty could be maintained even without a bonnet or cape found it hard to accept the importance of uniformity. Indeed, reacting to the apparel of a summer Bible school teacher whose cape dress had darts sewn in to make it 'so form revealing that I could hardly look at it,' one woman felt that 'plain dress' was not always the most plain.[29] A male layleader in the Mennonite Conference of Ontario also reasoned that if a woman wore a dress that covered her body properly, then the cape was 'as superfluous as the swearing of the oath.'[30]

While some women openly defied the dress code, and others became advocates of uniformity, still others grudgingly went along with conference regulations yet at the same time found ways of actively expressing their resistance. These small acts of rebellion include the minister's wife who, when her husband suggested that their eleven-year-old daughter should wear a bonnet even though she was not yet a church member, had a bonnet custom-made of pink straw for the girl.[31] Canadian women may well have identified with two American Mennonites who, *en route* by ship to mission work in Turkey, reportedly tossed their regulation bonnets overboard. Observing the resistance of Turkish women to regulations regarding veiling of the face, one of these women wrote, 'the Turkish women must be going through a process of liberation much as our Mennonite women have.'[32]

Some women, while not taking steps as drastic as those of the missionaries, nevertheless found ways to modify their bonnets so as to render them less unfashionable. At the turn of the century, Ontario Mennonite women were known for their 'hat-bonnets,' a type of headgear that tied under the chin like a bonnet but was covered in ribbons and had the shape of a hat. The gradual removal of the ties and brim from the plain bonnet so that it resembled a 'turban' was another way to adapt an outmoded style.

The cape dress was probably the easiest to modify in such a way that one could be within the guidelines and at the same time express one's defiance. For instance, cape dresses with short sleeves, lace, and fancy decorative buttons were not unheard of. Some young women owned one cape that they wore only to church over the bodice of dresses. Without the cape, they were fashionably dressed with bright colours and patterns. At one Ontario Mennonite church, only two women donned the cape; of these, one wore earrings with her cape dress.[33]

Wearing the head covering received the least open resistance, though rebellion was expressed by not tying the strings under the chin or leaving them off altogether. A female missionary who questioned the hierarchy implied by this particular doctrine, nevertheless used the teaching about the covering to her advantage. When approached by a minister to reprimand a female songleader for wearing a blouse he considered inappropriate, the missionary woman refused: She felt that 'If we didn't have the authority to teach, neither did we have the authority to correct.'[34]

Not all Mennonite women consciously resisted the dress standards imposed by the church. In fact, some of the strongest defences, particularly of the head covering, can be found in articles authored by women in Mennonite periodicals. One woman described, in poetry, the 'humble joy' she experienced in wearing her head covering, comparing it to a bridal veil, she being the 'bride of Christ.'[35] Another woman, a convert to the Mennonite church, similarly described her newly adopted headgear as a crown of thorns like that worn by Christ.[36] Nevertheless, whether for or against the practice, Mennonite women recognized that the witness of uniform dress applied to them more than to the men and carried a very specific message about women's role.

The dress question demonstrates that Mennonite women were expected to carry the banner of nonconformity for the entire church community. To the extent that the head covering and bonnet also served as symbols of woman's subordination, the mechanisms used to express Mennonite nonconformity also served to define woman's role by defining her dress. If the principle of nonconformity as expressed in plain dress presented a double standard for Mennonite women, the doctrine of nonresistance placed less direct demands on women than it did upon men. Nevertheless, the expression of a pacifist position during wartime presented problems and opportunities that were unique for women.

Historically, nonresistance has been the most distinctive aspect of Mennonite faith. The principle is based on the belief that warfare is wrong because it is contrary to Jesus' command to love one's enemies.[37] In the past the most tangible form of Mennonite nonresistance was their unwillingness to participate in secular warfare. The first Mennonites to immigrate to Canada in 1786 were Pennsylvania Germans who settled in Ontario in part because the government of Upper Canada promised them exemption from performing military service. During both world wars of the twentieth century, Canadian Mennonite men received, not without struggle, exemption from service enlistment. During the Second World War Mennonite leaders, together with other historic peace churches such as the Quakers and Brethren in Christ, negotiated an alternative service program: Conscientious objectors performed tasks such as tree-planting, road-building, and forest-fire fighting in work camps across the country.[38]

Obtaining the right not to participate in wars of the nation has been central to the Mennonite story. The fact that women were not conscripted into the military, however, meant that Mennonite women have by and large been left out of the great stories of nonresistance and alternative service. One Mennonite woman has remarked: 'Because the destiny of the Mennonites revolved around the way sons were involved in [conscientious objection] and not the way the women experienced the truth of scripture, women's contribution was not as significant.'[39] Another woman whose father was a church minister observed, 'My father did not quiz prospective daughters-in-law, as he did sons-in-law, on their attitude to pacifism.'[40]

War meant a number of things for Mennonite women. While their menfolk were struggling with the relation of nonresistance to military conscription, Mennonite women were grappling with what it meant, in a tangible sense, to be a nonresistant people. The exigencies of war brought new tasks and challenges to Mennonite women.

First, the war meant economic difficulty for some women. The small remuneration received by conscientious objectors, substantially less than that of enlisted men, created hardship for their families, particularly after 1942 when alternative service terms were extended for the duration of the war. Without the support of a father, son, or husband, some households had difficulty staying afloat. One Saskatchewan woman warned the local authorities that 'unless my son is permitted to return [home] for the term suggested [three months], it will have the effect of wrecking the health of myself and my children.'[41] In making requests for leave from camp in order to return home, some conscientious objectors (COs) outlined situations where mothers, sisters, and wives were attempting to run the family farm on their own. One young man in an alternative service camp in British Columbia wrote the following to the minister of his home congregation in Waterloo, Ontario:

By this time you have perhaps looked over the enclosed letter addressed to mother from the government including her remarks on the reverse side of the letter as forwarded to me. It appears as though she has already become quite discouraged and seemingly has taken rather drastic steps toward obtaining what she thinks her justice. What I would appreciate is that either you or some member of the welfare board would visit her sometime in the near future to see what suggestion could be offered toward getting the required help on the farm before she writes any more of these desperate letters. You of course will appreciate when I say mother has been operating under a strain heretofore unknown to her which would account for her persistent effort on the line of my release.[42]

Many women were undoubtedly quite successful on their own. Catherine Schulz of Manitoba wrote in her diary that during the war, when her bishop husband was often on the road negotiating with government officials and supporting young men in the work camps, her responsibility was 'to keep everything organized at home.'[43] This must have been no small task for the wife of a church bishop in the days of large families and labour-intensive household work. Like other Canadian women, many Mennonite women entered the workforce, both part time and full time, to bring more money into the household. Another letter to the minister in Waterloo complained of the 'rubber infection' received by a CO's wife as a result of her employment at the local rubber factory.[44] Other women depended upon such survival mechanisms as taking in boarders or moving in with family members.

Normally, Mennonites assisted those within their congregations who were in need; the tradition of mutual aid had long been practised in Mennonite communities. At the outset of the war, however, the plight of the conscientious objector often overshadowed the situations of their families. That the church may not always have helped its members is suggested by one CO in camp who wrote to his minister, J.B. Martin: 'I don't know what happened to the promises that were made to us before we left as far as support for our wives goes or that they would be looked after.'[45] Responding to similar requests from other men in camp, Martin promised to look into the matter. At the 1942 annual sessions of the MCO, in response to a request from the peace problems committee within the conference, a joint committee was formed to look after the needs of dependents of married men in alternative service camps. Composed of the peace problems committee and the conference welfare board, this joint committee appointed a committee of investigation the following year to act as liaison between congregations with needy members and the welfare board which administered a 'CO Dependent Fund.' The policy of the joint committee was that families should maintain themselves with their own labour and resources as much as possible.[46] In effect, women had to prove their own need in order to obtain assistance.

The problem did not go away. At a March 1943 meeting of the Non-Resistant Relief Organization (NRRO), the cooperating body of Ontario pacifist churches, the question was again raised of some form of relief for dependents of conscientious objectors. The problem, however, was deferred to the individual groups represented in the NRRO.[47] Other Mennonite conferences and congregations established their own funds for dependents of COs, confirming the existence of need, but it is difficult to establish the extent of the distress as well as the success of the churches in ameliorating the situation.

At the same time the government was also recognizing that a problem existed. Aware that a conscientious objector, receiving only $25 per month, could hardly provide adequately for a family, Order-In-Council P.C. 5130 was passed in July 1944 which legalized allowances for dependents. The exact amount of such an allowance varied according to individual circumstances and was subject to the discretionary power of the Alternative Service Officer in a specific locale. The average dependent allowance was $5 to $10 per month for a married man with an additional $5 for each child.[48] The source of the allowance was, in a sense, the conscientious objector's own earnings, because it was simply subtracted from that portion of his wages that went to the Red Cross; under the existing system, a CO working in agriculture or industry was paid $25, the remainder of the normal wage going to the Red Cross.

The fact remained, however, that this arrangement was put into place only six months before the end of the war. After the war, new measures were enacted to ease the home situation of those individuals who were still performing alternative service. On 1 June 1945 all married COs over thirty years of age were exempt entirely from Red Cross payments, though they remained under the jurisdiction of Alternative Service Officers. For the rest, the amount payable was reduced to $5 for those in agriculture and $15 for those in industry, as the work camps by this time had been emptied.[49] Clearly, many a woman with a husband, father, or son performing alternative service was forced to sustain her family during most of the war years by means of her own resources, without much organized help from the government or her church.

While in some households women were bearing the economic brunt of the CO position, they nevertheless found their own way of demonstrating their commitment to peace.[50] The *Canadian CO* noted that even though women were not required to perform alternative service, 'their pacifist stance can [be] and is being expressed conscientiously in many different ways.'[51] An American Mennonite woman whose sentiments were likely shared by her Canadian sisters listed twenty different methods. She raised the following challenge:

Have you ever wished that you could prove your convictions on peace and war as your boy friend, husband, brother, or son has? ... Girls and women of the Mennonite church groups! Our Christian responsibility, to our God, the world, the church, our boys in [alternative service] is tremendous. The challenge is before us; the projects await us; the question is, do we as girls and women want to serve? Are we willing to take time out to do the little things that count so much?[52]

Mennonite women expressed their nonresistance primarily by providing material relief, both to their men in alternative service camps at home and to war sufferers overseas. For many Mennonite women, sewing clothing and quilts and knitting socks and bandages became their unique contribution to their country. In 1939 women in Ontario organized local sewing circles into the 'Nonresistant Relief Sewing Organization,' an indication that they themselves viewed their material labour in the context of a faith principle. In describing the material assistance and moral support given to conscientious objectors in camps, Clara Snider, the secretary of this organization, said: 'We are representing a common cause and stand for the same principles ... United we stand, divided we fall.'[53]

Women organized and coordinated relief efforts early in the war in many other local congregations across the country. Mennonite women were knitting and sewing for the Red Cross well before their own church institutions took formal action with respect to exemption from military service or providing material aid. Mennonite women prepared care packages with writing paper, envelopes, warm socks, and gloves, and home baking for their own COs in camps. The Girls' Sewing Circle at Erb Street Mennonite Church in Waterloo, Ontario, wrote down minister J.B. Martin's sermons in shorthand during the Sunday service, transcribed them, and sent them to the alternative service camps.[54] Overseas relief, however, soon consumed the largest proportion of the material aid efforts. Collecting new and used clothing, sewing and mending, knitting, assembling care packages, and canning food became a giant undertaking for Mennonite women across Canada. Mennonite relief workers in England, the main recipient of Canadian material aid during the early years of the war, suggested that women in

North America adopt the slogan 'Non-Resistant Needles Knitting for the Needy' to underscore the 'magnificent opportunity' that their work represented.[55] One observer of the relief needs in postwar Europe noted that Mennonites now had the opportunity to perform a positive service out of conviction and interest and not out of compulsion as had been the case with the alternative service program.[56] Unfortunately, the writer did not acknowledge the fact that Mennonite women had already been performing this 'positive service' throughout the years of conflict.

Not only did women prepare and send material aid overseas, but several women themselves crossed the ocean to work at clothing distribution, in orphans' homes, and in other volunteer capacities. One of these workers, Arlene Sitler of Kitchener, compared the situation of women in England with that of Mennonite women at home in Canada. Writing in the *Women's Activities Letter*, a paper distributed to women's groups from Kitchener, Ontario, beginning in 1944, Sitler observed that during wartime English women had taken over many occupations previously occupied by men such as embassy staff, subway ticket agents, and bus conductors. Though the Mennonite woman in Canada had not undergone the trauma experienced by European women, nevertheless each of them had 'had to adapt herself to war conditions.' Sitler affirmed the material relief provided by Canadian Mennonite women, suggesting that through their giving, 'the bonds of peace and Christian fellowship may become stronger throughout the world.'[57]

It is clear that the living out of Mennonite principles of nonconformity and nonresistance created both problems and opportunities that were unique for women. To the extent that they were confronted with a glaring double standard as they attempted to live separate from the world, Mennonite women responded, on the one hand, by modifying their 'uniform' or disregarding the dress code altogether or, on the other hand, by viewing dress as their special Christian witness. Mennonite women also had to cope, sometimes without the help or moral support received by their menfolk, with the implications of being part of a pacifist church. Nevertheless, they put into action their own expressions of nonresistant love and thus participated wholeheartedly as conscientious objectors to suffering in the world.

NOTES

1 At one end of this continuum one would find the Old Order Mennonites and Amish of southwestern Ontario, whose horse-and-buggy transportation and uniform 'nineteenth-century' dress make them unique and peculiar in modern

society. At the other end is the much larger number of mainstream Mennonites who for the most part are indistinguishable from their neighbours. See J. Winfield Fretz, *The Waterloo Mennonites: A Community in Paradox* (Waterloo: Wilfrid Laurier University Press, 1989) for a sociological discussion of this continuum of Mennonite groups. Also Margaret Loewen Reimer, *One Quilt, Many Pieces: A Reference Guide to Mennonite Groups in Canada* (Waterloo: Mennonite Publishing Service, 1990).

2 Closely relating to the Swiss Mennonites of Ontario, and included in this discussion, were a group of Amish who had immigrated from Europe in the early 1800s. By the first part of the twentieth century they were calling themselves Amish Mennonites, and in the 1960s they dropped the Amish label altogether. The Old Order Mennonite community, which has most strictly adhered to nonconformist standards, is not dealt with here.

3 For overviews of Mennonite theological and doctrinal developments during this period, see the following: Frank H. Epp, *Mennonites in Canada, 1786–1920: The History of a Separate People* (Toronto: Macmillan, 1974), and *Mennonites in Canada, 1920–1940: A People's Struggle for Survival* (Toronto: Macmillan, 1982); and James C. Juhnke, *Vision, Doctrine, War: Mennonite Identity and Organization in America, 1890–1930* (Scottdale, Penn.: Herald Press, 1989).

4 Russian Mennonites did not develop specific regulations regarding dress to the same extent as the Swiss; the more conservative groups did, however, require women to cover their heads, whereas women in more modern congregations simply wore a bow in their hair upon baptism into the church.

5 For a discussion of Mennonite dress from an American perspective, see Melvin Gingerich, *Mennonite Attire through Four Centuries* (Breinigsville, Penn.: Pennsylvania German Society, 1970). A more detailed examination of the subject in Ontario is contained in my paper, 'Carrying the Banner of Nonconformity: Ontario Mennonite Women and the Dress Question, 1900–1960,' *Conrad Grebel Review* 8, 3 (Fall 1990), 237–58.

6 The Mennonite Conference of Ontario was part of a larger North American body called the Mennonite General Conference or simply the 'Mennonite Church.'

7 See Donald B. Kraybill, 'Mennonite Woman's Veiling: The Rise and Fall of a Sacred Symbol,' *Mennonite Quarterly Review* 61 (July 1987), 298–320. Beulah Stauffer Hostetler similarly places the head covering in the context of a movement towards 'codification of practice' resulting from denominationalism in the Mennonite church. See *American Mennonites and Protestant Movements: A Community Paradigm* (Scottdale, Penn.: Herald Press, 1987).

8 Harold S. Bender, 'An Exegesis of I Cor. 11:1–16' (Unpublished paper, Mennonite Historical Library, Goshen, Indiana, 1922), 19.

9 Ezra Stauffer, 'The Christian Woman's Spiritual Service,' *Christian Ministry* 2, 1 (Jan. 1949), 33–5.

10 Oscar Burkholder, 'The Devotional Covering,' *Gospel Herald* 23, 3 (17 Apr., 1930), 67–8.

11 Minutes, Annual meeting, Mennonite Conference of Ontario (MCO), 23–4 May 1901, MCO Collection II-2.A.1, Conrad Grebel College Archives (CGCA).

12 Minutes, Semi-Annual Meeting of MCO, 7 Sept. 1905, MCO Coll. II-2.A.1, CGCA.

13 Minutes, Annual Meeting of MCO, 29–30 May 1913, MCO Coll. II-2.A.1, CGCA.

14 Minutes, Annual Meeting of MCO, 30–1 May 1918, MCO Coll. II-2.A.1, CGCA. The experience of the First World War had undoubtedly strengthened the separatist position of the Mennonites in that they had been the target of public animosity because of their non-participation in military service. As well, the fact that single Mennonite women were filling factory jobs vacated by men who had volunteered for military service added to the breakdown of Mennonite isolation and the corresponding search for new forms of separation, and, quite possibly contributed to the fear that women were becoming too independent.

15 For a discussion of attitudes towards women after the First World War, see especially Veronica Strong-Boag, *The New Day Recalled: Lives of Girls and Women in English Canada, 1919–1939* (Toronto: Copp Clark Pitman, 1988). Also, Margaret L. Bendroth notes that fundamentalists in particular shared a 'general horror' over the 'new woman' who had appeared in the twentieth century and they were increasingly sceptical about the hitherto prevalent belief in woman's moral superiority. Indeed, certain premillenialists, among them Mennonites, came to believe that women's social freedom was a sign of the end times. See 'Fundamentalism and Femininity: The Reorientation of Women's Role in the 1920s,' *Evangelical Studies Bulletin* 5, 1 (Mar. 1988), 1–4.

16 'As It Was in the Days of Sodom, Attention Women!' *Christian Review* 2, 12 (Oct. 1928), 14.

17 Burkholder, 'The Devotional Covering,' *Gospel Herald* 23, 2 (17 Apr., 1930), 67.

18 S.F. Coffman to Absalom S. Snyder, 12 June 1922, S.F. Coffman Collection, 1.1.1.2.6, CGCA. S.F. Coffman was the Ontario bishop in charge of the Toronto Mission.

19 Investigating committee interview with Mary Snider, 8 Nov. 1922, MCO Coll. II-2.A.1, CGCA. The problems at First Mennonite Church are examined in detail in E. Reginald Good, *Frontier Community to Urban Congregation: First Mennonite Church, Kitchener, 1813–1988* (Kitchener: First Mennonite Church, 1988), chap. 8.

20 'Amendments to the Constitution and Discipline of the Mennonite Conference of Ontario,' MCO Coll. II-2.B.1, CGCA.

21 Clara Bechtel Shantz, Interview 7113, Fairview Mennonite Home Oral History Project, CGCA.

22 L.N. Snyder, Interview 7095, Fairview Mennonite Home Oral History Project, CGCA. Though the recollections coming from oral history do not generally pinpoint specific dates, the interviews chosen for this study for the most part refer to the period from the 1920s through the 1950s.

23 Leah Hallman, Interview 7125, and Myra Snyder Shantz, Interview 7111, Fairview Mennonite Home Oral History Project, CGCA.

24 Interview, Lorna Bergey, 14 Mar. 1990.

25 Malinda Bricker to John S. Coffman, 1 Mar. 1895, John S. Coffman Collection, Archives of the Mennonite Church, Goshen, Indiana.

26 Interview, Alice Buehler, 1 Mar. 1990.

27 Naomi Collier Martin, Interview 7122, Fairview Mennonite Home Oral History Project, CGCA.

28 Interview, Lorraine Roth, 14 Mar. 1990.

29 Interview, Lorna Bergey, 14 Mar. 1990.

30 S.C. Brubacher, to Gordon Bauman, 2 Feb. 1970, S.C. Brubacher Collection, Historical Manuscripts. 1.119.1, CGCA. Mennonites traditionally abstained from swearing the oath in a court of law.

31 Interview, Lorraine Roth, 14 Mar. 1990.

32 Juhnke, Vision, Doctrine, War, 251. In a study of dress among the Puritans in early America, Leigh Eric Schmidt observes that the extent to which women were inclined to adopt fashionable dress despite the injunctions of their ministers represented a challenge to men's 'prerogative to prescribe not simply female fashions, but women's roles.' See '"A Church-going People are a Dress-loving People": Clothes, Communication, and Religious Culture in Early America,' Church History 58, 1 (Mar. 1989), 36–51.

33 Ken Bechtel, Strangers within the Gate: Wanner Mennonite Church, 1837–1987 (Kitchener, 1987), 47.

34 Interview, Lorraine Roth, 14 Mar. 1990.

35 Margery Coffman, 'The Ordinance of the Devotional Covering,' Christian Monitor 31, 2 (Feb. 1939), 40.

36 As quoted in C.F. Derstine, 'Three Attitudes Toward the Bonnet and Hat Question,' Gospel Herald 30, 45 (3 Feb. 1939), 946–7.

37 The term 'nonresistance' itself is probably derived from Matthew 5:39: 'Do not resist one who is evil.' The scripture passage calling God's people to 'turn their swords into plowshares and spears into pruning hooks' (Micah 4:3) is often used in support of this position.

38 Several studies of the alternative service program have been done. They include popular depictions such as Lawrence Klippenstein, *Let There Be Peace*, as well as scholarly treatments such as David Fransen, 'Canadian Mennonites and Conscientious Objection in World War II' (MA thesis, University of Waterloo, 1977), and William Janzen, *The Limits on Liberty: The Experience of Mennonite, Hutterite, and Doukhobor Communities in Canada* (Toronto: University of Toronto Press, 1990).

39 Katie Funk Wiebe, 'Images and Realities of the Early Years,' *Mennonite Life* 36, 3 (Sept. 1981), 27.

40 Magdalene Redekop, 'Through the Looking Glass,' in *Why I Am a Mennonite: Essays on Mennonite Identity*, Harry Loewen, ed. (Kitchener: Herald Press, 1988), 239. The question of the meaning of Mennonite non-resistance as it affects women's lives is being asked with increasing urgency by contemporary theologians. See esp. the essays in *Peace, Theology, and Violence against Women*, Elizabeth G. Yoder, ed. (Elkhart, Ind.: Institute of Mennonite Studies, 1992).

41 National Archives of Canada, Record Group 27, file 601.3 (12), vol.1. Quoted in L.E. Westman, Chief Alternative Service Officer, to Allan M. Mitchell, Director, Employment Service and Unemployment Insurance Branch, 23 Aug. 1943.

42 H.S., Seymour Mt Camp, Dollarton, BC to J.B. Martin, Waterloo, Ont., 26 Aug. 1942, J.B. Martin Collection, CGCA.

43 Quoted in LaVerna Klippenstein, 'The Diary of Tina Schulz,' in *Mennonite Memories: Settling in Western Canada*, Lawrence Klippenstein and Julius G. Toews, eds. (Winnipeg: Centennial Publications, 1977), 232.

44 Letter to J.B. Martin, 1 Mar. 1943, J.B. Martin Collection, Historical Manuscripts (Hist. Mss.) 1.34.1.1.1, CGCA.

45 B.S. to J.B. Martin, 1 Mar. 1943, J.B. Martin Collection, Hist. Mss. 1.34.1.1.1, CGCA.

46 'Peace Problems Committee,' *Calendar of Appointments of the Mennonite Church of Ontario* (1943–4), 22.

47 Minutes, Executive Committee of Non-Resistant Relief Organization, 19 Mar. 1943, Non-Resistant Relief Organization Collection, Hist. Mss. XV-11.2.2, CGCA.

48 J.A. Toews, *Alternative Service in Canada During World War II* (Winnipeg: Canadian Conference of the Mennonite Brethren Church, n.d.), 90.

49 Thomas P. Socknat, *Witness against War: Pacifism in Canada, 1900–45* (Toronto: University of Toronto Press, 1987), 346. The alternative service program lasted until mid-1946.

50 Even while the war meant hardship for some women, the absence of young men ironically offered Mennonite women greater opportunities in some arenas. The enrolment of women in Mennonite-operated high schools and Bible schools

increased dramatically during the war years, and, indeed, some schools would
have not survived without this strong female enrolment. At Pniel Bible Institute
in Winkler, Manitoba, women first appeared in a graduating class in 1938. By
the 1943–4 school year they so outnumbered the men that people began to wonder whether Pniel was not becoming a school for girls.

51 Quoted in Socknat, *Witness against War*, 242.
52 Edna Ramseyer, 'Will Ye Heed the Call?' *Missionary News and Notes*, Nov.
    1943, 1.
53 Clara Snider to Workers of the Nonresistant Relief Organization, 16 Dec. 1942,
    John Coffman letters, CGCA.
54 Correspondence, J.B. Martin Collection, Hist. Mss. 1.34.1.1.1, CGCA.
55 *Missionary News and Notes*, Apr. 1941, 61.
56 'Nonresistance and Relief Service,' *War Sufferers' Relief Bulletin* 1, 4 (June
    1945), 3.
57 Arlene Sitler, 'A Challenge to Mennonite Women,' *Women's Activities Letter* 18
    (Feb., 1946), 1–3.

The Missionary Enterprise at Home and
Abroad: Taking Charge

4

Sharing a Vision: Maritime Baptist Women Educate for Mission, 1870–1920

H. MIRIAM ROSS

Maritime Baptist women formed a strong network to support the missionary work of women for women. Hannah Maria Norris initiated the effort; she enjoyed the advantages of a heritage of Baptist interest in missions, the encouragement of one particularly supportive man, and the aid of a close company of relatives and friends. By holding meetings and by publishing and disseminating literature, women like Norris sought to increase knowledge of missions and commitment to work for their 'heathen sisters.' Members of the societies set their boundaries and claimed their own space as volunteers who supported the work of full-time paid labourers whom they themselves chose.

'Go to your "Sisters" for support' advised the Foreign Mission Board as they set aside the request of Hannah Maria Norris, a single woman intent on mission work in Burma. And go she did! During ten weeks in the summer of 1870 Norris travelled hundreds of miles, 'met 41 appointments with different churches, organized 32 Societies (Circles), visited seven Sabbath Schools, attended Central and Eastern Associations and Convention.'[1] In August of that year she was commissioned as a missionary by the Baptist Convention of Nova Scotia, New Brunswick, and Prince Edward Island. Secure in the support of her 'sisters,' she left a few weeks later to join Minnie DeWolfe, another Maritime Baptist who had sailed for Burma in 1867 under the auspices of the American Baptist Missionary Union (ABMU). That was the beginning.

By 1920 Maritime Baptist women had sent thirty-one more single women missionaries to Burma and India and one to Bolivia, and had contributed substantially to home mission efforts. During those fifty years, the 'Sisters' at home had raised thousands of dollars for support of personnel (including a few men) and had underwritten projects ranging from construction of mission houses, hospitals, and schools to purchase of Bibles, lantern slides, meeting tents, and bullocks for missionaries 'on tour.' Believing implicitly in the validity of their task, many Maritime Baptist women tried valiantly to keep their goals of mission before the whole church. Their enterprise grew through a web of relationships, formalized into organizational modes planned to educate and enlist in the 'work' of mission persons of all ages and strata in the Baptist churches.

EARLY INFLUENCES

In North America evangelical Protestant women at home 'provided the support base for foreign missions' that emerged during the 1800s. Though confined to a wheelchair, Mary Webb, a young Baptist laywoman, formed the Boston Female Society for Missionary Purposes in 1800. Composed of seven Baptist and six Congregationalist women, this ecumenical group was 'the first woman's missionary society in the world.'[2] Although they separated in 1829 in order to support particular denominational missions, the Boston society provided the impetus for a proliferation of women's charitable and mission organizations in churches throughout New England and the Maritime Provinces. Foremost among these were Female Foreign Missionary Societies, Cent Societies (entailing dues of fifty-two cents per year), and Mite Societies.[3] During the latter half of the nineteenth century, churchwomen banded together to do 'woman's work for women.' This motto struck a responsive chord in the hearts of women across the spectrum of Protestant congregations in Canada and the United States as they formed a large number of mission organizations, most of them with the word 'woman's' appearing prominently in the name of the group.

Although women supported missions actively, at first unmarried women found it difficult to enter mission service abroad. But change was imminent. Because of various forms of segregation, rigid sex roles, and confinement of Asian women to family compounds, it became obvious that 'heathen women' could scarcely be reached by male missionaries. At the same time, Canadian women's options for education and work were widening, and some postponed marriage until they had attained specific educational goals or had worked in paid domestic service, industry, or the professions; others remained single, whether from personal preference, a sense of vocation, or assumption of responsibility for ailing or elderly family members. Recognition of these social trends had to be incorporated into the growing vision for mission of Maritime Baptist women.[4]

1870–84 WOMAN'S MISSION AID SOCIETIES (WMAS)

Hannah Maria Norris was an intelligent young woman determined to explore that vision. An experienced teacher with demonstrated competence in several languages, a devout Christian and a social activist, Norris volunteered as a missionary to Burma. Lacking adequate funds, the Foreign Mission Board (FMB) of the Maritime Baptist churches turned down her offer of service and advised her to appeal to her 'Sisters' in the Maritime Provinces for financial support.[5] Encouraged in this direction by men and women whom she trusted, Norris conferred with Dr Theodore H. Rand, a graduate of Horton Academy and Acadia College, and her former teacher at the Normal School in Truro where she had enrolled in 1861 and had distinguished herself as a 'young woman of unusual ability.'[6] After graduation Norris had taught school in her home town of Canso until the autumn of 1868 when she began teaching at the Female Department of Horton Academy. Meanwhile, as superintendent of education for Nova Scotia since 1864, Rand was known for his 'progressive views on education,' for keeping abreast of 'current thinking on education in North America and Europe,' and for his commitment to 'God-centred education.'[7] Together Norris and Rand wrote a constitution for Mission Circles based on that of the Woman's Union Missionary Society of America.[8]

Interest in missions was not a new phenomenon among Maritime Baptists. They were aware of Ann and Adoniram Judson, an American missionary couple who had been converted to Baptist principles *en route* to India in 1812. At an association meeting in Chester in 1814, money was contributed for the Auxiliary Bible Society in Halifax. A Mite Society was formed in Saint John in 1818 to collect funds for missions. In 1820 missionary committees were set up in New Brunswick and Nova Scotia to sustain home and foreign missions.[9] A circular letter to churches in that same year recommended 'the formation of missionary societies in every district' and further recommended to 'females in each district to imitate the good example already set – to form separate associations, and to appoint their own officers for the more effectual promotion of this object among themselves.'[10]

As Baptist churches grew, the topic of foreign missions 'was discussed at the fireside and in public, and called forth prayer from the secret closet, the pulpit, and social meetings.' In 1838 at the association in Chester, 'zeal for foreign missions seems to have broken out like a consuming fire.' By the next year Baptist churches of New Brunswick and Nova Scotia voted to accept the Reverend Richard Burpee as a candidate for work overseas and to support him during studies at Queen's (later Acadia) College. He and his wife went to Burma in 1845 to work among the Karen people there, under the auspices of the ABMU. Four years later, ill health forced their return home. Other candidates offered themselves for mission but were deterred by financial constraints or indifferent health. Finally in 1853 the Reverend A.R.R. Crawley, a graduate of Acadia College, was accepted as a missionary of the Maritime Baptist Convention, promised some monetary and prayer support, but advised to proceed under American Baptists. Crawley and his wife engaged in missionary work among the Karens until his death in 1876. At the convention of 1867, Minnie B. DeWolfe, the first single woman missionary from Canada, was accepted for work among the Karens under supervision of American Baptists. After five years in Burma, failing health forced her return to Nova Scotia.[11]

In 1870, against this background, Hannah Maria Norris planned her campaign to enrol her 'sisters' more deeply in mission effort. One reporter soars close to hyperbole: 'Miss Norris ... ripped through the Maritime provinces from end to end like an overdue hurricane, leaving in her wake the greatest furor of religious disturbance since the New Light Movement.'[12] Another author is more restrained in his assessment: 'Her peculiar contribution lay in drawing into a unified movement the wealth of talents, both intellectual and material, which had for many years been directed in a more diffuse form toward the support of Foreign Missions.'[13]

In August of 1870 the FMB recommended that the Woman's Mission Aid Societies (WMAS) form a central board in Saint John for Mission Circles in New Brunswick and another in Halifax for those in Nova Scotia and Prince Edward Island. Officers of the central boards were asked to collect funds and transmit them quarterly to the FMB. The women were also requested to publish items of mission interest in the *Christian Visitor* and the *Christian Messenger*, denominational magazines widely read in Baptist churches.[14] This reaffirmed a strategy already begun when the FMB approved the appointment of Minnie DeWolfe in 1867 and asked the editors of these papers to publish extracts of letters from women missionaries.[15] From 1871 onwards, reports from the central boards were appended to the annual report of the FMB and published in the *Year Book of the Convention*. The women also submitted material to the *Canadian Missionary Link*, a monthly publication of the Canadian Baptist Missionary Society in Toronto. Through these various avenues, women disseminated information across all sectors of Maritime Baptist churches. Nevertheless, they had special goals for women, as stated by Mrs Stephen Selden, who wrote 'that eventually every church in the Province shall have its Women's Missionary Society, and every woman in them shall have her name recorded as a member.'[16]

From the arrival of the Burpees in Burma in 1845, Maritime Baptist missionaries had worked under the auspices of the ABMU. Periodic discussion of the wisdom of inaugurating an 'independent mission' usually brought on heated debate among church members and missionaries. Finally in 1875 in Amherst at a convention 'composed of our leading men and women,' the decision was made to withdraw from Burma and join Ontario Baptists working among the Telugu people along the Bay of Bengal in India.[17] That decision affected Hannah Maria Norris. In 1871 she had begun her missionary career among the Karens of Burma. Among seven new missionaries arriving in Burma in 1874 was the Reverend William F. Armstrong whom Norris had known in Wolfville. The two were married shortly afterward. In 1875 they moved to India with other Maritime Baptist missionaries, but they were never fully satisfied with that decision. For health reasons the family had to return to Canada in 1880. Unable to resolve misunderstandings with the FMB, the Armstrongs resigned at the end of that year. Later they returned to Burma under American Baptist auspices and remained there until his death in 1918.[18]

Between 1870 and 1884 Maritime Baptist women had begun to see the 'Christianization of heathen females' as a task to which they were particularly called. Although careful to remain within their 'proper sphere,' women made opportunities to express themselves both within their own Mission Circles and also within meetings of the church at large. Legitimation for such efforts was established earlier in a circular letter read in churches in 1832 which emphasized that 'the force of the Great Commission ... rests not on ministers alone, but on all professing the Christian name.'[19] Furthermore, in the same year, the constitution drawn up by the Nova Scotia Association of Baptists stipulated that any church or ladies' Mite Society contributing funds to home or foreign missions could send delegates to the association. Any individual donor was also a member: 'This is the first instance in which women were given the privilege of representation in a Baptist Association.'[20]

Given the sparse financial resources, church leaders urged support of ordained male missionaries; nevertheless, recognizing the unique contributions of single women emissaries overseas, they did not obstruct the acceptance of women. But women were difficult to retain during the early years of the mission. Between 1845 and 1883 the FMB sent five couples and three single men to Burma and India. During that time the women's Mission Circles sent five single women: One returned to Canada because of ill health, one married a missionary from the Ontario board and transferred to his constituency, and the remaining three married the single males sent out by the FMB. By the end of 1883 the women's Mission Circles had no single lady missionaries under their care.[21] That situation changed the following year with the arrival in India of two single women recruits.

In their small scattered circles, women continued to inform themselves about missions. They read biographies; they organized mission bands and Sunday schools to imprint young minds with the importance of foreign missions. Baptist magazines for the whole church carried regular columns with reports from Mission Circles and news of missionaries. Outgoing or returning missionaries visited the churches; their letters were eagerly awaited and widely circulated. Through careful economies in their house-holds, women forwarded monetary contributions to support their mission-aries overseas. Somehow finding time to learn about and pray for their emissaries, these labourers at home lived out the observation that 'the sal-vation of the world belongs to kitchens as dynamically as to seminaries.'[22]

Women continued to pursue their vision of mission. By 1881 they sensed the need for more united action. In that year ninety-eight circles contrib-uted $2,068.99.[23] Such growth put heavy responsibilities on those women who formed the central boards. Travel was arduous. Most members in local circles had scant contact with their officers in the boards. Few of the women in the rank and file of the organization were able to attend the women's sessions held in conjunction with the churches' district and asso-ciation meetings or the annual convention. Although changes were consid-ered, definitive action was not taken until Mrs Mathilda Churchill, missionary on furlough from India, used her considerable energy and per-suasive powers to plan and rally support for the formation of the Woman's Baptist Missionary Union (WBMU) in 1884.[24]

1884–1906 WOMAN'S BAPTIST MISSIONARY UNION

Committed to united action, in 1884 the women broadened their new exec-utive board to consist of ten officers and twenty-four other delegates named as representatives of the WMAS across the three provinces. Set forth in the constitution and by-laws were procedures for conducting busi-ness at various meetings. Sensitive to possible criticism, the women care-fully delineated their object as 'the evangelization of heathen women and children and the prosecution of Home Mission Work.'[25] Shrewdly, they set their boundaries: to support Christian women whom *they* recommended as missionaries to the FMB, to support Native teachers and Bible readers (often women), to aid the FMB in ways that 'may from time to time seem to this Union necessary,' and to furnish funds to the Home Mission Board. These stipulations reinforced the women's determination to retain control over their own personnel and funds in the face of any attempts at diversion by men of the FMB.

The women's efforts provoked heated debate. In his published sermon 'How Shall Woman Work for her Saviour?' one male minister avowed that woman was created secondary to and dependent upon man; consequently, she 'is on a level with man, but not as regards the place she is to fill in the church ... The pastorate is not the sphere for woman's labors' because her 'mightiest power is her influence, not her authority.' Furthermore, in separating 'woman from man in the work for Christ,' the WMAS had turned 'woman's sympathy towards a *part* of Christ's work, instead of embracing it in its completeness ... so there has been considerable friction between the Aid Society and the General Board' (i.e., the FMB).[26] The editor defended these arguments and asked rhetorically, 'Have we reached the position where we hold that the sisters should preach and take full share in public business discussions of the church and Convention?' Believing that separate societies in the church for men and women were wrong, this writer pleaded that those 'earnest in the Lord's work keep with their sisters in the church ... and spread the fire among all ... The church of Christ must depend chiefly upon the sisters with their warm hearts, to do this, for the brethren are absorbed more in business and worldly work.'[27]

In the same issue Brother J. March rebutted the charges that the WMAS was outside the church, was composed of persons who should keep a secondary position, and was productive of friction. On the contrary, he maintained that friction between the WMAS and the FMB 'shows that the two bodies are at work, acting and reacting on each other,' stimulating rather than retarding.[28] Declaring 'woman vindicated,' Judge Johnston reminded readers that, according to their constitution, women of the WMAS were to furnish their support *through the Foreign Mission Board*. Furthermore, although one antagonist decried the fact that 'many of the most important subjects in Association and Convention have to be discussed while the sisters are holding separate meetings,' the judge retorted that 'the sisters are not delegates, and have no privilege of speaking or voting in the meetings of either of these bodies.'[29]

Apparently actual practice differed from official declarations. As already noted, according to the constitution of 1832 any church or ladies' Mite Society providing funds for home or foreign missions could send delegates to the Nova Scotia association, and any individual contributor could be a member. The constitution at the founding of the general convention in 1846 stipulated that 'any person paying annually ten shillings, or upwards, into the funds of the Convention shall be a member thereof.'[30] Five years later the term 'any person' was changed to 'every member of a Baptist Church, in good standing,' and the number of delegates per church, local union society, and association was stated.[31] Delegates named in attendance at the 1882 convention were 193 men and 5 women from churches and 17 men from associations.[32] But, given the financial requirement, the tenor of the times, and the disproportionate numbers in such an assembly, women may have been deprived of attending, speaking, or voting at these sessions.

While the 'Brethren' debated the legitimacy of female participation in the public sphere of the church and the dangers or merits of the WMAS, the 'sisters' proceeded. In 1885 at the first annual meeting of the WBMU, Mrs Williams as president entitled her address 'Woman's Work, and the Special and Important Position Filled by Her in All Ages.'[33] Four years later at the WBMU convention, Williams felt compelled to 'face this myth of ecclesiasticism,' to challenge hierarchies with 'their walls and gratings' and 'their enslaved adherents.'[34] Point by point, Williams refuted the men's charges, then flung out a challenge to her hearers to work as women,

not only because we owe so much to the gospel, but because, by virtue of our natures and experiences, woman's need of the gospels appeals especially to us. 'Tis to our woman's heart that the story of woman's suffering and degradation, of hopeless, sin-burdened lives, uncheered by 'earthly love or heavenly,' comes with greatest power; and it is from one woman's heart to another that the current of pitying love must flow, until every one of our entire sisterhood shall press into our ranks ... [to] work and pray and give.[35]

Ending on a more prosaic note, Williams suggested that annual meetings be held at a different date and place from those of the general convention to allow more time to deal with the growing 'work' of the WBMU and to ensure full attendance of women without drawing them away from meetings of the general convention. In 1896 this change was accomplished, establishing the independence of the WBMU and adding to its stature as a denominational body in its own right.[36] No doubt this was a greater show of autonomy on the part of the women than the 'brethren' had ever anticipated! Certainly it illustrates women's 'remarkable persistence in defending their prerogatives as independent entities within the church.'[37]

By various educational means, women were spurred to keep abreast of developments in home churches and in overseas enterprise and to realize their unique role in providing succour to 'heathen sisters.' In the devotional talk that usually preceded the business component of meetings at all levels, speakers often expounded on biblical texts that gave warrant for Christianizing and civilizing endeavours. Delivered at each WBMU convention and printed in the annual report for all to read, the president's address signalled the current state of the organization, reflected on events in the world at large, and proposed ways for local societies and individual members to further common goals.[38]

Noting in her first presidential address in 1889 that only four thousand of twenty-five thousand women in Maritime Baptist churches were members of the WMAS, Mrs Sarah Bigelow Manning called for increased determination to involve in mission every 'sister' who was a member of a Baptist church. In the 'Sabbath-school' and in the home, women could inform and influence, could seize the 'golden opportunity to make missionaries and mission workers of our children,' who are in that 'malleable state' that can be stamped to reflect 'our character and teaching.'[39] In addition to daily prayer and regular attendance at monthly WMAS meetings, 'sisters' had valuable contributions to make in the monthly public missionary meetings of the church. Manning suggested they should help the pastor through active participation: praying in the assembly of men and women, reading aloud letters from missionaries, relating stories from biographies of 'great and good men,' and circulating excerpts about missions from denominational publications.[40] While carefully extolling the virtues of proper feminine deportment in the private sphere of the home, Manning challenged women to extend their missionary influence to the public arena of the church, an area usually claimed by men as their exclusive jurisdiction.

In addresses, meetings, and reports of the WBMU, several themes recurred: the condition of women and children in India as motivation for action, the need for the engagement of more Maritime Baptist women in this enterprise, and the value of mission literature. After describing what they believed to be the condition of women and children in India, missionaries recounted their efforts to enter 'darkened sin-cursed homes' characterized by 'poverty, filth, jealousy, ignorance, and sin.'[41] Against such conditions Christian men were powerless: 'No man's presence can peer into that darkness, no man's voice break that silence, no man's hand loose those chains.'[42] Christian women were needed for 'crooked narrow places where only a woman can travel, sore places that only her touch can soothe – excesses of sin and sorrow where only her voice can be heard.'[43] Although it was felt that missions had made progress, 'the citadel, the home, where life is generated and character formed was untouched ... It avails little to purify the stream if we may not touch the fountain. When the women of heathen lands are won to Christ down goes heathenism and up goes the family, the country, the race.'[44] Manning asked, 'Out of the fulness of our glad lives have we nothing to give? ... What so fills our hearts with gratitude, and our lips with praise as contrasting our exalted positions with that of our down-trodden heathen sisters?'[45] Helping other women would carry reciprocal benefits: 'There will never be a full Christianity for women until every woman is working for some other woman; and when some women are working for many others.'[46]

In advancing their goals women of the WBMU agreed that literature was a prime agency for disseminating knowledge and promoting action. Manning characterized the 'cheap printed page' as 'the most powerful weapon which human ingenuity has devised.'[47] Besides contributing columns and letters to denominational and missionary magazines, these activists began to print their own pamphlets, lesson plans, and maps for use by women, youth, and children in mission meetings and personal reading. In 1892 they founded a Bureau of Literature to stock and distribute their materials. From a small leaflet first published in 1894, *Tidings* gradually developed into a monthly magazine with content particularly suited to the needs of the WBMU and affiliated groups. The WBMU and some forty other women's boards cooperated in sponsoring the *International Course of Mission Studies*. Topics ranged from a history of missions to intensive studies of peoples and conditions in China, Japan, Africa, and elsewhere. These books were supplemented by appropriate maps, charts, pictures, and pamphlets, and by studies for young people.[48]

Women of the WBMU placed high priority on education of children and youth for missions. While organizing the first thirty-three WMAS in 1870, Hannah Maria Norris had also visited seven 'Sabbath Schools.' To complement this outreach to children, the first Mission Bands were formed in 1874 and carried such names as 'Willing Workers,' 'Jewel Gatherers,' 'Cheerful Givers,' and 'Helping Hands.' In their meetings, children drew maps of India and located its cities and towns, learned about its topography and climate and resources, listened to stories of customs there, memorized the names of Maritime Baptist missionaries and their Indian helpers, heard of events on mission stations, and saved their pennies to contribute to the cause. In 1897 at the time of the appointment of the first WBMU Mission Band treasurer, one of the officers declared, 'I am convinced that, for its future good, no church can afford to be without a Band in which to train the children. If our denomination is to come up to its privilege in the future, the children must be trained in benevolence.'[49] Two years later, the WBMU appointed a Mission Band superintendent for each Maritime province. One of these officers later assessed the value of 'Christian activity': 'There is none more important than having our boys and girls, young men and maidens engaged in mission study and practicing self-denial to extend the Redeemer's kingdom at home and abroad.'[50] Seeing the need to enlarge and standardize programs for these age groups, leaders began in 1900 to publish special mission lessons that were later incorporated into *Tidings*.

In 1897 Manning challenged 'mothers, sisters, grandmothers': 'To begat [sic] an interest in missions we must begin as near the cradle as possible.'[51] To assure early contacts with infants and their mothers, the WBMU instituted the Cradle Roll (renamed Baby Band in 1906) and appointed three provincial superintendents to promote that outreach. By such careful organization, the women expected to assure the ongoing of their cherished 'work': 'Each child now led into sympathetic relations with the cause of the Redeemer will be almost sure to preserve that bias to the end of life.'[52] Sincere in their desire to plant the seed of missionary concern in boys and girls, many women put much effort into their endeavours. Rewards came as they watched their protégés grow into adulthood – many of the women to engage in the 'work' of the WBMU, a few members to become single women recruits or wives of missionaries, and some men as pastors or laymen to act as advocates for the claims of missions.

But results were sometimes discouraging. By 1896 only one-quarter of women in Maritime Baptist churches were members of the WBMU, and only one-quarter of those donated more than one dollar annually.[53] Three years later there were still only 248 WMAS in the 400 Baptist churches in the Maritimes. In closing her presidency, Manning expressed regret that many women and girls within the churches had not 'identified with this work.'[54] Nevertheless, in 1906 there were 280 WMAS and 169 Mission Bands and they underwrote estimates amounting to $13,000.[55] Manning had cause for hope as she reported with approval: 'It is generally acknowledged that the Women's Missionary Societies are today one of the most valuable aids to the evangelization of the world.'[56]

Leaders of the WBMU struggled to turn the concern and efforts of Maritime Baptist women towards amelioration of the difficult circumstances of distant 'sisters' – those in India and those immigrants and Native Canadians within reach of the Home Mission Board. Addresses and reports are devoid of consideration of conditions surrounding women in the Maritimes. Rather than railing publicly against restrictions on their own lives, spokespersons chose to find ways to reach their specific goals without unduly challenging social mores or male hierarchies.

Although many members of the WBMU lived isolated, poverty-stricken lives, their leaders expressed much optimism. The small coterie at the centre was closely bound by ties of kinship, marriage, or long-standing friendship, and they held exceptionally long but varied terms of office. Many of the leaders were married to or were relatives of ministers and professional men of considerable stature in the denomination.[57] Officers of the WBMU tended to be intelligent, well educated by standards of their day, well read, and convinced of their contribution to the salvation and uplift of their 'heathen sisters.' They were also persuaded of the value of education, both to assure the continuation of interest in missions on the part of their children and to enable women of India to improve their own lot in life and to bring about major changes in Indian society. As they moulded their organization to achieve these ends, the women of the WBMU matured in their own religious beliefs, enlarged their world far beyond the narrow confines of daily life, and set in motion forces that allowed them to carve out a wider place in the structure of the male-dominated church. Although the WBMU and sister organizations encouraged women to become teachers, nurses, and physicians and to exercise their talents overseas as teachers, evangelists, pastors, and church and hospital administrators, they did not express any desire to promote women in the recognized pastoral office in the church at home. Their records disclose no mention of yearnings of women to undertake formal study of theology or to receive ordination.

During this period two Free Baptist mission organizations had also been developing in the Maritimes. Organized in 1867, the Nova Scotia Free Baptist Foreign Mission Society included both male and female members, although women conducted most of the meetings. Established in 1875 the Free Baptist Woman's Missionary Society of New Brunswick received reports in 1905 from 72 branches, 24 Mission Bands, and 11 Cradle Rolls. These two groups had sent a total of four single women missionaries to India: Two were later invalided home, one married while overseas, and one (Elizabeth Gaunce) returned to Canada in 1902 to take a three-year course in nursing. In 1905–6 when these two Free Baptist denominations united with Maritime Baptists to form the United Baptist Convention of the Maritime Provinces, the three mission groups joined to become the United Baptist Woman's Missionary Union of the Maritime Provinces (UBWMU). In the basis of union provision was made to continue specific aspects of the work of the Free Baptist Missionary Society of New Brunswick, including the return of Gaunce to India as a missionary of the UBWMU. Although the uniting societies ceased to exist, they continued under another name to 'work, in larger, fuller, measure' than before.[58]

1906–1920 UNITED BAPTIST WOMAN'S MISSIONARY UNION

The structure of the UBWMU reflected those of the three founding bodies. During the first five years of union, however, names of only two former officers of the Free Baptist WMS of New Brunswick appeared among the UBWMU officers who were mostly former WBMU members, many of whom held long tenures.[59] Women at the core of the UBWMU were highly dedicated to its goals. The desire to lead a spiritual life was inculcated from one generation to the next. Manning's mother was remembered for her faithfulness at Sunday morning worship and the woman's weekly after-noon prayer meeting: 'no excuse but serious illness was allowed to inter-fere'[60] As secretary for the central board of Nova Scotia from 1870 until her final illness in 1887, Mrs Selden frequently reminded women that their gift of two cents a week to missions must be accompanied by regular prayer and by attendance at the monthly meetings. Of Mrs Parsons, found-ing member in 1870 and president or vice-president until her death in 1890, it was said: 'She never let anything but illness keep her away. To her that one hour a month of prayer was sacred to the Master.'[61] Manning's note-books contained long lists of intercessions, demonstrations of prayer as 'the habit of a lifetime,' and basis for her continual concern for the 'spiri-tual side' and 'prayer life' of the societies. Her final letter (1921) to the Wolfville Missionary Society contained an admonition: 'Let me intreat you to be faithful every day ... . Never allow anything but sickness to keep you from the place of prayer.'[62] Mrs David Hutchinson, UBWMU president from 1906 to 1921, 'for years' spent one hour at noon each day in prayer for missionaries.[63] To encourage others desirous of following this pattern, a 'prayer cycle' with current matters of concern in the mission 'work' was published monthly in *Tidings*, beginning in 1907.

Members of the UBWMU were stimulated by numerous contacts beyond the borders of the Maritime Provinces. Presidential addresses at annual conventions included references to missionary figures past and present and to current events within the world and the church at large. Women leaders attended international conferences. Among several thou-sand clergy, missionaries, and church members present at the Centenary Conference on Protestant Missions of the World (London, 1888) were 381 women, of whom five were Canadians. A few women spoke at small sec-tional meetings; only one woman – Hannah Maria Norris Armstrong – addressed the general assembly.[64]

One of the goals set in 1917 for the jubilee celebrations in 1920 was the establishment of fifty World Wide Guilds to interest young people over the age of fifteen in missions. Although these societies were mainly to bridge the gap between girls and young women and the older women, the superin-tendent hoped that young men would also join to pray, study, and give to mission work. By the 1920 convention, only twenty-five guilds had been organized but hopes remained high for later success.[65] Meanwhile, the women continued their concerted efforts to educate children in Mission Bands and Sunday school and many missionary and mission workers traced their interest 'to lessons taught and impressions received' in these groups.[66] But the full value of the Mission Bands lay beyond time: 'If we work upon marble, it will perish; if we work upon brass time will efface it; if we rear temples they will crumble into dust; but if we work upon immortal souls, if we embue them with principles, with the just fear of God and love of fellowmen, we engrave on these tablets something which will brighten eternity.'[67]

Having survived the trauma and terror of the First World War, women of the UBWMU were optimistic. In 1918, when women in Canada won the right to vote, leaders in the UBWMU saw the franchise 'opening greater opportunities for usefulness to those, who by their war-work experience, have demonstrated their ability to help in establishing righteousness in the world.'[68] Two decades previously a resolution at the WBMU convention decried 'intemperance' which 'blights our homes and destroys our children, and defaces the image of God in man.' It called women to 'put forth every effort in our power both by prayer and personal work to help forward the annihilation of the liquor traffic.'[69] Now women of the UBWMU again turned their attention to social problems at home: 'The liquor traffic must be outlawed, and social purity safe-guarded, Sabbath observance enforced, and unwholesome amusements must be made to give place to what will harmonize with the Ten Commandments, the Lord's Prayer and the Sermon on the Mount.'[70] Furthermore, having filled expanded roles during the war, women of the UBWMU were hearing the call of 'higher Christian stateswomanship' which envisioned 'a new woman's overseas service movement, Christ's woman movement ... ready to carry to 500,000,000 women overseas relief from sin and sickness and superstition within [which] they groan, being burdened.'[71]

Goals for the jubilee in 1920 included ten thousand prayer intercessors, fifteen thousand subscribers to *Tidings*, fifty new WMAS branches, fifty World Wide Guilds, one hundred new Mission Bands, fifty new Baby Bands, seven single women missionary recruits (including two physicians and two 'trained' nurses), $50,000 in contributions to the jubilee funds, and Home Mission work 'among foreigners in New Brunswick, and among colored people and others in Nova Scotia.'[72] Considerable advance was made towards each of these goals. Four single women recruits were sent overseas and another was under appointment. Special jubilee contributions amounted to $36,275.99.[73] Although somewhat disappointed that their full agenda had not been achieved, the more than four hundred delegates and visitors at the UBWMU convention in October 1920 found ample reasons for rejoicing and for looking confidently towards the future. Saddened by the absence of Manning because of her serious illness, the women recalled the distinction accorded Manning and Mrs Mary Smith (UBWMU general treasurer) in May of that year when Acadia University bestowed upon them the honorary degree of Master of Arts.[74]

ASSESSING FIFTY YEARS

For fifty years women in Maritime Baptist missionary societies were bent on educating themselves and others to share in their vision of mission. In spite of opposition, these women achieved many of their goals – and gained a wider place for themselves in the process.

Although women in her day had scant public voice in Baptist churches, Hannah Maria Norris organized women's Mission Circles and made her presence felt at Baptist associations and conventions. She enlisted the help of powerful men to attain the goals that she herself had set. Throughout her lifetime by addresses at local meetings and major conferences, and by letters in publications produced for general church readership as well as those specifically for women, Hannah Maria Norris Armstrong kept the audience informed about her missionary endeavours and challenged by her plans for evangelism, social action, and education. Although the Armstrongs transferred to the ABMU in 1884, Norris Armstrong is still highly revered as the founder of the UBWMU. Her acumen, boldness, and dedication have long served as models for members of the missionary societies and for women missionary candidates.

In trying to engage every Baptist woman in the 'work' of missions, members of the missionary societies showed their belief in the capacity of women, even those of limited accomplishment, to be part of the evangelistic outreach of the church and to instill in their children knowledge of the scope and importance of missionary endeavours. Visionary leaders at the core of the movement gradually evolved a vast organizational web that reached even into isolated outposts to mobilize women for the cause of missions. They expected members in their local constituency to keep the topic of missions before pastors and laymen as well as before women and children.

Whereas in the church financial support for missions had been limited to occasional desultory collections, the women planned for giving that would be 'individual, systematic, proportionate, cheerful and self-denying.'[75] Money was scarce; women had little control over family finances, but they did have proceeds from the sale of their own work – the egg and butter and knitting money. 'They could squander some of that on missions if they chose.'[76] Those small sums added up to ample amounts to support their own missionaries and projects. They gave the lie to 'the grave doubts and ominous shaking of heads' of the 'brethren' who awaited the collapse of the whole enterprise, since most of them deemed women incapable of being 'good financiers.' Proudly an anonymous chronicler proclaimed, 'Not *one dollar* of the thousands that have passed through the hand of the WBMU has either been *lost* or misappropriated, in all these years.'[77] In contrast, chagrined by less apt financial structures, the FMB sometimes had to turn to the women for help to meet embarrassing shortages. Ironically while Mrs Peabody, special speaker at the 1920 jubilee celebrations, reinforced traditional roles by showing that 'God intended women to be homemakers, to be teachers, especially of little children, and to take care of sick people,' members of the UBWMU that year had contributed and administered the substantial sum of $83,789.35.[78]

Participation in their missionary societies gave women opportunities to develop organizational and financial skills, to find personal satisfaction by engaging in 'work' that was well regarded by men and women in the church, and to attend meetings and conventions where they met and exchanged ideas with a wide range of persons from locations and perspectives far beyond those of their local community. This expanded vision was reinforced as the women exercised teaching skills and shared their knowledge of missions with adults and children in the church. The constant emphasis on education provided motivation for some young girls to seek advanced training – sometimes in the expectation of going to the mission field where they found greatly expanded opportunities to teach, preach, and practice medicine. In spite of circumscribing women's roles in the church in Canada, Maritime Baptist administrators, like similar ecclesiastical bodies, evidenced 'less concern about what women did [overseas] – in direct proportion to the distance they were from the home power base.'[79]

Although the missionary societies opened new vistas for many members, the reins of control from 1870 to 1920 were firmly in the hands of a small coterie of women who usually remained in office for decades. They seldom swerved from their main objective of evangelization and succour for their 'heathen sisters.' Except to advance that goal, they rarely challenged the ecclesiastical hierarchy. Although deeply moved by tales of destitution in India, they made few attempts to address poverty and related social issues at home until after the First World War. Nevertheless, through their own mastery of organizational skills and through their commitment to education, members of the missionary societies laid foundations for continued enlargement of roles open to women in the public sphere.

In the early twentieth century most Woman's Missionary Societies were merged into denominational mission boards, often with little or no prior consultation with the women.[80] By contrast, the UBWMU withstood this trend to be co-opted and engulfed; it continues today as a separate convention. Women of the UBWMU used several strategies to retain control of their own structures: acting as the first portal of entry in screening single women missionary applicants, designating specific personnel and projects that they would support for the FMB, insisting upon sending their own female representatives to sit on that board, and holding their convention at a time and place other than that of the general convention until the autonomy of the UBWMU was well established. Like the suffragists, members of the UBWMU turned the 'evocative symbols' of 'home' and 'motherhood' from 'boundaries of limitation' to 'channels of opportunity.'[81] They clarified goals that they deemed appropriate and valuable and initiated organizational structures and educational projects to share their vision with women and men, children, and elders within and beyond their church constituency.

NOTES

1 Mary Cramp, *Retrospects: A History of the Formation and Progress of the Women's Missionary Aid Societies of the Maritime Provinces* (Halifax: Holloway Brothers, 1891), 9.
2 Ruth A. Tucker, *Guardians of the Great Commission: The Story of Women in Modern Missions* (Grand Rapids, Mich.: Academie, 1988), 63.
3 R. Pierce Beaver, *American Protestant Women in World Mission: History of the First Feminist Movement in North America*, rev. ed. (Grand Rapids, Mich.: Eerdmans, 1986), 17–25; Helen Barrett Montgomery, *Western Women in Eastern Lands* (New York: Macmillan, 1910), 19.
4 H. Miriam Ross, 'Shaping a Vision of Mission: Early Influences on the United Baptist Woman's Missionary Union,' in *An Abiding Conviction: Maritime Baptists and Their World*, Robert S. Wilson, ed. (Hantsport, NS: Lancelot Press, 1988), 83–107; H. Miriam Ross, '"Sisters" in the Homeland: Vision for Mission among Maritime Baptist Women, 1867–1920' (in press).
5 *Minutes of the Twenty-Fifth Session*, Baptist Convention of Nova Scotia, New Brunswick, and Prince Edward Island (hereafter BC–NS, NB, PEI), 1870, 34.
6 George Edward Levy, *The Baptists of the Maritime Provinces, 1753–1946* (Saint John, NB: Barnes-Hopkins, 1946), 192.
7 Margaret Conrad, '"An Abiding Conviction of the Paramount Importance of Christian Education": Theodore Harding Rand as Educator, 1860–1900,' in *An Abiding Conviction: Maritime Baptists and Their World*, Robert S. Wilson, ed. (Hantsport, NS: Lancelot Press, 1988), 163–4.

8 Cramp, *Retrospects*, 9. This process contrasts with the description by John Webster Grant of the formation of the Woman's Foreign Missionary Society of the Presbyterian Church in Canada.

9 Edward M. Saunders, *History of the Baptists of the Maritime Provinces* (Halifax: John Burgoyne, 1902), 208–10.

10 Ibid., 228.

11 Ibid., 284, 294, 297–8. Burpee was often spelled Burpe or Burpé.

12 Earl C. Merrick, *These Impossible Women, 100 Years: The Story of the United Baptist Woman's Missionary Union of the Maritime Provinces* (Fredericton, NB: Brunswick Press, 1970), 13.

13 Levy, *Baptists of the Maritime Provinces*, 193.

14 Charles Tupper, 'Women's Aid Societies,' *Christian Messenger*, 31 Aug. 1870, 275.

15 *Minutes of the Twenty-Second Session*, BC–NS, NB, PEI, 1867, 29.

16 *Minutes of the Twenty-Ninth Session*, BC–NS, NB, PEI, 1874, 48.

17 D.A. Steele, *Our Pioneer: Impressions Regarding Mrs H.M.N. Armstrong* (Amherst, NS: n.p., 1920), 29.

18 Ibid., 30; *Minutes of the Thirty-Sixth Session*, BC–NS, NB, PEI, 1881, 39.

19 Saunders, *History of the Baptists*, 228.

20 Ibid., 293.

21 Cramp, *Retrospects*, 25.

22 Merrick, *These Impossible Women*, 29.

23 *Minutes of the Thirty-Sixth Session*, 42–5.

24 Cramp, *Retrospects*, 28.

25 *Second Annual Report*, Woman's Baptist Missionary Union of the Maritime Provinces (WBMUMP) (1885–6), 3. In response to an 1885 appeal by the Home Mission Board, the women thereafter directed some of their educational efforts and funds towards assistance to and evangelization of 'colored people' (especially in Nova Scotia), immigrants arriving at Canadian ports, immigrants settling in the prairie provinces, and French-Canadians. Reports from workers among these groups were made regularly at WBMU and UBWMU conventions, printed in *Tidings*, etc.

26 Reverend A. Cohoon, 'How Shall Woman Work for her Saviour?' *Messenger and Visitor* [St John], 29 July 1885, 2. Emphasis added.

27 'Woman's Work,' Editorial, *Messenger and Visitor* [St John], 12 Aug. 1885, 4.

28 J. March, 'Woman's Position and Work in the Church,' *Messenger and Visitor* [St John] 12 Aug. 1885, 4. Probably Brother March was the husband of Mrs John March, first corresponding secretary of the WBMU.

29 J.W. Johnston, 'Woman Vindicated,' *Messenger and Visitor* [St John], 26 Aug. 1885, 4.

30 *Minutes of the First Session*, BC–NS, NB, PEI, 1846, 4.

31 *Minutes of the Sixth Session*, BC–NS, NB, PEI, 1851, 26.

32 *Minutes of the Thirty-Seventh Session*, BC–NS, NB, PEI, 1882, 9–13.

33 Cramp, *Retrospects*, 29.

34 Mrs W.M. Williams, 'President's Address,' *Fourth Annual Report*, WBMUMP (1887–8), 21, 22.

35 Ibid., 23–4.

36 Mary Kinley Ingraham, *Seventy-Five Years: Historical Sketch of the United Baptist Woman's Missionary Union in the Maritime Provinces of Canada* (Kentville, NS: Kentville Publishing, 1946), 20; Levy, 196.

37 Wendy Mitchinson, 'Canadian Women and Church Missionary Societies,' *Atlantis* 2, 2, part 2 (Spring 1977), 69.

38 Over its duration of 22 years, the WBMU had only two presidents: Mrs Williams (1884–9) and Mrs Sarah Bigelow Manning (1889–1906). Having been a member of the central board for Nova Scotia, Manning became treasurer from the formation of the WBMU in 1884 until assuming the presidency 1889–1906, then editor of *Tidings* 1908–20. She was a cousin and early schoolmate of Hannah Maria Norris and a graduate of Grand Pré Seminary. Her husband, the Reverend J.W. Manning, was minister of several influential city churches, then secretary-treasurer of the FMB 1892–1906, later chairman of the board of governors of Acadia University. Mrs F.H. Beals, *Mrs J.W. Manning: A Tribute* (Kentville, NS: n.p., 1932), 23, 25, 29.

39 Manning, 'President's Address,' *Sixth Annual Report*, WBMUMP (1889–90), 26.

40 Ibid., 25.

41 Manning, 'President's Address,' *Seventeenth Annual Report*, WBMUMP (1900–1), 135.

42 Manning, 'President's Address,' *Fifteenth Annual Report*, WBMUMP (1898–9), 111.

43 Ibid., 110.

44 Ibid., 111.

45 Manning, 'President's Address,' *Eighth Annual Report*, WBMUMP (1891–2), 24, 25.

46 A Life Member of the WBMU, 'What Aid Society Has Done for Me,' *Tidings*, Mar. 1894, 4.

47 Manning, 'President's Address,' *Eighth Annual Report*, WBMUMP (1891–2), 29.

48 Clementina Butler, 'The Work of the Women's Foreign Missionary Societies,' *Missionary Review of the World* 18, 7 (July, 1905), 482–90; Central Committee of the United Study of Missions, 'Foreword,' in *Western Women in Eastern Lands*, Helen Barrett Montgomery (New York: Macmillan, 1910), xi–xiv.

49 Mrs P.R. Foster, *Thirteenth Annual Report*, WBMUMP (1896–7), 93.

50 Foster, *Twenty-first Annual Report*, WBMUMP (1904–5), 74.

51 Manning, 'President's Address,' *Fourteenth Annual Report*, WBMUMP (1897–8), 123.

52 Mrs W.E. McIntyre, *First Annual Report*, United Baptist Woman's Missionary Union (hereafter UBWMU) (1906–7), 76.

53 Manning, 'President's Address,' *Twelfth Annual Report*, WBMUMP (1895–6), 106.

54 Manning, 'President's Address, *Twenty-First Annual Report*, WBMUMP (1904–5), 23.

55 Mrs C.H. Martell, *Historical Sketch of the United Baptist Woman's Missionary Union of the Maritime Provinces* (n.p., 1920), 23–4. $13,000 budgeted as follows: $3,300 for salaries of seven single women missionaries; $2,895 for schools, hospitals, sea passages, etc.; $3,405 for salaries of male missionaries; $3,400 for home missions.

56 Manning, 'President's Address,' *Seventeenth Annual Report*, WBMUMP, (1900–1), 142.

57 Virginia Leison Brereton and Christa Ressmeyer Klein, 'American Women in Ministry: A History of Protestant Beginning Points,' in *Women in American Religion*, Janet Wilson James, ed. (Philadelphia: University of Pennsylvania Press, 1980), 176. 'Women missionary leaders represented an emerging elite within the denominations. Since these women were frequently the wives and relatives of male denominational leaders, the missionary societies created a virtual "interlocking directorate" of prosperous families.' In the thirty-five charter societies of the WMAS at least twelve of the presidents were wives of clergy and at least six of the presidents or secretary-treasurers were wives of deacons in the Maritime Baptist churches.

58 Clara R. Fullerton, 'Historical Sketch of the Free Baptist Woman's Missionary Society of New Brunswick [and Nova Scotia Free Baptist Foreign Mission Society],' in Martell, 32–3, 51, 57.

59 Martell, 66–70; Ingraham, 62–3. Mrs C.W. Weyman, corresponding secretary of Free Baptist Woman's Missionary Society of New Brunswick since 1877, was listed as vice-president for NB of UBWMU, 1907–8. Augusta Slipp, president of Free Baptist WMS of NB since 1902, served as NB provincial secretary of UBWMU, 1910–41. In 1910 she was a member of the UBWMU committee touring the three provinces to revitalize old societies and organize new ones.

60 Beals, *Mrs J.W. Manning*, 8.

61 Cramp, *Retrospects*, 35, 48.

62 Beals, *Mrs J.W. Manning*, 27, 34.

63 Flora Clarke, K.I.H., *Sisters: Canada and India* (Moncton, NB: Maritime Press, 1939), 447.

64 James Johnston, ed., *Report of the Centenary Conference on the Protestant Missions of the World*, 3rd ed. (New York: Fleming H. Revell, 1888), vol. 2, 595; vol. 1, 217–19.

65 Edna Wilson, *Fourteenth Annual Report*, UBWMUMP, 1919–20, 72–5.

66 Mrs David Hutchinson, 'President's Address,' *Second Annual Report*, UBWMUMP, 1907–8, 68.

67 Mrs Simpson, *Eighth Annual Report*, UBWMUMP, 1913–14, 22.

68 Martell, 86.

69 *Fourteenth Annual Report*, WBMUMP, 1897–8, 29.

70 *Tidings*, Mar. 1919, 2.

71 Caroline Atwater Mason, 'The "Rainbow" Campaign of the Women's Boards of Missions,' *Tidings*, May 1919, 2.

72 Hutchinson in Martell, 91; Beals, 27.

73 Hutchinson in Martell, 93.

74 Beals, *Mrs J.W. Manning*, 29. Only two other women had previously received this honour from Acadia.

75 Manning, 'President's Address,' *Seventh Annual Report*, WBMUMP (1890–1), 27.

76 M.L. Orchard and K.S. McLaurin, *The Enterprise: The Jubilee Story of the Canadian Baptist Mission in India, 1874–1924* (Toronto: Canadian Baptist Foreign Mission Board, n.d.), 23.

77 'Women's Missionary Aid Societies, Their Formation, Methods and Results' (Baptist Collection, Acadia University Library, Wolfville, NS, c. 1904), 6. Emphasis in original.

78 Hutchinson in Martell, 95.

79 Frances Hiebert, 'Missionary Women as Models in the Cross-Cultural Context,' *Missiology* 10, 4 (Oct. 1982), 459.

80 Brereton and Kline, 180–6.

81 Donald G. Mathews, 'Women's History / Everyone's History,' in *Women in New Worlds: Historical Perspectives on the Wesleyan Tradition*, Hilah F. Thomas and Rosemary Skinner Keller, eds. (Nashville: Abingdon, 1981), 45.

5

Two-thirds of the Revenue: Presbyterian Women and Native Indian Missions

JOHN WEBSTER GRANT

Like Baptists, Presbyterian women claimed a significant space for themselves in mission work. Presbyterians placed a strong emphasis on education, an area of responsibility often seen as particularly appropriate to women. Thus, Presbyterian women discovered one opportunity for Christian service in the needs of Native women and children in western Canada, and they responded by taking on the responsibility for an extensive educational work there. They supported their own missionaries, some of whom, like Lucy Baker, clearly gave the lie to the myth of female weakness. They also paid a large portion of the missions' expenses. Although members of the Presbyterian Woman's Foreign Missionary Society were in a more dependent position than, for example, those of the Methodist Woman's Missionary Society, they recognized and used the power that they did hold: the power of the purse. Over the years their board of management became 'steadily more discriminating' in its decisions to pay for the support of proposals made by the church's Foreign Mission Committee.

In 1895 Andrew B. Baird of Manitoba College wrote of the native Indian work of the Presbyterian Church in Canada that for several years the members of the Woman's Foreign Missionary Society (WFMS) had 'borne the entire cost of that part of the work which is especially directed to women and children, and this, since it includes the building and maintenance of schools, the payment of the salaries of matrons and teachers, and similar expenses, has amounted to about two-thirds of the Committee's whole revenue.'[1] Although Methodist and Anglican women also helped to support native Indian missions, the former from a slightly earlier time, neither accounted for such a significant share of their denomination's work. Methodist women confined their support almost entirely to a few institutions in British Columbia, while the givings of Anglican women were dispersed over an enterprise that dwarfed that of either Methodists or Presbyterians.[2]

The importance of the role of Presbyterian women is further underlined by the fact that Presbyterians, more than any other denomination, concentrated their efforts among Natives upon the educational work in which women specialized. One naturally asks why they were so deeply involved and what their involvement came to mean for them as women. Although the work in question is still being carried on to some extent by the United and Presbyterian churches, a terminal point for this study is suggested by the concurrence of three developments: agreement by the federal government in 1910 to meet a larger proportion of the costs of Native education, the transfer of Presbyterian work among native Indians from the Foreign Mission Committee (FMC) to the newly formed Board of Home Missions in 1913, and the union of the WFMS with its home missionary counterpart in 1914 to form the Women's Missionary Society.

The WFMS came into being at a meeting of women called together on 17 February 1876 at the request of the Foreign Mission Committee[3] of the newly formed Presbyterian Church in Canada. The possible scope of the committee's operations and some limitations on them were spelled out in a constitution approved by the church's general assembly that year: 'Its object shall be to aid the Foreign Mission Committee or Board of Missions, by promoting its work among the women and children of heathen lands, and to this purpose it shall receive and disburse all money which shall be contributed to the Society, subject to the action of that Committee or Board, in the appointment of Missionaries supported by the Society, and fixing their salaries and location.'[4] Women had been organizing similar societies in the United States for some time, often in the face of male opposition, and American precedents were influential in inspiring the Canadian effort. American Presbyterian women organized themselves for mission at first regionally rather than nationally.[5] The Canadian WFMS drew its inspiration most directly from an identically named society that had been formed in Philadelphia in 1870; at the first annual meeting of its board of management, on 2 February 1877, the president of the Philadelphia society was a guest speaker. Later that year the WFMS instituted a practice of exchanging visitors with the Chicago-based Woman's Presbyterian Board of Mission of the Northwest.[6] Despite an initial designation as the 'Woman's Foreign Missionary Society of Toronto,' its constitution authorized it to form auxiliary societies 'throughout the Church' on the American pattern, and in 1878 it was allowed to style itself as of 'the Presbyterian Church in Canada (Western Section).'[7]

The formation of the WFMS was intended in the first place to support the work of Margaret Rodger and Marion Fairweather, who in 1873 had gone under American Presbyterian sponsorship to what is now the state of Uttar Pradesh in India. In 1876 the Canadian Presbyterians opened their own field in Central India, now Madhya Bharat, and Rodger and Fairweather transferred their activities there. The constitution of the society reflected conditions in India, where women were segregated in zenanas and thus unapproachable by male missionaries. The concept of 'women's work for women' and by extension for children was, however, already in the United States a recognized justification of female participation in foreign missions, and has been noted as such in Canada by several other contributors to this volume. The WFMS soon extended its support to a Presbyterian mission in Formosa (Taiwan). At that time, and for some years thereafer, there was no suggestion that it might include North American Indians within the range of its operations. By 15 April 1885, however, it could state as its policy that 'efforts in the future as in the past shall be directed to the evangelization of women and in heathen lands, including our own Indians of the North West.'

Native Indian missions were brought to the attention of the WFMS in November 1878 by the first of a series of letters from George Flett, the country-born missionary at Okanase in Manitoba. In this correspondence one may suspect a deliberate attempt to involve the society, for it was instigated by Marion Bryce, the first woman president of the Manitoba Historical Society and wife of a professor at Manitoba College who frequently advised the FMC on Native matters.[8] Two personal contacts during the early 1880s may have given at least marginal encouragement. On 1 November 1881 a monthly meeting was addressed by Emma Baylis, a Montreal Congregationalist who worked among the Ojibwa along the north shore of Lake Huron. Baylis was noted as having 'aroused much interest and sympathy' and, perhaps significantly, as being known already to some of the 'ladies.'[9] Then at the annual meeting on 12 April 1883 a delegate from the newly formed Methodist Woman's Missionary Society brought not only greetings but an account of work among various peoples including 'Indians on the confines of Alaska.'

The actual decision to become involved was taken without warning at the tag end of what must have been a long meeting on 5 June 1883. It took the form of a resolution 'to state to the Foreign Mission Committee that we will gladly bear any expense in connection with the children of the Indians in our North West under the care of that Committee and also that Mrs Harvie [the corresponding secretary for foreign fields] correspond with Miss Baker at present teaching in Prince Albert.' This action was followed by such a long silence in the minutes that one might be tempted to regard it as stillborn, but such was not the case. On 6 November a letter was read from Flett listing educational needs, and by the next year the society reported that it was providing financial aid to all schools in the northwest.[10] Soon, in response to an appeal received on 7 October 1884 from Hugh McKay of the Round Lake Mission, the society also began to pack boxes of clothing for Native families suffering from the disappearance of the buffalo. Reserves were allocated to auxiliaries or regional presbyterials, the WMS equivalent of presbyteries, which set to work with a will and during the first year sent supplies valued at two thousand dollars.[11] This effort had the effect of drawing a further flood of letters from the field, expressing profound gratitude but also in many cases attaching detailed statements of educational needs.

So far the WFMS was merely assisting missionary work carried on by others, but on 1 September 1885 it noted the appointment to a native Indian mission of Isabella Rose of Woodstock, Ontario, the first under its sponsorship. Well qualified as a teacher, Rose had already spent time in the west and had acquired some knowledge of the Cree language. Her school on Piapot's Reserve north of Regina was successful enough to draw both local acclaim and tempting offers from American missionary societies.[12] In 1889, however, she married a farm instructor who had been denied a divorce from a native wife on the ground that their marriage lacked legal standing, and the resulting scandal led to Rose's withdrawal and the temporary closing of the school.[13] Meanwhile, other women had been appointed, and the society's missionary force gradually expanded.

The entry of the WFMS into native Indian work was neither novel nor surprising. In the United States single women had been admitted to this work long before they were regarded as suitable candidates for appointment overseas. As early as 1825, indeed, an African-American Presbyterian named Betsey Stockton is said to have taught in a Native school in Canada on her return from service in Hawaii, thus anticipating the WFMS by sixty years.[14] Canadian women would have been aware of similar connections through their contacts with American societies, especially the board of mission of the northwest. The association of the WFMS with the Foreign Mission Committee of the church pointed inexorably in the same direction, for missions among native Indians were its responsibility. As early as 1879 the presence of Lucy Baker as a missionary teacher at Prince Albert, under the direct sponsorship of the FMC, constituted an open invitation to involvement; she was the 'Miss Baker' with whom Harvie was instructed to correspond by the meeting that resolved to offer financial support to native Indian schools. The eventual participation of the WFMS in native Indian missions was thus practically a foregone conclusion.

The extent of that participation does, however, call for explanation.[15] On 7 June 1887 the WFMS agreed 'that the Foreign Secretary write to the F.M. Committee asking for the usual estimates for our work for the present year and stating that we will be glad to support all the schools under the care of our Church among the North West Indians, and will undertake to bear all the expense of maintaining the pupils at the school at Round Lake.' Although this resolution constituted something less than an offer to accept responsibility for the total support of educational work among native Indians, this interpretation seems to have been assumed in all subsequent correspondence between the WFMS and the FMC. The division of labour between the two was never clear cut, and individual items were often matters of negotiation, but in general the society left evangelistic work on the reserves to the committee while providing the bulk of the salaries and capital expenditures for Native schooling.[16]

A major incentive to this extension of effort was simply the financial success that made it possible. Beginning as a group of women in Toronto who met monthly in conjunction with the board of management to hear missionary letters, the WFMS expanded rapidly, like its Maritime Baptist counterpart, in both membership and givings as branch auxiliaries were formed in other cities and then in congregations. Before long, money was pouring in much faster than was required for the society's initial commitments. Within the first ten years, indeed, the budget rose from $1,000 to $13,000.[17] The result was a growing surplus that enabled the society, gradually and accidentally, to institute what was later to become a proudly self-conscious policy of budgeting on the basis of money on hand rather than borrowing against expected revenue. In the first expansive years the surplus was sometimes so great that it was felt necessary to authorize supplementary expenditures. During the 1880s the society had more money than it knew what to do with and was actively seeking new uses for its resources. The members of the FMC, several of whom were husbands of women active on the board of the WFMS, must also have been aware of this untapped source.

These early years coincided with a period of expanding opportunities for involvement in Native education. A report by the Canadian journalist Nicholas Flood Davin in 1879 recommended that the government should embark on a program of promoting industrial and other schools for the newly settled native Indians of the plains and added, significantly, that contracts should be made with the churches to provide them.[18] The Presbyterians, with fewer commitments to existing mission stations than some other denominations, were in an unusually favourable position to take advantage of the opportunity thus offered. In 1882 William MacLaren, the convenor of the FMC, visited most of the Indian missions in company with Hugh McKellar, who had served the pioneer Presbyterian mission at Prince Albert. Their report suggested no new global policy, but in its general tone it was a call to build new schools and enlarge existing ones, to hire additional teachers, and to seek out new areas of work. In 1883 the committee sought government aid for Native schools through a strong subcommittee that included the Honourable Alexander Morris, former lieutenant-governor of Manitoba and the North-West Territories. In 1885, when the end of the North-West Rebellion accelerated settlement on reserves, it took the further step of resolving that 'the mission work in the North-West be extended as rapidly as possible, consistently with economy and efficiency'[19] and sent Flett with Thomas Hart of Manitoba College to scout promising sites.[20] Here were tempting prospects for a society with money to spend.

These opportunities were forcibly brought to the attention of the WFMS in various ways. Like others of its kind, the society depended for the sustained interest of its members largely on the reading of letters from missionaries. At first these were mainly from India, but from 1884, letters of thanks for clothing bundles from the North-West increasingly competed for attention. Then in 1886 Mary McGregor returned from Central India after disagreements with other staff members similar to those Rosemary Gagan has noted among Methodists in Japan.[21] McGregor had been the society's most prolific correspondent, and when hers stopped, letters from western Canada began to predominate. On 6 July 1886 Hugh McKay was present at a meeting of the board of management, and the solicitude thereafter shown for his school at Round Lake suggests that he possessed considerable personal charm. Isabella Rose began to correspond, calling attention in a letter read on 5 October 1886 to the 'touchingly painful lot of the Indian women and girls.' Deepened interest suggested still greater involvement. On 7 April 1885 the society voted $600 out of its surplus to native Indian work. At the next two annual meetings it took similar actions, including the approval on 5 April 1887 of $2,000 for school buildings at Round Lake.

The WFMS, we should not forget, claimed a special mandate for work among women and children, justifying its separate existence by calling attention to the special needs of these categories. It resisted any suggestion of becoming a sort of all-purpose 'ladies' aid' of missions, and there are hints that it occasionally suspected the FMC of treating the contributions of women merely as subsidies for its regular work. On 5 December 1882 it asked pointedly, in relation to India and Formosa, whether all of its money was in fact being used for work among women and children. The education of Canadian Indian children met the requirements of the WFMS constitution, especially because, unlike its Anglican counterpart, the society had no objection to work among boys. The society also liked the satisfaction of paying in full for the work it sponsored, and 7 February 1882 was one of several occasions on which it sought estimates of the total cost of the work for which it was responsible. Once involved in native Indian education, therefore, the WFMS preferred to undertake its entire support.

Involvement in missionary work within Canada also furnished both a ready defence against frequent charges that the WFMS diverted money from the regular work of the church into foreign adventures, and a means of relieving constant pressure from some of its members to extend its charter to include home missions. Worries about the religious future of Canada's recently acquired west were also influential in directing attention there. Agitation within the Ottawa branch came to a head on 3 June 1884 in an appeal to the society to take more active steps to counteract the alleged success of Roman Catholic agents in the northwest, and in the following year there was a minor flood of requests for greater efforts in Canada. As auxiliaries were formed in western Canada, too, there was spontaneous local interest in native Indian missions; a residential school at Portage la Prairie was founded by an independent women's society there. Despite such efforts, the society never quite shook off the criticism that it lacked concern for domestic needs or even that it was deficient in patriotism. A brochure entitled *Answers to Erroneous Statements Concerning the W.F.M.S.* gave considerable attention to such charges,[22] and presidential addresses regularly cited the extent of involvement in native Indian missions in reply.

Opportunities for participation in missionary activities helped to allay discontents which, if unchecked, might have crippled the society. Preventing glib missionaries from cornering an undue share of money to the neglect of less eloquent workers and less spectacular projects has been a constant and universal problem in the financing of missions. The WFMS insisted on centralized control, but many auxiliaries preferred direct dealings with favourite missionaries. The society regularly advised the FMC against countenancing 'special objects' for local auxiliaries, warning on one occasion that 'any *organized* and *approved* scheme of that nature will tend to the disaffection and the ultimate disorganization of our Branches.'[23] The logistics of packing and mailing boxes for Natives were such, however, that there was no feasible alternative to assigning individual reserves to particular auxiliaries and presbyteries. Local groups were thus given the personal contacts that they craved, and, in many cases, correspondence with the local missionary ensued. These contacts were clearly not responsible for the society's involvement in Native work, for they began only after the crucial decision had been made. They must have done a good deal to stimulate and sustain interest, however, and to encourage the society to expand its original bridgehead.

The nature and effectiveness of the participation of the WFMS in native Indian missions depended to a great extent on the women who laboured under its auspices. Ruth Compton Brouwer has identified missionary candidates as an unusually homogeneous group, mostly 'in their late twenties or early thirties' and 'unusually well-educated by the standards of their time.' She adds: 'They came, overwhelmingly, from rural communities or from small urban centres, and while, in economic terms, their backgrounds were only marginally middle class, they were members of respectable, church-going families and had themselves played prominent roles in church and church-linked organizations.'[24] Those who entered the less glamorous native Indian work were similar in background. Few of them possessed the specialized qualifications that were common among those accepted for service abroad, however, and many seem to have been appointed on short notice as vacancies arose. Typical applications for educational positions offered the experience of teaching in rural school sections. Two missionaries stand out as in some respects exceptional, in others – despite a considerable overlap in time of service – as representative of succeeding eras.

Since her own time Lucy Baker has been without question the most celebrated Presbyterian woman to have worked among the native Indians of Canada. A superficial summary of her career leaves one wondering why. Described by Agnes Laut in *Collier's* as 'a little lady – one of the old school, the kind done up in ecru lace and black silk,'[25] she was sent to Prince Albert in 1879 to teach Native children. She taught a number and even boarded a few. As white settlers moved in and the native Indians moved away, however, the number of Native pupils dwindled until by 1884 her school could be described as 'simply the common school of Prince Albert supported by the people of the town and a grant from the North West Council.' During the rebellion of 1885 Baker so exhausted herself in nursing that she had to spend some time recuperating in Oregon. Plans for a girls' boarding-school of her own that would attract Native children from a distance and ward off the competition of a local convent came to nothing. In 1888 Baker appeared on the WFMS list for the first time as a teacher in the newly founded Nisbet Academy – again to compete with the Roman Catholics – but in the following year the FMC discharged her with the briefest notice.[26] By the fall Baker was employed again as a teacher for an 'outlaw' Sioux band in the neighbourhood. Although she had previously expressed interest in this band, the appointment seems to have been designed by others who were eager to reclaim her services. Baker's reputation rests largely on this phase of her career, which lasted with a brief intermission until her retirement in 1904. She was able to report no conversions, however, and her work was abandoned a few years later.

To follow Lucy Baker's story more closely is to recognize in her a person of distinctly superior quality. Born in Glengarry County, Ontario, in 1838, she grew up in Dundee Centre, Quebec. For a number of years she taught French at private schools in New Jersey and New Orleans. Caught in the latter by the American Civil War, she had a rather worrisome return home through the Confederate lines and spent the next decade or so teaching at a private school in her native county. Appointed to Prince Albert when her pastor was named missionary there, this hitherto rather protected woman made her way from Winnipeg with a convoy of strangers when her minister became ill there.[27] Baker's school at Prince Albert, although never very successful in attracting Native children, was universally praised despite living conditions that were a disgrace to the FMC. One missionary even reported of the rather dismal situation of the mission, 'Miss Baker's school is the only thing in the settlement that gives general satisfaction.'[28]

The Sioux band to which Baker was eventually appointed was camped on the other side of the North Saskatchewan River. Unable to persuade any band member to ferry her, she repeatedly rowed across herself. On one occasion she had a narrow escape from drowning, and after that she was able to hire an Indian oarsman. Our eyebrows are likely to be raised by such tactics of Baker's as scattering cookies to attract Native women as one might entice birds to a feeder, but she is said to have been so successful in winning the band's confidence that she was hailed as its 'queen' and had the Union Jack hoisted in her honour.[29] While we could not commend Lucy Baker as a model for the contemporary missionary, we can recognize in her one of those indomitable Victorian women who could settle down in any part of the world and impose proper English table manners on the natives. Baker would have made a credible, if perhaps not glamorous, Anna in *The King and I*.

Catherine (Kate) Gillespie was born in Teeswater, Ontario, in 1866, and after graduation from the local high school taught in Ontario for several years.[30] In 1889 her family took up a homestead in the Qu'Appelle Valley, and Gillespie moved her teaching career to their vicinity. As a result of contacts with Native children in a rural school there, Gillespie was moved to offer her services to the WFMS and took a short course in hospital work to qualify herself further. For a time she taught on the Cote Reserve near Kamsack and then on the Mistawasis Reserve west of Prince Albert. In 1901 the principalship of the File Hills residential school fell vacant. The school had the advantage of being near Gillespie's home, but it had a history of mismanagement and ineffectiveness. Gillespie applied with some diffidence, for such positions were normally reserved for men, and she insisted that she would not have applied if she had known of other candidates. Despite the objections of the previous principal and the local Indian agent, she received the appointment. When the FMC had second thoughts about sending a woman into a position of such difficulty, Gillespie showed another side of her nature. She was aware of all the difficulties, she insisted, and had her own ideas for overcoming them.[31] She remained at the school until her marriage in 1908 to the Honourable W.R. Motherwell, then Minister of Agriculture for Saskatchewan and later a member of several federal cabinets. Her husband's home was not far away, and she maintained close relations with the Natives around File Hills until shortly before her death in 1952.

Gillespie arrived at File Hills at an interesting and strategic time. In that very year William M. Graham, the local Indian agent, founded a colony nearby where young Natives could establish farms of their own and thus distance themselves from the traditions of the reserves. For recruitment Graham depended on the help of Father Joseph Hugonnard, principal of a neighbouring Oblate school, and despite his initial reservations he came to rely equally on Gillespie.[32] They made a curious troika. Gillespie loathed Hugonnard's Roman Catholicism and sought in every possible way to counteract his religious influence, while she noted that Graham was indifferent to religion of any kind.[33] Although the intent to distance native Indians from their traditional culture is obvious, a Native resident pronounced the colony still a success in the 1930s.[34] For the rest, Gillespie was happier with ambitious projects than the classroom. She had only a third-class teaching certificate, which did not rate for a government grant and may have made a principalship more attractive to her.[35] Gillespie soon gave over the teaching branch of the work into other hands to concentrate on mothering her charges and organizing a Native church.[36] Reports of the school during her tenure were uniformly favourable.

Whereas Baker never quite lost the patina of the private school teacher, Gillespie was a down-to-earth, small town Ontario woman who adjusted readily to life on the prairies. A fine horsewoman, she reported no hair-raising adventures but routinely made 'drives over distances that many a man, not supposed to be lazy, would think impossible for regular work.'[37] Where Baker remained throughout her life a lonely pioneer, Gillespie brought her own colony; at File Hills her sister Janet was matron, her father the farm instructor. And whereas Baker was shabbily treated by the church and went for several years without the money owed her, Gillespie knew how to look after herself and brooked no nonsense from the FMC. It helped that she was something of a religious enthusiast who made decisions only after she had checked with God, and did not hesitate to tell the mission secretaries so.[38] Most conspicuously of all, Gillespie illustrated in a very practical way the maternal feminism that previously had been so romanticized. She regularly visited her graduates, delighted to organize their weddings, and remembered their anniversaries with appropriate gifts. Eleanor Brass, a Native woman who later recalled the history of the File Hills colony, paid a glowing tribute to Gillespie's 'continued affection for the Indians of the area.'[39] In many ways she represented a stage of the mission when Baker's pioneering had given way to more settled institutions, but without the loss of the human touch this transition sometimes entailed.

No WFMS missionary – Baker, Gillespie, or any other – seems to have queried the now discredited belief that Christianization implies the eventual displacement of Native by Western culture. Among the elements of this mission of acculturation, indeed, none has been more bitterly condemned than the educational work that was the particular responsibility of the WFMS. In the long run, too, this enterprise proved to be unusually static in both extent and conception. After expansion on the prairies in the 1880s, the WFMS shared in work opened by the church in the 1890s among the Nootka on the west coast of Vancouver Island. In 1921, however, the author of a historical survey admitted that the Women's Missionary Society had opened no new native Indian work in twenty years and had not expanded the work previously established.[40] If a consistent difference in approach between the FMC and the WFMS is to be detected, it may have been – as in British Columbia – in the greater concern of the latter for personal well-being. Officials who visited the missions on behalf of the society pleaded for greater attention to the comfort of staff and students alike, matters to which male authorities often seemed blind or indifferent.[41] Typically of the times, the society also urged that no 'lady' should be sent alone to a new field without domestic help.[42] Many women as well as men, ill at ease in Native surroundings, made mission institutions into European ghettos into which Native children were admitted only as foreigners in the process of naturalization. The best, such as Baker and Gillespie, showed that they genuinely respected the people among whom they worked and received their confidence in return.

'From the beginning the organization and management of the Society has been entirely in its own hands, the executive business being vested in the Board of Management,' wrote Agnes F. Robinson in commemorating the first twenty-five years of the WFMS[43] That a measure of self-conscious feminism had been involved from the outset is evident from a statement in the foreign secretary's report of 1881: 'The nineteenth century is pre-eminently a century in which woman has shone in almost all the departments of life. She is crowding into business avenues, educational work, professional life, and the world of literature.'[44] This assertiveness was not apparent in the constitution of the WFMS, which declared that all of its actions should be 'subject to the action of' the FMC 'in the appointment of missionaries supported by the Society, and fixing their salaries and location' and went on to warn in the imperative mood, 'Do not interfere with other organizations. Make no appeal that will conflict with duties church members owe to any other benevolent work.'[45] In the minutes of its second annual report the society noted even more flatly that it had been organized 'at the request and under the direction of the Foreign Missions Committee,'[46] and no formal change was ever made in any of these provisions.

Like the parallel Methodist organization, the WFMS owed its formation largely to male initiative. Unlike counterparts in the United States, it was organized not in the teeth of male opposition but at the direct request of the FMC. Professor William MacLaren of Knox College has been credited with much of the initiative. The society chose his wife as its first president, and in the early years it turned to him for help in organizing meetings and selecting speakers. Those selected to address public meetings were at first exclusively men. As late as 1898 a representative of the society expressed strong disapproval of public addresses by any of its missionaries.[47]

If the WFMS was at all inclined to forget its place, there were men around to remind it. In 1897 A.B. Baird reported confidentially to R.P. MacKay of the FMC that the WFMS had offered to make possible the reopening of a school at Lakesend by bypassing the church treasurer. '*Of course* I declined such an offer promptly and decidedly,' he wrote, adding with perhaps a touch of wistfulness, 'but *that is one way* of evading the necessity of keeping within our estimates.' In the previous year he had apologized to MacKay for inadvertently failing to send the year's estimates to him as he had to the WFMS 'In any case,' he wrote, 'there is no misapprehension on our part as to the relation of our Committee to the Executive Board of the WFMS.'[48] On other occasions the WFMS itself used limitations of jurisdiction as an excuse for avoiding unwelcome requests. When R.N. Toms approached L.J. Harvie of the society for help in starting a new residential school, Harvie passed it on with the marginal note that Toms had evidently forgotten that this was the business of the FMC.[49]

This relation of dependence cannot be explained simply as a common feature of women's organizations, for in practice the Woman's Missionary Society of the Canadian Methodists was virtually autonomous. The same Presbyterian diffidence has been noted in the United States,[50] but even within Canadian Presbyterianism there were differences. The Women's Home Missionary Society had a great deal more freedom of action than the WFMS, perhaps because the Presbyterian Church in Canada had no home missionary arm with the wide-reaching powers of the FMC. The difference was graphically, if subtly, reflected in the constitution of the Women's Missionary Society that was eventually formed by the union of the two agencies. For 'mission work' the WMS merely recommended appointments, but in the home field it made appointments 'subject to the sanction of the [newly formed] Home Mission Board.'[51]

These inequalities in the relation of the WFMS to the FMC, though real, were by no means the whole picture. For one thing, the WFMS kept an increasingly close watch on the native Indian work. In 1894 it sent a deputation of two to investigate the schools to which it was contributing. As a result it made no less than twenty-one recommendations, many of them relating to specific institutions and many in considerable detail.[52] Significantly, a committee in Winnipeg through which the FMC then supervised its western missions accepted all of the recommendations in principle, demurring only to a request for specifications on all buildings in the case of those costing less than $400.[53] After a similar tour of inspection in 1906, Margaret Craig, then WFMS secretary for native Indian missions, was unsparing in her criticisms of some missionaries and some institutions. The condition of the mission house at Mistawasis was disgraceful. One missionary she described as 'Bombastic Beverley,' while of another she wrote that she had never met anyone 'so repugnant' to her.[54] That such reports carried weight is suggested by the urgency of a warning from E.A. Henry, then Presbyterian minister at Regina: 'Let me say just here, that not a great deal of stock sh'd be taken in the reports carried east by WFMS workers who come here for a few hours, look around, and then know more immediately about the whole thing than those living on the spot, and with experience covering months and years.'[55] On other occasions, too, the WFMS could give forceful expression to its views. In 1897, for example, when it was proposed to extend to Indian missions the mandate of James Robertson, the prestigious missionary superintendent for western Canada, the society objected strongly and apparently decisively.[56]

Over the years the WFMS gradually secured considerable control over the process of candidature. In 1882 it exacted a promise that it would be consulted before appointments were finalized.[57] In 1891 the FMC proposed that applications from single women should go in the first place to the women's board. Indeed, an anonymous handwritten note in the UCA copy of the booklet containing this information claims that such was already the practice in 1889 and that representatives of the society accompanied candidates when they appeared before the FMC.[58] As a result of these changes the society produced a manual setting forth qualifications and regulations.[59] Not all was clear sailing after that, for in 1894 Harvie complained that the FMC anticipated the WFMS by asking many of the questions in the *Manual* and objected further that applications from single women were being declined on financial grounds when the finances of the WFMS were 'in a remarkably prosperous condition.'[60] Despite occasional evasions on the ground of finance or urgency, however, the FMC seldom seems to have questioned the qualifications of candidates recommended by the WFMS.

Most effective of all in encouraging the assertiveness of the WFMS was the direct power of the purse. Theoretically, the FMC had the final say in determining the budget of the native Indian missions, but it could only disburse what it received. Paying over the money asked of it called for an annual vote of the WFMS board of management, and it became steadily more discriminating in its examination of proposals. In 1893 the WFMS would assist in providing school accommodation at Alberni but did not approve of a memorial building.[61] In 1897 it refused to grant four thousand dollars for an extension to the school at Birtle on the ground that there was enough accommodation at Regina.[62] In 1901 Craig sent the FMC a list of items passed and declined by the WFMS, noting that a proposal for a telephone at the Birtle school had raised 'a storm of opposition' in the society.[63] Although the FMC always insisted on its right to determine the allocation of funds, the WFMS could not be forced to pay for projects of which it disapproved.

The leaders of the WFMS were neither militant feminists nor shrinking violets. They had inherited a traditional view of the differentiation of gender roles and were not prepared to challenge it overtly. They were also committed believers in Christian missions, however, with strong opinions as to how they should be carried on and did not hesitate to express or even insist upon their ideas. In some ways the circumstances of the work among native Indians fostered their self-assertion, for it was of a type familiar to many of them and close enough for personal inspection. If they never overcame completely a deeply ingrained prejudice against female participation in missionary leadership, they learned to exercise a fair amount of power in a wider sphere than had previously been open to them.

NOTES

1 *The Indians of Western Canada* (Toronto: Canadian Presbyterian, 1895), 28.
2 In 1911–12 the Methodist Woman's Missionary Society (WMS) reported a total of $19,117.20 for native Indian missions, but from this one must subtract

$6,798.50 in government grants to the institutions it supported, *31st Annual Report of the WMS*, Methodist Church, 1911–12, xx, xxi. Roughly $13,000 may be inferred from a list of Anglican items that cannot all be clearly identified, but this includes only money spent in dioceses other than those in which it was raised, *1st Year Book of the Women's Auxiliary to the Missionary Society of the Canadian Church*, 1912, end page. Presbyterian figures for this year were $14,300.79 for the prairies and $6,335.92 for British Columbia, *36th Annual Report of the WFMS*, 1911–12, 89.

3 Minutes of the Board of Management of the WFMS of the Presbyterian Church in Canada (Western Section), United Church Archives (UCA). Occasional reference will be made to these minutes, without notes, by date of meeting.

4 Acts and Proceedings of the 2nd General Assembly of the Presbyterian Church in Canada, 1876, Appendix, 252.

5 A.J. Brown, *One Hundred Years: A History of the Foreign Missionary Work of the Presbyterian Church of the USA*. (New York: Revell, 1936), 110–27. Much of his information is derived from [Isabel Hart], *Historical Sketches of Woman's Missionary Societies in America and England* (Boston: Mrs L.H. Daggett, 1879), 122–30.

6 Minutes of the Board of Management, 7 May 1877, 7 Jan. 1880.

7 Minutes of the Foreign Mission Committee (FMC) of the Presbyterian Church in Canada (Western Section), 16 Apr. 1878, UCA.

8 Minutes, Board of Management, 5 Nov. 1878; Priscilla Lee Reid, 'The Role of Presbyterian Women in Canadian Development,' in *Enkindled by the Word* (Toronto: Presbyterian Publications, 1966), 116.

9 Emma Baylis's diary, 1872–85, is in UCA.

10 *8th Annual Report*, WFMS, 1884, 3.

11 *9th Annual Report*, WFMS, 1885, 22.

12 *Qu'Appelle Vidette*, 27 June 1889.

13 Baird to H. Cassels, 24 Aug. 1889, UCA, Indian Missions (IM).

14 R. Pierce Beaver, *American Protestant Women in World Mission: A History of the First Feminist Movement in North America* (Grand Rapids: Eerdmans, 1980), 59–60, 67.

15 Although the WFMS provided a larger proportion of Native missions than any other, the actual amount it sent to India was consistently larger.

16 This policy is stated explicitly in the *20th Annual Report*, WFMS, 1895–6, 37.

17 *1st Annual Report*, WFMS, 1877, 22; *11th*, 1887, 104.

18 'Report on Industrial Schools for Indians and Half-Breeds, Ottawa, 14 March 1879, to the Right Honourable the Minister of the Interior,' 13.

19 Minutes of the FMC, 23 May, 17 Oct. 1882; 20 Sept. 1883; 18 June 1885.

20 Thomas Hart to T.W. Wardrope, 23 Oct. 1885, IM.

21 On the circumstances, see Ruth Compton Brouwer, *New Women for God: Canadian Presbyterian Women and India Missions, 1876–1914* (Toronto: University of Toronto Press, 1990), 135–8.
22 No publishing details, but someone has added the date 1895 in ink to the copy in UCA.
23 L.J. Harvie to R.P. MacKay, 8 June 1894, Correspondence between the Foreign Mission Committee and the Women's Missionary Society (Corr), UCA.
24 Ruth Compton Brouwer, 'Presbyterian Women and the Foreign Missionary Movement, 1876–1914: The Context of a Calling,' *Canadian Society of Presbyterian History Papers*, 1984–5, 1.
25 Quoted in Elizabeth A. Byers, *Lucy Margaret Baker: A Biographical Sketch of the First Missionary of Our Canadian Presbyterian Church to the North-West Indians* (Toronto: WMS of the Presbyterian Church in Canada [Western Division], 1920), 20.
26 William MacWilliam to Wardrope, 15 July 1884; Robert Jardine to M.J. MacMurchy, 4 Apr. 1887; Baker to Wardrope, 12 Feb. 1889, all in IM.
27 Byers, *Baker*, chaps. 1, 2.
28 J. Sivewright to MacLaren, 21 Dec. 1880, IM.
29 Byers, *Baker*, 24–5, 28, 39.
30 Personal details from L.L. Dobbin, 'Mrs Catherine Gillespie Motherwell, Pioneer Teacher and Missionary,' *Saskatchewan History* 14, 1 (Winter 1961), 17–26.
31 Gillespie to MacKay, 10 July 1901; W.H. Farrer to MacKay, 27 July 1901; Gillespie to MacKay, 1 Oct. 1901, all in IM; Eleanor Brass, 'A Friend of the Canadian Indians,' *Missionary Monthly*, Nov. 1952, 498.
32 Jacqueline Judith Kennedy, 'Qu'Appelle Industrial School: White "Rites" for the Indians of the Old North-West' (MA thesis, Carleton University, 1970), 55, 133ff.
33 Gillespie to MacKay, 1 Oct. 1901, IM.
34 Eleanor Brass, 'The File Hills Ex-Pupil Colony,' *Saskatchewan History* 6, 2 (Spring 1953), 68.
35 Baird to MacKay, 20 Apr. 1897, IM.
36 *Missionary Tidings* 21 (Dec. 1904), 68.
37 Minutes of the Indian Mission Committee to Synods of Manitoba and Saskatchewan, undated but apparently 1906, IM.
38 Gillespie to MacKay, 1 Oct. 1901, IM.
39 'A Friend,' 498.
40 WMS of the Presbyterian Church in Canada, *The Planting of the Faith* (Toronto, 1921), 263.
41 For example, Margaret Craig to MacKay, 19 May 1906, IM.

42 Minutes of the Board of Management, 1 Sept. 1888; Harvie to Cassels, 3 Sept. 1897, Corr.

43 *A Quarter of a Century* (Toronto, 1901), 2.

44 *5th Annual Report*, WFMS, 1881, 17.

45 Acts and Proceedings of the 2nd General Assembly of the Presbyterian Church in Canada, 1876, appendix, 252–3.

46 2nd Annual Report, WFMS, 1878, 11.

47 Minutes of the Board of Management, 3, 6 Mar. 1877; Andrew Thomson, *The Life and Letters of Rev. R.P. MacKay, D.D.* (Toronto: Ryerson, 1932), 63; M. Shortreid to MacKay, 4 Feb. 1898, Corr.

48 Baird to MacKay, 17 Nov. 1897, 7 July 1896, IM.

49 Toms to Harvie, 15 Oct. 1887, IM. At least the handwriting of the note closely resembles Harvie's.

50 Patricia R. Hill, *The World Their Household: The American Women's Foreign Mission Movement and Cultural Transformation, 1870–1920* (Ann Arbor: University of Michigan Press, 1985), 51.

51 *38th Annual Report*, WFMS, 1913–14, 13. However, from this time all work in Canada counted as home missions.

52 'Recommendations of the deputation from the Bd of the WFMS (W.D.) to N.W. to FMC,' undated but 1894, IM.

53 Baird to Harvie, 12 Nov. 1894, IM.

54 Craig to MacKay, 4 June, 14 July 1906, IM.

55 Henry to Mr Martin, 19 Feb. 1907, IM.

56 Cecilia Jeffrey to MacKay, 2 June 1897, Corr.

57 Minutes, Board of Management, 5 Dec. 1882.

58 Robinson, *Quarter of a Century*, 10: cf. M.J. MacMurchy to Cassels, 15 May 1889, Corr.

59 *A Manual for the Use of Women Offering for Foreign Mission and for Missionaries in Connection with the Woman's Foreign Missionary Society of the Presbyterian Church in Canada (W.D.)* (Toronto: WFMS, n.d.).

60 Harvie to MacKay, 8 July 1894, Corr.

61 Ibid., 25 Apr. 1893, Corr.

62 Jeffrey to MacKay, 26 May 1898, Corr.

63 Craig to MacKay, 3 Oct. 1901, IM.

6

'Let the Women Keep Silence': Women Missionary Preaching in British Columbia, 1860s–1940s

MARGARET WHITEHEAD

The frontier of British Columbia offered women of several denominations non-traditional opportunities for Christian ministry. Many who came to undertake both domestically oriented and educational mission work found themselves called upon to preach either temporarily, when the usual preacher was ill or briefly absent, or for a longer period when no man was available. Their preaching activity might meet with opposition in the hierarchies of their churches, a situation that tended to vary according to denomination. The women, however, were frequently supported in their work by their husbands or by other men on the mission fields. They also relied on the encouragement they received from the women's pages of missionary periodicals, pages that not only linked them to a network of supportive women, but also sometimes provided theological justification for their expanded ministerial roles. Yet even when their preaching was encouraged, women found it difficult, for they bore a double burden: Preaching was usually not substituted for, but added to, women's other responsibilities.

On 15 September 1947 Elizabeth MacVicar, recently appointed missionary at the Presbyterian Ahousaht Mission on the west coast of Vancouver Island, took the Sunday evening service for the local, primarily Native, population. She was somewhat apprehensive. Because there was a First Nations celebration held earlier in the day, only one child had appeared for MacVicar's afternoon Bible class. She wondered whether the feast would have an equally negative impact on the regular Sunday service. However, approximately fifty men, women, and children attended the church to hear their missionary preach the word of God. MacVicar wrote to her family: 'The children were quiet to my relief, it being my first service.'[1] In this Native community, Elizabeth MacVicar's 'first service' testified to a continuous tradition of missionary women preachers in British Columbia that dated back to the earliest days of missionary activity in the province. In spite of biblical and Pauline edict, Canadian church intransigence – or, at least, reluctance – and societal limitations, missionary women of the Methodist, Presbyterian, and Anglican churches in British Columbia expanded on their prescribed domestic role. With open support from women sponsors and at least the tacit approval of some male colleagues and the church hierarchies, missionary women clearly engaged in a wide spiritual ministry; they were joined in this task by First Nations women catechists who also undertook vital preaching work in spreading the Christian message.

In 1857 William Duncan, a lay missionary representing England's Church Missionary Society, and the Oblates of Mary Immaculate, a Roman Catholic missionary order, arrived in British Columbia to begin permanent missionary work among the colony's Native peoples. Their arrival marked the beginning of a general missionary thrust by several major denominations that sought to 'save' the Native peoples by converting them from 'pagan-ism' or 'heathenism' to their particular branch of Christianity. The reaction of the native Indians to the missionaries appears to have been, for the most part, quite positive, and, according to anthropologist Wilson Duff, by 1904 90 per cent of the province's Native population was nominally Christian. Indians such as the Chilcotin, who fiercely resisted all other aspects of white culture, accepted Christianity; the Kwakiutl of northern Vancouver Island who resisted, initially, Catholic missionary efforts, accepted the Anglican faith. According to the 1939 census 57 per cent of British Colum-bia's Native population was Roman Catholic, 20 per cent Anglican, 20 per cent United Church, and 3 per cent belonged to other denominations – mostly Salvation Army. It must be noted, however, that although only twenty-eight among the Native population were recorded as still holding aboriginal beliefs, many retained their old beliefs even while they practised Christianity.[2]

The first missionaries were men. With the exception of one or two Anglican priests who combined white parish work with missionary efforts among Victoria's Native population, these male missionaries worked for several years without women to share the daunting task of evangelizing ten major ethnic groups spread over the colony. Then, in the 1860s, British Columbia missionary women began their work among the province's Native peoples. And while most Canadian Protestant women remained primarily locked into traditional roles, Methodist, Presbyterian, and Angli-can missionary women in British Columbia had the opportunity to shatter the norm. This was a reflection of at least two very different realities: the larger struggle for women's expanded and equal role within the churches, and a progressive Christianity that 'in obedience to [the] Lord's commis-sion to make disciples of all nations,'[3] welcomed necessary innovation in the mission field.

British Columbia's missionary women were encouraged to widen their ministry. One strong measure of support for their right to preach came from the Methodist Woman's Missionary Society (WMS) through the women's pages of the *Missionary Outlook*. This journal was widely read and much appreciated by women in the field. Through the 'Women's Mis-sionary Pages' section – which began as one page in 1884 and increased to a full section within a few years – women were able to link up with their sis-ters not only in Canada but throughout the missionary world. British Columbia missionaries Caroline Tate, Emma Crosby, and Reba Kissack all welcomed what Crosby referred to as 'almost [her] only source of informa-tion.'[4] In this publication, both Methodist and Presbyterian women promoted women's right to expand their evangelical role.[5] Their theologically based arguments regarding that right presaged the arguments of modern church feminists and their supporters.[6] Revealing what John Webster Grant has termed 'A measure of self-conscious feminism,' Mrs Harvie, secretary of the Presbyterian Woman's Home Mission Board, clearly angered by suggestions that 'the progressive age' was alone responsible for inspiring women's interest in mission work, drew her audience's attention to the historical continuity of woman's work for the churches. Harvie focused on the preaching of both the woman of Samaria, who told friends and neighbours that Jesus was the Christ, and Mary Magdelene, who received 'a special commission at the tomb of the risen Saviour.'[7] Mrs T.J. Jackson, wife of a Methodist minister, addressed the 1889 conference of the Woman's Missionary Society of the Methodist Church of Canada on the topic of woman's right to preach. Jackson based her arguments on both the presence of women on the day of Pentecost and the apostle Peter's use of the Old Testament saying, 'I will pour out of my spirit upon all flesh, and your sons and your daughters shall prophesy.' Attacking those who would deny women their rightful role in spreading God's word, Jackson denounced their arguments: '[Peter] had not learned to say with a certain Doctor of Divinity of the nineteenth century "Every woman you let in will keep some man out." While some quote Paul as saying "Let the women keep silence in the Churches," they forget that he gave instructions in other places as to how women should be attired when they prophesy.' Like Harvie, Jackson drew attention to the prophetic role of Mary Magdelene and finally declared to her audience, 'It is high time that somewhere in her creed the Christian church should teach her children to say, "I believe in godly, intellectual, consecrated, Holy Ghost baptized, womanhood."'[8]

The editors of the woman's pages of the *Missionary Outlook* did not hesitate to print or promote literature that supported woman's right to preach. A paper read by Mrs William Casey at the Uxbridge (Ontario) district convention of the Methodist WMS in the summer of 1902 was printed 'by request.' It stressed that according to Matthew 22, 'a woman was the first missionary'; the paper went on to challenge the literal interpretation of Paul's admonition regarding women's silence in church and stressed the lack of discrimination against women by the Holy Spirit: 'on them the tongues of fire descended as well as on the men.'[9] The editors also promoted Frances Willard's *Women in the Pulpit*[10] and urged that it be introduced into every Sunday school. The *Outlook* published some strong statements, although these were not necessarily the views of all WMS members: for example, a review of Willard's book stated that woman's 'truest sphere will not be reached until her place is made at man's side in every department of activity.'[11]

The male ministers of British Columbia, both colleagues in the mission field and the church hierarchy, frequently supported women preaching and even conducting complete religious services. Practicalities determined that women might undertake a wider ministry in the mission field than they would be allowed in either urban or rural situations. Male missionaries gave no indication that they saw anything unusual in women preaching. Nor is there anything in their writings to suggest that they felt threatened by this apparent usurpation of a traditional male role. There is no evidence that British Columbia's women missionaries had to engage in a power struggle with male clergy in order to preach or that they were considered 'interlopers on essentially male terrain.'[12] When the demarcations between lay and ministerial roles blurred, neither the men nor the women involved appeared to find it particularly unusual. The Reverend Mr William Allen reported to his superiors that during his illness both his wife and the missionary teacher Emily Butchard conducted Methodist funeral services.[13] And the Reverend Mr Francis Swan did not object to his sister and his missionary colleague Lavinia Clarke taking Sunday services when he was incapacitated by blood poisoning.[14] But the most enthusiastic supporter of the expanded role of women was the Reverend Thomas Crosby. During a revival among the Port Simpson Indians in September of 1877, while Crosby was in Vancouver, the evangelical work of the women proved invaluable. According to Crosby, 'the church was crowded night and day, and Mrs Crosby, Miss Knott [schoolteacher] and Kate [Dudoward, a Native catechist] had as much as they could do to carry on the work and direct these poor people to Jesus.'[15]

In the tradition-bound Anglican Church women could expect little support if they ventured outside their prescribed 'handmaiden' role. It is unlikely, for example, that Bishop George Hills, in spite of what has been referred to as his 'new episcopal style' would have countenanced Anglican women in a role other than that of 'helpmate,' a term he applied to his wife.[16] Hills's diary indicates that he had decided views on the place of women:

At the end of our walk met with two young ladies with whom we returned. I was not a little amused to hear one of them who professed to be very religious and a great admirer of schismatic teachers declare that she was about to study the newspaper! And to get up the subject of politics! ... The idea of a lady studying politics! I do think it a most absurd idea, especially for a young person. In my opinion a lady should never read a newspaper – they are too full of everything that is violent and bad, they are too ungentle for a lady who should do nothing nor say what is not perfectly gentle. Besides I think it is meddling too much with the world – it is violating in spirit the scripture precept concerning them. Let them be 'Keepers at home.'[17]

Whether or not Hills's experiences in British Columbia ever modified his strong feelings on the issue of the place of women remains unknown. But there is evidence that even the Anglicans eventually accepted the reality of missionary women preachers. A woman in the pulpit of Christ Church Cathedral, Victoria, would scarcely have been tolerated,[18] but the preaching of Kate Dibben and Kathleen O'Brien at Alert Bay in the 1920s, Eva Hasell and her companions for several decades in the province's interior, and Dorothy Thomas in the Peace River Country in 1943, were reasons for rejoicing.[19]

Preaching was important to these and other missionary women of British Columbia because there is some evidence they viewed the saving of souls as their primary task. Any practical application of the gospel, teaching and nursing, for example, had to go hand in hand with preaching the gospel message. While they valued their caregiving and nurturing capacities, missionary women saw a larger responsibility. For teaching missionary Lavinia Clarke, the spiritual needs of the Native peoples were a priority and always took 'first place.'[20] Emma Crosby concurred. Speaking for both herself and her fellow women workers in the Indian Girls' Home at Port Simpson, she wrote, 'What we desire most of all is that the heart of each girl who may enter the Home may be brought under the power of the Gospel; without this we fail, whatever else may be accomplished.'[21]

In the 1890s Presbyterian missionary Bella Johnston, matron of the Alberni Indian Girls' Home, undertook not simply the material care of Native children but also the care of their 'neverdying souls.'[22] Johnston's Methodist counterpart at the Chinese Rescue Home in Victoria understood her role as a 'genuine work of the converting grace of God.'[23] On her return to the Kitamaat Mission after a month's vacation, Elizabeth Lang reported to her superiors, 'I feel more than ever what a privilege it is to minister.'[24] Miss Reid, Presbyterian missionary hired as a nurse at the Ahousaht Mission considered herself 'a nurse evangelist.'[25] And young Agnes Knight, Methodist missionary on the Pacific northwest coast made it absolutely clear how she perceived her role; in 1885 she began her journal on her mission work in British Columbia with a quotation from Matthew 28:20 – 'The Lord said unto me, Go and preach the gospel to every creature.'[26]

There is little doubt that British Columbia missionary women followed this directive. Caroline Tate, a Methodist missionary who worked in British Columbia for close to forty years, noted several times in her diary that she conducted services and preached the gospel.[27] Emma Crosby, whose missionary work was equally extensive, preached regularly.[28] Agnes Knight recorded in her journal that on her second Sunday in the mission field, she conducted the morning service at Bella Bella; with Mrs Culyer, wife of the male missionary, acting as interpreter, she spoke to the Indians 'from the text Matt. 21.'[29] And in 1899, once the Native school at Kitamaat closed for the summer, missionary teacher Kate Nicholas travelled with her husband up and down the numerous inlets of the northwest coastline 'proclaiming,' she wrote, 'the glorious Gospel of our Blessed Redeemer to the different tribes of Indians, whites and Chinamen.'[30]

Among Presbyterian women, it is clear that Elizabeth MacVicar and her female co-worker regularly took Sunday services, including 'the great festival days.'[31] There is some evidence that MacVicar was following a tradition of Presbyterian women preachers. Both May Swartout and her daughter Nina, missionary teachers at Ucluelet, Vancouver Island, preached regularly for several years in the 1890s,[32] and, in 1905, Ellen Christine Mackay and Miss MacNeil were running the Ahousaht Mission together.[33] Although there appears to be more evidence from the writings on Methodist women preachers, witnesses indicate that even the Anglican church allowed some license to its women missionaries. An unidentified fellow-worker claimed that Kate Dibben, an Anglican missionary at Village Island in the 1920s, regularly held Sunday morning and evening services.[34] And Anglican Sunday school missionaries Eva Hasell and Kate Sayle impressed the Bishop of Kootenay by travelling 1,750 miles throughout his diocese every year, not only visiting over eight hundred homes, but also 'taking many services.'[35]

Discovering and documenting the extent to which missionary women preached presents difficulties, primarily because of the paucity of written sources on their role in the mission field, but evidence indicates that preaching was far from a novelty. It was clearly not so for Emma Crosby,[36] and there is no indication of the unusual in Caroline Tate's diary entries. In April 1911, for example, when the Tates paid a return visit to Port Simpson, the scene of some of their earliest missionary work, Caroline Tate noted that they spent a day 'at conference' where she and her husband were married thirty-five years earlier, and 'where many times [she] preached to a congregation.'[37] Not even Agnes Knight, who was required to preach so soon after her arrival on the Naas, records any surprise at this turn of events.

Certainly women appear to have preached regularly in the absence of male missionaries who were itinerating, travelling to provincial or national conferences, or on fund-raising tours. Continuity in missionary work was essential to success, and services could not be allowed to lapse. The Reverend Robert Culyer was away visiting an Indian village when Agnes Knight preached to the Bella Bella; throughout his absence, Agnes and Mrs Culyer held the 'usual Tuesday evening preaching service.'[38] Alice Jackson noted that during the absence of George Raley at Kitamaat, the two missionary women 'conducted the church services.'[39] At the Kitamaat Mission, during the appointed missionary's absence 'the ladies of the Home Staff had to conduct the Sunday services ...'[40] Both Emma Crosby and Caroline Tate mention that they held services in their husbands' absence.[41] Kate Druary, who worked with the Tates at Duncan, on Vancouver Island, noted that 'during Mr Tate's absence at District Meeting and Conference, I took full charge of all his services. On Sunday ... I had Sunday school, preaching service and class meeting at Quamichan in the morning, the same at Chemilemahts in the afternoon and then preached at Khnipson ... in the evening Sunday school service and a short prayer and class meeting at Somina. I preached to the people through an interpreter.'[42] Druary felt confident enough to offer services the following week without an interpreter. Thomas Crosby was much in demand in central and eastern Canada as a guaranteed fund-raiser[43]; consequently his wife Emma Crosby and other female workers were frequently called upon to fill the gap. Kezia Hendry wrote that during Thomas Crosby's two-month absence in 1884, she and her co-worker Susannah Lawrence had 'full charge' of the Port Simpson Mission and held the religious services.[44]

Male missionaries apparently needed to share preaching responsibilities with their female counterparts simply because confining women to a practical role would have retarded missionary expansion. Thomas Crosby was grateful for the help of his wife Emma Crosby, as well as to Susannah Lawrence, Kezia Hendry, and Reba Reinhart; their ability to take over his spiritual charges enabled him to travel farther afield in search of converts.[45] Robert Culyer depended upon his wife and a female missionary to move with the Kitamaat Indians to their summer camp and continue the work of evangelization while he visited other Native groups.[46] The need for expansion, coupled with a shortage of male missionary help, not only enabled women to preach intermittently but also to take complete charge of mission centres and to offer a full range of missionary services, including evangelical preaching.

A woman might take over the appointment given originally to her now-deceased husband, as May Swartout did when she was appointed to what the Presbyterians considered a vital work of preaching and teaching at Ucluelet, Vancouver Island.[47] Like Reba Reinhart, a woman could remain at a mission post during a male missionary's illness and carry on the work until someone else was appointed; or, as in the case of Ellen Mackay and Miss MacNeil at Ahousaht in 1905, women could take control when there were difficulties finding replacement male missionaries.[48] But women like Kathleen O'Brien and Kate Dibben at Village Island, Carrie Gunn, missionary to the Chinese in Victoria, and Susannah Lawrence at Kitamaat are examples of women who worked on their own, thus avoiding, or at least curtailing, male supervision or control. This allowed women to add more than simply preaching to their regular missionary work. Susannah Lawrence is an interesting case study in that her evangelical work appears to have succeeded where an experienced male missionary's had failed.

Visits by Thomas Crosby and attempts by him to place a Native catechist among them had failed to impress the Kitamaat Indians. They refused to be converted. In 1883 Lawrence volunteered to work with these 'recalcitrant' people and to establish and run a mission post 160 miles from the nearest centre at Port Simpson, in an area where, according to Emma Crosby, 'no white woman was known to have set foot.'[49] There, with the assistance of two Indian catechists, a wife and husband team, she offered a full range of missionary activity, including the church services and Bible classes.[50] Lawrence's efforts were rewarded when, in the spring of 1884, the Kitamaat experienced 'a powerful revival' that caused Susannah Lawrence to rejoice 'over the spiritual prosperity' of her charge.[51] Her ministry was considered 'one of much power.'[52]

Having once experienced the freedom offered by this individual effort, Lawrence felt confined and restless when she was replaced at Kitamaat. After two years teaching school at Port Simpson, feeling 'anxious to go into another field of labor,'[53] Lawrence volunteered to work alone again at Nanaimo. There, living in a two-room mission house that Emma Crosby referred to as 'a light in a dark place,' she preached the gospel for six years.[54] While centred at Nanaimo, Lawrence was active as an itinerant preacher. She became particularly concerned about one Indian village that had never been visited by a missionary; she wrote to a friend, 'I could not think of the poor things perishing for want of the bread of life ... so every Sunday morning I go, or send Cushan [a Native preacher] to hold a service among them.'[55]

Contrary to the findings of Canadian scholars Rosemary Gagan and H. Miriam Ross, the American writer R. Pierce Beaver regarding foreign missions, and researcher Olive Anderson regarding British women preachers, there is no evidence that in British Columbia women missionaries confined their preaching exclusively to women and children.[56] Caroline Tate, Emma Crosby, and Kate Nicholas obviously preached the gospel to all those whom their husbands were evangelizing. Susannah Lawrence, Reba Reinhart, Kathleen O'Brien, and Kate Dibben, as the sole missionaries in their particular fields, reached out to all who would listen. In the writings of missionary women, only Kate Nicholas and Caroline Tate mention preaching to white settlers but this shortage of written confirmation does not necessarily mean that most women who preached confined their work to Native congregations. From the earliest years, lack of church personnel combined with the mobility of many whites – for example miners, cannery workers, loggers, and railway workers – led missionaries to act as spiritual guides to both Euro-Canadians and Native peoples; it is therefore probable that at least on some occasions women also preached to combined congregations.

Preaching in the mission fields, whether by women or by men, was not confined to church pulpits. Although eventually the major mission centres had churches, many areas continued to rely on intermittent visits by missionaries. The Indians of Fort Rupert, for example, were still without a church in 1934, after more than sixty years of Anglican missionary activity in the area.[57] Therefore women missionaries, like their male counterparts, preached the gospel whenever and wherever the opportunity presented itself. From the pulpit preaching of Caroline Tate, Emma Crosby, and Elizabeth MacVicar to the outdoor Bible classes of Margaret Minnes, Bella Johnston, and Emma Marion Kenmuir,[58] from Susannah Lawrence's itinerant preaching to 'the quiet talks ... on religious subjects' Elizabeth Long gave to young Native women,[59] missionary women in British Columbia engaged actively in a preaching and ministerial role.

In this work they were joined by women First Nations catechists. From the early years of missionary activity, Native women exercised an evangelical role for the major Protestant denominations. Theirs was a purely catechetical role, although missionaries also hoped that simply the example of converted Indian women would draw others to lead 'happy Christian lives.'[60] Proselytization by Native peoples remains an understudied aspect of Indian/white missionary contact history.[61] But in British Columbia where missionaries were few, prospective converts numerous, Native migratory habits commonplace, diversity of languages problematic, and interdenominational rivalries keen, the need for Native preachers was acute. Some of the first clergy dispatched to British Columbia, recognizing 'the vast missionary field to be worked' and the limitations imposed on their efforts, hoped that the Native peoples would themselves facilitate missionary activities and 'spread the Word.'[62] The Methodists were enthusiastic regarding the utilization of Native preachers and, as Thomas Crosby noted, in British Columbia 'it was Native or lay agents who first commenced practical mission work and so prepared the way for the regular missionary.'[63] Crosby actively promoted 'general use of the talents of ... Native converts' and, regardless of whether or not they were educated, urged the church to use them in 'evangelistic efforts of every kind,' including preaching: 'When Amos Cushan, our first Native preacher at Nanaimo, went out he could not read, but he could tell of the disease and the cure. When Sahlosalton commenced his work on the Coast the people marvelled and asked "Where did he get this wisdom?" Many others of our Native brethren, like Capt. John Sua-lis and August Jackson, have been mightily used of God in spreading the Gospel among their people.'[64] Crosby's fellow-worker Cornelius Bryant also had praise for Indian catechists, crediting one with attracting as large a congregation as Crosby himself.[65] Only a few weeks after her arrival at Bella Bella, Agnes Knight also determined that 'the more effectual way of reaching the people would be thru [sic] Native preachers.'[66]

Although apparently the most enthusiastic, the Methodists were not alone in promoting the use of Native preachers. As early as 1868 Bishop George Hills was calling on friends of the Anglican mission efforts in British Columbia to finance at least two institutions for the training of Native teachers.[67] In spite of this early enthusiasm, however, the Anglican Church appears to have had indifferent success.[68] According to one long-term Anglican missionary, the difficulty lay in finding 'Indians of ability to run regular services in the outlying villages.'[69] But one Anglican bishop, although reluctant to push for a Native ministry, did recognize that some Indians were doing 'good missionary work in their own villages.'[70]

There were difficulties inherent in the use of Native preachers, particularly in the years when neither missionary nor prospective convert was knowledgeable of the other's language. Theological concepts totally unfamiliar to the Native peoples could not be readily translated into Native dialects. This undoubtedly created problems for local preachers whose role was to interpret missionary teachings and continue missionary work. It could also prove less than satisfactory for the dependent missionary. During her research among the Tlingit, anthropologist Laura Klein was informed by a Native woman that when the Presbyterian church missionary was giving a sermon, the translator was actually telling 'a traditional

Raven story.' Klein notes the irony: 'The natives believed the minister was telling Raven tales while the minister believed the natives were being enlightened by the gospel.'[71] Despite these obvious limitations, Native preachers were considered essential to the continuity of missionary endeavours. In 1884, for example, almost one-fifth of the Methodist missionaries in British Columbia were Native people.[72]

The task of discovering the extent to which Native women actively participated in evangelical work is a formidable one. Women missionaries left behind at least a partial record of their active preaching role, but Native women committed little to paper. Another major problem is simply one of identification. Had Christian Native women both retained and been identified by their tribal names, they would have been more easily identifiable, but those received into the Church were given new Christian names[73]; and others, either because they were women of mixed blood, or had married mixed-blood men (or, later, Indians who had white surnames) became, in the written records, indistinguishable from white women. Unless it had been indicated by a missionary, who would know, for example, that Mrs Gladstone, vice-president of the Skidegate Woman's Missionary Society, and Mrs McKay, the society's recording secretary were (unlike the president, Mrs Allen) Native women? The names Mrs Jane Cook and Mrs Joe Harris do not indicate the Native lineage of these Anglican Native catechists.[74] And Katherine Derrick is hardly a name one would associate with the profession of medicine woman.[75]

Fortunately, some missionaries were willing to give recognition to the work of Native women evangelists, and it is from their letters, many published in missionary journals, that we learn something of these obscure mission workers. In 1875 Methodist missionary Charles Tate gave equal weight to the successful preaching of Kate and Alfred Dudoward.[76] Over a decade later, Reverend Alfred Green gave credit to Sarah Russ, who 'faithfully helped her husband in his mission work ... enduring exposure and privations without a murmur that they might preach Jesus in distant villages.'[77] Thomas Crosby lavished praise on Elizabeth Deex, 'a chieftainness of the Tsimpshean nation who ... entered into the work of bringing others to Christ,'[78] Mrs Hamblet, 'a Native of Port Simpson who was preaching Christ and doing a great good amongst the lowest of the city,'[79] and Kate Dudoward who worked with Emma Crosby and teacher Miss Knott during a revival at Port Simpson in 1877.[80] Anglican Bishop Schofield singled out Jane Cook and Mrs Harris who preached to the women at Alert Bay. He informed the secretaries of the Church Missionary Society in London of the 'new spiritual efforts' these women were making preaching among their own people.[81] According to Kwakiutl Indian chief James Sewid, his godmother, Jane Cook, 'used to preach in the church' in the Kwakwala language, and Mrs Harris 'used to read the lessons.'[82] Agnes Knight praised the 'missionary spirit' of a Weekano woman called Lucy who worked hard to convert her people and 'often got up and talked to them herself' about the gospel.[83]

Lucy and also Elizabeth Deex apparently worked alone among their people, but some of the Native women mentioned by missionaries worked in partnership; Lydia Cushan, Sarah Russ, and Kate Dudoward all travelled missionary circuits with their husbands. How often these women were called upon to preach remains unknown. The Reverend Mr Dennis Jennings, however, gives an indication that, like their white counterparts, Native women preached when their husbands were taken ill. In a letter from Port Simpson, 23 October 1883, he wrote, 'Our Native worker [Russ] was ill; his wife on this account had to address the people. While speaking she felt such power, her heart strongly warming within her, she exclaimed, "The spirit of God I believe is come into my heart." Her words touched the hearts of the people.'[84]

Allowing for the passionate rhetoric of a man who wanted to impress potential missionary supporters, it is clear that Sarah Russ rose to the occasion. Whether it was Russ's impromptu outpouring from the heart, Agnes Knight's explanation of a New Testament chapter,[85] or Elizabeth MacVicar's Thanksgiving sermon, which, as she 'didn't have a thing on Thanksgiving,' was 'out of [her] head with blood and sweat,'[86] the gospel message was given by women.

Since women left few records that expressed their feelings about their work, it is impossible to determine how many women found their new experiences exhilarating and liberating and how many perceived this new, sometimes unexpected, role to be burdensome and, sometimes, a little nerve-wracking. Alice Jackson was grateful for her Sunday school experience as it prepared her for 'taking the services with greater ease.'[87] Certainly not all missionary women relished their new opportunities, as these imposed new burdens. Male missionaries could be single-minded in their evangelical work primarily because they had the help of women; at least one, most often two or three, women missionaries provided for both the basic material well-being of these men and the material and educational care of prospective converts. Women missionaries, however, added such activities as preaching, Bible classes, funeral services, and visiting to their domestic roles. For some the combination proved to be too much. Methodist missionary teacher Reba Reinhart offered to take over the Bella Bella

Mission until a new appointment was made by the missionary board.[88] There appears to have been no official complaint from Reinhart, but, according to Thomas Crosby, although Reinhart had 'done well' at the mission station, she was eagerly awaiting the new missionary who would 'take from her such a care.'[89] And there is a sense of desperation in a letter written by Miss Alton from Kitamaat in the spring of 1912: 'We are all anxious to hear of the appointment of the missionary for Kitamaat village as it will relieve the Home Staff of the responsibilities of the three Sunday services and prayer meeting and the visiting which we feel should be carried on.'[90] These women were not rejecting a wider ministry; they simply found the double load too heavy to enable them to work effectively.

Other women desired to expand on their traditional roles and were denied the participation they desired. Bella Johnston, who ran the Alberni Mission with the mission's female teacher until a male missionary arrived, pressed the Presbyterian superintendent of missions to send a man as soon as possible. Johnston noted that in spite of their best efforts, they were limited; she complained that there was 'work to do that however willing we are we cannot touch.'[91] The two women were obviously constrained in their outreach, although in what manner is not clear. When the Reverend Mr Swartout, a replacement missionary finally arrived, he proved to be opposed to women taking an active ministerial role. When the superintendent of missions suggested that a female missionary be sent to assist him, Swartout resisted on the grounds that a woman would not be able to take the 'Sabbath services.'[92] Nine years later, however, Swartout had softened his stand. In a letter to his superior he expressed relief at the return of his wife because he found it difficult to get away in her absence, as his female missionary companion Mrs MacKay was 'not yet able to take a service in anything but English.'[93] It is ironic that this missionary who repeatedly stressed his need for a male assistant was, upon his death, replaced by his wife Mary and daughter Nina.

In 1901 another Presbyterian missionary was making life difficult for a woman worker at Alberni. Kate Cameron, who taught at the Alberni Mission, clearly felt that she was unjustly restricted from taking a more active evangelical role. Writing in anger to the superintendent of missions, Cameron expressed her dissatisfaction with the restrictions a newly arrived missionary had placed upon her: 'I am permitted to take no part in the Sabbath Services for the Indians except teach a S[unday] Sch[ool] and the evangelistic work is not spoken of around me.'[94] When she did not receive a favourable reply from McKay, Cameron hammered home her point in a second letter: 'All who are fitted for it should take part in the evangelistic work.'[95] It is clear that however much she desired a more active role in the spiritual work, unless empowered by the local missionary, Cameron could only complain.

The pressing needs of frontier missionary endeavours clearly determined that in British Columbia the fullest use be made of women's abilities. Women who had entered the mission field in domestically oriented and/or educational roles found the opportunity to take an active part in the spiritual advancement of their charges. But it was an opportunity 'subject to the constraints of male power.'[96] Preaching, Bible classes, visiting, even funeral services, were added to, not substituted for, 'women's work,' a situation that effectively limited the scope of women's preaching ministry. And while some women worked with progressive male colleagues willing to share, as far as possible, their evangelical work, others had to contend with more traditional-thinking co-workers. Within the limits imposed by domesticity and male control, however, the missionary women of British Columbia proved that on the mission frontier they could experience a new power.

NOTES

1 Elizabeth MacVicar to her family, 15 Sept. 1947, United Church Woman's Missionary Society (WMS), Home Missions, Indian Work, box 1, file 13, United Church Archives, Toronto (hereafter cited as UCA).

2 Wilson Duff, *The Indian History of British Columbia*, Vol. 1, *The Impact of the White Man*, Anthropology in British Columbia, Memoir No. 5 (Victoria: Provincial Museum of BC, 1964), 87; Margaret Whitehead, *Now You Are My Brother: Missionaries in British Columbia* (Victoria: Province of British Columbia Sound Heritage Series, Sound and Moving Image Division), 1981.

3 John Webster Grant, *The Church in the Canadian Era* (Burlington, Ont.: Welch, 1988), 21.

4 *Missionary Outlook*, June 1883, 91; Aug. 1881, 91; Apr. 1903, 94 (hereafter cited as *MO*).

5 Although a Methodist publication, the *MO* was often ecumenical in content.

6 See, for example, Elizabeth Carroll, 'Women and Ministry,' *Theological Studies* 36, 4 (Dec. 1975), 665–79; Raymond E. Brown, 'Roles of Women in the Fourth Gospel,' *Theological Studies* 36, 4 (Dec. 1975), 688–99; Margaret Brackenbury Crook, *Woman and Religion* (Boston: Beacon Press, 1964); Barbara Brown Zikmund, 'The Struggles for the Right to Preach,' in *Women and Religion in America*, vol 1, Rosemary Radford Ruether and Rosemary Skinner Keller, eds. (San Francisco: Harper and Row, 1981), 193–241.

7 *MO*, Mar. 1882, 39.

8 *MO*, Oct. 1889, 153.

9 *MO*, Oct. 1902, 154.

10 Frances Willard, *Women in the Pulpit* (Boston: D. Lothrop, 1888).

11 *MO*, Aug. 1888, 116. It has been argued, however, that the WMS of the United Church offered no support for the ordination of women; see Alison Prentice, Paula Bourne, Gail Cuthbert Brandt, Beth Light, Wendy Mitchinson, and Naomi Black, *Canadian Women: A History* (Toronto: Harcourt Brace Jovanovich, 1988), 275.

12 Veronica Strong-Boag, 'Pulling in Double Harness or Hauling a Double Load: Women, Work, and Feminism on the Canadian Prairie,' *Journal of Canadian Studies* 21, 3 (Autumn 1986), 32–52.

13 *MO*, Jan. 1919, 23.

14 *MO*, Mar. 1913, 71.

15 *Missionary Notices of the Methodist Church* (Nov. 1877), 274.

16 Hills to Mr Mackinney, 9 May 1886, Bishop Hills's Correspondence, Text 57, box 2, file 1; Hills to Mr Rivet, 4 June 1888, Bishop Hills's Correspondence, Text 57, box 2, file 11, Anglican Church Archives, Victoria (ACA).

17 Bishop Hills's Journal, 1841, Text 57, vol. 1, file 3, ACA.

18 For Anglican attitudes on the expansion of women's role within the Anglican communion see, Reports on Synod: 25th Synod of the Anglican Church, Victoria, BC, Feb. 1925, 5–8; 32nd Synod of the Anglican Church, Victoria, BC, Feb. 1932, 16–17; 35th Synod of the Anglican Church, Victoria, BC, Feb. 1935, 7, ACA.

19 Bishop Schofield to Canon Gould, Toronto, 16 Feb. 1927; Bishop Schofield to Miss Francklyn, 4 June 1936, Schofield Correspondence, Text 203, box 1, file 5, ACA; F.H.E. Hasell, *Canyons, Cars, and Caravans* (Toronto: Macmillan, 1930), 113; Margaret Whitehead interview with Dorothy Thompson, May 1990. Thompson believes, however, that her preaching was not well received by the men simply because she was a woman.

20 *19th Annual Report of the Woman's Missionary Society of the Methodist Church*, 1901, 86.

21 *MO*, Nov./Dec. 1881, 140.

22 Bella Johnston to Mr Cassells, 10 Apr. 1893, Presbyterian Foreign Mission Society Correspondence, Western Division, box 1, file 24, UCA.

23 Annie Leake Tuttle, 'Reminiscences,' 114, British Columbia Archives and Record Service (BCARS).

24 *MO*, Dec. 1903, 287.

25 Mrs C.A. Wicken to Executive of the Presbyterian Woman's Mission Society, 20 Feb. 1930, United Church WMS, Home Missions, Indian Work, box 1, file 13, UCA.

26 Diary of Agnes Knight, July 1885 – Oct. 1887, 23 Oct. 1887, BCARS.

27 Caroline Tate Diary, 12 Mar., 16 Apr., 2 July 1911, BCARS.

28 *MO*, Nov./Dec. 1881, 139.

29 Diary of Agnes Knight, 18 July 1885, BCARS.

30 Kate Nicholas to the Methodist WMS, published in *MO*, Aug. 1899, 127.

31 Elizabeth MacVicar to family, 16 Oct. 1947, United Church WMS Home Missions, Indian Work, box 1, file 13, UCA.

32 May Swartout to Reverend Dr R. Mackay, 13 Oct. 1894, Foreign Missionary Society Correspondence, box 3, file 67, UCA.

33 Ellen Christine Mackay to Presbyterian Woman's Foreign Mission Committee (WFMC), 8 Oct. 1903, Presbyterian WFMC, Home Missions, Indian Work, box 3, file 79, UCA.

34 Historical Notes and Bylaws, Text 237, ACA.

35 Hasell, *Canyons, Cars, and Caravans*, 112–13.

36 *MO*, Nov./Dec. 1881, 139.

37 Caroline Tate Diary, 16 Aug. 1911, BCARS.

38 Diary of Agnes Knight, 14 July 1885, BCARS.

39 *MO*, Nov. 1905, 263.

40 *MO*, June 1912, 120.

41 Caroline Tate Diary, 12 Mar. 1911, BCARS; *MO*, Nov./Dec. 1881, 139.

42 *MO*, Sept. 1904, 215.

43 Carence Bolt, 'Thomas Crosby and Tsimshian of Port Simpson, 1874–1897' (MA thesis, Simon Fraser University, 1981), 90.

44 *MO*, Feb. 1885, 24–5.

45 *MO*, Jan. 1887, 15; *MO*, Nov. 1886, 174.

46 *MO*, June/July 1886, 109.

47 May Swartout to Reverend Dr R. Mackay, 13 Oct. 1894, Foreign Missionary Society Correspondence, box 3, file 67, UCA.

48 *MO*, Jan. 1887, 15; Miss Mackay to McKay, Oct. 8, 1905, Presbyterian Foreign Mission Society Correspondence, Western Division, box 1, file 79, UCA.

49 *MO*, Apr. 1899, 92.

50 Ibid.

51 *MO*, Apr. 1884, 59; *MO*, July 1884, 106.

52 *MO*, Feb. 1906, 41.

53 *MO*, Feb. 1885, 25.

54 *MO*, Apr. 1899, 92.

55 *MO*, June/July 1886, 98.

56 See the chapters by Gagan and Ross in this volume; R. Pierce Beaver, *American Protestant Women in World Mission: A History of the First Feminist Movement in North America* (Grand Rapids: Eerdmans, 1968), 117–43; Olive Anderson,

'Women Preachers in Mid-Victorian Britain: Some Reflexions on Feminism, Popular Religion, and Social Change,' *Historical Journal* 12, 3 (1969), 468.
57 Reverend C.K.K. Prosser to Bishop Schofield, 19 Jan. 1934, Text 503, box 1, file 3, ACA.
58 Bella Johnston to Cassels, 11 Apr. 1894, Presbyterian Foreign Mission Society Correspondence, Western Division, box 1, file 6, UCA; Columbia Branch Woman's Auxiliary (WA) Minutes, 15 June 1928, ACA.
59 *19th Annual Report of the Woman's Missionary Society of the Methodist Church*, 1901, 88.
60 See, for example, Thomas Crosby's comments in Crosby, *Among the An Ko Me Nums of the Pacific Coast* (Toronto: William Briggs, 1907), 229–31.
61 Margaret Whitehead, '"A Useful Christian Woman": First Nations Women and Protestant Missionary Work in British Columbia,' *Atlantis 18*, 1 & 2 (1992–3), 142–66.
62 *Wesleyan Missionary Notices*, Feb. 1870, 82–3; see also *Missionary Notices of the Methodist Church of Canada*, Jan. 1877, 215–16; *Mission Field* 8 (Jan. 1863), 7.
63 Crosby, *Among the An Ko Me Nums*, 233–4.
64 Ibid., 234–5.
65 *Missionary Notices of the Methodist Church* Jan. 1877, 177.
66 Diary of Agnes Knight, 1 Sept. 1885, BCARS.
67 *Mission Field* 13, 8 (Aug. 1868), 212–15.
68 A letter from Bishop Schofield to Reverend O.T. Hodgson, 9 Aug. 1934, attests to a lack of success in the recruitment of Native ministers. After over sixty years of Anglican missionary endeavour, Schofield wrote, 'Regarding training natives for the ministry, I agree with you we must proceed very slowly.' Text 203, box 1, file 4, ACA.
69 Reverend C.K.K. Prosser to Bishop Schofield, 8 June 1931, Text 203, box 1, file 2, ACA.
70 Bishop Schofield to L.F. Earl Anfield, Principal, St Michael's Indian Residential School, Alert Bay, 16 Dec. 1932, Text 203, box 1, file 3, ACA.
71 Laura T. Klein, 'Contending with Colonization: Tlingit Men and Women in Change,' in *Women and Colonization: Anthropological Perspectives*, Mona Etienne and Eleanor Leacock, eds. (New York: Praeger, 1980), 99.
72 *MO*, Apr. 1884, 51.
73 *MO*, July 1888, 109.
74 James P. Spradley, ed., *Guests Never Leave Hungry: The Autobiography of James Sewid, a Kwakiutl Indian* (Kingston and Montreal: McGill-Queen's University Press, 1969), 48.
75 *MO*, July 1888, 109.
76 *Missionary Notices of the Methodist Church of Canada*, June 1875, 55–6.

77 *MO*, Apr. 1885, 61; *MO*, Aug. 1889, 127.

78 Crosby, *Among the An Ko Me Nums*, 235.

79 *MO*, Oct. 1883, 160.

80 *Missionary Notices of the Methodist Church of Canada*, Nov. 1877, 274–5.

81 Bishop Schofield to Church Missionary Society, 11 Dec. 1914, Synod Office General file, Alert Bay, Text 63, box 1423, file 10, ACA.

82 Spradley, *Guests Never Leave Hungry*, 49.

83 Diary of Agnes Knight, 19 Aug. 1885, BCARS.

84 *MO*, July 1884, 110.

85 Diary of Agnes Knight, 18 July 1885, BCARS.

86 Elizabeth MacVicar to family, 16 Oct. 1947, United Church WMS, Home Missions, Indian Work, box 1, file 13, UCA.

87 *MO*, June 1912, 120.

88 *MO*, Jan. 1887, 15.

89 *MO*, July 1887, 110.

90 *MO*, Sept. 1912, 214.

91 Bella Johnston to McKay, 18 Aug. 1893, Presbyterian Foreign Mission Society Correspondence, Western Division, box 1, file 3, UCA.

92 Reverend Swartout to McKay, 23 Feb. 1894, Presbyterian Foreign Mission Society Correspondence, Western Division, box 1, file 4, UCA.

93 Swartout to Mr McKay, n.d. 1903, Presbyterian Foreign Mission Society Correspondence, Western Division, box 3, file 57, UCA.

94 Kate Cameron to Mr McKay, 1 Nov. 1901, Presbyterian Foreign Mission Society Correspondence, Western Division, box 2, file 33, UCA.

95 Cameron to McKay, 16 June 1902, Presbyterian Foreign Mission Society Correspondence, Western Division, box 2, file 33, UCA.

96 Sylvia Van Kirk, 'What Has the Feminist Perspective Done for Canadian History?' in *Knowledge Reconsidered: A Feminist Overview*, Ursula Martius Franklin, Michele Jean, Sylvia Van Kirk, Andrea Lebowitz, Meg Luxton, Susan Sherwin, and Dorothy E. Smith, eds. (Ottawa: Canadian Research Institute for the Advancement of Women, 1984), 54.

7

Two Sexes Warring in the Bosom of a Single Mission Station: Feminism in the Canadian Methodist Japan Mission, 1881–1895

ROSEMARY R. GAGAN

Some women, like many who preached in British Columbia, accepted unexpected calls to service, while others were more aggressive in their search for Christian work. Women of the Methodist Woman's Missionary Society seized the opportunity to establish themselves in an area denied to men, namely working with women and children in Japan. These missionaries enjoyed an unusual degree of independence, developed strong feelings of sisterhood, and gained considerable leadership and administrative experience. Yet the 'Japan affair' demonstrates that this enterprise was not without its difficulties. The women paid a price for working outside accepted societal roles. There were tensions in the Methodist Japan mission as women had to work out ways, for which they had no pattern, of relating to male colleagues. The male missionaries often ignored or disregarded the women and rarely sought out their opinions on issues that affected them. Also, higher ethical standards were demanded of women than of men. Independent, assertive women were most likely to succeed in such a setting, but the same traits that gave success might upon occasion inspire strong resistance, as Eliza Spencer Large and other women of the Japan mission discovered to their dismay.

As one of several exclusively female organizations established in the last quarter of the nineteenth century by evangelical Canadian women responding to the fervent Anglo-Celtic enthusiasm to extend Christianity throughout the world, the Woman's Missionary Society (WMS) of the Methodist Church of Canada inaugurated a wide range of programs designed to improve the spiritual and material welfare of women and children in Canada and overseas. In retrospect, however, especially if measured in lasting conversions to Christianity, the impact of their endeavour proved less significant and enduring than the eager WMS membership anticipated. After the First World War, an increasingly secular society now responsive to cultural relativism censured both churches and missionaries as intrusive agents of Western imperialism; by the 1930s the missionary calling no longer attracted large numbers of zealous candidates.

In the past decade historians have begun to re-examine the role of missionaries as agents of Western cultural imperialism, but they have also tried to provide an understanding of the religious and material incentives mobilizing these men and women. In particular, to evaluate women's status in the Protestant churches and to appreciate the relevance of religion to women's lives in the nineteenth century, Canadian historians have studied the home-base organization of several women's missionary societies and the experience of their female workers in the field. Consequently, nineteenth-century women's missionary societies can now be appreciated as avenues for many thousands of Canadian women to move beyond their domestic roles, to acquire business and administrative skills as well as knowledge about the wider world, and to become part of a far-reaching network of like-minded activists. Equally important, women's missionary societies provided a singular opportunity for devout, dedicated, and ambitious single Canadian women to pursue missionary careers as an alternative to marriage and domesticity, to exercise personal confidence and freedom, and to further their status as professional women within an admittedly male-dominated institution.[1]

The record of the Woman's Missionary Society of the Methodist Church of Canada provides substantial evidence of the evolution of missionary work from a 'calling' in the 1880s to a self-regulating profession sustained by women determined to direct their own enterprise by the end of the century. From its founding in 1881 until 1925, when it became incorporated into the WMS of the United Church of Canada, the Methodist WMS recruited more than three hundred women as its home and overseas representatives. Employment with the society enabled these carefully chosen women to embrace Christian activism as more than a voluntary pursuit and to earn public appreciation for their altruism, to support themselves financially and to lead an independent existence, often in exotic settings only imagined by their more domesticated sisters. Freed by isolation, distance, and the self-sufficient nature of their organization from much of the sexual tension and professional jealousy that inhibited women's entrance to, and subsequent success in, male-dominated professions in Canada, WMS missionaries developed their own professional standards and work-related skills and seized an opportunity afforded few Canadian women of the day to acquire leadership and administrative experience. At the same time, the intimate friendships among the missionaries and the sense of sisterhood throughout the society forged an assertive gender solidarity that enabled the women in the field to follow their mandate in the face of physical and emotional danger as well as overt hostility to their undertaking.

Within the parameters of this distinct sphere, the WMS missionaries secured a place in the corporate structure of the Methodist Church closer to equality with men than was usually granted women of their generation and background. The operation of the WMS and its fiscal acumen were admired and envied by the men employed by the debt-ridden General Board of Missions (GBM) of the Methodist Church.[2] Sometimes, however, the WMS missionaries' determination to act autonomously in the mission field and to advance their own professionalism had unanticipated and potentially disastrous consequences. The Japan Affair of 1895, a humiliating episode for the Methodist Church, which demonstrated that in spite of their sacred calling missionaries were, after all, men and women motivated by the prerogatives of gender, is a case in point.

In October 1895, responding to vicious gossip that had devastated 'missionary contributions in [Canada] and ... spiritual results in Japan'[3] and stunned Methodist administrators and members alike, the Methodist Church reluctantly was forced to investigate a crisis in its Japan mission. After several years of quarrelling and discontent, the male employees of the GBM and the female personnel of the WMS stationed in Japan no longer maintained satisfactory personal or working relationships; most missionaries were not on speaking terms. Several senior representatives from each mission in Japan submitted their resignations; work in the field was almost at a standstill; and the Canadian Methodist Church feared that it might have to abandon the Japanese enterprise.

To the casual observer of the day, the central issue seemed to be two missionary societies in competition for Japanese souls. In the long run, however, the Japan affair lays bare the tangled and unpredictable nature of gender relations in late-Victorian Canadian society, the emerging feminism of WMS missionaries and administrators when the parameters of their work were jeopardized, and the hesitancy, perhaps inability, of the Methodist hierarchy to resolve the gender issues until the confrontation of feminism with male entitlement had seriously undermined the Methodist Church's credibility in Japan. Put another way, the Japan affair provides a tidy microcosm of late-Victorian Western gender controversies sharpened by the alien cultural context in which the episode unfolded. What follows is an analysis of the sexual dynamics within the Methodist missions that provoked and fed the Japan affair.

Although each missionary had a personalized interpretation of the origins and course of the crisis, the dispute between the GBM and the WMS was long standing; it probably began in 1882 when the first WMS overseas missionary, Martha Cartmell, arrived in Tokyo where the GBM had opened a station almost a decade earlier.[4] Japan had been avidly endorsed by the WMS board of managers as the society's initial overseas base. In 1873, as part of a comprehensive modernization policy to advance Japanese competition with the West on more equal terms, the Meiji government had launched an ambitious program of social and political reforms. Encouraged by the government, the Japanese people became intensely curious about Western culture and technology. The middle class copied Western social habits.[5] University students read the classics of Western literature; J.S. Mill and Samuel Smiles seemed to hold the formulae for success in the contest with the West.[6] Because the government also lifted the Tokugawa edicts against Christianity, Western missionaries became the source of much of this new scholarship. If not always enthusiastically welcomed for their proselytizing, the hundreds of missionaries who arrived in Japan in the

1870s were at least tolerated for the superior Western-style education they offered children of the enterprising Japanese middle class.[7] In the vanguard of this Western offensive were GBM missionaries Davidson Macdonald and George Cochrane who opened a station in Tokyo in 1873.[8] Their apparent success, as well as the Methodist Church's urgent appeals for women missionaries to begin work among Japanese women were major considerations in the decision of the WMS to launch its first overseas enterprise in Tokyo.[9]

Encouraged by Alexander Sutherland, the general superintendent of missions, and by the general conference's recommendation that women should be part of the contingent in Japan, in 1881 Canadian Methodist women formed their own single-sex missionary society. The next year, under the supervision of Martha Cartmell, a Hamilton, Ontario, teacher, the society launched its mission in Tokyo on the crest of a serendipitous wave of Japanese interest in Western culture and buoyed up by its members' support and the Methodist Church's enthusiasm for female workers in Japan. By contrast, the men of the GBM were bitterly disappointed; they had blindly assumed that to initiate the essential work among Japanese women their board would simply hire female missionaries to be supervised by the men already in the field. The financial difficulties of the General Board curtailed this plan. Consequently, as far as the men were concerned, their appeals for women workers had floundered from the start.[10]

Nonetheless, for several years there was cooperation between the two missions. Cartmell often conferred with Macdonald, the *pater familias* of the Japan mission,[11] although she ignored the men's suggestion that, as a woman, she 'ought not to do too much.'[12] Instead, Cartmell immediately began to visit Japanese women in their homes and to establish a girls' boarding-school, opened in 1885, to accommodate 250 students and four missionaries.[13] When Cartmell became ill, apparently from stress and overwork, Eliza Spencer, another Ontario teacher and the daughter of a former editor of the *Christian Guardian*, shouldered the school's administration.[14]

Exhibiting an astute sense of *realpolitik*, Cartmell and Spencer recognized that in Japan, where political and social changes could not be achieved without the endorsement of the governing class, their mission's fortunes depended on the good-will of those adjacent to power. To attract the daughters of the elite, the WMS Tokyo girls' school (Toyo Eiwa Jo Gakko) adopted a broad Western curriculum encompassing mathematics, sciences, history, and instruction in English – subjects that Japanese critics of mission schools later attacked as irrelevant to the experience of Japanese women.[15] Western influences pervaded the school's academic, social, religious, and moral activities.[16] Whatever the motivation of parents who sent their daughters to the school, within a year it was filled to capacity,[17] though converts were few; in the first year, just seventeen girls became Christians – 'exotics, transplanted from a heathen soil to a Christian garden.'[18] In 1887, a second station, also structured around a school conceived for the daughters of the affluent and influential class, was opened in Shizuoka, 130 miles south of Tokyo.

The girls' schools became the first line of attack in the WMS's program to improve the circumstances of Japanese women whom the missionaries concluded were 'unwelcome at birth, untaught in childhood, enslaved when married, accursed as widows, unlamented when they died.'[19] Living for even a few months in this still semi-feudal and patriarchal country prompted the Canadian women to question the nature of Japanese society; they condemned arranged marriages, concubinage, and prostitution, but, above all else, they denounced the deficiencies of female education and the limited opportunities in the workforce for the girls whom they were carefully grooming to be more self-reliant than their mothers. Like other Westerners in Japan at the time, the WMS representatives argued that women's secondary status sustained by 'the doctrine of "triple obedience" to father, to husband, and when old to son' was 'disastrous' for Japan.[20]

Recent studies of the Meiji period tend to substantiate some of the missionaries' impressions about Japanese women's social status. As Christian missionaries, the WMS personnel emphasized Buddhism and Shintoism as the sources of Japanese women's oppression, but the primary factor was, in fact, a legal system that sustained female dependency. Moreover, the renewed emphasis during the Meiji period on the family as the basis of a strong empire reinforced the submissive role of women within the household.[21] To support this patriarchal order and to withstand Western intrusion, public education for women was reshaped to 'produce the good wife and wise mother for the maintenance of the family system.'[22] Meiji administrators stressed the value of education in the modernization process, but in the decade after 1868, while 40 per cent of Japanese boys attended school, just 10 per cent of girls entered the educational system and even there for them cooking and sewing took precedence over science and mathematics.[23] Most girls were educated at home in preparation for marriage, motherhood, and family life.[24]

The WMS Board conveyed its missionaries' impressions of the disadvantaged situation of Asian women to the membership-at-large. In one especially explicit evocation of the Victorian 'cult of true womanhood' that embodies the messages of cultural imperialism and ethnocentrism as well as maternal feminism and the WMS's sense of *noblesse oblige*, the society contrasted its members' privileges with the suffering of women 'where the religion of Christ is unknown. For them, no light of homelife has ever shone. *Slaves* to brutal masters – not loving and beloved *wives* – have they been. Even motherly love – that precious and most enduring of all earthly loves – has been crushed and bleeding under the direful superstition of their so-called religions.'[25]

The majority of Japanese women did not challenge tradition, but a handful of feminists, led by Kishida Toshiko, founder of the Kyoto Women's Lecture Society (whose first meeting in 1883 was attended by more than 2,000 women),[26] identified education as the key to improving the condition of women. This early feminism dwindled after Kishida was arrested in 1884; the Liberal party that promoted the women's lecture societies dissolved, leaving Japanese feminists ideologically isolated and their educational plans adrift.[27]

In the absence of other channels for women's reforming impulses, Christian schools, like the Toyo Eiwa Jo Gakko, filled the void, 'offering intellectual challenges and a humanistic view to their women students.'[28] The WMS missionaries, themselves well-educated women determined to pursue a professional life, became committed activists on behalf of Japanese women. For example, Mary Jane Cunningham, director of the Shizuoka girls' school, hectored civic leaders for their indifference to female education. Her 'audacity – standing up and telling the governor and other official men of Shizuoka that their wives were inferior to American ladies' – astounded F.A. Cassidy of the GBM who, Cunningham reported, feared 'they would be offended, but no such thing. My "lecture" quite pleased them.'[29] Eventually Cunningham's effrontery 'provoke[d] comment from Japanese,' and forced her recall in 1908[30]; but in the 1880s her feminist testimony was expedient to the WMS cause.

By the end of the 1880s WMS correspondence suggests that the work was not flourishing as anticipated because the Japanese were becoming uncertain about any benefits of westernization. Now out of fashion, Christian schools were suspect as instruments of Western imperialism designed to erode Japanese cultural values. Girls' schools were specifically censured for disregarding the 'special characteristics' of Japanese women and their traditional virtues.[31] After 1894, when the war with China and the intervention by Russia, France, and Germany in the subsequent peace negotiations galvanized Japanese sentiment against the West, the consequences for Christian missionary work in Japan were catastrophic. At some mission schools, registration fell more than 50 per cent.[32] The WMS experience reflects these general developments. Whereas in 1886 'thirty to forty women would gather around us to hear the word of God,' by 1893, according to Eliza Spencer, 'only by constant, untiring work ... can [we] get a half dozen to hear us ... foreign ways are not things to be desired ... the harvest of souls does not appear.'[33]

After several years of success, rejection was hard to accept. In 1889 the WMS extended its operations to Kofu, between Tokyo and Shizuoka,[34] but during the 1890s there was little growth, especially in the society's educational facilities in Japan. Instead, in 1892, the society's next project at Kanazawa, an industrial city on the Sea of Japan, centred on a night school, a Sunday school, and a workshop where children were paid to make matches and handkerchiefs to be sold in Canada.[35] The working class was no more receptive than the elite. Cunningham was 'mocked to her face, [and] called [a] foreign devil.'[36] Abby Veazey concluded that she and her colleagues were resented simply as foreigners, not missionaries, but it seems likely that they were increasingly assigned to the periphery of Japanese life because of their gender.[37] It was in the midst of this escalating marginalization of WMS work in Japan that the shrill strains of disharmony in the Canadian Methodist ranks began to be heard.

The mounting tension between the men and women was complicated by disputes among the men themselves over salaries and their own institution's hierarchical structure; while the WMS employees were often at odds over allegiance to their putative leader, Eliza Spencer (Large). Now senior representative in Japan, Spencer had been permitted to retain the principalship of the Tokyo School after she married Alfred Large of the GBM in July 1887. In spite of its rules against employing married women, as a testimony to Spencer's executive skills and also as a strong endorsement of Christian marriage, the WMS board gave 'a hearty consent, believing that benefit may arise as the pupils have a somewhat near view of the privilege accorded by Christianity to women as the companion of man.'[38]

Until 1886 the two missions in Japan appear to have reviewed, albeit informally, matters of mutual concern. But in 1886 the GBM inaugurated its own council to which the women were not invited. Their exclusion might not have been contentious, given that women were not represented on Methodist councils in Canada until 1914.[39] But it appeared to the WMS missionaries that the GBM's disregard of them was intentional. As senior GBM administrator and spokesman in Japan, Davidson Macdonald later acknowledged, 'after [6 Feb. 1886] [the women] never received any notice of our meetings ... In the constitution of the Council no provision was made for any representation of the Woman's Missionary Society workers

... the ladies did not withdraw from us, but we seem to have, unwittingly, dropped them.'[40]

Under Spencer Large's direction, the women began to build an administrative structure to promote their professional needs and ambitions. With the board's approval, in September 1888 the women formed their own council (the WMS Japan Council), explicitly designed to evaluate their particular work, to impose uniform standards, including a common curriculum, for the Japanese schools, and to direct the posting of personnel. The women met monthly and an executive in Tokyo handled emergencies.[41] The annual meeting at a resort hotel became the highlight of the year; it was a pleasant experience where the women discussed problems and simply enjoyed themselves in relaxing surroundings.

The WMS Japan council was a vehicle for the gradual redefinition of WMS work as a self-regulating enterprise and for making autonomous decisions. For example, in September 1890, citing their heavy workloads, the women petitioned the WMS board to increase salaries from $600 to $700 per annum for the first five-year term and to $800 for subsequent terms. The WMS Japan Council argued that trained workers who had now mastered Japanese and probably would remain with the society needed more money for retirement,[42] but the nature of missionary work also justified the raise. Missionaries needed expensive books and, like other professional women, their busy schedules prevented them from economizing 'in the way of clothing or household expenses, since we are expected to give to the Society ... our whole time, except what is necessary for rest or recreation.'[43] Although the request was rescinded when the widespread Depression in Canada curtailed the society's spending,[44] it demonstrates directly not only the women's perception of their work as a viable profession with unique demands on its members but also their willingness to assume responsibility for their futures within their chosen vocation with its singular liabilities and risks.

The women's anxiety about their situation as Christian missionaries in Japan intensified in April 1890 after a terrifying incident that unsettled Western missionaries in Japan: that is, the murder of Alfred Large during a robbery at the Tokyo girls' school. In the attack Eliza Large lost two fingers and suffered a disfiguring sword cut to her face.[45] Her colleagues worried more about her emotional stability than her physical injuries. While Alfred Large's death destroyed any complacency the Canadian Methodist community had accumulated about its welcome in Japan, it also cast the redoubtable Eliza Large into a position of great distinction in the missionary community. The ordeal earned her a furlough in Canada until the summer of 1891,[46] an interval later characterized by the most outspoken GBM combatant, F.A. Cassidy, as 'the golden period of pleasant relations between the missions.'[47] In fact, the discord between the men and the women was simmering even during Large's absence.

Defining the boundaries of their respective areas of work, disagreement over whether the women should help the men whenever their services were requested and personality clashes and power struggles among veteran missionaries kindled the hostility between the societies. The confrontation over authority and power (a word often used by both sides) ought not to have shocked the Methodist hierarchy given the situation in Japan where men and women with little or no experience either working or interacting with members of the opposite sex were now in direct competition for the reluctant Japanese converts on whom their jobs depended. Fed by unfamiliar, often inhospitable surroundings where the missionaries' social activities were limited almost exclusively to the small Western community and where the women were acutely aware of patriarchal attitudes and the men of female submissiveness, petty disputes and idle gossip grew to alarming proportions. The women's resolve to protect their work inspired a strong feminist reaction directed at the GBM missionaries, who remained oblivious to the intensity of the women's drive for autonomy and its centrality to their professional identity. The dissension accelerated while credulous administrators from both boards refused to concede that, dedication to Christian objectives notwithstanding, their employees in the field could react so aggressively, even abusively, when their territorial rights were threatened.

The most constant source of aggravation for the WMS was the men's assumption that the women were always willing to help with their work. For example, in September 1891, Charles Eby and John Saunby asked the WMS Japan Council to provide personnel to assist at the Tabernacle at Hongo, about four miles from the WMS school, and at the GBM boys' school in Kanazawa.[48] The WMS refused unless the GBM's council in Canada approved the request and the recommendation was communicated to the WMS by the secretary of the GBM. In the interests of professionalism, the WMS Japan Council rejected ad hoc arrangements between the societies though the women were careful to reassure the men that the WMS would adhere to its constitution and seek the GBM's approval before initiating new projects.[49] Apparently the GBM complied, because Lizzie Hart was sent to the Tabernacle and Cunningham to Kanazawa.[50] But a critical disagreement arose when Saunby demanded that Cunningham teach more than the daily hour previously agreed to. When the WMS council protested, Saunby relieved Cunningham of all her teaching duties, even though, under Japanese immigration regulations, she was required to teach some English classes in order to remain in the country. Because the WMS did not operate the requisite classes in Kanazawa, Cunningham suggested an arrangement with the American Presbyterian mission. In retaliation, Saunby threatened 'to expose [the WMS] Council and ... ladies to the Presbyterians in such a way that they would in no case take her in.' Eventually a rapprochement was reached and Cunningham continued at the boys' school.[51]

In another inflammatory incident, the General Board of Missions tried to persuade the women to allow Japanese ministerial candidates to conduct WMS Sunday schools, even though the WMS, recognizing Japanese mores, refused to permit male teachers in its institutions. Moreover, some GBM missionaries wanted WMS Sunday school members included in their records, a scheme that the women immediately construed as interference.[52] There was even an ideological dispute when the WMS Herbie Bellamy Orphanage opened in Kanazawa in December 1893.[53] Speaking for his colleagues, Macdonald opposed the project 'as a pampering,' incompatible with Methodist designs to 'train the Japanese to go forth and take up their work.'[54] The WMS envisaged the orphanage as the logical extension of its work with the poor in Kanazawa and vital to counterbalance the Presbyterians' inroads in the area.[55]

At the annual Japan Council meeting in July 1892, attended by WMS president Sarah Gooderham and corresponding secretary Elizabeth Strachan (on a mission inspection), the women made a conspicuous effort to promote good working relationships with the General Board of Missions in spite of recent allegations that the WMS was ignoring Methodist discipline,[56] and had 'failed to give' the men 'rights that are theirs.'[57] For its part, the GBM council appointed three men to consult with the WMS council 'with a view to a harmonious adjustment of the work and a satisfactory understanding between the workers.'[58] Although the women received the men politely enough, no solution was realized. As the WMS minutes tersely noted, 'the main difficulty apparently [was] that the women were not under the control of the Council of the Japan Mission of the Methodist Church of Canada.'[59]

Complicating the issue of who determined the disposition of WMS missionary work in Japan was the women's well-founded suspicion that the men disliked, indeed hated, Eliza Large for her ability to galvanize her associates. In a dramatic gesture just before Gooderham and Strachan left Tokyo, Large tendered her resignation. When her colleagues pledged their support, the WMS board rejected the request, citing her 'superior executive ability, strict adherence to duty and her earnest devotion to the work' as critical to the mission's success.[60]

This demonstration of gender solidarity did not improve relationships with the men. Six months later, they attributed the failure of the work at Hongo to Lizzie Hart, 'a nice but utterly inexperienced girl ... getting more good from the Tabernacle than giving.'[61] The WMS then withdrew its personnel from GBM work, demanding substantiation of the complaints through a full-scale investigation attended by members of both missions.[62] Macdonald criticized this strategy, fearing 'unnecessary publicity to matters which belong[ed] to the two missions only.' In a conciliatory gesture, he assured the WMS that the GBM had no 'wish or intention to interfere with [its] ... autonomy as a mission.' It sought consultation, not control.[63] For the time being, the women agreed to 'put the past out of sight and memory' and to confront the missions' mutual problems.[64]

At this point, just when it seemed that the missionaries could reach a reasonable compromise, Cassidy sent Large a letter that 'had the effect of arresting further progress in the way of reconciliations, and stirring up very bitter feelings.' What indeed may have been, as Cassidy later insisted, a demonstration of goodwill was interpreted as an offensive insult, aggravated because the message arrived on the anniversary of Alfred Large's death. In an effort to alleviate Eliza Large's apparent paranoia and suspicion, Cassidy advised that 'the phantom that has embittered your life is "self-protection." As a lone lady in a hard world this has formed one of the chief elements of your anxiety.'[65] Until she abandoned the notion that she was surrounded by enemies, 'there [was] no hope of ... remaining here with comfort to yourself or profit to the work.'[66]

The letter, which Large considered 'neither gentlemanly nor Christian-like,' received no reply; instead, copies were forwarded to the WMS board of managers and to Alexander Sutherland. Cassidy tried to make amends in subsequent correspondence with the WMS Japan Council. But his insistence – compounded by his unfortunate phraseology – that he was not 'at war with a lot of hopeless shrews' but 'in a bad tangle with a lot of noble and respectable ladies who are working for the glory of God, and who are my sisters in the Gospel' worsened the situation.[67] The WMS prohibited its employees from communicating with Cassidy.[68] In May 1893 the WMS accepted Cassidy's apology, but in the meantime Large had tendered her resignation, again declined, because the failure of the Hongo tabernacle was ascribed to her excessive authority.[69]

Social and business associations between the two missions disintegrated during the next six months. The perpetual squabbling provoked John

McArthur to seek a transfer to the Methodist West China mission because, he contended, Large had accused the GBM council of dishonesty and squandering missionary funds 'for the devil.'[70] In disgust, she had refused to shake hands with GBM's William Elliott because he believed rumours about her sharp tongue.[71] Elliott apologized, blaming Large's belligerence on a 'nervous condition,' but he thought 'it would certainly be better every way to pay her to stay at home than to pay her to work here.'[72]

By March 1893, from his vantage point in Canada, Alexander Sutherland had also identified Eliza Large as a major source of dissent. Though 'personally, [he would] be very sorry to have [her] leave,'[73] the WMS should have accepted her resignation. Sutherland's advice was ignored. Until 1895 the WMS board steadfastly endorsed Large despite recurring rumours, never satisfactorily disproved, about her cruelty and her abrasive personality and that she had 'caused ill-health' to Hannah Lund, a furloughed colleague who had recently died at her home in Brantford, Ontario.[74] Likewise, the women in the field firmly denied that the estrangement between the men and the women was rooted in personal enmity and antagonism; they had merely acted 'in defense of their work.' 'Outwardly friendly relationships' were approved, but the WMS certainly sought 'no ground for closer friendship.'[75]

In December 1894, the WMS Japan Council sent an impassioned vindication of its collective reputation to the board of managers with the following demand for immediate action: 'We indignantly resent the idea that a band of women mostly experienced in Christian work before leaving home should be so lacking in strength of character as to submit to unjust treatment of themselves or stand passively by and see it imposed upon others; or should be so lacking in integrity as to refrain from expressing our conscientious convictions on all vital points.'[76] The board did not interpret this declaration of independence in the same light; 'to restore harmony,' Large was relieved of her duties when the school year ended.[77] In a counterattack six months later, the WMS Japan Council challenged the Methodist concept of justice and solicited sympathy from the WMS membership: 'Does God ask us to come here to offer to Him our all for the good of His work, and after spending the best years of our lives in His service, does He desire us to submit to be called home before we know the charges brought against us or have had an opportunity to defend ourselves against them: With our hearts bound up in the work we have left, with health, reputation and fitness for work in Canada impaired or gone, yet most of us are obliged to work for our daily bread.'[78] The message did not reach its intended audience. The concerted efforts of the church and its missionary organizations to suppress rumours of a crisis had already failed and in October 1895 the Japan affair came before the General Board of Missions of the Methodist Church of Canada.

Before the official hearing, the WMS conducted its own review because by now four WMS missionaries had submitted resignations. The WMS inquiry exposed, among other things, Large's abuse of her colleagues by hypnotism and her ruthlessness to Hannah Lund, who had been confined to her room in the mission home and fed only bread and water.[79] Large admitted that she and Lund had quarrelled when they were on furlough, a situation confirmed by former WMS president Sarah Burns, who had visited Lund's home. Other missionaries on furlough conceded that the situation in Japan was 'almost more than [we] could bear'[80]; they refused to return until the tension subsided. Isabella Blackmore believed she had 'done what was right, and as I know Mrs Large had done what was right ... I felt it was useless for me to go back.'[81]

The GBM hearings covered all aspects of the controversy. Although the inquiry concentrated on the complex internal problems of the General Board of Missions that had precipitated six resignations, the all-male tribunal could not avoid the relationships between the men and women. During the interrogation, the missionaries introduced some new evidence about personal bitterness and rivalry, especially between Cassidy and Eliza Large, but most of the issues were already familiar to those present. The failure of the GBM's initiative in Hongo, attributed to WMS incompetence, was much discussed. So was Nellie Hart's association with Cassidy, who had pressured her to accompany him on overnight trips, arguing that a Western woman would attract an eager audience to his evangelist meetings.[82] Hart had declined because the junkets involved Sunday travel. The tribunal persisted in quizzing her about the possible sexual impropriety involved in her relationship with Cassidy. 'That thought never came into my mind,' Hart replied.[83] But the tribunal found it improbable that a Victorian woman, even a Methodist missionary, would not have understood and been shocked by the undertones of Cassidy's proposal.

Eliza Large was the principal WMS witness. Her testimony disclosed a spiteful feud with Agnes Wintemute who resigned in 1892 to marry a GBM employee. Large alleged that Wintemute had turned many of the women against her; in retribution, Large returned her invitation to Wintemute's wedding. Large was evasive about her other male and female colleagues, preferring to direct the questions to the Hongo Tabernacle issue which, she contended, established 'the evident desire on the part of some of the agents of the General Board to get control of the work of the Woman's Missionary

Society.'[84] At the inquiry's close, at least one member of the tribunal was thoroughly disgusted by the 'trifles' that 'humiliated [the] Church from ocean to ocean.'[85]

The tribunal voted (with one dissension) that Cassidy and Eby, whom the WMS had singled out for intervening in its work, be recalled for the time being. Nor did Sutherland consider it expedient for Large to return because if missionaries 'cannot help quarrelling over things that ought not to set children quarrelling – it does become a question whether they ought not to be brought out of the field.'[86] As Sutherland astutely concluded, the acrimonious rift between the mission societies had 'begun in little sparks of misunderstanding that, fanned by the breath of gossip and talebearing, kindled smouldering fires of mutual suspicion and dislike, and rendered more difficult the adjustment of wider differences.' The personal vendettas were intensified by 'the persistent endeavor of certain [men] to dominate the work and workers of the Woman's Missionary Society.' Sutherland sharply reprimanded the men because if they 'could not agree with lady missionaries, they had still the alternative of quietly letting them alone.'[87]

After visiting the Japanese missions three years later, Sutherland reiterated his confidence in the WMS personnel as 'faithful workers ... rendering our beloved Zion a very noble and valuable service.'[88] But he also pointed out that many missionaries had erred in 'the pride of opinion. The Methodist Church ... [was] running a two-wheeled vehicle without any connection between the whole but the invisible bond of piety and good sense, which are not always present in large quantities. The riders on the separate wheels sometimes make vaulting sprints and dash in collision.'[89] The impulsive assertiveness of the WMS was partially to blame: 'Its workplans, not of a set purpose but of an unguarded evolution, greatly accentuated and increased the difficulties ... and may in some instances have even been the occasion of their development. The spirit of a sensitive independence did not conduce to harmony and cooperation.'[90]

While Sutherland's is a perceptive appraisal of the immediate origins of the Japan affair, it failed to acknowledge the broader context and circumstances of the issue. Cut off by thousands of miles and three months' delay in communication from those whose guidance might have proven helpful, the women felt vulnerable to the demands of men who treated them unprofessionally and assumed that, like Victorian wives, female missionaries should have been flattered to assist them. Instead, the women acted on their own initiative to safeguard their work and defend their reputations. As they understood it, their paramount obligation was to the WMS and their charges in Japan, not to male missionaries.

Ironically, one of the chief offenders, F.A. Cassidy, perhaps best understood the essence of the dispute. Though he did not explicitly exercise the rhetoric of feminism, correspondence after the hearings suggests that Cassidy was convinced that the WMS's feminist drive for autonomy had triggered the confrontation. The women were 'primed with the idea of independence, and with a latent prejudice against the missionaries of the General Board and charged to resist any encroachment by the missionaries of the Gen Board.'[91] Moreover, WMS president Sarah Gooderham had actively encouraged 'the same ambition for absolute independence.'[92] One discerning tribunal member reproved the Methodist Church itself: 'The friction ... would never have happened if men and women had been placed upon equality long ago in the Methodist church, and we had no Women's [sic] Missionary Society.'[93] It was an impractical proposal given the nature of Victorian gender relationships. In spite of John Wesley's recognition of female participation in Methodist spiritual matters, since the 1830s most Canadian Methodists had endorsed Victorian society's patriarchal principles and discouraged female preaching.[94] Until 1881 when the WMS provided Canadian Methodist women with the opportunity to join similarly inclined women to promote the ideals of Christian service and womanhood, with few exceptions, Methodist women had been limited to educational, custodial, and charitable work at the congregational level.

As the shock troops in the mission field, the WMS Japan missionaries' responses embody the frustrations of determined women challenging the ordering of Victorian society which, in spite of its allusions and deference to women's unique qualities, subscribed to patriarchal authority over women in the home and the workplace. For public consumption, the women and men chose to define the problem in terms of the success or failure of their work of salvation which, in the eyes of the church, its membership, and God, was beyond reproach. But, in the final analysis, even pious and committed missionaries proved vulnerable to the sexual tensions and jealousy that frequently followed when women began to infiltrate a male preserve.

As proof, even after the tribunal's ruling, each mission society supported its guilty associates. The WMS petitioned Sutherland to reinstate Eliza Large, but the request was denied. This time the board of managers acknowledged that Large's withdrawal was in the best interests of everyone in Japan. In reality, the WMS had no constitutional authority to act further.[95] The decision was not universally accepted. A few months later, Sarah Gooderham, now 'out of harmony' with the WMS over Large's fate, resigned as president to accompany Large to Japan where they worked for several years on behalf of the Woman's Christian Temperance Union (WCTU).[96] Large frequently solicited the WMS for money until 1909, when she was given a small pension. Bitter to the end, Large contended that 'the WMS no less than the General Board ... had wrecked her life and that of her daughter.'[97]

In the aftermath of what Methodists termed the 'imbroglio' – a fitting word denoting a 'confused entanglement' – the WMS began to repair the damage in Japan. Consultation arrangements were set up between field secretaries in both Japan and the new station in Szechwan and the home base. Procedures were also adopted to settle personal disputes among missionaries in the field. Each mission was designated as a 'little community in which the will of the majority should rule. Each member of it should do her utmost to promote its peace and unity, and to submit gracefully and not merely because she cannot prevail.'[98] By 1898 Isabella Blackmore believed that 'peace and confidence like that of the old days before the mission trouble, are coming back to us.'[99] But the WMS administration and its personnel in Japan had been severely tested and their vulnerability as professional women exposed.

The affair and the ugly allegations about the women altered the future course of the WMS Japan mission. For example, the WMS board concluded that some employees in Japan had, indeed, proven immature in their responses. They needed 'experience in life and work! The average girl of 24 is *very* young ... too young to be a real strength to the work.'[100] After 1896, with one exception, all WMS missionaries posted to Japan were above the minimum age requirement of twenty-five. For many years after the crisis, women selected for Japan were known personally to the board of managers or the regional secretaries. Sixteen of the thirty-six women recruited for Japan from 1896 to 1914 were ministers' daughters or sisters, perhaps because the board assumed they would be more subservient to the church's authority. Moreover, after 1896 WMS missionary candidates were required to attend the Methodist Training School, or an equivalent, to guarantee that they understood the essential theological foundations and to be observed interacting with their future co-workers in an institutional setting.

The consequences of these tighter standards on WMS missionary work and the atmosphere within the mission community are hard to measure, but the intensive screening seems to have paid dividends for the society, at least in terms of length of service. The thirty-six women hired between 1896 and 1914 remained in Japan an average of 24.4 years; two-thirds of them worked until retirement. These statistics confirm the WMS missionaries' deep commitment to their profession and reinforce their own testimony about the rewarding nature of their employment in Japan once their 'sensitive independence' was no longer in dispute.

ACKNOWLEDGMENT

I wish to acknowledge the support provided for this paper by the Social Sciences and Humanities Research Council of Canada.

NOTES

1 See Wendy Mitchinson, 'Canadian Women and Church Missionary Societies,' *Atlantis* 2, 2 (Spring 1977), 58–75; Ruth Compton Brouwer, *New Women for God: Canadian Presbyterian Women and India Missions, 1876–1914* (Toronto: University of Toronto Press, 1990), esp. chap. 2; K. Ridout, 'A Woman of Mission: The Religious and Cultural Odyssey of Agnes Wintemute Coates,' *Canadian Historical Review* 71 (June 1990), 204–44; Rosemary Gagan, *A Sensitive Independence: Canadian Methodist Women Missionaries in Canada and the Orient, 1881–1925* (Kingston and Montreal: McGill-Queen's University Press, 1992). See also Bettina Bradbury, 'Women and the History of Their Work in Canada: Some Recent Books,' *Journal of Canadian Studies* 28, 2 (Autumn 1993), 159–78 for a discussion of recent work on women and religion in Canada.
2 Gagan, *A Sensitive Independence*, 154.
3 Stenographic Report of Proceedings re the Japan Affair at the Annual Meeting of the General Board of Missions of the Methodist Church of Canada, Montreal, 3–11 October, 1895 (Toronto: Methodist Mission Room, 1895), 78, Methodist Church of Canada (MCC), Japan Mission Collection, General Correspondence, 1894–1915, box 2, file 27, United Church Archives, Toronto (herein cited as UCA).
4 Biographical file of Martha Cartmell, UCA.
5 W. Scott Morton, *Japan: Its History and Culture* (New York: Thomas Y. Cromwell, 1975), 156.
6 Toshio Yokoyama, *Japan in the Victorian Mind* (London: Macmillan, 1987), xxii.
7 Chitoshi Yanaga, *Japan Since Perry* (New York: McGraw-Hill, 1949), 126.
8 Reverend John W. Saunby, *Japan: The Land of the Morning* (Toronto: William Briggs, 1895), 280–95; Hamish Ion, *The Cross and the Rising Sun* (Waterloo: Wilfrid Laurier University Press, 1990), 38–40.

9 J.E. Sanderson, *The First Century of Methodism in Canada*, vol. 2, *1840–1883* (Toronto: William Briggs, 1910), 365.

10 Mrs H.L. Platt, *The Story of the Years: A History of the Woman's Missionary Society of the Methodist Church of Canada 1881–1906*, vol. 1, *Canada* (Toronto: Woman's Missionary Society of the Methodist Church, Canada, 1907), 13–14.

11 Strachan-Cartmell Papers, box 1, file 6, UCA.

12 *Christian Guardian*, 11 Apr. 1883.

13 Mrs H.L. Platt, *The Story of the Years: A History of the Woman's Missionary Society of the Methodist Church of Canada 1881–1906*, vol. 2, *Beyond Seas* (Toronto: Woman's Missionary Society of the Methodist Church, Canada, 1907), 9–11.

14 Biographical file of Eliza Spencer, UCA. Cartmell was furloughed to Canada in 1888, but she returned to Japan in 1892 where she remained until 1896.

15 Sharon Sievers, *Flowers in Salt: The Beginnings of Feminist Consciousness in Modern Japan* (Stanford, Calif.: Stanford University Press, 1983), 105.

16 Platt, vol. 2, 13.

17 *Annual Report of the Woman's Missionary Society of the Methodist Church of Canada*, 1885–86 (hereinafter cited as *ARWMS*), 12.

18 Platt, vol. 2, 17.

19 *Missionary Outlook*, Oct. 1883, 156.

20 Sidney Gulick, *Working Women of Japan* (New York: Missionary Education Movement of the United States and Canada, 1915), xi.

21 Susan Pharr, 'Japan: Historical and Contemporary Perspectives,' in *Women's Roles and Status in Eight Countries*, Janet Giele and Audrey Smock, eds. (New York: Wiley, 1977), 229; Joy Paulson, 'Evolution of the Feminine Ideal,' in *Women in Changing Japan*, Joyce Lebra, Joy Paulson, and Elizabeth Powers, eds. (Boulder, Col.: Westview Books, 1976), 13.

22 Paulson, 'Evolution of the Feminine Ideal,' 15.

23 Ibid.

24 Pharr, 228.

25 *Missionary Outlook*, Nov. 1884, 175.

26 Sharon Sievers, 'Feminist Criticism in Japanese Politics in the 1880s: The Experience of Kishida Toshiko,' *Signs* 6, 4 (Summer 1981), 605–13.

27 Ibid., 613; Dorothy Robins-Mowry, *The Hidden Sun: Women of Modern Japan* (Boulder: Westview Press, 1983), 62–3.

28 Sievers, *Flowers in Salt*, 105.

29 *Missionary Outlook*, Feb. 1888, 26.

30 Report of Annual Meeting, Sept. 1908, MCC, Woman's Missionary Society (WMS), WMS Executive Minute Books, UCA.

31 Sievers, *Flowers in Salt*, 104–5.

32 Richard Drummond, *A History of Christianity in Japan* (Grand Rapids: Eerd-mann, 1970), 200.

33 *Missionary Outlook*, Feb. 1893, 46.

34 Platt, vol. 2, 52.

35 *Christian Guardian*, 14 Sept. 1892.

36 *Canadian Methodists in Japan, 1911–1912* (n.p., n.d), 50.

37 *Missionary Outlook*, Sept. 1893, 14.

38 *Christian Guardian*, 17 Aug. 1887.

39 In September 1914 delegates to the general conference voted to admit women to Methodist church councils. *Christian Guardian*, 7 Oct. 1914.

40 Report of Proceedings re the Japan Affair, 61.

41 Minutes of the First Annual Meeting of the Council in Japan of the WMS of the MCC, Tokyo, 3 Sept. 1888, 3–4, MCC, WMS, Japan, box 1, Council Minute Books, UCA.

42 Ibid., 53.

43 Ibid., 60.

44 *ARWMS*, 1892–3, 13.

45 *Missionary Outlook*, June 1890, 84.

46 WMS Japan Council Minutes, 82.

47 F.A. Cassidy, St Catharines, Ontario, to Dr Carman, 29 Jan. 1898, MCC, Japan Mission Papers, box 1, file 1, UCA.

48 WMS Japan Mission Council Minutes, 1 Sept. 1891, 86.

49 Ibid., 91–5.

50 Ibid., 3 Sept. 1891, 93; 10 Oct. 1891, 114.

51 Proceedings re: Japan Affair, 138.

52 Ibid., 135.

53 'History of Herbie Bellamy Home, 1893,' 6, MCC, WMS Overseas Missions, Japan, Correspondence and Papers, 1883, 1909–25, box 2, file 1, UCA.

54 Report of the Board Meeting of the WMS re: Japan Affair, 16 Oct. 1895, 13, MCC, WMS Correspondence, Miscellaneous, UCA.

55 Ibid.

56 WMS Japan Council, 121. What the women had done was never made explicit.

57 Ibid., 122.

58 Ibid., 120.

59 Ibid., 136.

60 Ibid., 143; *ARWMS*, 1892–3, 5.

61 Proceedings re: the Japan Affair, 71.

62 WMS Japan Council Minutes, 10 Jan. 1893, 144–5.

63 Ibid. Macdonald to E.S. Large, 4 Mar. 1893. The letter from Macdonald is included in the WMS minutes.

64 Ibid., 154.
65 Proceedings re: the Japan Affair, 72.
66 Ibid., 73.
67 Ibid.
68 WMS Japan Council Minutes, 157.
69 Proceedings re: the Japan Affair, 74.
70 Ibid., 76.
71 Ibid., 77.
72 Ibid., 78.
73 Alexander Sutherland to Elizabeth Strachan, 4 Mar. 1893, Alexander Sutherland Papers, box 6, file 11, UCA.
74 WMS Japan Council Minutes, 3 Dec. 1894, 25–6.
75 Ibid., 29.
76 Ibid.
77 ARWMS, 1894–5, vi.
78 WMS Japan Council Minutes, 18 July 1895, 52.
79 Report of the Board Meeting of the WMS re Japan Affair, 16, 19.
80 Ibid., 21.
81 Ibid., 32.
82 Proceedings re: the Japan Affair, 135.
83 Ibid., 136.
84 Ibid., 139.
85 Ibid., 147.
86 Ibid., 145.
87 Ibid., 84.
88 Confidential Report of the General Superintendent's Official Visit to the Mission in Japan, Apr.–June, 1898, 11, Methodist Church, United Church of Canada, Missions Pamphlets, box 1, UCA.
89 Ibid., 17.
90 Ibid., 42.
91 F.A. Cassidy, St Catharines, Ontario, to Carman, 19 Jan. 1898, Japan Mission Papers, box 1, file 3, UCA.
92 Cassidy to Carman, 29 Jan. 1898, ibid., file 1.
93 Proceedings re: the Japan Affair, 189.
94 Elizabeth Gillan Muir, *Petticoats in the Pulpit: The Story of Early Nineteenth-Century Methodist Women Preachers in Upper Canada* (Toronto: United Church Publishing House, 1991), 3–4.
95 ARWMS, 1896–7, vii.
96 WMS Board of Managers Minute Books, 10 Oct. 1897; ARWMS, 1897–8, viii.

97 Elizabeth Ross to Sutherland, 4 Sept. 1909, Alexander Sutherland Papers, box 10, file 196, UCA.
98 *ARWMS.*, 1896–7, 201.
99 *Monthly Letter*, May 1898, 1.
100 Blackmore to E. Strachan, 16 June 1898, Methodist Church, WMS, Miscellaneous Papers, Isabella Blackmore Letterbooks, UCA.

Pastoral Ministry and Professional Status: Developing Occupational Roles

8

Beyond the Bounds of Acceptable Behaviour: Methodist Women Preachers in the Early Nineteenth Century

ELIZABETH GILLAN MUIR

Methodist women were supported by a tradition that had long allowed them leadership roles including some preaching. It was not surprising, therefore, that women of various Wesleyan denominations preached in Canada in the early decades of the nineteenth century. Yet they laboured at a disadvantage. Many of them felt a great reluctance about speaking in public which they overcame only with great difficulty. Their salaries were much lower than those of men doing the same work. Women with families carried the burden of combining their home responsibilities with their ministry and sometimes took young children with them while they conducted their services. By the middle of the century, however, most women were no longer given the opportunity of preaching even under these hardships. Indeed, the memory of their occupational role was lost, as their obituaries either omitted all references to the women's preaching activity or named it differently, commending them for 'rendering valuable aid' to the church or to their male partners.

Of late I've been requested in silence for to keep,
Because I've grieved the Pastor and likewise his dear sheep;
But if my Savior calls me to speak in his dear name,
I can't obey the Pastor, although a man of fame.
I do respect his person, his faults I can forgive,
But to refrain from speaking, I cannot do and live;
If I am called to speak for Jesus and his cause,
I can't obey the people which make such human laws.
...
I must join with Mary and tell to all around
That Jesus Christ is risen, for I his grace have found,
And if I am reproached because these things I say,
My work is to forgive them and humbly watch and pray.
Polly M. Stevens

L.I. Sweet, *The Minister's Wife*, 107.

For a few decades in the nineteenth century in Canada, Methodist women held active preaching roles, both in local areas and as itinerants on official circuits. In the Methodist Episcopal denomination, women preached in Upper Canada (Ontario) until the early 1830s. In two smaller Methodist streams – the Bible Christian and the Primitive Methodist Churches – women continued their preaching activity well into the second half of the century, but in a limited capacity. Primitive Methodist women worked on circuits in Upper Canada; Bible Christian women preached in Prince Edward Island, as well.[1]

Early Methodist Church polity and doctrine had not only allowed leadership positions for women, but encouraged women to take an active role. At the heart of the Methodist Church organization were the small class meetings and the even smaller bands. In the early eighteenth century John Wesley had organized his followers into classes in order to check up on their morality and spiritual progress. Each class had approximately six or seven members with a designated leader. Smaller groups called bands, of no more than four people, were set up for prayer and spiritual growth.

Wesley believed that segregation of the sexes had been the practice in the early Christian Church, and the Moravians, a denomination he greatly admired, used a similar small-group model. Classes were restricted to either men or women, especially at the beginning of the Methodist movement. This policy, coupled with the fact that there were many more Methodist women than men, immediately thrust large numbers of women into positions of leadership as heads of women's classes. In April 1742 the first year classes were held, forty-seven women were class leaders at the Foundry, the official Methodist worship centre in London, England; only nineteen men held that responsibility.[2]

Wesley had initiated the policy of segregation, but he favoured flexibility. In a letter to 'Miss B.,' he asked if she would be willing to lead a small class at Bath where there had been a society for thirty years. Half of the thirty Methodists there wanted to meet with Joseph Harris. But, Wesley wrote, 'I had rather that the single women in both Classes who desire it, should meet with you.'[3]

Later Canadian and American societies adopted segregation, but whether or not the classes were mixed was often dictated by the availability of leadership. The original 1803 Stanstead, Quebec, class consisted of a male leader, four women, and four other men. Yet around the same time in Upper Canada, Ann Dulmage (b. ca. 1777), the talented wife of the controversial Methodist Episcopal itinerant Samuel Coate, held classes for women only, in her home. In 1836 the Canadian *Book of Doctrines and Discipline of the Wesleyan Methodist Church* included the rule of segregation in church services, but not in classes. The rule book stipulated, however, that the smaller bands must consist only of men or women, and more specifically, only of single or married people. Some women led mixed classes, for in the 1840s the Bible Christian itinerants Ann Vickery Robins (1800–53) and Elizabeth Dart (Eynon) (1792–1857) led classes of both men and women in the Cobourg and Peterborough areas in Ontario. Male and female leadership were interchangeable; at one time Brother Cosper, a male member of Robins's class, felt slighted when Robins selected someone else to lead her class in her absence, instead of choosing him.[4]

Early Methodists did not always adhere to segregation of classes, but where they did, it provided not only an opportunity for women to assume leadership roles, but an obligation. Idleness, Wesley had pointed out, was a sin. All Methodists, and especially preachers, were required to be diligent, never to be unemployed, and never to be 'triflingly employed.' Talents, Wesley stressed, had been given by God to be used. 'I fear you are too idle,' he wrote Elizabeth Bennis (1725–1802) in 1773 in Ireland. 'Do not loiter. See that your talent rust not.' The next year he wrote again with a similar rebuke: 'You are not sent to Waterford to be useless. Stir up the gift of God which is in you; gather together those that have been scattered abroad, and make up a band, if not a class or two.' Bennis evidently heeded Wesley's challenge. On her death in the United States, it was noted that she 'had called people to repentance.'[5]

In fact, all the women itinerants must have taken this dictum to heart, for the amount of work they accomplished was prodigious. In England, where she had begun her itineracy in 1815 as the first Bible Christian itinerant, Elizabeth Dart opened a society at Bristol, although she mainly travelled around Devon and Cornwall. Later, she initiated the Methodist movement in Wales. Dart ministered to the sick, preached outdoors, and trudged miles through 'storms and opposition, frosts and floods' sometimes with severely blistered feet. In addition to preaching three times on Sunday and usually every evening except Saturday, Dart supplemented her meagre income by dressmaking and teaching school. When she and her husband, John Hicks Eynon, came to Canada as missionaries, they often went their separate ways on a two-hundred-mile circuit, speaking in fields, homes, woods, and schools. At times they conducted services together. At one point Eynon was ordered by his doctor to rest in bed for several months, and Dart did as much of his work as she could along with her own responsibilities.[6]

During the 1820s the lively Methodist Episcopalian Eliza Barnes (Case) (1796–1887) was involved in constant activity – teaching, preaching, and coordinating women's projects on the Methodist Indian missions in Upper Canada. The year 1829 was typical of Barnes's busy and rigorous life. In February she travelled north with male missionaries on an exploratory trip to Holland Landing to discuss establishing a mission on Snake Island in Lake Simcoe. In March she set out on a two-and-a-half-month tour of the New England states to raise funds and arrange for the translation of worship materials into a Native language. By the middle of May she was at the Rice Lake Mission, and two months later she began a mission tour of Lake Simcoe and Lake Huron. In September she was working at the Grape

Island Mission. In October she was at York, collecting supplies for the Credit River Mission, and in December she organized a benevolent society for the Indian women at the mission.[7]

Many of the women preachers were married and brought up children in addition to undertaking an extensive ministry. Ann Copp (Gordon) (1837–1931) did her own housework and made over clothes for her five children, sewing in the evenings after long days as a Bible Christian preacher. Part of a ministerial couple, Copp and Andrew Gordon, her husband, shared in worship services, preaching in cities and towns, indoors and on the streets throughout central Ontario.[8]

Elizabeth Trick (Henwood) (1801–72) and her husband Charles Henwood preached in the Cobourg area, where Trick took her share of assignments even though she gave birth to twelve children, including one set of twins. Ann Vickery Robins, itinerating in the same area, prepared her Sunday meals in advance to avoid 'bustle on the Sabbath.' She preached, visited the sick, led classes and prayer meetings, and often filled in for other itinerants, making special arrangements for the care of her family. Robins's husband remarked that she had no sympathy for preachers who were 'held back because of disagreeable weather.' Indeed, she allowed very little to stand in the way of her ministry. After her marriage, she kept on preaching; many times she carried an infant to an appointment miles from her home, and handed it to one of the congregation while she conducted the service. Afterwards, she picked up the child, and walked with it back home.[9]

While it appears that the women threw themselves into their work with zealous abandon, it was, in fact, very difficult for most of them to begin speaking in public. Although women had been speaking and travelling throughout Great Britain and North America since the seventeenth century, much of society was not receptive to women in the pulpit. Nineteenth-century women had been conditioned to remain in the home to serve and submit, as the press reminded its readers over and over again. In 1830 the *Christian Guardian* pointed out that 'the wife is not expected to go into the field, the workshop or the counting house ... To the middling class of life there is no female accomplishment more valuable than housewifery.'[10] A woman preaching could be doubly offensive. The English Earl Edward Bulwer-Lytton explained in 1833 that 'the aristocratic world does not like either clergymen or women to make too much noise.'[11]

Many of the women who did preach in the eighteenth century in Great Britain had no intention of assuming this role, but circumstances thrust them into this position. Sometimes their classes were so large that they unwittingly became public speakers or preachers. Sometimes their talents and spiritual gifts were so obvious that the people pressed them to speak, often because there was no other preacher available. The women's correspondence with Wesley points up their dilemma. In 1761 Wesley answered Sarah Crosby's questions about whether she should speak in public by telling her that she had not overstepped the bounds of propriety. He advised her to tell the people of her difficulty, that Methodists did not allow women preachers and she did not wish to become one. Read them notes or sermons, he advised, and just tell them what is in your heart 'as other women have done long ago.'[12]

By 1771, however, Wesley had sanctioned women preaching and actively encouraged them. Still they hesitated. Elizabeth Dart believed that she had been called by God to be an itinerant and could not disobey. Yet it was hard for her, at first, even to lead in prayer. In her diary Dart admits that she had 'a great struggle' before she could decide 'to speak for Christ in a public way.' At times Dart was tempted to leave the 'work' because she felt that there were others who could do it much better. Ann Copp Gordon still retained a nervousness when she had to speak, even after years of preaching in England and Canada. Copp described her fear on one occasion when she discovered that she was sitting on the same platform with Chief Justice Benson of the Supreme Court of Canada. Quickly she slipped off the platform and ran to the parsonage where she gulped down the whites of two eggs – one whipped, and the other plain. She had heard that the white of an egg loosened 'muscular tension,' but was not quite sure how the white should be eaten.[13]

The Wesleyan Methodist preacher William Bramwell explained in a sermon that there were not more women preachers because they were 'not faithful to their call.' But many of the women, like the eastern Canadian Mary McCoy Morris Bradley, had no support at all, and never could summon up enough courage to speak. Bradley was convinced that God had called her to be a preacher and was aware of biblical examples of women 'prophetesses.' Still she felt bound to yield to the restrictions her church placed upon women. Bradley's diary explains how she struggled to come to terms with these conflicting demands all her adult life: 'I thought if I had been a man, nothing could hinder me from going abroad to proclaim salvation to a dying world. O, how I longed to declare what God had done for my soul, and to invite Sinners to flee from the wrath to come, and lay hold on eternal life.' But Bradley lacked the courage and self-confidence to act against the church's expectations for women. 'I was many times afraid lest the fear of offending man, kept me from obeying the operation of the Spirit of God, which I felt in my heart,' she confessed in her memoirs. Finally, believing it to be her only recourse, Bradley decided to write her autobiography as a testimony to God's call.[14]

Most of the women who preached did so because they could not help it. At the heart of Methodist doctrine was the experiential knowledge of the forgiveness of sin. When men and women believed that their burden of guilt and sin had been removed, they were filled with a joy that could not be contained and that had to be shared. Ann Copp Gordon described the experience as feeling a 'weight' that she had borne for months being 'lifted like the sun breaking through the cloud.' She claimed that afterwards she was filled with a 'light' that never left her through 'persecution, loneliness and years of dire poverty.' In 1776 Wesley had written Elizabeth Bennis that if God had given her this 'light,' she must not hide it under a bushel. 'It is good to conceal the secrets of a King, but it is good to tell the loving-kindness of the Lord.' Everyone, said Wesley, should declare what God had done for them.[15]

Because of this compulsion to share their 'good news' and because of a genuine concern for the 'unconverted,' Methodist women preachers endured long days, difficult and treacherous journeys, ill health, and primitive living conditions. But the demanding missionary life took its toll.

Elizabeth Dart (Eynon) had never been physically strong. Often when she preached, her body was 'racked with pain.' In 1819 in England, four years after she began as an itinerant, she was listed on the preachers' plan 'to travel as her health will permit.' For the last twenty years of her life in Canada, Dart suffered from asthma, yet she kept up her ministry until she was sixty-two years old. 'No doubt the rigour of our climate with the toils and exposure of pioneer missionary life, had the effect of hastening the collapse of her delicate physique,' the Bible Christian *Observer* editor wrote in a later testimonial to her.[16]

Ann Vickery Robins also suffered from the climate, particularly the Canadian winter. In their house, a thick cake of ice covered everything Robins and her family put in the indoor cupboards. Their breath froze on the bedclothes. They had no well of their own, and Robins carried water from her neighbours. She cared for her husband Paul when he became critically ill soon after he arrived in Canada, even though she herself was sick with rheumatism brought on by the frost and snow.[17]

On the Indian missions where a few of the women preached, housing was often primitive, supplies were scarce, and loneliness was part of many of the women's daily existence. Susannah Farley Waldron (1802–90) was often short of food. Once she was unable to offer a visiting minister anything at all to eat. Waldron lived on Indian missions for twelve years, and on one trip from Whitby to the Muncey Mission, she travelled with two children by canoe and on horseback through mire and bush and over logs, harassed continually by mosquitoes, only to reach a vermin-infested mission house which had to be turpentined completely to be made livable.

Eliza Barnes (Case) and another missionary taught in a seventeen-foot-square schoolhouse on Rice Lake in 1828. The six-foot high sides and roof were made of ash and cedar bark fastened to upright posts. Native women wove bark carpeting, and the men built a clay oven. The two women not only taught twenty-five girls 'domestic economy' and how to read, sew, knit, and braid straw in this tiny building, but they lived in it as well. Shortly after it was built, the house caught fire, and the women had a narrow escape. That summer, Barnes lived in a wigwam on an island because of virulent fever on the mainland. In his early history of the Methodist Church, James Youngs reported a fire at the mission on 'Lake Simco' [sic] that forced the missionaries to flee to canoes in the water, and it may have been that Barnes was threatened again.[18]

An early death or retirement from the preaching field because of ill health was not uncommon. Hetty Ann Hubbard (ca. 1796–1831) died three years after she arrived at the Indian missions, when she was about thirty-five. Both Elizabeth Dart and Eliza Barnes lost their only children at childbirth, Dart at Cobourg the year she arrived there, and Barnes nearby on the Indian missions.[19]

But while the women preached, they evidently did so with great skill, and received much popular acclaim. In England, where Elizabeth Dart began her itinerancy, crowds flocked to hear her. In Cornwall, she was told that the people only came to listen to her because she was a woman, and once their curiosity was satisfied, she would have no congregation. 'But, blessed be the Lord,' she exclaimed, 'I found it otherwise.' Later when Dart came to Canada, she was considered to be the best missionary the Bible Christians had ever had. Another of the early Bible Christian preachers who emigrated to Canada from England, Elizabeth Trueman Hoskin (1807–82), was held in such regard in her community in Ontario that she became known as the Reverend Mrs Hoskin.[20]

Of all Eliza Barnes's talents and accomplishments, witnesses were most impressed by her preaching ability. At one time she created a 'sensation' preaching in York. There had been a number of revivals at the Indian missions from their beginning in 1823 until 1827, and Barnes may have taken part in this activity. The New England states, where Barnes had grown up, were ablaze with religious revivals as part of the Second Great Awakening, and women were taking a leading role. When Barnes and her friend Hetty

Hubbard arrived together at the Grape Island Mission in May 1828, both of them spoke, Barnes at a prayer meeting the first evening and Hubbard the next day. Barnes's speech was 'much to the feelings of the assembly,' and she spoke very 'fluently.' At a camp-meeting in Haldimand in June Barnes gave a theological 'discourse' that covered a wide range of Christian thought – the 'incarnation, death, resurrection and ascension of our Lord and Saviour.' Barnes was responsible for a great religious revival, such as was not seen again in the area for thirty years; perhaps this sermon precipitated it.[21]

Barnes undertook a number of speaking engagements in 1929 and caused a mild 'Pentecost' at Yellowhead's Island in Lake Simcoe. Of that occasion the Canadian Indian missionary Peter Jones recorded in his journal that it seemed as if 'the very gates of heaven were opened to our souls, and the spirit of God descending upon our hearts.' Jones saw a footpath appear 'like a blaze of fire,' and the whole camp 'manifested the presence of God.' One evening in February, Barnes preached to a large gathering of Indians at Holland Landing 'with her usual eloquence' and also exhorted. Later that month she 'addressed' the 'whites' in the mission house at a meeting on Grape Island, although it is recorded that at the same time Jones 'preached' to the Indians in the chapel. And in May Barnes spoke in the John Street Church in New York City to the Dorcas Missionary Society about her 'trials and sufferings' on the Indian missions. The next year she spoke twice in that same church with 'simplicity and artfulness' and so 'fervently' that many of the congregation were reduced to tears.

The historian John Carroll wrote that Barnes was 'tolerated' as a preacher. And William Case, the general superintendent of Indian missions – and later Barnes's husband – at first refused to sit on the same platform with her. Many of the other male preachers objected to her preaching. But the Methodist educationist and temperance worker Letitia Creighton Youmans reported that Barnes had been a successful preacher in the United States, and when she came to Canada she was greatly sought after for camp-meetings and services in private homes. Youmans recorded the reminiscences of one woman whose doorway became the 'pulpit' for one of Barnes's sermons. The inside of the house was filled with women; the men stood in the large yard in front of the house. The text Barnes took was from Ezekiel's 'vision of the waters.' '"When the preacher [Barnes] spoke of the spread of the Gospel, and quoted in raptured accents *the waters were still rising*," said the old lady, "I fancied I could still see the waters of life flowing in until the earth was filled with the *glory of God*."'[22]

Indeed, it was often claimed that the women's preaching was superior to that of their husbands. The Methodist Episcopalian Ellen Bangs Gatchell (d. 1857) was exhorting in the Niagara region in 1810, 'like a streak of red-hot lightning.' It is said that Gatchell's speaking gifts surpassed those of her husband, also a Methodist preacher, to the delight of members of their congregation. The Primitive Methodist preacher Jane Woodill Wilson (1824–93) and her husband Isaac Wilson both drew crowds when they preached north of the present Toronto area. Jane, however, was described as being intellectually 'superior' to Isaac. Ann Copp Gordon and her husband Andrew often shared services as a ministerial couple in the Bible Christian Church, and their listeners judged Ann to be the better preacher.[23]

The historian Jane Agar Hopper describes a number of women who held leadership positions in the Canadian Primitive Methodist Church in the first part of the nineteenth century. Among these was a Mrs Stephenson who, Hopper wrote cryptically, 'had great help in her husband.' Evidently Mrs Stephenson was the more prominent individual in that ministerial couple. Unfortunately, there is no record of what she did except that she 'brought much of the early Primitive Methodist fire across the ocean.' It seems highly likely, though, that she preached, for Hopper does tell us how her husband helped: 'He could arouse a prayer-meeting or class-meeting wonderfully.' It was not uncommon for ministerial couples to work together, but historians usually recorded that it was the wife who led prayer meetings or classes to assist her husband who preached the sermons.[24]

In Prince Edward Island, Frances Calloway took a number of preaching appointments, drawing particularly large congregations. According to her husband's journals, however, Calloway appears to have been more adept at preaching than at some household chores. In describing her attempts to put up a 'Moschetto [sic] blind around the bed,' William wrote that Frances was 'not so well skilled in putting them up as the Americans are.' Evidently, 'numbers of them [mosquitoes] found their way in, just as it was getting light.'[25]

But even though secessionist Methodist denominations were open to women preachers, and some of the women did surpass their husbands in ability, an examination of preaching plans indicates that often women were not given an equal share of preaching appointments. For example, in 1860 and 1861 both Elizabeth Trick and her husband Charles Henwood were listed on the Cobourg circuit plan as preachers, Henwood third in seniority and Trick fourth out of a list sometimes as long as twenty-nine. From January to July and October to December of 1860 and from January to

July of 1861, Trick was assigned only sixteen preaching appointments, whereas Henwood was allotted forty-one. The discrepancy could have been the result of the fact that much of Trick's time would have been spent managing their large household. However, in 1860, their youngest children were the twins, then fourteen years old, well able to care for themselves and help with domestic chores.[26]

Often the women were invited to preach at anniversary services or other celebrations rather than regularly on circuits, granting the women preachers a special yet unequal status. This pattern can be seen developing as the century progressed, as the more radical Methodist denominations became imbued with Canadian conservatism. Mary Ann Lyle had begun her preaching career in England in 1817, first for the Bible Christian Church, and later for the Primitive Methodists. In 1833 she and her husband William emigrated to Upper Canada as a missionary couple, where they continued preaching on circuits around the present-day city of Toronto. She was listed on preachers' plans, at least in 1836, 1839, and 1843, years for which plans are available. Later on it appears that she was invited to speak mainly on special occasions. She preached at the opening of the chapel in the Nassigoway Township on the Guelph circuit in 1846 and again at the opening of a church in Claremont.[27]

The widowed Bible Christian preacher Mrs Andrew Cory spoke only infrequently, as well. Cory was invited to participate in the dedication services for a new church at Darlington in 1855. It was reported that as part of the celebrations, Mrs Cory 'made remarks,' whereas Mr Draper and Mr Frayner 'preached.' Two Sundays later, however, there were three special 'sermons,' by Mr John Hooper, Mr Henry, and Mrs Cory.[28]

Another Primitive Methodist preacher, Mary Ann Towler, was evidently much sought after, but again only as an anniversary speaker. As a full-time schoolteacher, however, she would have had little time for a full itineracy. Towler and her husband William had emigrated to the United States from England in 1846. Her husband, a general superintendent, soon became ill, and Towler looked after his extensive correspondence and preaching when he was sick, in addition to taking care of seven children. A short time later he died, and soon Mary Ann Towler moved to Toronto where she opened a day school in 1848 and continued preaching on special occasions. In June of that year Towler was the guest speaker at the anniversary of the Yorkville Sunday schools, and later she preached at least three times at the opening of a chapel on the Hamilton Mission, on Sunday, Monday, and Tuesday. Each successive appearance seems to have drawn larger crowds than before, yet the newspaper report of the services continued to state that her audiences were astonished at her 'calmness and ability.' In 1851 Towler preached the anniversary sermons for the Hope Chapel Sunday school. Other Methodist groups also accepted her as a speaker, for at least on one occasion she appeared on the same platform with Wesleyans and members of the New Connexion.[29]

As well, the salaries for Primitive Methodist women preachers were less than those for men. In 1832 male itinerants received between £16 16s and £21 8s, while females were paid only £10. It was, of course, common to pay women less than men in all areas of society, but a good female domestic servant could earn up to £18, almost twice the amount paid to a female itinerant. Men were paid on a sliding scale, receiving the higher amount if they were married. But if a male preacher's wife carried on his business while he travelled, his needs were felt to be less, and his salary was reduced. Clearly, it was assumed that women were quite capable of managing businesses.[30]

The women may have been denied equality, yet most of their husbands apparently took pride in their wives' accomplishments and offered them encouragement. In fact, it is often only through published excerpts of the men's journals that we learn of the women's activities, for the women's writings were not generally printed. For example, the *Bible Christian Magazine* published very little of Elizabeth Dart's journal describing her terrifying forty-two-day ocean crossing from Padstow to Quebec City in 1833, although the editor included sizeable excerpts from her husband's diary. Much of Dart's journal was omitted, the editor noted, because it was similar to Eynon's.[31]

Not only were the women's diaries generally not quoted in the denominational magazines and newspapers, but the biographies and memorials of the women in both the religious and secular press usually omitted references to their preaching activity or named it differently. In 1862 the historian George Playter noted only that Eliza Barnes Case was an adventurous missionary woman, although John Carroll included in his history scattered references to her preaching activity. Her 1887 obituary in the *Christian Guardian*, however, pointed out only that she 'labored for 8 or 10 years among the Indians at Grape Island as a pioneer missionary.' And when Annie Stephenson wrote her history of Methodist missions in 1925, she mentioned simply that 'Miss Barnes' was a teacher at Grape Island and 'Miss Hubbard' at Rice Lake.[32]

Ann Copp Gordon appears to have been the only Bible Christian woman preaching regularly as late as the 1870s, and her exploits did find their way into twentieth-century Canadian newspapers. Copp's story illustrates well how Canadian society erased the idea of women in the pulpit from its history.

When Copp died in 1931 in Winnipeg at the age of ninety-seven, she was well known. Local newspapers had printed a story about her almost every year on her birthday when she was in her nineties. They referred to her preaching career, even noting that she had preached at three circuit points on Sundays. Believing, however, that women preachers were almost unheard of in the early days of Methodism, a journalist explained that as one of the first women to preach, Copp attracted wide attention. Indeed, another writer noted, she was probably the first woman to preach in Canada. In fact, Copp was among the last of the nineteenth-century Methodist women who preached in Great Britain and in Canada, beginning her career in both countries in the late 1850s. Only a very few women in the Bible Christian and Primitive Methodist groups were still active in the pulpit at that time.

The newspaper stories also emphasized Copp's role as a mother and homemaker, for this was where society believed women were meant to be. 'Outside the Church the centre of her life was in the home, which she loved and cared for, and here was where she really reigned,' one biographer wrote. Another indicated only that she took 'the pulpit herself when the need arose – which she did for one whole year.' These twentieth-century journalists could not conceive of a woman preaching except to fill in, in an emergency.[33]

Earlier when Elizabeth Dart died in 1857, the *Bible Christian Magazine* noted her death, but described her only as the wife of John Hicks Eynon and a 'devoted Christian.' The denominational paper, the *Canadian Statesman*, mentioned that she was a 'very devoted Christian,' a 'superior woman,' and a 'superior teacher,' making no reference to her itineracy. As time went on, Dart generally received even less recognition. In 1883, on the eve of the union of all the Methodist Churches in Canada, a series of *Observer* articles pointed out this gap in the official church records, placing Dart's contribution to the Bible Christian Church before its readers. But in a memorial to John Hicks Eynon who died in March, 1888, the *Canadian Statesman* referred to his wife briefly and anonymously only as a 'heroine in the missionary cause.' The *West Durham News* devoted two long columns on its front page to Eynon's life and work in the 'christian Ministry.' Dart is described as a 'great worker, and untiring in her effort to do good' and a 'fit companion' for Eynon. The *Minutes* of the London Methodist conference also paid tribute to Eynon, noting that a 'lady evangelist' who later became his wife had given him 'advice, encouragement, and aid in proclaiming ... the message of Divine mercy.' Who she was, the *Minutes* do not say. And in a biographical sketch of Eynon, complete with photograph, in the *Christian Guardian* in 1904, there is no mention at all of Dart.[34]

Although the line between preaching and evangelism was not clearly defined, the difference between an evangelist and a preacher was evidently important. A mid-nineteenth-century historian wrote of Mary Barritt Taft, one of the more iconoclastic of the English Wesleyan preachers, that 'her employment as an evangelist led to her employment as a preacher.' As Marilyn Whiteley notes in the following chapter, in the late nineteenth century, a few unordained 'lady' evangelists were tolerated when women preachers were considered to be an aberration. By then the designations of 'minister' and 'preacher' had become interchangeable, and a minister had to be ordained. Women as evangelists were less threatening than women as preachers because evangelists generally travelled from place to place, invited to preach or speak only on special and specific occasions. As instruments of spiritual growth, they held roles suitable for women at that time. Preachers or ministers, however, were settled in one location, and they undertook all the sacramental and pastoral duties inherent in that position.[35]

Articles, letters, and journal excerpts in newspapers and periodicals indicate that there had been discrimination against women preaching in all the Methodist movements in Great Britain and North America throughout the whole of the nineteenth century, even in the denominations more open to women in leadership such as the Bible Christian Church. Elizabeth Dart recorded male opposition to her itineracy in England on a number of occasions. Once when she arrived at the house where she was to preach in Tavistock, the people were afraid to let her come in because some 'great man' had threatened them with punishment if they did. So Dart preached in the doorway. Another man told her that all preaching women should be burned, but a few days after his 'abuse' of her, Dart noted in her journal that his house had been burned.[36]

There are no similar recorded instances of opposition to Dart in Canada. Only a few extracts from her Canadian letters and journals are extant, however, and according to legend, when she was challenged as to whether she had been properly ordained to preach, she replied, 'No, but I was foreordained.' But in 1847 Paul Robins, another Bible Christian itinerant in Upper Canada, wrote from Peterborough, 'The Sunday I am in the country there is no person to address the people but Sister Heard and my wife, and there seems to be a prejudice against female preaching.'[37]

Ann Copp experienced hostility all her life – first from her family and later from her co-workers – as well as from society at large. Her father, a pillar in the established church, had forced her to leave home when she joined the Methodists. However, when he finally heard her preach on the eve of her departure to Canada in 1857, he was overawed. Eleven years later in Canada when Copp was asked to preach the conference sermon to all the ministers in the area, a few male ministers suggested that 'it was too much to ask of the little woman,' even though by that time she had established herself as a successful preacher. Others said, 'let the little woman win her spurs.' And 'win her spurs' she did – in a black silk dress which she had made especially for the occasion.[38]

Many of the male preachers found it difficult to accept women in a preaching role, believing that femininity and preaching were simply not compatible. A number of Canadian men reacted the same as James Garfield, later president of the United States, who responded in the 1850s when the American Antoinette Brown was ordained, 'There is something about a woman's speaking in public that unsexes her in my mind, and how much soever I might admire her talent, yet I could never think of the female speaker as the gentle sister, the tender wife or the loving mother.'[39]

Members of Mary Ann Lyle's family evidently felt the same way. While proud of the stature she had attained as a 'prophetess' in the Primitive Methodist Church, they had misgivings as to the propriety of her profession. In a funeral tribute to Lyle in 1862, her son-in-law, R.L. Tucker, expressed his concern to the other mourners that 'female preachers' generally lacked 'meekness, charity and domestic qualities.' Tucker hastened to point out, however, that this was not the case with his mother-in-law, a preacher who had attained 'a position of some prominence' in the church. Even though she 'occasionally expounded the Word, and exhorted sinners to flee from the wrath to come,' Lyle was never 'dictatorial and assuming' but always 'modest and diffident.' Tucker, himself a preacher, continued that it could be useful for a woman to speak in 'public' occasionally as long as she could also 'blend' this with a domestic life and a 'meek and quiet spirit.' Tucker explained that his mother-in-law was so correctly 'diffident' that she was 'unwilling to address the public while ministers were present,' and 'for many years she refused to preach in the presence of her own husband.' Another son-in-law and preacher, William Clarke, confirmed that indeed Lyle was 'modest and retiring,' and although she 'frequently addressed public assemblies ... she looked upon this as a sort of exception to God's usual way of working, and only felt justified in it when there was apparent need for her help ... Only a sense of duty,' he reported, 'could have overcome her natural diffidence and nerved her for this work.'[40]

At least Lyle's sons-in-law did acknowledge her preaching activity. Generally, women's preaching was ignored or denied. Two years earlier, an anonymous writer who described Methodism in Canada from 1820 to 1860 insisted that Methodist women 'never presumed to preach.' The 'good' they accomplished, the writer explained, was in visiting in houses, gathering together in classes, and praying at prayer meetings. A Methodist woman might have read other women a sermon or added an exhortation of her own, but never had she stepped beyond the bounds of acceptable behaviour by preaching.[41]

By 1860 most Canadian Methodists were genuinely unaware of the legacy of several hundred women preaching over one hundred years in the Wesleyan tradition in Great Britain and North America. Indeed, many of these women were still active. Even in the conservative atmosphere of Canada, there is firm evidence that forty Methodist women were preaching in the five decades between 1810 and 1860 and beyond, and tantalizing reports indicate that the number may have been even much greater.

The women's preaching activity in Canada was relatively short-lived, however, compared with that in the United States of America. In the Canadian Methodist Episcopal Church, women stopped preaching at the beginning of the 1830s. In the Bible Christian and Primitive Methodist denominations, women's preaching continued into the second half of the nineteenth century. Yet as the century progressed, women held fewer regular preaching appointments; instead, they were invited to speak as guest preachers on special occasions. By 1884, when the Canadian Methodist Churches were reunited, the long history of women preaching had been virtually forgotten.

By contrast, Methodist women fared much better in the United States. In the Primitive Methodist Church, women had achieved equal rights with men in two conferences by the early 1880s, and by the end of that decade, the first woman minister had been ordained. The Bible Christian Church never took hold in the United States, but many British Bible Christian women from England preached in the American Methodist Protestant Church and the Methodist Protestant conference ordained Helanor M. Davidson in 1866. The Methodist Episcopal Church offered a preacher's licence to Margaret Newton Van Cott in 1870. Although the next two decades were a confusing era of invoking, granting, and revoking licences and ordination for women in the various denominations, by the late 1880s women had been accepted for ordination in the majority of American Methodist Churches.[42]

It should not be surprising that nineteenth-century Canadian women held less powerful and less prominent positions in the church than their American sisters did. In 1833 two Canadian women had written that women in other countries had much greater opportunities, 'Women in this country are not sufficiently considered, they who in every other land have attracted to themselves the consideration of all, have here been neglected and left in oblivion.'[43]

While this was no doubt an exaggeration, it was true that the climate in the United States was more liberal than in Canada, and American women were considered to be much less subservient and more assertive than Canadian women. Whereas the United States had been born of revolution and peopled by radicals seeking freedom from restraint and authority, the governing body of Upper Canada was bent on preventing rebellion and preserving the status quo. The results of this difference can be seen clearly in how both men and women preachers were received in the nineteenth-century Methodist Episcopal Church in Canada.

Itinerants from the Methodist Episcopal Church in the United States had been warmly welcomed in Upper Canada when they first arrived at the end of the eighteenth century. Whereas other Protestant denominations generally expected the people to come to their church buildings to worship, the Methodist preachers took their services to the people. In a pioneer country of bad roads, extreme weather conditions, and sparsely populated areas, the Methodists met with resounding success. Indeed the emotionally charged Methodist meeting was often the only social opportunity available to isolated settlers.

The itinerants, however, were much less well received by the governing elite of Upper Canada, most of whom had come from Great Britain and belonged to the Church of England. Ever since Wesley had begun preaching in England in the early eighteenth century, relations between the Methodists and the parent church had been severely strained. An ordained Church of England minister himself, Wesley had attempted to bring new life into the established church in England, but his actions ultimately resulted in the formation of a new denomination.

The attitude of the Upper Canadian governing body to Methodism in the 1800s was coloured not only by the past, but by recent political events as well. First the American Revolution, and later the invasion by the Americans of Canadian territory during the War of 1812, led Upper Canadian government officials to fear any American connection. Methodist itinerants were suspect, Methodist doctrine was considered to be seditious, and Methodist charismatic worship experiences were judged a less than legitimate form of religious expression. In 1814 General Gordon Drummond, the administrator of the government of Upper Canada, reported that the Methodists were 'itinerant fanatics, enthusiastic in political as well as religious matters,' who came from the United States to Upper Canada deliberately to disseminate 'their noxious principles.' As a result, Canadian officialdom denied the Methodist Church religious status and permission to perform official acts such as valid marriage ceremonies.[44]

The Canadian Methodist Church devised its own plan to counter these attitudes. In 1828 it separated from the American Methodists to form an independent Canadian Methodist Episcopal Church. One year later the Canadian Methodists were given permission to conduct marriage ceremonies. Presumably with this separation from the United States, the Canadian Methodist Episcopal Church was perceived as having acquired more 'sober and regulated modes of thinking' which the Upper Canadian legislation had specified as the criteria for granting that privilege to religious denominations. Still, there was hostility towards Methodist preachers, and believing further action was needed in order to be received better by the governing establishment, Egerton and John Ryerson, two prominent Canadian Methodist itinerants, spearheaded a move to join with the British Wesleyans in 1833. The move was a disastrous one for women preachers. The British Wesleyan Methodist Church had already passed formal legislation in 1802 and 1803 forbidding women to preach, as part of an attempt to become more respectable and hence more acceptable to the British government. After this legislation was enacted, some of the women preachers in Great Britain had reluctantly stopped preaching. A few defied the legislation and kept on preaching for a number of years. Some organized their own Methodist denominations. But most of them joined other Methodist movements such as the Primitive Methodist and Bible Christian denominations which had sprung up as a result of the increasing legalism and hierarchicalism in the Wesleyan Church.

In Canada, after the union which formed the Wesleyan Methodist Church in Canada, women preachers were not welcome in that denomination. Whereas a number of women had been preaching for the Methodist Episcopal Church, after the union active preachers such as Eliza Barnes 'settled down' to a lifestyle more appropriate for women.[45]

Canadian Methodism had provided preaching opportunities and paid positions for women early in the nineteenth century, mainly because of theological doctrines and church structures. Yet in the last few decades, these positions were severely limited. Not only did they eventually disappear, but even the memory of Canada's Methodist women preachers was lost.

NOTES

1 For a fuller account, see Elizabeth Gillan Muir, *Petticoats in the Pulpit: The Story of Early Nineteenth Century Methodist Women Preachers in Upper Canada* (Toronto: United Church Publishing House, 1991), passim.
2 George J. Stevenson, *City Road Chapel London and Its Associations* (London: George J. Stevenson, 1872), 29ff.
3 *Methodist Magazine*, 1803, 34, undated letter.
4 Nathan Bangs, *The Methodist Episcopal Church*, vol. 1 (New York: Carlton and Phillips, 1856), 205. George F. Playter, *The History of Methodism in Canada* (Toronto: Anson Green, 1862), 55–6. *Minutes of Elders' Meetings*, Cobourg, Ontario, 21 Feb. 1852, United Church Archives (hereafter UCA). J.E. Sanderson, *The First Century of Methodism in Canada*, vol. 2, (Toronto: William Briggs, 1908), 213. *The Doctrines and Discipline of the Wesleyan Methodist Church in Canada* (Toronto: Matthew Lang, 1836), 33.
5 John Wesley, *Letters*, 1 Apr. 1773; 18 Jan. 1774. C.H. Crookshank, *Memorable Women of Irish Methodism in the Last Century* (London: Wesleyan Methodist Book-Room, 1882), 20.
6 Frederick William Bourne, *The Bible Christians: Their Origin and History* (n.p.: Bible Christian Book Room, 1905), passim. *Observer*, weekly articles from 28 Mar. to 25 Apr. 1883. *Cobourg Star*, 3 July 1833, 196. *Bible Christian Magazine*, 1833, John's Journal, passim, Mar. 1834, 109ff. Elizabeth Muir, 'Elizabeth Dart (Eynon),' in *Dictionary of Canadian Biography* 8, gen. ed. F.G. Halpenny (Toronto: University of Toronto Press, 1985).
7 John Carroll, *Case and His Cotemporaries or the Canadian Itinerants Memorial*, vol. 3 (Toronto: Samuel Rose, 1871), 219, 279. Sanderson, *The First Century of Methodism in Canada*, vol. 1 (Toronto: William Briggs, 1910), 220. Peter Jones, *Life and Journals of Kah-Ke-Wa-Quo-Na-By* (Toronto: Anson Green, 1860), 205, 216, 263. *Christian Advocate*, 6 Mar. 1829, 106, report from W. Case; 15 May 1829, 145. *Christian Guardian*, 12 Dec. 1829, 27. For more details on Eliza Barnes Case's activities and other women on the Indian missions, see Elizabeth Muir, 'The Bark Schoolhouse: Methodist Episcopal Missionary Women in Upper Canada, 1827–1833,' chap. in *Canadian Protestant and Catholic Missions, 1820s–1960s*, John S. Moir and C.T. McIntire, eds. (New York: Peter Lang, 1988).
8 Annie R. Gordon, 'Whither Thou Goest – Ann Copp, a Devon Maid,' UCA, passim.
9 Bible Christian preachers' plans, UCA. Trick-Henwood Papers, private collection of Howard Harris. *Bible Christian Magazine*, 1853, 474ff., memorial tribute by Paul Robins.

10 *Christian Guardian*, 4 Dec. 1830, 10; 5 June 1830, 230.

11 As quoted in Deborah M. Valenze, *Prophetic Sons and Daughters: Female Preaching and Popular Religion in Industrial England* (Princeton: Princeton University Press, 1985), 7.

12 Wesley, *Letters*, 14 Feb. 1761.

13 Wesley, *Letters*, 13 June, 1771. *Observer*, 25 Apr. 1883, 1. Gordon, 'Whither Thou Goest,' 48ff.

14 Zechariah Taft, *Biographical Sketches of the Lives and Public Ministry of Various Holy Women* (London: Mr Kershaw, 1825), 175. Mary McCoy Bradley, *A Narrative of the Life and Christian Experience of Mrs Mary Bradley of St John, New Brunswick* (Boston: Strong and Brodhead, 1849), passim esp. 150, 163.

15 Gordon, 'Whither Thou Goest,' 14. Wesley, *Letters*, 29 Mar. 1766.

16 *Observer*, 28 Mar. 1883, 1.

17 *Bible Christian Magazine*, Oct. 1847, 403, journal of Paul Robins; May 1847, 200, letter of John Eynon.

18 James Youngs, *History of the Rise and Progress of Methodism in England and America* (New Haven, Conn.: H. Daggett, 1830), 417. Solomon Waldron, 'A Sketch of the Life, Travels, and Labors of Solomon Waldron, A Wesleyan Methodist Preacher,' UCA. *Christian Guardian*, 14 Aug. 1833, 158; 3 Dec. 1890, 779. *Christian Advocate*, 19 Sept. 1828, 10; 1 Mar. 1833, 106; 12 July 1833, 182; 13 Dec. 1833, 62.

19 William Case biographical file, UCA. *Bible Christian Magazine*, 1834, John's Journal. Some of the women did live to a remarkably old age in spite of the conditions, or perhaps toughened by them. Eliza Barnes Case died at age ninety-one, Ann Copp Gordon at ninety-four.

20 *Observer*, 15 Mar. 1882, 3; 2 May 1883, 4. Jas B. Fairbairn, *History and Reminiscences of Bowmanville* (Bowmanville, Ont.: Bowmanville Newsprint, 1906), 42.

21 Carroll, *Case and His Cotemporaries*, vol. 3, 177, 184, 220–1, 227. Playter, *History*, 342. Jones, *Life and Journals*, 139–40, 157, 216.

22 Letitia Creighton Youmans, *Campaign Echoes* (Toronto: William Briggs, 1893), 64–5.

23 Carroll, *Case and His Cotemporaries*, vol. 1, 223–4. Jane Agar Hopper, *Primitive Methodism in Canada, 1829–1884* (Toronto: William Briggs, 1904), 52–3. Gordon, 'Whither Thou Goest,' passim.

24 Hopper, *Primitive Methodism*, 102, 210, 217–18.

25 *Bible Christian Magazine*, 1847, Canadian Missionary Reports.

26 Bible Christian Preachers' Plans, UCA. These are months when plans are available on which they are both listed. Trick-Henwood Papers, private collection of Howard Harris.

27 *Primitive Methodist Magazine*, 1834, 280, Journals of William Summersides;

1846, 423, Journals of M. Nichols. Hopper, *Primitive Methodism*, 29. Primitive Methodist Preachers' Plans, UCA.

28 *Bible Christian Magazine*, Jan. 1857, 42–3. *Canada West Missionary Chronicle*, 16 Sept. 1855; 5 Oct. 1855.

29 Hopper, *Primitive Methodism*, 29. *Evangelist*, Jan. 1848, 14; July 1848, 29; Oct. 1848, 134, 138; Dec. 1851, 191. John A. Acornley, *A History of the Primitive Methodist Church in the United States of America* (Fall River, Mass.: R.R. Acornley, 1909), 48–9.

30 *The Doctrines and Disciplines of the British Primitive Methodist Connexion* [Canada] (York: W.J. Coates, 1833), 40. William Cattermole, *Emigration: The Advantages of Emigration to Canada* (London: Simpkin and Marshall, 1831) reprinted (Toronto: Coles, 1970).

31 *Bible Christian Magazine*, 1833, letters from Elizabeth and John, and John's diary.

32 Mrs F.C. Stephenson, *One Hundred Years of Canadian Methodist Missions*, 1824–1924 (Toronto: Missionary Society of the Methodist Church, 1925), 70–1.

33 Andrew Gordon Biographical File, UCA.

34 Bible Christian Church (Canada) *Year Book*, 1857, 2. *Canadian Statesman*, 22 Jan. 1857, 2; 11 Apr. 1888, 8. *West Durham News*, 20 Apr. 1888, 1. Methodist Conference, *Minutes* (London: 1888). *Christian Guardian*, 6 Apr. 1904, 1, 6.

35 James Porter, *A Compendium of Methodism* (New York: Carlton and Porter, 1851), 487–91.

36 *Observer*, 1 Aug. 1883, 4.

37 J.E. Sanderson, *The First Century*, vol. 2, 427. *Bible Christian Magazine*, 1848, 123, letter from Paul Robins, 2 Dec. 1847.

38 Gordon, 'Whither Thou Goest,' 16, 39ff.

39 Sweet, *The Minister's Wife*, 140.

40 W.F. Clarke and R.L. Tucker, *A Mother in Israel: Or Some Memorials of the Late Mrs M.A. Lyle* (Toronto: W.C. Chewett, 1862), 4–5, 6–7, 14–15.

41 A Spectator of the Scenes, *Past and Present or a Description of Persons and Events Connected with Canadian Methodism for the Last Forty Years* (Toronto: Alfred Dredge, 1860), 49. *The Cyclopedia of Methodism*, ed. Matthew Simpson, defines exhorting as a form of preaching, a 'sort of probation to the ministry.' At the end of the sermon, an exhorter aroused the people to their 'sense of duty.'

42 William T. Noll, 'Women and Clergy and Laity in the 19th Century Methodist Protestant Church,' *Methodist History* 15 (1977), 110ff. Janet S. Everhart, 'Maggie Newton Van Cott: The Methodist Episcopal Church Considers the Question of Women Clergy,' in *Women in New Worlds* vol. 2, R.S. Keller, L.L. Queen, and H.F. Thomas, eds. (Nashville: Abingdon, 1982), 303ff.

43 *Christian Guardian*, 17 Nov. 1833, 108.

44 Gerald M. Craig, *Upper Canada: The Formative Years, 1740–1840* (Toronto: McClelland and Stewart, 1963), 165–6.

45 C.B. Sissons, *Egerton Ryerson – His Life and Letters*, vol. 1 (Toronto: Clarke and Irwin and Co Ltd., 1937), 77ff. Craig, *Upper Canada*, 56, 175. Carroll, *Case and His Cotemporaries*, vol. 3, 169.

9

Modest, Unaffected, and Fully Consecrated: Lady Evangelists in Canadian Methodism

MARILYN FÄRDIG WHITELEY

By the latter part of the nineteenth century most women in Canada were no longer able to fill the occupational role of Methodist minister. Yet for a brief period a few were able to work as evangelists. This was made possible in part by a mythology concerning the place of women in Methodism, and it was encouraged by the desire of Methodists to adopt techniques that the rival Salvation Army was using so successfully. Women were also accepted as evangelists because they were seen as peculiarly qualified for the work: It called upon many of the very traits that were deemed characteristic of women. Evangelism offered women little financial security, for they had to rely on discreetly given collections and offerings; even the discussion of remuneration for women appeared somehow unseemly. This limited opportunity for women was brief. Early in the new century, when the character of evangelism changed and the occupation became professionalized, women were no longer able to minister in the Methodist Church as evangelists.

The St Thomas, Ontario, *Daily Times* for 5 October 1888, reported that 'Grace Methodist Church was crowded to the doors last night to hear the evangelists view of dancing. On the platform were Revs. Best, Griffin, Whiting, Ranton, and Hunter, the latter receiving a warm welcome. All took part in the meeting.' All took part in the meeting, but the evangelist whom the crowd had come to hear was not one of the notable ministers present. It was instead a young Ontario woman of about twenty-five, from the village of Bell Ewart on the shores of Lake Simcoe. Her name was Elizabeth Hannah Dimsdale; familiarly known as Libby, she was most often referred to as L.H. Dimsdale. She was in the midst of a month of revival services in St Thomas; in the past three or four years she had been engaged in evangelistic work in more than fifty places.[1] Dimsdale was well known and much sought after. Nor was she unique: Between 1885 and 1910 more than thirty Methodist women worked as evangelists.[2]

Yet a century later the labour of these women is forgotten. Their activity was not the type recorded in the official reports of their denomination, and thus it has not been noticed by historians who focus their attention on traditional denominational history. Yet it is a distinctive part of Canadian Methodism, for it was the Methodist heritage that helped to make evangelism a career option for late nineteenth- and early twentieth-century Canadian women; it was the character of Methodism which contributed to the acceptability of evangelism as an appropriate field for woman's work; and it was a change in Methodism in the twentieth century that meant that the option had almost closed prior to church union in 1925.

Canadian Methodists pointed with pride to the Christian usefulness of Methodist women. Women gained a leadership role in the early years of the Wesleyan movement, and in this volume Elizabeth Gillan Muir has described how a number of Methodist women had preached in Upper Canada in the first part of the nineteenth century. As she explains, however, by the latter half of the century, little remained of this distinctive heritage. Yet Methodists continued to express satisfaction about the situation of women in their denomination: It had become a constituent of the mythology of Methodism.

Members of the Methodist Woman's Missionary Society (WMS) were able to maintain more independence in their mission work than those of other denominations.[3] In 1885 Sarah Gibbs Gooderham, president of that group, acknowledged the difficult situation of women in churches that 'have raised a formidable barrier in the way of our sisters in these denominations, who found themselves moved by the Holy Spirit and prompted by the indications of divine Providence, to actively enter upon this work.' She continued,

Happily, we, as Methodist women have had little to complain of in this respect. Our denomination from the beginning recognized the right of women to exercise their gifts, as God gave themopportunity, for the conversion of sinners and the edification of believers. With the history of the labours of Susannah Wesley, Mary Bosanquet and a host of others, whose names are in the book of life before it, Methodism could not be true to its traditions and lay a straw in the way of any Christian woman who felt herself to be divinely called to evangelistic work.[4]

While Gooderham was speaking of the opportunity of Methodist women to do missionary evangelism, others argued in more general terms. In 1891 E.H. Dewart, editor of the *Christian Guardian*, wrote that its class meetings, prayer meetings, and love feasts were a distinguishing feature of Methodism: 'By affording an opportunity for confessing Christ, [they] become "schools of the prophets," in which even timid women and young converts may learn to exercise their gifts for the edification of others.'[5] Dewart went on to list some of Methodism's 'noble sisterhood,' including Susanna Wesley, Mary Bosanquet Fletcher, Barbara Heck, Phoebe Palmer – and Miss Dimsdale. According to the perception that late nineteenth-century Methodists had of their heritage, their church offered unusual opportunities to women, and it had been blessed through women's work.

One of the women on Dewart's list had a particular role in paving the way for the Canadian lady evangelists of the late nineteenth century. Although she was from the United States, Phoebe Worrall Palmer was well known in Canada, especially for her work in the Hamilton revival of 1857. She showed clearly that a woman could be a powerful force in evangelism, and her writings spread her influence and her ideas. Palmer insisted that it was not merely permissible but necessary to obey the command of the Holy Spirit: to resist the prompting of the Spirit was to risk condemnation. For the followers of John Wesley, both conversion and the further experience of sanctification might lead Methodists, both women and men, to feel a sense of call. The views of Palmer gave to women constrained by their traditional roles the permission they needed to respond to that call.[6] Palmer's work provided a basis for the evangelical feminism that enabled women to take initiatives in religious activities.

Methodist women empowered by evangelical feminism might move beyond their commonly prescribed roles to take on some uncommon activity. In this they could claim the support of an attitude common in Canada in the late nineteenth century, a society strongly influenced by evangelical Christianity. While the responsibility of women had been seen to lie in the private, domestic sphere as wives and in particular as mothers, in a gradual expansion of these roles, 'true women' were called upon to act as mothers to the world, and to work for those improvements to society that would serve to protect their homes and families. Thus, the women's missionary societies were born in order to do 'woman's work for women and children,' and thus also many women became involved in temperance work, in order to provide 'home protection.'[7] The heritage of Methodism supported this expansion of woman's role: Wesley's view of Christianity as a social religion and his own example of Christian usefulness influenced his followers to be active in both mission and reform work. Through these activities women obtained experience in conducting meetings and speaking in public, and they also gained greater acceptance as speakers on church and reform platforms.[8] Good Christian women could be heard in public so long as they were speaking on behalf of an appropriate cause, a cause that was an extension of their natural role as mother.

Thus, by the early 1880s several factors set the stage for the acceptance of Methodist woman evangelists: Methodist mythology ascribed to women an active role; Methodist evangelical religion recognized that anyone experiencing conversion or sanctification might receive a call to Christian usefulness; and evangelical Canadian society in the late nineteenth century supported an expansion of woman's role to fulfil the duties incumbent upon 'true womanhood.' Then something happened to give impetus to a sudden flowering of female evangelism: The Salvation Army entered Canada.

Methodists felt ambivalent about the work of the Salvation Army. They rejoiced that this child of Methodism was saving lost souls, and recognized

its 'aggressive spirit' and its ability to 'revive many of the methods of early
Methodism, and repeat many of its triumphs.'⁹ While they objected to the
more sensational methods of the Salvationists, their discomfort probably
had a deeper root: the Salvation Army was successfully evangelizing many
whom the Methodist Church had been unable to reach.

Some Methodists saw that they might learn from the Army 'the larger
employment of lay agency for Christian work.'¹⁰ Salvation Army converts
quickly became involved in the evangelistic activity of the movement, and a
large number of these workers were women. If the energy of committed
young Methodists could be harnessed in the same way, what a power for
revival that would be! Reports appeared in the *Christian Guardian* and the
Canada Christian Advocate.¹¹ David Savage, Methodist minister in Petro-
lia, was impressed by reports of the work of a Methodist 'Hallelujah Band'
in Belleville. One Sunday he 'announced that at the close of the service a
similar "Band" would be organized for Petrolea [*sic*].'¹²

Savage found his people's 'hands stretched out for work,' and he put
work into their hands. It was not an entirely new kind of labour, for
throughout Methodist history laypeople had participated in evangelism.
One feature of Phoebe Palmer's revivals was that she had mobilized the
laity for work.¹³ Even as Savage was organizing bands and taking them to
assist at one revival and then another, so were other ministers tapping this
rediscovered resource of lay talent and energy. Yet Savage's enthusiasm
and his organizational skills made his bands the model for the rest.

Bands worked at home and travelled on invitation to assist with revivals
at other churches. Sometimes Savage accompanied his band; at other times
he named a 'second in command' to lead them. As his own members
became more experienced, he was able to send them out 'in companies of
from two to four ... where a local 'band' is available to support the more
experienced workers.'¹⁴ Thus, band membership spread. It gave valuable
training; it also lent legitimacy to the work of the members, since they were
seen as being under the control of a minister.

Gradually references in the *Guardian* to the work of Savage's bands gave
way to reports of leadership by individual band members, both men and
women. In 1887 the following notice appeared: 'Rev. David Savage writes
that several young ladies qualified for evangelistic work, and for whom he
can vouch both as to gifts and grace, will be available for work in Ontario
about the end of August. Applications for their services made to him will
receive due attention.'¹⁵ Methodist band work had trained some young
women for evangelistic activity and had also helped them gain acceptance
in that role. Now a few were ready to work more independently.

The challenge of the Salvation Army was at its height around the year 1884. This was also the year of the union of the several branches of Canadian Methodism. The newly united Methodist Church was eager to demonstrate the validity of its union through successful evangelism.[16] That fall Methodist ministers Hugh Crossley and John Hunter began working together as an evangelistic team, and at about that time also an extraordinary young woman was beginning to conduct revivals without the apprenticeship served by her band-member contemporaries. This was L.H. Dimsdale, the evangelist at work in Grace Methodist Church, St Thomas, in 1888; the *Guardian* first reported her activity in February of 1885.

L.H. Dimsdale was one of the seven children of Alfred Dimsdale and Hannah Henry. Both parents were Methodist converts from the Church of England, Alfred 'through the influence of his wife.'[17] In England Alfred Dimsdale had practised law; in Canada he was a schoolteacher and became a local preacher and Sunday school superintendent. According to L.H. Dimsdale's account, she was sent to Muskoka for her health. While her father was there with her, he did some preaching since there was no church nearby. When he was called home, he announced without her knowledge that his daughter would fill his appointments the following Sunday. She hesitated, but did so; before she left Muskoka, the young woman schoolteacher had about one hundred names to present for church membership.[18] Soon she began assisting at revivals at Bracebridge, Gravenhurst, and Huntsville, and gradually farther afield.

In June of 1885 the Toronto conference of the Methodist Church commended Dimsdale to ministers 'who may desire her services in evangelistic work, but with the distinct understanding that she shall be under the direction of the superintendent of the district in whose district she is laboring.'[19] She was about twenty-two at the time. Apparently she was never a member of an evangelistic band, although she had another connection with the evangelism of laywomen: from the fall of 1884 until March of 1885 her younger sister Gertrude was in Orono as a captain in the Salvation Army. By December 1885 Gertrude was assisting her older sister in revivals, and until each of them married a Methodist minister in 1891, they conducted evangelistic services, sometimes separately and sometimes together.

Reports of these revivals appeared in the *Guardian* and in various local papers. The young lady evangelists aroused interest and apparently tended to win over those who initially questioned the propriety of evangelism by a woman. Thus, they helped prepare the way for the band workers and others who soon began to appear as revivalists. In the fall of 1887 Lyda Hall and Sadie Williams worked together in Marsville, Ontario.[20] Hall was about twenty-two years old, from Guelph, Ontario. Williams was older, about twenty-six. Her family lived on a farm in Simcoe County near Tottenham. Hall and Williams had both served as band workers,[21] and briefly they pioneered together as an evangelistic team.

Hall and Williams did not remain co-workers. Lyda Hall soon gained her younger sister Annie as a partner. Williams was capable of preaching and of leading the song service as well, and she laboured alone. She and the Hall sisters continued to work as evangelists for many years. By the end of 1900 each had figured in the *Guardian* reports of more than fifty revivals, and those apparently covered only a small portion of the revivals in which these women had participated.

As months and years passed, the names of many other female evangelists appeared in the columns of the *Guardian*, some only once or twice, others many times. At least twenty-five lady evangelists were mentioned more than once between 1885 and 1900; these women gave leadership in about three hundred series of meetings. Between 1901 and 1910 there were reports of at least half a dozen new Canadian lady evangelists, and of meetings at well over one hundred locations. While some of these women worked only briefly, others made an extended career of evangelism: Sadie Williams and the Hall sisters laboured for about twenty years, and Kathleen Morton of Toronto continued as an evangelist for almost thirty years, until after the Methodist Church became part of the United Church of Canada in 1925.

The revival reports on which this information is based were printed in order to encourage the faithful, so they spoke routinely of the gifts of the evangelist and the success of the revival. Only a serious problem could elicit a negative report. When the secular press in this period reported on Methodist revivals, it, too, tended to look on them with favour, and to speak positively about the leaders. Thus, it is not surprising that the testimony about female evangelists, like most of that concerning male evangelists, is strongly complimentary.

A few reports acknowledge that a female evangelist was a special case. A letter in the Orillia *Packet* admitted that 'Some object to a lady preaching and a few are not satisfied in other ways. Of course if a fault is wanted, it is very easy to find it, in not only Miss Dimsdale, but in any other minister of the gospel.'[22] The writer went on to say, 'As to a lady preaching, about the best test is, does God bless the means?' Like Captain Maggie Barker of the Salvation Army, who had worked in Orillia a few years before, L.H. Dimsdale was having results which should cause people to 'honor and give encouragement.'

A report about services in Wallaceburg later that year showed that a female evangelist could be either a liability or an asset. It explained that 'at the very beginning large numbers were attracted by the novelty of hearing a lady speak in public. Some, however, remained away on account of the prejudice that they entertained against ladies appearing in that capacity.' Later 'those who had come merely through curiosity began to be impressed.'[23] At Wallaceburg Dimsdale had proved herself. She continued to do so, and in November of 1890, the Strathroy *Age* commented: 'Indeed, if the Misses Dimsdale are a fair specimen of lady Evangelists, would there were more of them.'[24] The women came to be accepted.

They were accepted, and in many respects they were described in the same terms used for men who engaged in evangelistic work. Both men and women were 'earnest,' one of the characteristic virtues of the Victorian age.[25] They were consecrated: thoroughly consecrated, or fully consecrated, or wholly consecrated, or entirely consecrated – the variations seem endless. In 1886 J.R. Jaques listed seven principles of successful evangelists. The final cause of success was the evangelist's 'utter consecration.' Jaques went on to say, 'We know of no successful evangelist who is not a subject of sanctifying grace. Without this, he could do little in this office.'[26] Consecration in this sense was a necessary characteristic for any evangelist, male or female. It was not distinctive to women. Neither were the claims for their talent, their hard work, or their efficiency.

There were also many statements that the lady evangelists were sound in doctrine. Some correspondents reported that the women were 'scriptural in teaching,' others that they were 'Methodist in doctrine.'[27] It was especially important to note of women that they were thoroughly Methodistic. While many of the men active in evangelistic work were ministers, obviously none of the women were under this discipline.

For the same reason, some reports spoke of the relationship of an evangelist, male or female, to the local pastor. An evangelist who desired 'to run the minister' could be a problem.[28] Many reports praised the women's cooperation with the pastor. In this respect women were probably very acceptable evangelists, for they were well trained to be cooperative and subordinate.

Lady evangelists were cooperative. They were not, however, always subordinate. While L.H. Dimsdale, in particular, was commended for working with the minister and the people, reports show that she took charge of the meetings.[29] The Dimsdales may have been more independent than many of the later evangelists, but others, too, were often seen as conducting, rather than assisting in, revivals. Yet whether they conducted or assisted, there is never any hint of insubordination on their part.

A number of the reports comment on the mental abilities of the evangelists. According to the Woodstock *Evening Standard* on 17 January 1888 the Misses Dimsdale were 'neat, intelligent ladies,' and while we may wonder about the precise meaning of 'neat' at that time and in that context, there does not seem to be any question about the meaning of 'intelligent.' L.H. Dimsdale was 'logically sound,' and the discourses of the two sisters 'luminous and argumentative.'[30] Williams was 'systematic,' Katherine Morton's sermons 'well thought out,' and Annie Greene had a 'keen intellect.'[31] Those reading the reports were reassured about the intellectual qualities of the various women evangelists.

Other reports stressed the evangelists' powers of illustration. L.H. Dimsdale was particularly skilled at this. While many brief reports spoke of her 'apt illustration' and use of 'pointed incidents,'[32] some daily papers delighted in giving examples. On her second evening at Kingston, Dimsdale spoke to those within the church, but she reminded 'those outsiders who railed so much at the inconsistencies of members and like to hearthem "getting it," that a stain on a clean tablecloth was much more conspicuous than on a soiled one.'[33] She put common experiences to theological use in a way that suggests she had developed her skill as a teacher. Although this was a special ability of Dimsdale, it was mentioned of others, too.

Doctrinal soundness, cooperation, intelligence, and power of illustration are all characteristics that tend to be used more in describing woman evangelists than in speaking of their male counterparts. The most distinctive characteristics of the descriptions of women, however, are the references to emotion and personal relationship. It was in the nature of evangelists' work to make appeals, but the appeals of the women were much more frequently described. They could be earnest, of course, and tender, fervid, pointed, loving, touching, affecting, patient, persistent, or pathetic. Each of these was part of a positive, complimentary description of the work of a woman evangelist. Since women were perceived as being more emotional than men, they might be peculiarly suited for work as evangelists.

Emotion was an accepted component of revivals, yet this was a delicate matter. By the latter years of the nineteenth century, there were patterns of emotional behaviour that were no longer acceptable in Methodist evangelism. Thus, the reports offer assurance that both the revivalist and her congregation retained the necessary control. L.H. Dimsdale 'never loses her self-possession,' and the preaching and singing that she and her sister did were 'calculated to stimulate those better emotions of lapsed Christian professors and lost sinners.'[34] Morton might 'so [move] the hearts of the large congregation, that in every pew many were in tears who could not find room at the communion rail,'[35] but she 'does not aim at sensationalism or excitement.'[36] The St Thomas paper spoke approvingly of the Dimsdales' 'quiet, orderly' meetings with 'an absence of all excitement.'[37]

Women also displayed tact. Two references to the tact of the Hall sisters help to explain this puzzling terminology. According to a report from St Paul's Church, Avenue Road, Toronto, 'They are unassuming in manner, scriptural in their teaching, Methodistic in methods, and they display in their management of the inquiry meeting, exemplary tact and sanctified common sense.'[38] Tact was again connected with the inquiry meeting in a report from Kincardine: 'These young ladies have special gifts for this work; their singing is attractive, their exhortations and sermons persuasive and powerful, their tact in conducting the after-meeting equal to any emergency, while all their talents are fully consecrated to the Master.'[39] The women displayed particular sensitivity to those inquirers with whom they met following the main revival meeting.[40]

In addition to pathos and tact, a third characteristic was much more common in descriptions of woman evangelists than in those of men. That is the tie of affection between the evangelist and the people. An early example of this is the description of Gertrude Dimsdale departing from Kettleby: 'On Monday evening last she bid the people, whose hearts were filled with deepest regret, farewell, imploring them to continue their trust in the Lord; and from the many tears that coursed down we can safely assert that the whole community will unanimously wish Miss Gertie Dimsdale all the health, hope and happiness that may be bestowed upon a child of God wherever her lot may be cast.'[41] In Aurora the Dimsdales were familiarly styled 'our girls,' and in Guelph many accompanied them to the train station. The Strathroy *Age* printed a poem dedicated to them. The long story in which that paper reported their farewell service showed that affection was not all on the side of the people. The older sister told the congregation that the two of them regretted that they could not stay longer because 'we have become attached to this church and its people.'[42] While the Dimsdales received more extensive press coverage than their co-workers, the others, too, developed ties of affection with the people they served.

All three of these characteristics of the women's evangelistic work – pathos, tact, and affection – are connected with what had come to be seen during the nineteenth century as the nature of woman. As men had become associated with the public and rational spheres, women were seen as belonging to the domestic and emotional. Their talents were ones that enabled them to provide for the moral and spiritual welfare of their families.

Evangelistic work also spoke to moral and spiritual needs, and thus the same talents were useful in evangelists. While women might be unacceptable in some roles, or tolerated through necessity in others, the role of evangelist was one for which a talented and consecrated woman might seem especially suited. She was, after all, only doing what a Christian woman ought to do within her own family, using her special skills to encourage spiritual and moral development. She was simply doing this for a wider family, and in this era, that motivation made a broader role acceptable.

The suitability of women for evangelism was supported by the experiential, or 'experimental' nature of Methodism at the time. While the Methodists were extremely wary of any emotional excess, they were nevertheless convinced that religion must be based in the heart, in the personal experience of the believer. Thus, 'pathetic appeals' were appropriate to evangelism just as it was appropriate to women to make them.

For those women whose sense of call overcame their culturally trained reticence, evangelistic work was a suitable activity. For a few, it could even be a career. In the 1891 census, both the Halls and the Dimsdales were listed as evangelists. While both Dimsdales married that year, Lyda and Annie Hall continued work for another sixteen years, and others, too, had long careers.

A certain discretion was necessary, however. Letters to the *Christian Guardian* show that fees paid to evangelists could be a source of tension. A shadow of this controversy was cast over the proceedings at Kingston. The minister made it clear that 'never since Miss Dimsdale had been invited had she suggested that any remuneration was required.' The *Whig* went on to say that Dimsdale herself 'did not like talking about such matters, but as she had been subjected to indignities by persons saying she entered the work for the sake of making money it was necessary to defend herself.'[43] Whereas during the first two years she had borrowed money to meet her expenses, she was now able to pay them 'out of the gifts of those among whom she laboured. She loved the work and would go forward even if she got nothing.'

This delicate mention of money took place at the farewell service in Kingston; on that evening 'the collection was lifted, and as it was a thank-offering to Miss Dimsdale, a large sum, was realized, which has been further augmented.' This is how the evangelists were paid. Occasionally the amount was listed, ranging from $36.40 for Williams after three weeks at Chiselhurst, to $150 for the Hall sisters after five weeks in London. In addition the Epworth League there gave Lyda Hall a gold watch and her younger sister a purse containing a twenty dollar gold piece. Reports of gifts to woman evangelists regularly showed affection towards them, and a touch of local pride at the generosity of the community. Yet delicacy required that the money be seen as gift and not as payment.

This generosity is difficult to evaluate. During a revival evangelists probably stayed at a home in the community, so their earnings appear to compare favourably with those of many working women. However, the reports are so incomplete that there is no way to estimate how much an evangelist worked during a year, or how much money she received.

Like the question of money, the matter of a woman's making herself available for evangelistic work was delicate. For example, in 1887, after Dimsdale had conducted services in Guelph, W.S. Griffin wrote to the *Guardian* a high commendation of the youthful evangelist he had invited. He said in closing, 'Her name is L.H. Dimsdale; her address is Bell Ewart. It is perhaps unnecessary, but still it is true, to add, this communication is sent entirely without her knowledge.'[44] It would not do for a lady to appear to seek that kind of recognition! A woman's success in obtaining invitations depended on her reputation. That would be promoted mainly in the revival reports of the *Christian Guardian*, and the more detailed and enthusiastic of these frequently included information on how to reach the evangelist.

In the 1890s the *Guardian* printed notices of the availability of evangelists, but these announcements were always for men. The closest thing to an advertisement for a woman appeared very discretely in the *Guardian*'s column of personal news, giving Williams's address for any who might wish to secure her.[45] In 1914, when Morton was the only woman whose evangelistic work was reported in the *Guardian*, the notice was only slightly more direct. It, too, appeared as an item of personal news: 'Miss Kathleen Morton opens her evangelistic campaign this season with Rev. J.W. Totten at Prince Albert, Ont. Any of the brethren who wish to secure Miss Morton's services this winter had better write at once to 67 Maitland Street, Toronto, as she is now arranging her fall and winter's programme.'[46]

Despite this ambivalence concerning both payment and advertising, evangelism became the career of a small number of dedicated Methodist women. In 1891 the *Guardian* mentioned the names of seventeen women who conducted or assisted in a total of twenty-nine revivals. This is the largest number for any one year. Both Dimsdales married that year; one of the active evangelists died that December, and another the following year. A few, like Ella Birdsell and Inda Mason, became connected with Ralph Horner's holiness evangelism, and after 1894 their work received no further mention in the *Christian Guardian*.[47] Other women simply disappeared from the reports. Some new evangelists entered the work in the 1890s and in the first decade of the new century, but they never again rushed in as they had during the pioneering era of the Dimsdales and the band movement. There were changes going on in Canadian Methodism.

The situation for young women in the church was changing. A consecrated woman could now fill a new professional role, that of deaconess. The Methodist Deaconess Society was founded in 1894, and although women's response may have disappointed the promoters of deaconess work,[48] certainly the new occupation provided an outlet for the religious zeal of many young Methodists. There were no longer the evangelistic bands that had proved a training ground for young evangelists. Instead there was the structured, institutionalized Epworth League. As one of its activities, it allowed young women and men to take part in revival work. Consecrated young women could find outlets within the church for their energies, outlets that might not require such a bold commitment as the travelling evangelist had to make.

At the same time that revival work was becoming a part of the structured program for young Methodist men and women, evangelism tended to be professionalized. One sign of the times was the lay training institute opened by Dwight Moody in Chicago but commended to Canadian Methodists. While Moody favoured evangelistic work by both men and women, this kind of professional training required resources as well as commitment to make serious preparation for a career. The *Christian Guardian* in 1897 reported on the work in Canada of two men who had attended the school, but there were no reports of women.[49]

In 1907 eleven evangelists met in Toronto at the home of Hunter and Crossley to form the Canadian Association of Evangelists (Interdenominational). According to the report of the meeting, 'it is expected that all accredited Evangelists in Canada will join the association.'[50] Although a number of Methodist women were still actively engaged in revival work, all eleven founding members were men.

At the very close of the nineteenth century there were also signs of the institutionalization of evangelism. According to plans for the Twentieth Century Revival Movement, duly enacted at the general conference of 1899, a revival sabbath on 14 October 1900 would herald revival services at the beginning of the new century, in 1901. Those women who were still doing evangelistic work participated in this well-planned period of evangelism. This program, however, demonstrated a shift away from the kind of local initiative and enthusiasm that provided a congenial setting for much of the evangelism by women. The pattern continued in the church's plans in 1903 to observe the bicentenary of John Wesley's birth and in the increasingly structured and official attention given to evangelism.

Evangelism was changing as Methodism changed. As Phyllis Airhart has shown, the new progressivist piety continued to value revivalism, but transformed its emphasis.[51] The resulting 'new evangelism' stressed 'the need of personal religion in order that men may be prepared to assist in Christ's great work of redeeming the world.'[52] Thus, it included a strong interest in ethics and moral reform indicative of the developing Social Gospel. Mass evangelism differed in focus from that of an earlier generation. And so in Stettler, Alberta, in 1912 the conference field secretary for the department of Sunday school and young people's societies held evangelistic services twelve days. The central theme was 'service.' Those moved by the appeals could specify their intentions by filling out a pledge card which said:

Believing in the triumph of right,
Believing in a life of Service,
     I will enlist in the great cause of working for the good of humanity:
     1 Department of Citizenship ...
     2 General Practical service ...
     3 Missionary Efforts ...
     4 Sunday School Department
          (a) Cradle Roll ...
          (b) General School ...
          (c) Teacher Training ...
          (d) Home Department ...
     5 Young People's Work ...[53]

Evangelism had become organized by the denomination, and the energies of those responding were channelled into institutional structures.

For this new evangelism, women no longer possessed the advantages that had enabled them to enter the field in the late 1880s and early 1890s. Briefly, around 1910, there was such a flurry of interest in evangelism that the decline in the numbers of evangelistic women was temporarily reversed, but by 1914 virtually no women remained besides Kathleen Morton, faithfully arranging her annual program. Yet her work, too, had changed, for in 1920 she was described as working under the Brotherhood Federation, and in 1924 as 'sometime evangelist under our Department of Evangelism and Social Service.'[54]

In the mid-1880s several factors in their heritage and in the immediate situation had given Methodist women permission to become evangelists. The historic role of women in Methodism and the current activity of women in mission and reform movements helped set the precedent, and the success of the Salvation Army challenged the Methodists to make increased use of laypeople and especially women in evangelism. That many of the women succeeded was the result, of course, of their own consecrated talents. Yet they also owed their success to the fact that some of the characteristics considered uniquely feminine were also especially suitable for evangelists. They could address the realm of emotion and show sensitivity and affection.

As evangelism became part of the structured program of the denomination, revivalism by women declined. Those feminine characteristics that had seemed appropriate for evangelism in the 1880s were not relevant to the new evangelism. In addition, much of this new evangelism was carried out by those in professional church positions, positions to which women had scant access. Thus, the day of the female evangelist was past, and the memory faded quickly. As the Methodist Church became part of the United Church of Canada, there was little impetus to develop the Methodist mythology for a new generation of women, and this distinctive episode in their history was forgotten. Yet for more than two decades a unique set of circumstances within the Methodist Church and Canadian society had allowed a small but dedicated group of women to express their religious calling by forging careers as lady evangelists.

ACKNOWLEDGMENT

An earlier version of this paper, concentrating on the work done by female evangelists until the close of the nineteenth century, was presented to the Canadian Methodist Historical Society in June, 1987.

NOTES

1 Kingston *British Whig*, 5 Mar. 1888.
2 Reports of evangelistic work in the Methodist weekly newspaper the *Christian Guardian* (hereafter *CG*) form the basis of this research; where possible, this has been supplemented by local newspaper reports of revivals mentioned in the *Guardian*.

3 Wendy Mitchinson, 'Canadian Women and Church Missionary Societies in the Nineteenth Century: A Step Towards Independence,' *Atlantis* 2, 2 (1977), 62; Katherine Ridout, 'A Woman of Mission: The Religious and Cultural Odyssey of Agnes Wintemute Coates,' *Canadian Historical Review* 71, 2 (1990), 212–13.

4 *Woman's Missionary Society Annual Report*, 1885, 14.

5 E.H. Dewart, *CG*, 25 Feb. 1891.

6 See esp. Nancy Hardesty, *Women Called to Witness* (Nashville: Abingdon Press, 1984), 34–5.

7 Frances Willard credited the phrase 'home protection' to the Canadian temperance leader Letitia Youmans, but while Youmans used it only in a limited sense, in the United States it served to justify the diverse reforms in addition to temperance in which the WCTU in both countries became involved. *Campaign Echoes* (Toronto, 1893), introduction by Frances Willard.

8 Youmans's report of her anguish the first time she spoke in public gives some indication of what a radical step this could seem (*Campaign Echoes*, 127). A Presbyterian minister, hearing her conduct a meeting in 1883, observed that 'it was like an old fashioned Methodist revival' (*CG*, 19 Dec. 1883).

9 *Canadian Methodist Magazine* 5, 19 (1884), 372.

10 Ibid., 561.

11 See, for example, in the *CG* the letter by John B. Clarkson, 2 Apr. 1884, and an editorial 'New Methods of Work,' 9 Apr. 1884; in the *Canada Christian Advocate* see the lengthy article 'Special Evangelistic Effort,' 16 Apr. 1884.

12 *CG*, 16 Apr. 1884.

13 Charles Edward White, 'The Beauty of Holiness,' *Methodist History* 25, 2 (Jan. 1987), 70.

14 *CG*, 26 Nov. 1884; cf. 1 Oct.

15 *CG*, 10 Aug. 1887.

16 For example, *Canadian Methodist Magazine* 5, 19 (1884): 560; also *Observer*, 14 Feb. 1883; *Christian Journal*, 2 Mar. 1883; *Canada Christian Advocate*, 16 Apr. 1884.

17 *CG*, 5 July 1916.

18 *British Whig*, 5 Apr. 1888; cf. A. Sutherland's report to Toronto conference, *CG*, 24 June 1885.

19 *CG*, 24 June 1885.

20 *CG*, 9 Nov. 1887.

21 *CG*, 12 Dec. 1888; cf. *CG*, 10 Mar 1886; 13 Oct. 1886; and 10 Nov. 1886. Williams later used a collection of songs by Savage (*Manitoba Daily Free Press*, 31 July 1890).

22 Orillia *Packet*, 11 Feb. 1887.

23 *CG*, 28 Dec. 1887.

24 Strathroy *Age*, 13 Nov. 1890.

25 Walter E. Houghton, *The Victorian Frame of Mind, 1830–1870* (New Haven: Yale University Press, 1957), chap. 10.

26 *CG*, 24 Mar. 1886.

27 For example, *CG*, 30 Dec. 1896 and 29 June 1898.

28 *CG*, 27 Mar. 1889; 13 Mar. 1889; cf. 29 July 1891.

29 For example *CG*, 4 May 1887. The Strathroy *Age*, in fact, stated plainly of the Dimsdale sisters, 'They were not here to assist, as has been represented by an unfortunate item in the London papers of the 11th inst., but from the first took entire charge – preached all the sermons and conducted the services throughout' (13 Nov. 1890).

30 *CG*, 18 Apr. 1888 and 24 Apr. 1889. The description 'argumentative' would have been intended as a compliment; see, for example, *CG*, 28 Dec. 1892.

31 *CG*, 1 Jan. 1890; 23 May 1900; and 18 July 1900.

32 *CG*, 19 Nov. 1890; *British Whig*, 17 Mar. 1888.

33 *British Whig*, 6 Mar. 1888.

34 *CG*, 22 Oct 1890.

35 *CG*, 9 Nov. 1898.

36 Strathroy *Age*, 3 Mar. 1898.

37 St Thomas *Daily Times*, 24 Oct. 1898.

38 *CG*, 15 Apr. 1896.

39 *CG*, 24 May 1893.

40 This understanding of the word is corroborated by an article on 'Women's Work' printed in the *Christian Guardian* on 2 Jan. 1899, reprinted from the *Church at Home and Abroad*.

41 *CG*, 27 Apr. 1887, reprinted from the Newmarket *Era*.

42 Strathroy *Age*, 23 Oct. 1890; 13 Nov. 1890.

43 Kingston *British Whig*, 5 Apr. 5, 1888; for criticism of the financial demands of some evangelists, see *CG*, 9 Dec. 1891.

44 *CG*, 4 May 1887.

45 *CG*, 27 July 1898; 7 June 1899.

46 *CG*, 22 July 1914. Similar announcements appeared periodically throughout the rest of her career; see, for example, *CG*, 23 Apr. 1924.

47 See the chapter in this volume by Helen Hobbs for their impact on the life of Frank Goff in 1895. During the summer of 1893, they were among seven evangelists (six women and one man) examined by a Montreal conference committee concerning their methods of work and their relationships with the local pastors (box 5, file 18, Montreal Conference of the Methodist Church, Montreal-Ottawa Conference Archives, Montreal. I thank George Rawlyk for calling my attention to these records).

48 John D. Thomas, 'Servants of the Church: Canadian Methodist Deaconess Work, 1890–1926,' *Canadian Historical Review* 65, 3 (1984), 382. The United Church heirs of the Methodist deaconess movement are discussed by Mary Anne MacFarlane in this volume.

49 *CG*, 3 Mar. 1897, and 13 Oct. 1897.

50 *CG*, 11 Sept. 1907.

51 Phyllis Airhart, *Serving the Present Age: Revivalism, Progressivism, and the Methodist Tradition in Canada* (Montreal and Kingston: McGill-Queen's University Press, 1992), esp. chap. 3.

52 *CG*, 14 Apr. 1909. At the general conference of 1910, a general conference committee on evangelism was formed, but this soon became the committee on evangelism and social service.

53 *CG*, 7 Feb. 1912.

54 *CG*, 19 May 1920; 23 Apr. 1924.

10

'What She Could': Women in the Gospel Workers Church, 1902–1955

HELEN G. HOBBS

Women in the Gospel Workers Church were also beneficiaries of the Wesleyan tradition of women's work. Spirit-led women felt called to preach, and they were encouraged to do so. They tended to function in a shared leadership or collegial working style, forming teams of evangelists as they travelled from one revival meeting to another. In a very basic way, however, women who felt called to be workers in the Gospel Workers Church were placed in a difficult position: because marriage was considered to be women's ultimate fulfilment, those who did not marry suffered social stigma and emotional turmoil. Yet women were restricted by the expectations that they would raise a family and look after the household, and their opportunities as married church workers were severely curtailed. As the Gospel Workers Church became a denomination, it focused its energy on parishes rather than evangelism and accepted ordination as the norm for its workers. In this process women lost their earlier opportunity for ministry.

One of the most notable characteristics of the Gospel Workers Church in Canada[1] was that one-third of its leaders were women. For the first two decades of this century, Gospel Worker women exercised their gifts as preachers and evangelists to an extent that suggested virtual equality with men. Like many other evangelical and holiness denominations that trace their theological lineage to John Wesley, and for whom personal religious experience is central, the Gospel Workers gave substantial recognition to women's capabilities and authority, particularly in spiritual matters. As the movement grew past the fervour and enthusiasm of its formative years, however, limitations emerged that restricted women's formal participation and channelled their work into less visible spheres. Records of the early years indicate a positive and forthright attitude towards women as preachers; yet traditional views on the role of women, along with a shift in identity towards denominational respectability, subtly undermined the professional possibilities open to women. Within this context, however, with its distinct opportunities as well as its limitations, there emerges an account of a number of women who carried out significant ministries with an unusually high degree of recognition, given the time and the place of their activity.

The Gospel Workers Church began as a revival movement in the rural regions of Grey County Ontario at the beginning of this century. It flourished for some fifty years as an independent holiness denomination and then joined the Church of the Nazarene. Apart from a few evangelistic efforts further afield, its geographic range encompassed the area bounded by the towns of Owen Sound, Meaford, Collingwood, and Shelbourne, with concentration in the Beaver Valley area. At its peak, its members and adherents numbered four or five hundred, and its Workers, about twenty.

The group was well named. In spite of their small size, by 1903 the Gospel Workers had instituted a Bible school for the training of their leaders, and the next year they began publishing an eight-page religious monthly called the *Holiness Worker*. A ten-day camp-meeting near Clarksburg quickly became the major event of the year in the area. From 1902 to 1910 the Workers conducted almost continuous revival campaigns throughout the region as well as pastoring their growing number of churches.

Publications include a *Discipline* of 1909; *The Promised Enduement of the Baptism of the Holy Ghost*, a booklet explaining their doctrine of holiness; and a journal, the *Holiness Worker*, which appeared monthly from 1904 to 1955. In addition to annual conference minutes, some circuit reports, and a few examination results from the Bible school, we have a personal journal of one of the first Workers, Albert Mills. Here Mills assiduously records the details of the group's activities from 1902 to 1909.

The immediate background to the formation of the Gospel Workers Church provides insight into some of the factors that contributed to its openness in welcoming women and men as equal partners. Shortly after several denominations came into union to form the Methodist Church of Canada in 1884, Ralph C. Horner spearheaded a movement for spiritual renewal within the church. Horner refused to accept a pastoral appointment after ordination by Montreal conference, and became instead an independent evangelist, conducting revival campaigns throughout the Ottawa Valley. His continued defiance of church authority led to his removal from ministry in the Methodist Church in 1895, and he formed the Holiness Movement Church.

Horner's independent evangelical style furnished an example that inspired imitators. One such young Methodist was Frank Delormey Goff, who in turn founded the Gospel Workers Church in Canada. Born in 1873 on a farm in Sand Bay, near Gananoque, Ontario, Goff was first converted as a lad in a Methodist Sunday school class. In about 1894 he encountered Horner's movement, was 'reclaimed,' and a year later, was 'sanctified, and shortly after, baptised with the Holy Ghost' under E. Birdsell and J. Mason, two Hornerite women evangelists.[2] For the next few years Goff worked as an evangelist with a Hornerite colleague, holding meetings in tents and schoolhouses in Quebec and in Eastern Ontario. It is likely that at this time he was affiliated with Horner, if not in an official capacity, at least in doctrinal and spiritual alliance. There is some evidence to suggest that he eventually severed his affiliation with Horner over the same issue that had caused Horner's break with the Methodist Church: Goff believed that divine guidance as to where he should preach should take precedence over any human authority.[3]

This element of direct divine guidance is still central in the story of Frank Goff's call, as told some eighty years after the event by his son. Goff was in the field one day, cutting grain with a cradle, when he was overwhelmed by the feeling that he should go to Meaford to preach. Unable to resist any longer, 'He threw the cradle down, and said to the old cradle, "Stay there! I've got to go and preach." He had a message to go to Meaford. Now that was a word that came to him. Never heard of the place, didn't know anything about it: Meaford.'[4]

Frank Goff arrived in Meaford in 1898, set up a tent, and began to preach. A number of people were converted, and some were seized with a burning zeal to emulate the lifestyle and dedication of the dynamic young evangelist. Before long a handful of women and men left homes, schoolhouses, and farms, and threw themselves into evangelical work around the countryside. They called themselves the 'Holiness Gospel Workers.'

Goff's own Spirit-led, independent venture, and his roots in the Hornerite defiance of church authority set the stage: The movement was at first unstructured and charismatic, and individuals were guided only by the Holy Spirit. This equalizing force meant that women as well as men were free to follow the call to preach the gospel.

The group first conceived itself to be a renewal movement within Methodism,[5] and thus it also inherited the tradition of women leaders from John Wesley himself. Though initially cautious, Wesley had recognized women as preachers and evangelists because he saw souls won to Christ as a result of their ministry. This practical evidence he understood to be the sign of endorsement from God. Women had also been active in preaching ministries in the earlier years of Methodism in Canada.[6] In this regard, as in others, the Workers saw themselves recovering the almost forgotten paths of 'old-time Methodism.'

The Gospel Workers also considered themselves to be imitators of the primitive church. 'God is trying to get us entirely on Apostolic lines,' Albert Mills remarked in his diary. Though he was referring here more specifically to the need for unity of spirit rather than to a non-hierarchical structure, he also comprehended the latter as integral to the apostolic model. The Workers at first operated without a system of authority and without ordination; the Eucharist was celebrated by the laity.

Thus, the foundations were laid enabling full participation of women. During the first few years of the movement, women and men shared equally in the spontaneous activity of evangelism. Someone would 'feel led,' or receive a 'burden' for a particular area, and after prayer and consideration, join forces with another Worker who felt similarly guided. Together they would procure a tent or the use of a building or church and begin revival services. A sampling of the teamwork of women between 1902 and 1905 demonstrates something of the extent of their activity.

In October of 1902 Mary McCort and Fannie Comley conducted services in Riverview that lasted for a month. At the same time Elize Jolley and Mary Carruthers assisted in revival meetings held in a tent in Vamphlew's Grove, near Heathcote. The next year Elize Jolley and Fannie Comley teamed in a series of meetings in Vandeleur, of which they reported 'a grand revival and great interest.'[7] During June of 1904 Fannie Comley and Annie McCort held a revival campaign in Rome.[8] In July Annie McCort moved on to Markdale, where a United Brethren Church was at her disposal. She 'expect[ed] Millie Shunk to go along to help her.'[9] During this same summer, Nellie Wright and Elize Jolley were in Collingwood, conducting services at a 'mission' in the downtown. From January to March 1905 Annie McCort and Elize Jolley held a revival in Violet Hill.

Women and men also conducted evangelistic meetings together. From the evidence available, it is apparent that the women took a prominent role when they teamed with men. Albert Mills's diary provides a running account of each service in which he participated – complete with Scripture text of the sermons, the names of those who preached, the number of people converted or sanctified, and his own opinion on the success of the meeting. One such campaign was conducted in Bajeros in July and August of 1902 in which Mary McCort, Albert Mills, and Herb Wilcox were the leaders. Of the forty-one services, McCort preached at twenty-two, Mills and Wilcox each preached seven times, and five other visiting Workers (all male) took one service each. At another event in Osprey, in October and November of 1905, the roster for fifty-two services shows Albert Mills preaching twenty-one times, Nellie Wright twenty times, Albert Armstrong and Ben Heslop each five times, and a visiting Mennonite pastor once. Although these two campaigns are the only ones during this time in which Mills shared leadership with women Workers, such division of labour is probably representative of other meetings in which men and women shared preaching responsibilities.

It would seem that women were well accepted as co-Workers. Cautious both in criticism and in commendation of his colleagues, Albert Mills usually confined his record to brief summaries of their sermons. The occasional evaluative comment, however, reveals no discrimination between men and women in terms of their preaching ability. He criticized 'Brother

Wilcox' for 'going from Dan to Beersheba' in a sermon, and reported that 'Sister Wright had but little liberty this evening' as she preached. Wright apparently regained her 'liberty' in a subsequent sermon, however, and Mills was quick to commend her. 'Sister Wright takes morning service,' he wrote. 'She launches out well and is well filled. Glory to Jesus. She is running on a straight course to glory. Says sister Jolley and she feel like worms in Collingwood and God is using them to thresh a mountain.'[10]

Also on record are the comments of another male Worker regarding a sister Worker. In the spring of 1903 Reg Allan began revival services in Sundridge, and Elize Jolley later arrived to assist him. 'Miss Jolley is wading into the work,' Allan wrote to a friend. 'I know of no other at present that I would rather have with me as a Worker. She is strait and solid.'[11]

The decision to organize as a group and draw up guidelines by which the evangelists would be mutually governed laid the basis for the Gospel Workers as a separate denomination. In developing their structure and definition of ministry, they also established the place of women in preaching and pastoral roles.

In May of 1902 the Workers gathered, naming themselves the 'Holiness Gospel Workers,' a group of independent evangelists who formed a sort of specialized, autonomous lay order of ministry. It was not long, however, before they made the decision to organize yet more formally. Responsibility for the spiritual welfare of those who had been saved and sanctified in their services weighed heavily. Left to go back to the 'ordinary churches,' the 'deadly leaven of lukewarmness' would surely erode the new-found fervour of their converts. Even yet, however, 'organization' was not meant to produce a separate 'church,' though the construction of several places of worship was already being planned. It is necessary to keep this curiously ambiguous ideal in mind as it is consistent with who they felt themselves to be: Spirit-directed evangelists. Eventually somewhat attenuated, this perception persisted for nearly two decades, expressing itself in the mobile, evangelizing character of their work. It is encoded in the words of the Introduction to their Discipline, published about 1909: 'We have but one aim in organizing, and that was not to form another church, but to maintain a high standard of purity and uprightness among ourselves, and those who might unite with us, and to spread scriptural holiness throughout the land.'[12]

This self-understanding, with its reticence to be considered an actual denomination, is reflected in their attempt to simplify and equalize the definition of their ministry. They formally recognized themselves as 'members of conference,' a group of professional lay ministers, called 'Workers.' During 1902 and 1903 they revised the *Discipline of the Holiness Movement Church* for their own purposes. Their choice of terminology is noteworthy, as it demonstrates their effort to minimize hierarchical levels of ministry.

The categories of 'deacon,' 'elder,' and 'deaconess' were eliminated as unnecessary. Workers were 'ministers': 'preachers' and 'evangelists.' There was no need to distinguish between these terms, since all were engaged in preaching and evangelism. They drew up a certificate which provided for the ordination of preachers and evangelists, though it appeared that ordination was not meant to become normative. They rejected the title 'Reverend,' opting for the simple 'brother' and 'sister.' As a concession to legal requirements, they ordained Frank Goff at this point, so he could be licensed to perform marriages. This ordination, in 1903, did not affect the terminology: 'brother Goff,' though president of their conference, and their recognized spiritual leader, was a 'Worker.'

Thus, 'Worker' functioned as the common designation for everyone in full-time ministry. Though it can hardly be termed an 'order' of ministry, to all intents and purposes the system they devised places it in this category. Would-be Workers had to go through a probationary period as candidates. Following examination on religious commitment and character, they were admitted on probation, and expected to work in evangelistic efforts, thereby proving themselves worthy of their calling. After a year or two they were examined again as to spiritual well-being, personal lifestyle, and habits, and recommended to conference for acceptance as full-fledged members of conference: official Workers.

It appears that structures had been set up that would enable women to continue to function as full partners in ministry. But the issues of relationships and marriage soon began to draw a dividing line between the sexes. With men and women working together in such proximity, the Workers were aware that this closeness could risk bringing accusations of sexual impropriety. They devised a list of rules that 'Workers be advised to observe.' The first five of these cautioned against such things as staying in the same home with Workers of the opposite sex, remaining after meetings, driving, or travelling together unaccompanied. In general, they were to 'avoid all undue familiarity' with those of the opposite sex. The last two rules concerned marriage: 'Remain single til you have three or four years experience in the work' and 'Take no steps towards marriage without first consulting with the brethren.'[13]

Besides guarding the Workers against possible damaging rumours from the outside, these rules represented protection for the internal integrity of the newly born ministry that the group had undertaken. Marriage and its responsibilities would reduce mobility and dedication to the work for both men and for women. Marriage for women, however, 'naturally' involved virtual cessation of commitments outside the home, as pregnancy, child-rearing, and home-making took precedence. For the Gospel Worker women, marriage in itself did not automatically disbar them from being Workers, but in practical terms, it meant that by taking this step they were seriously jeopardizing, if not totally abdicating, their call to ministry. Thus, the 'call to preach' over against 'tempted to marry' was on occasion the subject of dynamic exhortation from the pulpit. Frank Goff spoke of the dangers of being 'trapped by the devil in the matrimonial snare.' Women who had 'fallen' into this trap had become 'monuments of misery' and thus stood as 'warning posts for all ladies, especially those called to preach the gospel.'[14]

This position was reiterated in another sermon by Alex McReady in a camp-meeting in September 1904. Here it was made abundantly clear that birth control was not to be considered as an option: 'If means are taken to prevent the natural results of marriage God will require precious blood at the hands of such murderers.' Albert Mills concluded his summary of this sermon with his own passionate plea: 'O that God would give us lady workers who would be straight on these lines and follow their holy calling, crucifying the flesh and all its lusts.'[15]

Thus, the position enjoyed by the women at the beginning of the movement was often dependent upon their remaining single. One woman recounted the spiritual and emotional anguish this caused her, as she struggled between the call of God to full-time 'active work' and the desire to marry. 'Satan took advantage of my affections and they became divided,' she wrote. Yet the call of God to 'live a single life for him' was clear: 'It was the most trying time of my life, and as I resisted the Spirit on this point, he left me, and "light became darkness". I not only held back from confession but held back from taking the step for God. – I was going to say 'make the sacrifice,' but it is a privilege God gives us of leaving all else to follow him hard though it may be.'[16]

Such was the difficult choice for women Workers. A few remained single and continued in full-time service until retirement. Others married their male colleagues and continued in active, though somewhat attenuated ministry. Still more drifted away, and the records give no indication as to the causes of their defections, but we may surmise that some of these women chose marriage and thus gave up the practical possibility of full-time service in the church.

Within these limitations – celibacy, or marriage to a Worker colleague –

the women fared relatively well in the ranks of recognized preaching minis-try. Compared with women's status in the Methodist Church at this time, for example, the Gospel Worker women enjoyed somewhat greater free-dom in the areas of preaching and serving pastoral charges.

The high profile of the Gospel Worker women may have occasioned some opposition, simply because women preachers were becoming more uncommon in established churches. The 1905 camp-meeting featured Bird-sell and Mason, two of the Holiness Movement women evangelists. In one of the services, after Birdsell preached and Mason gave the exhortation and invitation, 'a crowd at the altar' gathered which 'broke out in an uproar of prayer.' One observer remarked, 'I wonder what made those old women come around; before they came the meetings were all right but now they have set them all crazy.'[17] Both the style of evangelism and the preaching of women were under attack on this occasion.

Such instances of opposition prompted the Workers to defend their position on women from time to time in the *Holiness Worker*. The first of these articles was written in 1905 by George Short, one of the Workers. Entitled 'Should Women Preach?' it began, 'We meet some people who are opposed to women preaching, and do not receive the benefit they would, if they knew it to be scriptural. Let truth and error grapple on this as well as other subjects.' First offering examples of biblical women in leadership such as Miriam, Deborah, Anna, and Phoebe, Short moved on to some of the thorny passages in St Paul's writings. He concluded that these passages that opposed women in leadership applied only to the specific situation when they were written. Citing other Pauline passages, Short demonstrated that Paul had accepted women as co-workers in the gospel. In the manner of John Wesley, the writer summoned the witness of experience as defini-tive: 'One unanswerable proof in favour of women preaching is that God sets his seal on it by saving sinners and edifying the church.'

An expanded version of the same arguments appeared in the *Holiness Worker* in 1918, and again in 1934, in an article called 'Women's Sphere in the Church,' written by Albert Mills. His introductory invective against the opposition was scathing and direct. The 'foolish notion' that women should not preach was 'a relic of the dark ages and of heathenism.' He went on to affirm that 'Women's sphere is not limited to the duties of the family or household since she is often by nature and grace pre-eminently adapted for wider service.'[18]

Even though the Gospel Workers stood firm on this issue and upheld women's right to preach, yet their views on women's nature introduced a subtle yet growing conformity to cultural attitudes regarding woman's 'natural' role. As Mills's article indicates, woman's main sphere was indeed home and family, but this could be extended, since by 'nature and grace' woman was also suited for ministry. The extension beyond the domestic realm was an important concession, in keeping with their stated position and practice of women in ministry. But it did not challenge the fundamental premise that woman's main place was in the home.

As the years advanced, the pages of the *Holiness Worker* indicate a shift in the image of women. These changes reflect patterns and issues discernible in society at large. Changing fashions and looser mores in the years after the First World War resulted in an entrenchment in the Gospel Worker's position of modesty of dress and purity of conduct. The Gospel Workers had always been very strict in their notion of what constituted modest, appropriate dress. Wesley's advice[19] on simplicity of clothing had become a moral code: Plainness of dress was a standard which measured spiritual well-being. When men and women were converted, they frequently shed at the altar their tie-pins, ruffled shirts, jewellery, the feathers from their hats, and 'unnecessary' buttons. The Gospel Workers were filled with moral outrage by the daring and flamboyant dress of the postwar period. Their writings were aimed at women and implied an image of woman as seductress. Articles in the *Holiness Worker* blamed young girls for enticing men by their dress. 'The immodestly dressed woman is an enemy to society, a menace to the purity of our homes, and the integrity of our young manhood.'[20] One article quoted Finney: 'What does that gaudy ribbon and those ornaments upon your dress say to every one that meets you? It makes the impression that you wish to be thought pretty. Take care! You might just as well write on your clothes "No truth in religion."' Another addressed women in an imitation of Jesus' lament over Jerusalem in Matthew 23:37: 'O women, women, thou who uncovereth thy nakedness and enticeth strong men with thy cunning smiles, how often would I have covered thy fair neck and limbs and adorned thee with virtue, modesty and purity – and ye would not.'[21]

Regarding the temperance issue, the Gospel Workers also followed prevalent trends as expressed in articles from other religious publications. Woman's role was pivotal in the stabilization of family values. She was to nurture and guard the virtue of her husband and children and provide a loving environment so her husband would not be tempted to frequent the bar and saloon. The articles strongly reinforced the view of woman as the spiritual and moral chatelaine of the home.

These changing images of women no doubt had an impact on the consciousness of women who might have aspired to become Workers. By the time of the First World War, new women recruits had virtually disappeared. Of the thirty people who had been accepted by conference as full-time Workers between 1902 and 1908, ten were women. Two more women joined in 1916, and after this, only one more. This last woman worked sporadically as an evangelist during the six years of her probationary period, was admitted to conference in 1945, and resigned two years later.

The First World War and postwar period was also a time of general difficulty for the Gospel Workers. The denomination declined as the Pilgrim Holiness Church grew in the same area. Because of a decision to close the Gospel Workers school in 1922, young people wishing to be trained for ministry were sent to other holiness Bible schools. Many did not return, but became ministers in denominations such as the Free Methodists, the Holiness Movement, and the Pilgrim Holiness. It would have been more difficult for the women to follow this route, for these groups offered them a tenuous future.

In 1918 the Gospel Workers incorporated as a denomination, and this milestone marked a turning point in the development of denominational consciousness. This shift in identity also had anadverse impact on the professional possibilities for women. From a group whose primary activity was evangelism, the Workers became more and more focused on the ongoing work of the parishes they had established. Though their religious distinctiveness continued unabated, the desire to be recognized and respected within the community moved them towards conformity in matters of church structure.

At the beginning of the work, few Workers had been ordained. Ordination became more frequent, however, eventually resulting in an unmistakable hierarchy whose lines became coterminous with those of gender. All Workers were expected to complete the three-year program of study at their Bible school. Yet success – or failure – in this cannot be correlated with ordination. Conference records are silent on the reasons for the choice: A motion was simply passed that a particular brother be ordained. He was then examined for character and spiritual standing, and a service of ordination was held. Several women were also pastors on charges and were eligible. Yet none was ever put forward as a candidate, nor was a woman ever ordained in the Gospel Workers Church. Two years after Frank Goff's ordination in 1903, Albert Armstrong was ordained in 1905. Like Goff, Armstrong was married, with a family, and was settled on one of the larger charges. One more man was ordained in 1908, another in 1909, and one more in 1914. Then in 1917, the year before incorporation, the rest of the men were ordained. Even from the outset, then, it would appear that there existed an unspoken understanding that ordination was not appropriate for women.

In the conference records there continued to be no distinction between ordained and unordained: All Workers were simply listed under 'members present' until about 1912, when they were recorded under 'ministers present.' This remained the terminology to the end of the denomination's existence, with the important exception of the special conference held in May 1918 to deal with incorporation. Here, Workers were classified under 'ordained ministers present' (all male), and 'evangelists present' (all female except one man who was on probation). Ordained men had become an important mark of the credibility of their organization as it prepared to enter into full incorporation as a denomination.

Though dropped again in the conference minutes, the distinctions had been named, and they were significant. The use of titles became increasingly common in the pages of the *Holiness Worker*. 'Rev. Goff' was reported to have conducted a certain burial service, while 'Evangelist E. Jolley' preached at a given revival meeting.

By this time evangelism was no longer viable as a full-time profession, and the pastoral positions were increasingly filled by men. After Nellie Wright retired from the pastorate in 1922, only one more woman served briefly as minister of a parish. Bertha McAuslan pastored the Williamsford church for two years in the early 1930s. She eventually returned to her nursing profession to support herself, continuing however to preach in revival services or camp-meetings.

Although the women Workers became professionally marginalized, the status of the Worker meant that women retained some stature within the ranks of ministers in the denomination. Workers wererecognized as ministers even after the Gospel Workers merged with the Church of the Nazarene, as the inclusion of Bertha McAuslan in the 'preachers meeting' of the Nazarene conference attests.[22]

It is mainly from articles in the *Holiness Worker* that we have access to the voices of the women themselves. Several of them wrote brief articles for this paper almost every month over a number of years, and many others made significant contributions.

The contents of the paper are strictly of a religious nature, with articles that explain the doctrine of three works of grace: salvation, sanctification, and infilling by the Spirit.[23] Attacks on higher criticism and biological evolution occur from time to time, as well as articles on such issues as dress, white slave traffic, and temperance. For these, the paper depended heavily on reprints from other journals of like-minded denominations. There is almost no mention of historical events except as they touch on moral or religious questions. The years of 1914–18 and 1939–45 pass by with very little comment. One article by Louise Fletcher in 1914 entitled 'War Notes' begins by announcing, 'The war is on!' The war, however, is spiritual: It is between darkness and light, sin and righteousness. The Workers concentrated on doctrinal issues and spiritual values; in this, the women and the men were equally single-minded in their focus.

In expositions on the central theme of sanctification, women's writings carry a personal touch which testifies to their own spiritual journey into this experience. For example, the relationship between emotional state and spiritual well-being, a question that hounded the lives of many of the Workers, was resolved for Nellie Wright. 'Faith is not a feeling. You may have very strong faith in God and at times very little feeling,' she wrote. 'True holiness is the soul's haven of rest. Where there is faith there is rest, and when our faith is perfect there is perfect rest.'[24]

Annie McCort wrote of 'Loving as Jesus loved': 'Jesus' love knows no bounds. It embraces the earth, wrapping the entire world in a mantle of charity ... possessed with the same love as Jesus had, we will love largely and tenderly, with all harshness swept away.'[25]

A fuller account of the precise nature of sanctification appeared in an article by Louise Fletcher Mills. Here too, a theology of love emerged: 'Christian perfection or holiness is not absolute perfection,' she wrote. 'It is not the being perfect in knowledge, wisdom, or judgment.' Rather, it is the 'perfection of love,' in which 'the love of God fills the heart and flows out unhindered to God and to our fellow men.'[26]

A theme runs through the women's writings, reflecting a strong and confident spirituality in the midst of whatever limitations the women may have experienced: the importance of faithfulness in 'small things.'[27] 'In the vineyard of the Lord there is a place for each and every one of His creatures,' wrote Elize Jolley. 'Wherever we can labor for God, that is where He wants us, and whatever we can do, that is what He wants us to do. There is surely somewhere a lowly place where there is something we can do, and whatever our hand findeth to do, let us do it heartily as unto God.'[28] In an exhortation called 'Clay in the Hands of the Potter,' Louise Fletcher scolded those who did not use their talents because the results were insignificant. 'Shame on such expressions or thoughts! If the tiny dew-drops refused to refresh the drooping flower, because it wasn't a great downpour of rain, how many plants which today cheer us with their beauty and refresh us with their fragrance would have drooped and died?' she wrote. 'However small the mission, God needs you to fulfil it, and as the Father hath made us and we are all to be moulded by Him, surely he will not make any mistake in the moulding.'[29] In the same vein, Elize Jolley reminded her readers, 'It is the continual drip, drip, drip, of the rain that wears away the stone. Trifling efforts persisted in will accomplish more than spasmodic endeavours of greater pretensions.'[30]

In an article entitled 'God's Notice of Small Things: She Hath Done What She Could,' Nellie Wright commented on the story in Mark 14 in which a woman anointed Jesus' head with costly ointment: 'It may seem a small thing to have in your heart daily, that meek and quiet spirit and yet it is in the sight of God of great price ... These words, 'She hath done what she could' must have been precious to the woman to whom our text refers, as they came from our Saviour. I know of no other way to have the words of the text repeated of us, than by doing our best for God every day. Our best always pleases him. If you cannot go into the heat of the battle you can pour ointment on those who do, by holding up their hands in prayer.'[31]

What these women could and did accomplish was not insignificant. The original group of women spent from three to six years in evangelistic effort, preaching in tent meetings and doing pastoral work. A number of women married fellow Workers, and continued their ministry in teams. They worked in the same parish as their husbands, and during the early years, at least, the two were considered as co-Workers. They shared preaching, conducting of prayer meetings, and pastoral visiting. Both of them signed the monthly reports, they both studied the prescribed curriculum and sat examinations, and each was questioned by Worker colleagues in the annual 'private session' at conference. The ministry of these women in married teams was officially recognized.

One of these women, Mary Arthur, married Abe Shunk in 1902, and after farming for a short time, they felt the call to full-time service. They sold their farm, procured a large tent, and began revival services. 'She wholeheartedly went into the work and with her husband won many for the Lord.' After holding 'successful meetings in which many souls were saved,' they were stationed at Shelbourne, and then Collingwood.[32] Eva Latter Camplin and her husband pastored the Collingwood Mission from 1905 to 1909, then they returned to farming. Gertrude Black and Louise Fletcher each spent some years in evangelism, married fellow Workers, and continued as ministerial teams.

Sources provide very little information about the specific work of these women, except for the occasional report of preaching on special occasions. Recognition tended to diminish over the years. Louise Armstrong Goff, for example, had been a Worker at the beginning of the movement. Though she did not officially retain this status, she nevertheless spent a lifetime in ministry. Her obituary in 1942 reported that in the early years she had 'assisted her husband in evangelistic work, taking charge of the music and singing.' More recently, 'She was an active member in the home church, being an organist, Bible Class teacher, and frequently conducting services.'[33]

Slightly more data are available for those women who remained single and continued as Workers for life. Two such women are outstanding in this regard.

After the first few years in evangelistic campaigns, Nellie Wright spent all of her active ministry (1903–ca. 1922) in small parishes. She and Elize Jolley struggled to maintain the 'mission' in Collingwood from about 1904–5. Wright reported that 'it was a good place to work to have your faith increased for there was much to try it, but best of all was God was with us.'[34] After this she was stationed at Bayview, and later on a number of other charges. For several years she pastored along with Albert Mills on the Osprey circuit. Ill health forced her into an early retirement, but she continued from time to time to assist in revival services. Wright's almost monthly contributions to the *Holiness Worker* during her active years of service reveal a strong, dedicated woman, with an 'untiring spirit.' She believed in witnessing by example as well as verbally: 'We find it adviseable in working for God, not to say a great deal about dress, but if we live according to God's word, our dress will preach sermons to the unsaved.'[35] According to Albert Mills's assessment, Wright was a good preacher: 'She could preach, and when she did it was no soft gospel but a rugged, whole-souled message that would stir your heart and bless your soul.'[36]

Elize Jolley left her teaching profession to become a Worker in 1902. After her work with Nellie Wright at the mission in Collingwood, she took on the tasks of administration of the Bible school, and the production of the *Holiness Worker*. Both school and newspaper were housed in the Goff manse in Clarksburg, which in effect became the headquarters of the denomination. Together with Albert Mills and Frank Goff, Jolley devised the three-year curriculum for Workers and administered examinations. Responsibility for oversight of the various courses was divided among them, with Jolley in charge of grammar and composition, Old Testament history, and New Testament history. It is not clear whether classes were taught formally or whether there was an ad hoc tutorial system where Workers dropped in as they could, to study and be advised in their reading. Jolley lived in the Goff household, as did a number of other Workers for various periods of time. The second floor acted as dormitory for women

Workers, for whom Jolley functioned as 'housemother.' The third floor was for the men, and the attic housed the printing press for the paper. Jolley and Mills were assistant editors, while Frank Goff was the editor. It is reasonable to assume, however, that Jolley did a great deal of the work, since Goff's lack of formal education meant that he relied heavily on editorial assistance.[37] In addition, he was fully engaged in his comparatively large pastorate at Thornbury, as well as the smaller country point, Peniel. Albert Mills, too, was pastoring, though his work on the *Holiness Worker* should not be minimized: Its issues bear much of his stamp as well as that of Elize Jolley.

Jolley wrote regularly for the journal, both articles and editorials. She received and edited submissions from Workers and church members, read other journals extensively and selected articles from them, and assisted or managed the production process itself. She also continued her work as an evangelist, taking her place as preacher at revivals and the annual camp-meeting. Evidently she acted to some extent in the capacity as assistant pastor with Goff as well, since there are some records of her yearly number of pastoral visits. 'We should aim at being too busy to stagnate,' Jolley wrote. 'It is better far to wear out than to rust out.'[38]

Elize Jolley certainly did not rust out. As one of her many tasks, she was in charge of checking the women Workers' skirt lengths to make sure they adhered to the required modest length. On one occasion she made the mistake of asking Frank Goff's opinion if the skirt of a certain Worker could not be a little further from the ground. In order to pass judgment on this suggestion, Goff asked the Worker to raise her skirt a little to demonstrate the effect, and was soundly rebuffed. 'I've never raised my skirts for any man, and I'm not going to do it for you either, brother Goff!' declared Bertha McAuslan. The subject was dropped, and Jolley thereafter exercised her own control on the length of skirts.[39]

Jolley's marriage in 1929 to a prominent widower in the community, without consultation of her co-Workers, was in defiance of the rules. Yet she commanded such respect that when the issue was raised at the following annual conference, it was agreed immediately that she should remain a member of conference. She continued in her work as assistant editor and signed her name E. Jolley Dinsmore for another eight years, shunning the customary form, Mrs G.W. Dinsmore, which, however, she eventually adopted.

Jolley did not leave any writings on the role or the nature of women. A single phrase of commentary on Eve in the Genesis creation story sums up her position: 'God saw that it was not good for man to be alone, so He made him a helpmeet, gave him a wife one of whom Adam said, "this is bone of my bone and flesh of my flesh," neither an inferior nor a superior.'[40]

Jolley's strength lay in the area of spirituality. In one of her last editorials, she wrote: 'As we behold the beauty of the spring-time upon nature we are led to aspire unto the more glorious things of God in our spirit. We long to go from one stage to another until we are clothed with our house which is from heaven, until we can worship God in the beauty of holiness and until glory shall crown what grace has begun in our souls.'[41]

NOTES

1 The group first called themselves Holiness Gospel Workers (ca. 1900–1902). After organization (1903), they took the name the Holiness Worker's Church; at incorporation in 1918 they officially became the Gospel Workers Church in Canada. I choose to use this final name.

2 Albert Mills, 'Obituary' of Frank Goff, in the *Holiness Worker* (hereafter *HW*), Sept. 1944. Birdsell and Mason's roots were also in the Methodist Church, where they had formerly been engaged in evangelistic work.

3 Christopher McNichol, taped interview with R.G. and H. Hobbs, June, 1978.

4 Sam Goff, taped interview with R.G. and H. Hobbs, July 1978.

5 See R. Gerald Hobbs, 'Stepchildren of John Wesley: The Gospel Workers Church of Canada,' in *Papers of the Canadian Methodist Historical Society*, [CMHS] *1988 and 1990*, (Toronto: CMHS, 1991), 174–88.

6 See the chapters by Elizabeth Muir and Marilyn Färdig Whiteley in this volume.

7 Albert Mills's Diary, vol. III, 29 (hereafter abbreviated as AMD).

8 This must have been a very small community, as Albert Mills finds it necessary to describe its location: 'on the townline between Artemesia and Euphrasia, one mile east of the fourth line' (AMD IV, 97).

9 AMD IV, 55.

10 AMD IV, 38. This curious metaphor in fact represents a positive statement on the part of Nellie Wright. The allusion is to Isaiah 41:14, 15.

11 Letter from Reg Allan to 'Emma' (Shunk?), June, 1903; loose leaf in AMD at II, 63.

12 'Introduction,' *The Doctrine and Discipline of the Holiness Worker's Church* (Office of the Holiness Worker, Clarksburg, Ontario. n.d.).

13 Minutes of Conference, May 1902.

14 AMD IV, 140.

15 AMD IV, 82.

16 Mary McCort, 'Testimony,' *HW*, July 1907.

17 AMD VI, 34.

18 Albert Mills, 'Women's Sphere in the Church,' *HW*, Feb. 1918.

19 John Wesley, *Advice to the People Called Methodists with Regard to Dress* (London: John Parmore, 1780).

20 H.C. Morrison, 'Immodesty in Dress,' *HW*, Oct. 1917.

21 *HW*, Mar. 1926. untitled, unsigned.

22 Letter from Bertha McAuslan to Annie Kirk Short, Dec. 1959.

23 The Gospel Workers were rare but not unique among holiness churches in this particular doctrinal refinement.

24 Nellie Wright, 'Faith,' *HW*, Feb. 1907.

25 Annie McCort, 'Loving as Jesus Loved,' *HW*, Sept. 1905.

26 Louise Fletcher Mills, 'Christian Perfection,' *HW*, Apr. 1925.

27 Cf. Zechariah 4:10; see Nellie Wright, 'For Who Hath Despised the Day of Small Things?' *HW*, Oct. 1905.

28 Elize Jolley, from 'Editorial,' *HW*, Jan. 1925.

29 Louise Fletcher, 'Clay in the Hands of the Potter,' *HW*, Feb. 1904.

30 Elize Jolley, 'Perseverance,' *HW*, July 1914.

31 Nellie Wright, 'God's Notice of Small Things: She Hath Done What She Could: Mark 14:8,' *HW*, Sept. 1906.

32 'Obituary,' *HW*, Mar. 1954.

33 'Fallen Asleep,' *HW*, Mar. 1942.

34 Nellie Wright, 'Report from Collingwood,' *HW*, Aug. 1905.

35 Nellie Wright, 'Dress,' *HW*, Sept. 1905.

36 Albert Mills, 'Obituary,' *HW*, July 1951.

37 This detail was obtained orally from Annie Kirk Short, who worked extensively with Frank Goff on his booklet, *The Promised Enduement of the Baptism of the Holy Ghost*, n.d.

38 Elize Jolley, 'Editorial,' *HW*, Jan. 1925.

39 Oral tradition from Annie Kirk Short, who observed the scene.

40 Elize Jolley Dinsmore, 'Editorial: The Missionary Movement,' *HW*, Mar. 1940.

41 Elize Jolley Dinsmore, 'Editorial: Spring-Time,' *HW*, May 1940.

11

The Motor Caravan Mission: Anglican Women Workers on the Canadian Frontier in the New Era

MARILYN BARBER

Some women developed new roles in voluntary ministries such as the Anglican Sunday school caravan mission that served the frontier of western Canada. Most of its workers were advantaged and single British churchwomen who embraced both the adventure and the occasion for service that it afforded. The mission came to the prairies in part because the Anglican Church lacked pastors for its western work, and women seized the opportunity. The women workers were more effective than men in working with lonely women in isolated settlements, and they were therefore welcomed in this work. Probably no female church worker in Canada gave the lie to the myth of woman's weakness more strongly than did Eva Hasell. She not only initiated the mission and publicized it through her writing, but she also drove her own van around hairpin curves on the edge of mountains and over muskeg and corduroy trails, and made major repairs to the vehicle herself. Yet effective as the women were, they were seen as substitutes for male preachers, and they always occupied a subordinate position in their denomination.

After the Great War a few dedicated British churchwomen took the initiative in promoting women's work within the Anglican Church in the frontier regions of western Canada.[1] Through an itinerant Sunday school caravan mission and subsequent permanent community work, they reached out to Anglican settlers, especially women and children, who seemed abandoned by the church. Motivated not by feminism but by a concern for people's spiritual welfare, they did not directly challenge the male church authority. Yet, because of the shortage of Anglican clergy in western Canada, they acquired some of the powers traditionally reserved for men in the Church of England. The work might form an interlude before marriage, but it also offered an alternative to marriage at a time when popular culture celebrated companionate marriage and denigrated the spinster as an unfulfilled failure. An image of the woman churchworker on the frontier emerged, an individual who enjoyed travel and adventure, who embraced the independence symbolic of the frontier as well as the New Era, but who accepted the responsibilities of service, repudiating the pleasure-seeking consumer orientation of urban mass culture. Nevertheless, these women workers continued to occupy a subordinate position in a patriarchal church. Excluded from ordination, they might substitute for clergy but they could never carry the full spiritual ministry of the church to isolated settlers. Although professionally trained, they worked for little or no pay, reinforcing the tradition of women's voluntary religious service.

Ironically, on the western Canadian frontier where men outnumbered women, the Anglican Church suffered from a severe shortage of men for church work. The rapid expansion of settlement in the decade before the Great War left all the major Canadian churches struggling to provide for the spiritual welfare of the people. There were fewer Anglicans than Presbyterians or Methodists in western Canada at the beginning of the century, but the Anglican Church experienced the greatest percentage increase in membership before the war.[2] Escalating numbers of immigrants from England, many of whom at least nominally belonged to the Church of England, explain the magnitude of the task confronting the Anglican Church. Although the war created a hiatus in the immigration movement, the call to wartime service stripped Anglican dioceses in western Canada of their workers. With close ties to England, Anglican clergy and laymen alike hastened to enlist. Many never returned. The carnage of the Great War, which destroyed thousands of men, crippled the Anglican Church as it attempted to meet the challenges of the postwar era.[3]

The lack of clergy and male lay workers opened the way for women to extend their ministry within the Church in western Canada. It was not by accident that most pioneer women workers were English rather than Canadian. The majority of Anglican dioceses in western Canada were not self-supporting and relied on aid from the Church of England and English missionary societies such as the Society for the Propagation of the Gospel (SPG) and the Colonial and Continental Church Society (CCCS). Only gradually during the interwar period did the Missionary Society of the Church of England in Canada (MSCC) and the Women's Auxiliary (WA), based in Toronto and drawing primarily upon the resources of the eastern Canadian church, begin to share more equally in the support of the western Canadian mission field. The episcopal structure of the Anglican Church, which vested considerable power with each bishop, also enabled individuals to undertake mission work through the authority of a bishop rather than necessarily through the aegis of a central church body or missionary society. In England there were women of well-established families whose financial independence, religious commitment, and social confidence empowered them to use the opportunity for service.

Beginning in 1920 churchwomen took religious education to outlying districts through the innovation of an itinerant Sunday school caravan mission. Towards the end of the decade, they undertook more permanent community work in frontier regions that were not adequately served by a resident clergyman. Their offers of service built on the established foundation of women's sphere of work in the church in both Britain and Canada – Christian education and home visiting. Since the women most influential in initiating the work and the majority of the bishops in western Canada came from Britain, their assumptions were shaped by British traditions.

In England, from the Victorian period, the Church of England depended on female volunteers to teach the Church Sunday schools and to assist the parish priests with district visiting. Middle and upper class ladies had the leisure time to devote to the church. Religious training, an extension of domestic child-rearing, seemed an appropriate activity for them. Home visiting also fitted into women's domestic sphere. In both cases the work drew upon qualities that ladies were assumed to possess by virtue of their class as well as their gender. Churchwomen, sustained by their culture and their religious commitment, could give of themselves in the evangelization, care, and moral reformation of the poor.[4]

In tandem with secular society, as the Church of England moved into the twentieth century it placed greater importance on the formal training of workers. Training, however, did not significantly alter the nature of women's work within the church nor did it eliminate the reliance on volunteer labour. Education and social service, including nursing and reform work, formed the twin pillars of women's outreach activity. Beginning in the 1860s the establishment of deaconess institutions provided training and some recognition for full-time women workers in the English church. Best known was the Mildmay Institute in London founded in 1860 by an Anglican clergyman, William Pennefather. By the twentieth century deaconesses received a two-year course of training, including religious study, devotional instruction, and considerable practical experience in parochial work such as visiting, Sunday school activity, and mothers' meetings. While some deaconesses entered foreign missions or specialized in nursing, most became parish workers, assisting the local clergyman with parochial visiting, the care of the poor and sick, moral reformation, and religious education.[5]

The concern for training and the twentieth-century veneration of experts also led to the establishment of a specialized church training college for religious education. St Christopher's College, Blackheath, founded in 1909 by the Reverend William Hume Campbell, offered women a certificate course, originally of one year but then lengthened to two years. At St Christopher's, women combined theological study (New Testament, church doctrine, church history, prayer book) with the theory and practice of education (psychology, method of teaching, Sunday school organization, history of education, and practical teaching in local day schools and parish Sunday schools). As an alternative form of academic study and teacher training, St Christopher's attracted women with religious interests who sought more professional preparation. Often they came from the higher social echelons, entering St Christopher's as a result of personal contacts or recruiting in fee-paying girls' schools. Upon graduation, some worked as diocesan Sunday school organizers in England, giving leadership, support, and training to the volunteer teachers. Others used their training in missions overseas, especially in other countries of the British Empire such as Canada, Australia, New Zealand, South Africa, and India.[6] Not surprisingly, St Christopher's College became the main training and recruiting centre for those Englishwomen who developed women's ministry on the western Canadian frontier.

The St Christopher's graduate most active in promoting women's work on the western Canadian frontier in the 1920s was Eva Hasell, founder of the Sunday school caravan mission.[7] In 1920, at age 33, Hasell began the caravan mission which she controlled until the year before her death in 1974. Hasell purchased and equipped vans for the mission in part with her own money, generally using a van herself for a season before donating it to the appropriate diocese. In addition to scouting new territory in each diocese to be served by other vanners in subsequent years, she recruited women to work with the caravan mission and solicited funds for its support. Through an onerous speaking schedule in both Canada and Britain, articles in church periodicals, and the three books that she wrote about her work in the 1920s, Hasell publicized the Sunday school caravan mission.[8] She also used her influence to direct trained women to frontier regions where she perceived the need for more permanent community workers. Although all the vanners may not have fully shared Hasell's views, Hasell's voice dominated the portrayal of women's work in the caravan mission. More than any other individual, she shaped Canadian and British perception of Anglican women workers on the frontier in the 1920s.

Hasell came to the caravan mission with the advantages of a privileged class background as well as the training of a Sunday school expert. The daughter of the squire of Dalemain, Cumberland County, she enjoyed an active girlhood, riding horses, playing tennis, going on long walking tours, and travelling with the family. Independently wealthy after the death of her parents, Hasell could volunteer for church work without worrying about earning a living or support in ill health or old age.

Growing up in an intensely religious family, Hasell from girlhood felt called to serve the church overseas. She learned about western Canadian needs while raising money for the Archbishop's Western Canadian Fund (AWCF), a special appeal launched in 1910 to send itinerant priests and laymen to Alberta missions and the Regina railway mission. Enrolling at St Christopher's College in 1914, Hasell became friends with Aylmer Bosanquet and Nona Clarke who shared her Canadian interests.[9] Although the AWCF appealed for men, Bosanquet and Clarke negotiated to be included. In 1915 they were stationed at the railway mission centre at Kenaston, Saskatchewan, to begin Sunday school work and visitations in order to 'promote the spiritual welfare of the children on the prairie.'[10] The Secretary of the AWCF was reluctant to send gently nurtured women to the hardships of a prairie shack – and Bosanquet left behind the luxuries of an upper class lifestyle, well-trained servants, and a car and chauffeur. Undoubtedly both Bosanquet's offer to finance the expedition entirely herself and the general agreement that children's religious welfare was most appropriately women's work were important in securing acceptance for the two women.[11] Similarly, Hasell could implement her friend Bosanquet's idea for a Sunday school caravan mission not only because Sunday school activity conformed to women's sphere but because she had the money to finance the work. Taking a leave of absence from her position as diocesan Sunday school organizer in Carlisle, Hasell sailed with a companion from England in February 1920 to undertake the first Sunday school van tour.

Hasell designed the caravan mission to carry religious education to the scattered settlements of the west which were deprived of regular church services. The vanners travelled in pairs during the summer season, a trained expert in religious education being teamed with a companion primarily responsible for driving the van and coping with repairs, cooking, and washing. The exception was Hasell herself who with her extraordinary energy, dual qualifications, and desire to be in control served both as Sunday school expert and van driver. Vanners sought out the children in each district and taught them Scripture lessons using the books, pictures, and other Sunday school teaching aids which they carried in the van. If possible, they organized a Sunday school, enlisting a local teacher to carry on with instructional materials which would be provided. Otherwise, they enrolled the children for the Sunday School by Post, a correspondence school in religious education administered by the dioceses.[12] As a member of the Sunday School by Post, a child received lessons for study and mailed the answers to a central diocesan office for correction. Parents were asked to pay for the lesson materials, but the vanners enrolled a child without charge if the family could not afford the cost.

Hasell was convinced that only a sound religious education gave a child the moral foundation essential for life and for citizenship. Frequently, she deplored the restrictions on teaching religion in the state schools of the west, asserting that it was a hopeless task to try to train character if you were not allowed to teach the only thing that really mattered.[13] In her view, the Sunday school work was not supplementary but rather of primary importance in the education of the next generation.

Hasell sought to improve the lives of women as well as children. In her words, 'the van work was started by women for women.'[14] She insisted that the vanners must be women, and they were welcomed with gratitude by lonely women on isolated homesteads. As they travelled across prairie and mountain, the vanners found many dwellings where the woman was bearing the harsh burden of pioneer settlement. Confined by the care of young children and cut off from the nearest neighbour by almost impassable trails, these women seldom left their homesteads or had visitors. The chance to talk to another woman, especially one who had come partly to offer sympathy and support, allowed them to share their fears and problems. As Hasell reported, 'a large part of the caravaners' work is to try to cheer lonely women, who are very glad to see one of their own sex.'[15] To counter the emotional stress of isolation, vanners might connect the lonely woman with a friend in another part of Canada or in Britain who would correspond with her. For example, in a particularly tragic case, where a sad-looking woman had lost her two young children because their shack burned while she was taking her husband his dinner, the vanners brought some happiness to the woman by linking her to an outside friend.[16] Hasell claimed that there were many cases where 'one woman could best help another.'[17] Certainly, she herself frequently arranged medical or material assistance for worried or needy women who confided their troubles to her.

While she felt a strong bond of sympathy with those of her own sex, Hasell also believed that the van work had important national significance. She wished to give support to women for their own sake and for the building of a Christian country. A visit from vanners might provide a pleasant break in the lives of women who were coping successfully with pioneer conditions, refreshing and encouraging them. Such was the case of one woman in the Peace River block who walked a mile with her van guests when they departed, although she knew her husband and sons would laugh at her. It was, she said, so nice to see another woman.[18] Others, more unfortunate, possibly might be saved from mental breakdown brought on by loneliness as well as overwork and privation. At the Ponoka, Alberta, mental hospital where there were about seven hundred patients, Hasell saw some who had succumbed. To her, the women looked particularly pathetic as they sat with listless, drooping heads. Doctors informed her that only about 30 per cent recovered.[19] The Royal Canadian Mounted Police also told Hasell that the part of their work they disliked most was bringing lonely women down to mental homes.[20] To reach and reinforce both the strong and the weaker women seemed critical to Hasell because 'it is the woman who is faced with the essential problem of the nation, the rearing and training of the child.'[21] She argued that women vanners could carry out this church work more effectively than male clergy or students because a woman would discuss crucial moral problems only with another woman. Such confidences occurred most easily among women, not only because of the common bonds created by gender, but because intimate details could be shared in a less formal way with female vanners as they participated in meal preparation or household chores.[22]

To implement her plans for the Sunday school caravan mission, Hasell had to secure the approval of western Canadian bishops. With its focus on the religious education of children and visitation with women, the women's caravan mission conformed most acceptably to the established pattern of women's work within the church. After the Bishop of Qu'Appelle set the example in 1920, other western Canadian bishops in succession welcomed and indeed requested the presence of van workers in their dioceses. Because of the scarcity of qualified men, the caravan mission also became defined more broadly. Bishops and vanners agreed that the van workers must hold the ground for the church. Therefore, most vanners received special episcopal permission to take services where no clergyman or layreader was available. Since they could not give Communion, usually they held shortened matins or evensong. Hasell herself generally gave an address relating to the training of character, using Christ as the perfect model. The services might be held in a school or hall but also in the small local churches.[23]

While van workers on the frontier preached and led in public worship, women generally were excluded from these aspects of church ministry in both England and Canada. By the twentieth century, laymen could be licensed as layreaders and preach at regular services.[24] Laywomen, even those well trained in theology, did not have the same opportunities. Women might address audiences, usually limited to congregations of women, in schoolrooms or mission halls but not in consecrated churches. With the rise of church feminism in England during the First World War, a few militant churchwomen preached from Anglican pulpits at non-statutory mid-week services with the support of sympathetic rectors. Pressure for reform persuaded the bishops gathered at the Lambeth conference in 1920 to recommend that laywomen should be allowed to preach at non-liturgical services in consecrated buildings. Even this resolution, however, proved too radical for the lower house of Canterbury convocation which pushed church feminists back towards their proper sphere by limiting their right to preach 'normally to women and children.' Although English bishops differed in their interpretation of the ruling through the 1920s, at best they regarded women's preaching as an exceptional occurrence.[25] The Lambeth conference of 1930, which insisted that it wished to offer women

of ability, education, and training full scope for their powers and real partnership with those who directed the work of the church, produced only the
limited recommendation that 'Bishops give Commissions to women of
special qualifications to speak at other than the regular services.' In Canada,
too, church regulations in the interwar years continued to restrict women
from giving addresses or sermons in church as reported by the committee
on women's work in the church which responded to the Lambeth resolutions in 1935.[26]

The issuing of layreader's licences to women of the caravan mission
clearly gave them rights not normally granted to women within the church.
A number of considerations probably influenced the bishops' action.
Necessity undoubtedly was the most compelling. The women vanners
were the only workers available for many districts, and the need was
urgent. Clergy and vanners alike reported that neglect by the church led to
apathy and indifference towards the church among the people. Alterna-
tively there was grave danger of 'leakage' to the union movement which
produced the United Church of Canada in 1925. Vanners found that once
children had entered a Union Sunday school, parents naturally were reluctant to withdraw them. United Church students also attracted Anglicans in
districts lacking clergy. The most pernicious threat, however, seemed to be
the itinerant preachers of various sects such as the 'Holy Rollers' (Pente-
costal) and International Bible Students. As in the emergency of the Great
War when women temporarily took over work from men in both England
and Canada, so women were allowed to fill in for absent men in the western Canadian church. The difference was that the church crisis in the west
was not temporary but lasted until after the Second World War.

The same conditions which created the need for women's services made
the acceptance of women in non-traditional roles less difficult. Elizabeth
Jameson, examining women's history in the American west, has argued
that although work continued to be divided along gender lines, the spheres
were permeable. 'Men could and did cook, do housework, care for the sick
and dying, even deliver babies. Women could and did plow, plant, and harvest.'[27] Often the men had to be away from the homestead for lengthy periods, leaving the women in full charge. In such an environment, some
deviation from formal church procedures often seemed less important than
the practical ability to carry out the work. Hence, in the United Church,
the strongest pressure leading to the ordination of women in 1936 came
from western Canada.[28] Similarly, in the more conservative Anglican
Church, women workers on the western frontier were allowed a much
more limited but nevertheless real extension in their ministry. Van workers

who came to the bishops as Sunday school teachers and home visitors, rather than as militant or even moderate feminists demanding equal rights, did not appear threatening to the established order. Bishops could grant them layreaders' licences more readily because their main work remained convincingly within women's sphere.

Van workers also received a warm welcome from bishops and settlers in part because they volunteered their services. They worked full time during the summer, and winter placements were incorporated later to save the cost of transportation if possible. Vanners were asked to pay their own way if they had the resources. Those unable to donate more than their hard work received return travelling expenses, their board, and insurance against accident and sickness.[29] In a society that so often equated the value of work with monetary recompense, voluntary service normally lacked the status of well-paid employment. The church, which relied so heavily upon volunteer activity, tried to promote a different value system, one emphasizing the importance of giving as opposed to the materialism of twentieth-century society. Men as well as women might be asked to volunteer their services. For example, the clergy and laymen sent to Canada by the AWCF received their travel expenses, an outfitting grant, board, and only £2 a month for purely personal expenses.[30] Similarly, the Fellowship of the West, founded in 1929 to send itinerant clergy and laymen to the northwest following the example of the women's caravan mission, asked men to work without being paid.[31] Nevertheless, the men volunteered their services within a church structure which assumed that they should receive an adequate salary for permanent work; women did not.

Women provided most of the volunteer labour for the church; therefore, the lack of salary for the vanners diminished the distinction between the full-time trained expert and the part-time untrained volunteer. In the 1920s when single women sought greater economic independence, the caravan mission perpetuated older assumptions that middle-class women would depend on others for support. Hence, unpaid women vanners were sent to districts that could not afford the stipend for a resident clergyman. Hasell, with her independent income, did not recognize the problems and echoed church complaints against the materialism of the modern age. While some Anglican teachers volunteered during the summer holidays, van work appealed particularly to well-born women who, like Hasell, had family resources to compensate for the lack of salary.[32] Hasell tried to recruit in Canada through speeches and advertisements in the *Living Message*, the periodical of the Women's Auxiliary, and agreed to give priority to Canadian applicants. Nevertheless, the majority of the vanners in the interwar period were British, perhaps because, as noted by the Canadian committee on women's work in the church, 'The situation in Canada and in England [is] not parallel. The great majority of the outstanding women workers in England belong by birth to the leisured class and have had the opportunity not open to many for leisurely education, for informative contacts, for personal experiment.'[33] Canadian women with professional training could find more financially attractive opportunities outside the church in the 1920s.

Although the caravan mission did not provide a salary, it did offer single women travel, adventure, and considerable independence in their work. Western Canada may not have seemed as exotic a missionary destination as Japan, China, or India, but, especially for British women, it had the attraction of a distant, if less foreign, land. Many van workers ventured into regions only recently settled by Europeans. Unlike British travellers who crossed the country on the trans-Canada railway, visiting major cities and the resorts in the recently developed national parks of Alberta and British Columbia, vanners followed trails which were often poorly marked, and visited people in their homes. As vanners camped, hiked, and rode horses when necessary to reach remote settlers, the work appealed to those who enjoyed the outdoors.

Although definitely not a lyrical writer, Hasell in her books referred many times to the beauty of nature: the broad dome of the prairie sky, brilliant sunsets reflected in the sloughs, and a kaleidoscope of colourful prairie flowers competing with the spectacular mountain scenery. In addition, frontier conditions gave the vanners more autonomy than enjoyed by most female church workers such as the deaconesses employed in urban centres as assistants to parish priests. Their situation resembled that of public health nurses who had more freedom of action than hospital nurses. Vanners sometimes obtained advice and direction from clergymen whose territory they passed through, but they worked under the authority of the bishop. Freed from close supervision, they assumed the responsibility for organizing and implementing their own work.

Life as a van worker challenged individual stamina and endurance. Recounting her own experiences in the three books which she wrote, Hasell conveyed in considerable detail the hardships and difficulties of the work. To ensure that the women who applied for van work were physically fit, they were required to have a recent doctor's certificate stating that they were strong enough to undertake the work in any altitude, especially regarding their heart and nerves.[34] Hasell wanted vanners to be self-sufficient and not impose on the people whom they hoped to help. Vans were equipped with mattresses, non-perishable food, and a portable burner for cooking meals. Because of the cramped conditions in the van, vanners also carried a tent which they pitched whenever possible beside public buildings, in private yards, or open fields. While some of the weather was delightful for camping, Hasell and her companions suffered from drenching rains, scorching heat, frost at the beginning and end of the season, and hordes of mosquitoes and blackflies. Hasell described numerous occasions when she had to meet adversity with fortitude. One time when forced to camp at the bottom of a hill because the van was stuck in the mud: 'It was pelting with rain and we could not light the primus though we were soaked to the skin and very cold. We remembered, however, that there was a post office a few miles ahead, so we walked to it. It was hard going in our heavy rubber boots, with waterlogged skirts, and we could scarcely keep our feet on the slippery clay. On such occasions Blanche [her teammate] reminded me that I was a Guider.'[35] Determined not to miss isolated settlers, Hasell would tramp twelve, fourteen, or even twenty miles in a day to reach families inaccessible by road. The mosquitoes that plagued settlers in the northwest attacked the vanners too. Hasell tried to secure an undisturbed sleep by putting up netting on the van and killing large numbers of insects inside the van before retiring. Outdoors, protection proved more difficult. Walking for nine hours in the cool of the night to visit isolated families near the Peace River, Hasell and her companion Iris Sayle met clouds of mosquitoes. 'We could not talk for fear of swallowing them. As we walked the mosquitoes settled on our legs in brown masses.'[36] Sayle marched along with her macintosh over her head sacrificing vision for protection. Thinking of the long hikes through difficult terrain in adverse conditions, Hasell declared that her present occupation was much harder than farm work during the war.[37]

The driver of the van also needed mechanical skills more commonly acquired by men than women. Not only did the driver have to be able to manoeuvre the van on primitive and often dangerous roads, but she had to repair the vehicle if it broke down in the middle of the prairie or on the side of a mountain. The use of motorized vans identified the Sunday school mission with the technological progress of the twentieth century. Although the wealthy owned cars before the war, the more common use of motor vehicles during the 1920s made the automobile an important symbol of the postwar era. Hasell had considerable practice driving as she had been allowed to use the family cars during the war years for her diocesan Sunday school work in the steep hills of England's Lake district. Since their chauffeur had been called up and mechanics were scarce, she learned to do her own repairs. She acquired additional expertise when she drove an ambulance for the Red Cross in England. This practical familiarity with motor vehicles led her to substitute motorized vans for the horse-drawn Sunday school vans initially suggested by her friend Bosanquet. With a motor vehicle, vanners could cover a much greater territory and did not have to depend on borrowing farm horses during the busy agricultural season. Hasell ordered the first van to be copied from a couple already being built in Saskatchewan for travelling missionaries. She chose a Ford truck chassis because Ford parts could be obtained at small village garages and hardware stores, and she had spare gas tanks added for more fuel capacity in sparsely settled regions.[38]

It was not unusual for women to drive cars in North America in the interwar period. Ruth Schwartz Cowan, who investigated the impact of technology on women in the American home, states that 'automobile driving was not stereotypically limited to men,' and concludes that the work of middle class American women increased as they became chauffeurs for family needs.[39] Nevertheless, in 1920 it was not customary for women to drive long distances across the prairie. Hasell reported that the men in the Winnipeg shop where she took repair lessons 'seemed to think it was not fit for two women to go out alone on the prairie, as in Western Canada women hardly ever drive outside the towns, and never do their own running repairs.'[40] Hasell tried to recruit Canadian ex-service women who had driven motor ambulances or transports in the war to serve as van drivers but found that most required a salary. She was more successful in England where driving motor vehicles during the war tended to have been an occupation of upper class women who already knew how to drive a car. Hence a number of van drivers during the 1920s were English ex-service women.[41]

Driving a van, particularly in the mountainous regions, could be almost as dangerous as war work. In her books, Hasell dwelt more on the difficulties and perils of the road than she did on the religious activity. On one level she presented a realistic serial account of the discouraging trials which vanners might encounter. Simultaneously, though, her books read like travel adventure literature with the women travellers heroically overcoming great obstacles in pursuit of their goal or quest. Travel formed an integral part of the mission, absorbing much of the energy of the vanners. A number of the trails which Hasell followed were too new to be marked on a motor map. Made of earth only without any stone, the trails were heaped in the middle with a steep drop on either side so water could drain. Frequently, gopher burrows, loose soil or roots, and large holes, some five feet deep, impeded progress. On the prairies, fierce duststorms driven by high winds created almost impassable drifts on the trails. When the roads became greasy, Hasell put heavy chains on the wheels to try to cling to the top of the trail. In areas of muskeg or swamp, she drove over rough corduroy trails which were very destructive of the van's springs. Crossing streams caused even more concern because the only bridges were logs simply laid in place and often broken or prone to roll. The vanners felt the greatest fear on the steep narrow mountain tracks cut into the edge of cliffs. Hasell described how, on a particularly bad descent, she managed to negotiate the van around two hairpin turns by driving almost over the precipice, only to fail at the third and lowest. The van slid off loose gravel down the twenty-five-foot drop, hit a boulder, and landed on its roof. Yet Hasell crawled unharmed through the broken window, her face protected by her panama hat from the dripping battery acid which had burned holes in her clothes.[42] Unfortunately, the vanners did not emerge unscathed from another accident. Although westerners often used the railway tracks as a road for their vehicles, Hasell found the tracks to be a danger rather than an assistance. When the van broke down once at night on a level crossing, she had to execute repairs to the transmission very quickly in order to avoid the Edmonton to Calgary express train. Later in the same tour, at another level crossing with a steep gradient, a freight train struck the van gravely injuring Hasell's companion, although Hasell herself was less seriously hurt.[43]

Hasell supplied quite detailed information on the mechanical operation of the vans. 'Onlooker,' who introduced her second book, felt compelled to explain that Hasell was writing for other practical motorists, but Hasell obviously derived satisfaction from her mechanical knowledge and skills. She remarked that she was the only woman in the Winnipeg shop where she took lessons on Ford running repairs and rather snidely added that, judging from the sound, western women seldom even oiled the engines of their vehicles.[44] Hasell clearly conveyed her own competency in diagnosing and fixing problems and her frustration when garage mechanics did not prove so efficient. For example, while on tour in Alberta: 'Before tackling the steep hills of our next route, I took the van to a garage to have the transmission bands renewed. I stayed to watch this being done, to make sure that the mechanics did it properly and did not charge me for a longer time than they worked. The man was a very poor mechanic, and kept dropping and losing the bolts and screws. Whenever this happened he always exclaimed "Jesus Christ!" till I could stand it no longer and told him that I would finish the work myself.'[45] The rough jolting journeys necessitated frequent repairs. In addition to mending tires which burst on sharp stones, Hasell had to cope with more complicated problems such as a broken spindle controlling the steering or a worn sleeve in the drive-shaft. Even ordinary maintenance required constant attention. In storms, Hasell covered the engine with a waterproof sheet to protect the wires and spark plugs. In colder weather, she drained the water from the radiator each night. She had little control, however, over the gas which often contained water because it came from barrels outside small country stores. Consequently, she had to lie under the van to drain the contaminated gas from the carburettor, a horrid experience, because first water and then gas trickled onto her face while she was prone, usually on a very muddy road.[46]

The image of the vanner created by this publicity had qualities very appealing to the symbolic 'new girl' of the 1920s who was athletic and adventuresome. Yet in other ways this image contrasted sharply with the dominant cultural ethos of the 1920s. At a time when popular culture emphasized female sexuality and much of the glamour of the working girl came from her proximity to men, vanners continued the older tradition of bonds with women. While modern fashion dictated slim trim lines and the careful application of cosmetics for an attractive appearance, vanners required sturdy boots and durable clothing, and when they toiled through the mud, they had little chance even to wash. Because Hasell herself dominated so much of the publicity, the contrast appeared even more striking. A short but hefty woman, Hasell did not have the figure for the new styles, nor did she worry about fashion. The first year she brought an English landworker's outfit, a smock and breeches, but found that some Canadians objected to the display of 'limb.'[47] Thereafter, she appears in photographs in a felt hat and baggy skirt, with a blouse or jacket of khaki. There is a hint in the books, however, that not all vanners followed Hasell's lead in abjuring modern fashion. Doris Miller of Toronto joined Hasell for a summer after her mother heard Hasell at a Toronto WA meeting and mother and daughter together read *Across the Prairie in a Motor Caravan*. A photograph of 'Doris doing chores' in *Through Western Canada in a Caravan* shows Doris, young, pretty, with fair curly bobbed hair, wearing a low-necked gown of satiny sheen.[48] Even an absence of sexual allure did not deter western bachelors, more than one of whom, seeking a strong useful helpmate, asked Hasell whether she was married. Yet the dominant image of the asexual spinster missionary may help to explain why Hasell had difficulty recruiting Canadian women for the work.

By 1930 the caravan mission had expanded to fourteen vans and twenty-eight workers, with twenty-one of the twenty-eight vanners from Britain. With the needs of the Depression and war period, the mission continued to grow during the next two decades, peaking in the 1950s.[49] Complementary to the itinerant caravan mission, permanent settlements of Anglican women workers also developed on the frontier. Recognizing the need for continuity in the work begun by the vanners, Hasell was instrumental in recruiting Marguerita Fowler, who began the Order of St Faith's in the Diocese of Brandon, and Monica Storrs, who became the guiding light for women's work in the Peace River block. Fowler and Storrs, both English-women in their forties when they came to the frontier in 1928 and 1929 respectively, extended the kind of community services begun by the van-ners. They carried on weekly Sunday schools, started youth groups such as Guides and Scouts, and organized summer camps. In the absence of a cler-gyman, they took services, baptized babies, and buried the dead. Because they served a scattered population, they, too, spent much time in difficult travel, on foot, by horse, and by car. Sponsored to a large extent by a Brit-ish organization, the Fellowship of the Maple Leaf, which took up wom-en's work in the 1930s, communities of women workers spread from these centres into other western dioceses. Like the vanners, the community workers also came primarily from England and volunteered their services in return for expenses and a small honorarium if necessary. Although ini-tially recruited for a short-term service of two or three years, many of the women, like Hasell, devoted their life to the work.[50]

Anglican women workers represented the church for many isolated set-tlers on the Canadian frontier in the interwar period. They extended wom-en's ministry in the church to include taking services, an intrusion into the male domain which could raise fears of the feminization of the church. One correspondent of the *Canadian Churchman* who strongly advocated the need for more caravanners nevertheless foresaw disastrous consequences if the women were allowed to preach: 'Many godly young women, enthusias-tic over the scheme when it is fully grasped, and mechanically inclined young women to drive and care for the cars would be forthcoming were a greater effort made to place this form of service before our virile young adventurous Canadian womanhood. Instruct them to baptize wherever the need. No ordination is needed for this and there is no need for licensed women preachers. When that comes we will lose the rest of our men from Church.'[51]

Although Hasell once characterized frontier congregations as a preach-er's paradise, she did not place emphasis on the importance of women preaching. A true educator, she valued most highly the work of guiding and moulding the next generation. Often described as dominating and autocratic, Hasell fought when necessary to maintain control of the Sunday school caravan mission, thus asserting female leadership in her chosen field.[52] Rather than asking equal rights for women, she implicitly worked for a re-evaluating of women's sphere. Yet the continued voluntary nature of women's work on the frontier diminished its professional status and directed its appeal primarily to well-born Englishwomen.

NOTES

1 Throughout the chapter, I have used the modern title, the Anglican Church (of Canada) rather than the earlier more cumbersome title, the Church of England in Canada.
2 *Fourth Census of Canada*, 1901, I, 144–5; J. Burgon Bickersteth, *The Land of Open Doors* (Toronto: University of Toronto Press, 1976), xii–xiii.
3 David J. Carter, 'The Archbishops' Western Canada Fund and the Railway Mission,' *Saskatchewan History* 22 (Winter, 1969), 19–21.
4 Brian Heeney, *The Women's Movement in the Church of England, 1850–1930* (Oxford: Oxford University Press, 1988), chap. 2, 'The Volunteers'; Martha Vicinus, *Independent Women* (Chicago: University of Chicago Press, 1985), 74.
5 Heeney, *Women's Movement*, chap. 3, 'Paid and Professed Workers,' 68–74; Vicinus, *Independent Women*, chap. 2, 'Church Communities: Sisterhoods and Deaconesses' Houses.'
6 Heeney, *Women's Movement*, 36–7; Certificate and Newsletter No. 46, Jan./Feb. 1979, St Christopher's College Association File, Muriel Hooper Papers, 1:18, Anglican Diocese of Ottawa, Synod Archives.
7 Vera Fast, *Missionary on Wheels: Eva Hasell and the Sunday School Caravan Mission* (Toronto: Anglican Book Centre, 1979) provides a good biographical study of Hasell and her work, but it does not analyse the mission from the perspective of women's place in the church.
8 The books are *Across the Prairie in a Motor Caravan* (1922), *Through Western Canada in a Caravan* (1927), and *Canyons, Cans, and Caravans* (1930).
9 Fast, *Missionary on Wheels*, 18–24.
10 Carter, 'Archbishops' ... Fund,' 21.
11 *Across the Prairie*, 4, 21.
12 G.A. Kuhring, ed., *The Church and the Newcomer* (Toronto: Church House, n.d.), issued by the Joint Committee on Education of the Church of England in Canada, explains the origins and work of the Sunday School by Post, 105–11.
13 *Through Western Canada*, 23, 41, provides examples of this conviction.
14 Fast, *Missionary on Wheels*, 44.
15 *Canyons, Cans, and Caravans*, 204.
16 Ibid., 229.

17 Ibid., 42.
18 Ibid., 207.
19 *Through Western Canada*, 131–2.
20 Fast, *Missionary on Wheels*, 77.
21 *Through Western Canada*, 58.
22 Ibid.; *Canyons, Cans, and Caravans*, 204.
23 *Through Western Canada*, 11–12, 23–5.
24 Heeney, *Women's Movement*, 79.
25 Ibid., chap. 6, 'The Last Barrier: Pastors and Preachers'; Sheila Fletcher, *Maude Royden: A Life* (Oxford: Basil Blackwell, 1989), 173–200, 239–40.
26 *Women's Work in the Church*, Report by a Committee of the House of Bishops, 1935, Anglican Church in Canada, General Synod Archives.
27 Elizabeth Jameson, 'Women as Workers, Women as Civilizers: True Womanhood in the American West,' in *The Women's West*, Susan Armitage and Elizabeth Jameson, eds. (Norman: University of Oklahoma Press, 1987), 150–1.
28 Mary E. Hallett, 'Nellie McClung and the Fight for the Ordination of Women in the United Church of Canada,' *Atlantis* 4, 2 (Spring 1979), 2–16.
29 Fast, *Missionary on Wheels*, 47.
30 Carter, 'Archbishop's ... Fund,' 14.
31 Mary Naylor, *The Fellowship of the West*, published by the Bishop of the Anglican Diocese of Montreal.
32 Fast, *Missionary on Wheels*, 44–8.
33 *Women's Work in the Church*, Report by a Committee of the House of Bishops, 1935, 10.
34 *The Living Message*, Feb. 1939, 59.
35 *Through Western Canada*, 99.
36 *Canyons, Cans, and Caravans*, 195–6.
37 *Through Western Canada*, 129.
38 *Across the Prairie*, 5–7, 30–1.
39 Ruth Schwartz Cowan, *More Work for Mother* (New York: Basic Books, 1983), 82–5.
40 *Across the Prairie*, 28.
41 Ibid., 107–8; Arthur Marwick, *Women At War, 1914–1918* (Fontana Paperbacks in association with the Imperial War Museum, 1977), 75–8.
42 *Through Western Canada*, 191–3.
43 Ibid., 139, 149–56.
44 *Across the Prairie*, 28.
45 *Through Western Canada*, 48.
46 Ibid., 93.
47 *Across the Prairie*, 8.

48 *Through Western Canada*, 176.
49 Fast, *Missionary on Wheels*, 44, 120.
50 The Fellowship of the Maple Leaf also sent British teachers, doctors, and nurses to western Canada. See also W.L. Morton, ed., *God's Galloping Girl: The Peace River Diaries of Monica Storrs, 1929–1931* (Vancouver: University of British Columbia Press, 1979) and Marguerita D. Fowler, *The Story of St Faith's* (London, Society for the Propagation of the Gospel, 1950).
51 *Canadian Churchman*, 19 Jan. 1928, 'Letters to the Editor.'
52 See Fast, *Missionary on Wheels*, 54–62 and 95–100, for an examination of Hasell's conflict with the Joint Van Committee and the Colonial and Continental Church Society, as well as for an assessment of Hasell's personality.

12

Faithful and Courageous Handmaidens: Deaconesses in the United Church of Canada, 1925–1945

MARY ANNE MACFARLANE

In some Protestant denominations women could be employed as deaconesses. They tended to be viewed as handmaidens or angels of mercy who brought help to those in need. Thus, they laboured under poor conditions and with low pay. For decades, those in the United Church of Canada also worked under the disadvantage of a 'disjoining' regulation that required them to resign from the deaconess order if they married; fulfilling what was considered to be their natural destiny abruptly ended their professional career. Some were able to seize the opportunity of the moment. During the Second World War, a number of congregations hired deaconesses as ministerial assistants because of the shortage of male ministers. Yet this episode demonstrates the fragility of such occasions: when the moment ended and the men returned from the war, the women discovered how transitory their opportunities had been.

The work and the political struggles of deaconesses in the United Church of Canada, a group of professional female workers specializing in education and pastoral care, show a pattern in common with other types of women's work. Diaconal tasks were both defined by and subtly limited to a persuasive theological and functional understanding of women that described them as servants or assistants: workers whose purpose was to meet the immediate, various, and ever-shifting needs of the growing church. Because of this, deaconesses were consistently located in low-status, behind-the-scenes, and supportive work that served to enhance the public, visible ministry of the male ordained clergy.

Deaconesses were originally referred to as 'handmaidens' in the United Church's service for their installation; though the term was eventually dropped, the image continued to structure both the expectations and the treatment of deaconesses as workers in the church. The understanding of handmaiden turned on constant availability to others and included all of the following aspects: limitless quantities of work, emphasis on responding to needs, invisibility of the work, separation from decision-making processes, and low status and remuneration.

This gendered and hierarchical ordering of work in the church proved remarkably difficult to dislodge. Over the years, the church actively rejected many of the attempts by deaconesses and their supporters to raise their status, expand their roles significantly beyond that of servants, and gain access to the decision-making positions in the church. The story of deaconesses illustrates how both the structures and the ideology of the United Church, with its liberal tenets and its emphasis on cooperation and equality of the sexes (without an accompanying analysis of its own structures, teachings, and practices), tended to operate against the interests of women workers and to maintain powerlessness, oppression, and invisibility for both lay- and professional women.

During the evolution of the deaconess order in the United Church from 1925 to 1945, questions of strategy, of how to maximize efforts for recognition and fair treatment, and how to be heard within an essentially patriarchal institution became large issues for deaconesses. They showed great creativity and patience as they worked for recognition both for themselves and for other women in the church: It took forty years for them to receive fair salaries and to be 'given the vote' in the courts of the church. In 1964 thirty-seven years after the first report to general council had recommended their inclusion within a diaconate as part of the order of ministry, and after many years of political work on their own behalf, deaconesses were made members of presbyteries in the church and became part of the 'unordained personnel' salary scale of general council. The beginning years of their struggle – and their triumph – are recorded here.

At the time of church union in 1925 the new United Church of Canada inherited two well-established deaconess groups with very different histories, self-understandings, and educational centres. The work of uniting the three denominations, Methodist, Presbyterian, and Congregational, offered the church an opportunity to remedy some existing and well-documented problems in deaconess work. But, instead, it perpetuated old structures and practices.

Methodist deaconesses came into church union with an accumulated variety of grievances resulting from poor working conditions, low salaries, no visibility, and no linkage to the official courts of the church. Expectations of their work were unusually high. Their duties, voluminous and only loosely defined, were usually oriented towards education and social service: deaconesses met the needs of the disadvantaged. They visited the sick and bereaved; found people housing, employment, and money; looked after travellers and immigrants; conducted Sunday schools, clubs, and domestic education classes for women and children; did secretarial work; provided country or 'fresh air' experiences for poor inner-city families; taught reading and Bible classes; and led Sunday services when necessary.[1]

For all of this, they were guaranteed minimal living expenses and provision for old age, and they received only a small spending allowance in lieu of salary, often as low as $8 to $10 a month.[2] In 1923 a Commission established to investigate the problem had confirmed the deaconesses' accounts of their experiences and attributed their dissatisfaction to an insensitive administration, poor salaries, and unrealistic expectations by employers. The report also suggested that many of the problems occurred because of the narrow way in which such women were perceived as mere 'servants' of the church.

Although the evolution of Presbyterian deaconess work was less tumultuous than that of its Methodist counterpart, evidence suggests that the Presbyterian Church, too, had problems associated with the salary, working conditions, and status of deaconesses. Presbyterian deaconesses had been working for salaries for many years and had more autonomy both in their choice of work and their personal living conditions, but they were still restricted to 'servant' roles. They were expected to plan for their own futures and to provide for themselves in old age; therefore, they received slightly higher salaries than did their Methodist counterparts.[3]

The new United Church quickly established an inter-board committee on women workers to take responsibility for directing the deaconess order and 'for studying the whole question of a permanent policy regarding the scope and supervision of the Deaconess Order and of other trained women workers in the United Church.'[4] The committee took on the task of preparing a service for the 'setting apart' of deaconesses for the *Book of Common Order.* The term chosen to describe deaconesses in the service of designation was that of 'handmaiden.' Drawing heavily on the scriptural account of Mary and the Magnificat, and on the story of the Last Judgment in which Christ rebukes those who do not give assistance to those in need, the service included within its description of deaconess work a wide variety of 'feminine' ministrations:

To you are accorded peculiar privileges and opportunities. Released from other cares, you give yourselves without reservation, according to the will of God, to the service of the Lord and of His Church, wherever your lot may be cast ... You are to go about doing good, ministering to the wants of a suffering, sorrowing and sin-laden world. You are to be angels of mercy to the poor, to visit the sick, pray with the dying, care for the orphan, seek the wandering, comfort the afflicted, save the sinning and ever be ready to take up any other duty proper to your calling.[5]

A prayer in the service asked that, in order to accomplish such work, deaconesses be given 'singleness of heart, simplicity and humility.'[6] Naming deaconess work in this way both drew upon and reinforced the tradition in which the church perceived and treated women as humble servants, constantly available and responsive to the needs of individuals and groups.

In 1926 the new committee on employed women workers began to gather information about women's work in the church. Though the committee members had suspected that there were many women at work in a variety of enterprises and that some working situations were bad, the results they uncovered amazed them. The committee located a total of 951 women employed in the work and institutions of the United Church. Over one-third were employed by the Woman's Missionary Society (WMS) and worked in other countries or in Canada in community missions, hospitals, Native schools, French-Canadian churches, missions in Nova Scotia, and in Chinese and European communities. In addition, they were employed in social service work in Montreal, Timmins, and Winnipeg, and in children's work in Vancouver and Toronto. An additional 106 worked in clerical and secretarial positions at church headquarters, and 212 within educational institutions. Of the total, only thirty-one did congregational work that was not secretarial.

One hundred and sixteen of these women were members of the deaconess order. Twenty-four deaconesses worked in self-supporting congregations, their duties ranging from church secretary to outreach worker. Other deaconesses worked in urban social service centres, in hospital visitation programs, at schools for girls, in the Toronto Strangers' Department, and in the production of educational and pastoral radio programs for isolated communities.[7]

All women workers for the WMS came under the organization's salary scale. For 1927 the annual starting salary was $800 with $25 increases for each year of previous service, to a maximum of $1,000. Salaries for overseas workers varied from one country to another, but were, like the earnings of their counterparts in Canada, consistently lower than those of other women in comparable occupations.[8] The committee also reported a lack of adequate general educational background and specialized preparation among many workers and stated that 'on the whole the standards have been low in light of the significance and importance of the tasks assigned.'[9]

The report also gave details of remarkably diverse salary and working conditions, some extremely poor. Individual employing bodies set their own policies for employment, salary, furlough (that is, paid leave), and superannuation, and they rarely cooperated with each other. As a result, women performed the same work under different conditions for radically varying rates of pay, and there was no procedure or structure to monitor such in-equalities and deal with them.[10] Women were not only isolated one from the others, but they also were on their own in securing fair treatment from their employers. Such a chaotic system kept many women isolated in places where their contributions and skills were neither respected nor valued.

To deal with these massive problems the committee recommended to general council that there be one level of preparation for women workers in the church, and that the women be united into a diaconate that would create a second part of the order of ministry. All women who had the necessary qualifications would be members and could participate more fully in the work and decision-making parts of the church. The recommendation, however, was turned down by general council. Instead, the council created another committee to recruit women workers, promote their employment, and initiate and maintain standards for their training and work. The new committee had no power to legislate changes in salaries or working conditions, but was to work instead through consultation and moral persuasion. The same general council established a minimum annual salary of $1,000 with increases for experience to a maximum of $1,200, 'the full remuneration to be paid to the Deaconess monthly, she being responsible for her own living expenses.'[11]

The new committee began its work with the help of an executive secretary who interpreted church policy, screened applications, and helped with the placement of new deaconesses and those wishing to change their work. In addition, she acted as a confidante for churchwomen across the country by maintaining contact through newsletters and visits. She advised them on personal and job-related problems, shared information about marriages and family deaths, and referred to herself as a friend: 'Be sure to drop me a note if you need a friend any time.'[12] Her work helped to break down some of the loneliness of the women who worked in congregations and social agencies and who had little contact with other deaconesses.

The new committee's first task was to review a number of policies agreed to during the period 1926 to 1928. One regulation that the board supported was that deaconess candidates must be 'not less than twenty-three, and not more than thirty-five years of age.'[13] The committee also reaffirmed that deaconesses could not continue to work or maintain membership in the order once they married. Constructed originally when deaconess orders were modelled on sisterhoods and included communal living arrangements, this rule proved difficult to dislodge, even though deaconesses now had much more independence and were expected to provide for themselves and live in the secular community.

The regulation required a deaconess to resign from her position and from the order by letter previous to, or on, the day that she was married. The procedure was called 'disjoining' and remained a part of the manual and constitution of the deaconess order until the late 1950s. Its effect on women was softened in 1953 when the committee on the deaconess order and women workers, the successor to the inter-board committee, began to allow individual deaconesses who married to keep their positions and remain in the order, if both they and their employers wrote letters formally requesting it.

The rule was kept in place by a theology and a societal expectation that a woman could not and would not want to combine the roles of wife and of paid worker outside the home. For all women, marriage was seen as the natural and legitimate primary commitment, and extra-domestic work was never to be permitted to interfere with it. Such a rule also applied to other caretaking professions such as nursing and teaching, though both of these won concessions for married women long before deaconesses did. The dominant ideology in each case proclaimed that women's nurturing and caretaking capabilities were, first of all, given for the 'calling' of family care and maintenance; only secondarily, in cases of spinsterhood or widowhood, could they be applied to wage-earning. Marriage and motherhood were seen, by definition, to include economic, social, and emotional dependence on a man. The church's theology on this was made explicit in the 1932 report entitled 'The Meaning and Responsibilities of Christian Marriage.'

Because of regulations such as the disjoining rule, issues of workload and inadequate remuneration were not taken seriously. It was assumed that deaconess work was not a career or a long-term occupation. In the short term, women were to endure poor working conditions and salaries because marriage, the real vocation, was not far ahead for most of them. Many saw deaconess work as some kind of preparation for real life, that is, for marriage, and the women who were deaconesses were frequently characterized as young and immature, less experienced than their ordained colleagues, and less serious about their work. Because of this, many believed that deaconesses needed supervision and constant advice to do their jobs and could be paid poorly and given little autonomy or authority in decision-making. In actuality, almost half of the deaconesses at any given period in the church's life did not marry, and ended up spending their entire lives in church work.

The disjoining rule disadvantaged women in several ways. It kept them out of contact with other deaconesses and out of the workforce for long periods of time. Because of this, deaconesses found it difficult to get back into the order and to secure positions if they were widowed or divorced. A number of women left deaconess work to care for members of their families such as ageing parents, a caretaking role that was assigned by society to single women. They, too, found it difficult to return to paid church work. As a result there was a constant decrease in the numbers in the order every year, and the creation of an impression that deaconess work was not long term, not seriously a vocation, and definitely secondary in importance to the ordained male profession.

Though in the years immediately after church union well over nine hundred women had been employed within the church, in the 1930s these job opportunities began to disappear. An excess of ministers resulting from the closing of some churches after church union, and the beginning of the Depression years combined to decrease women's work opportunities. Deaconess boards, autonomous organizations within the church that employed deaconesses to do social work, were also forced to disband in the early 1930s, curtailing even further the opportunities for deaconesses to do traditional types of community and benevolent work. The whole church was experiencing serious financial difficulties and had to struggle to hold the line in relief work, to continue vital social work, and to keep open as many as possible of the home mission fields across Canada. Though the WMS managed to keep most of its projects going throughout these years, many other employing boards did not. Many large congregations cut their staff to one ordained man.

By 1932 the situation was so critical that the committee stopped actively recruiting diaconal candidates. By 1936 the admission process to the United Church Training School included writing to prospective candidates, even those who were the most qualified, to inform them that their prospects of any employment after graduation were not very great. The staff of the school was cut back and the principal remained the only full-time member of the academic staff during the Depression and the Second World War.

When assessing the employment situation for deaconesses, the committee saw a potential for women's jobs as ministerial assistants in congregations and began promoting deaconesses as Christian education specialists, as secretary-deaconesses, and as social ministry assistants. Yet there were several problems associated with positions in local churches. The structuring of congregations frequently left deaconesses subject to the whims and evaluation of one person, the ordained minister, who had very different training and understandings of the church from those of deaconesses. Ordained ministers often had little comprehension of deaconess work in Christian education and social service, and little appreciation of deaconesses's enabling and supportive leadership styles. Yet they supervised deaconesses and represented them on the church committees and boards where deaconesses still had no official position.

In addition, those women who helped with Christian education programs could not be present for Sunday worship held at the same time, and thus they were not visible or known to many church members. In some congregations few men and women had direct knowledge of the work of deaconesses. To deal with this, some churches formed deaconess committees to assist in the work and publicize it, to raise funds, and to work for better salaries and working conditions.

Secretarial duties had often been a component of deaconess work. During the Depression, deaconess jobs could be saved by assigning clerical work that was both visible and indispensable in the eyes of the congregation. Though the United College in Winnipeg, Manitoba, had taught secretarial skills as a part of its curriculum for deaconesses since before church union, it was not until jobs became scarce that clerical work was formally incorporated into descriptions of deaconess work, and given official recognition with the title of 'secretary-deaconess.'[14] While the creation of this position did save some jobs for women, it also led to the overwork of many who were expected to accomplish a complete range of deaconess duties plus a whole new set of secretarial tasks. In many cases, this was not a new job, but the addition of a whole new set of responsibilities to a job that was already too large and diverse. Combining secretarial and educational functions also blurred the congregation's perceptions of diaconal work. In some cases, the deaconess came to be seen as a glorified secretary, very expensive and not particularly qualified, rather than as a skilled professional with specific training in Christian education and social ministry.

In 1936 the same general council that approved the ordination of women moved to create a new standing committee to deal with deaconesses in the church. Within it was lodged considerable power concerning recruitment, policy-making, and supervision of the working conditions of all deaconesses. The committee was staffed by a full-time secretary and was to publish a manual on the deaconess order that would both interpret the history and self-understanding of deaconesses and put into print all of the regulations concerning their candidacy, work, and retirement. In addition, the committee was to devise ways to keep in closer contact with deaconesses and to support them during difficulties on the job. Deaconesses were expected to consult with the committee concerning all appointments and transfers, to submit yearly reports of their work, and to seek the committee's advice on all job-related problems.[15]

The job description for the executive secretary focused on recruitment, administration, representation of deaconess's interests on committees and boards of the church, liaison with churchwomen's associations, and production of publicity and press releases related to deaconess concerns. For the first time, the secretary was to sit on all the boards of groups that employed deaconesses. It was hoped that this direct representation would lead to more effective work on salaries and employment conditions and would increase the opportunities available for deaconesses in the church. The secretary was to visit universities, presbyteries, normal schools, and high schools to recruit deaconess candidates.

In 1938 Lydia Gruchy, the first woman to be ordained in the United Church, left her work in the pastorate to become the executive secretary of the committee on the deaconess order and woman workers. Contributions towards her salary were solicited from women's groups across the country. Promoters of the deaconess order saw the formation of this committee and its financing by the women of the church as a vote of confidence in their work and as the beginning of a stronger movement for justice for women workers. Though initially unfamiliar with the specific workings of the deaconess order, Gruchy was very concerned about the absence of women from leadership and policy-making positions in the church. In a 1939 editorial in *Women and the Church*, she observed: 'What we find is that women are active in the work of the Church but not to any appreciable extent in the formulating of its policies. Sunday Schools are staffed preponderantly by women. Yet while women are on the committees dealing particularly with Children's and Women's Work, the general boards which consider the principles governing Christian Education are composed mainly of men. The same is true of community work.'[16]

Beginning in 1939 the employment prospects and work done by deaconesses and other women changed dramatically, partly because of a shortage of male ordained personnel created by their enlistment in the armed forces and by their resignations to take other employment. By 1942 the shortage of ordained clergy was so critical that the executive of general council was asked to stop the resignations of ministers, to prevent clergy from taking secular jobs, and to enlist women as assistants who could serve in large congregations in place of a second ordained minister. Furthermore, the executive was urged to declare that 'the preservation of such institutions as the Christian Church is of supreme importance, and ... its ministry is as vital to the well-being of the nation as any war industry for which manpower is needed.'[17]

As early as 1939 individual churches, unable to secure an ordained minister, hired deaconesses as lay supply ministers. Such women were asked to do all of the work of an ordained minister, yet were given none of the privileges of the clergy. They could not vote in presbytery or be involved in any of the decision-making processes of the church. Nor could they administer the sacraments during worship. For this, an ordained minister was called in to officiate. Though many of the women employed in these positions performed admirably and were respected in their congregations, they were seen as exceptional, as temporary, as 'less than' an ordained minister. They were praised publicly for 'holding down the fort' while the shortage of ordained men continued, but there was little understanding that their work had an integrity within itself and was making a distinct contribution to the practice of ministry. It was always assumed that when the war was over, things would return to normal, every church would want a 'real' minister, and deaconesses would quickly be replaced.

The shortage of ordained ministers and the rapid development of new churches in war-industrial areas led church officials to re-activate their recruitment policies of the past and to create new programs and training models that would place women workers quickly into both established and new places of work. The committee on the deaconess order and women workers promptly authorized the production of folders and posters, and set up meetings in high schools and universities across the country. In print and in speeches, promoters of work for women used images that both militarized women's work and appealed to women's patriotism and faith. Thus, the executive secretary of the committee on the deaconess order and women workers, in a 1944 radio broadcast, urged women to 'be a part of the spearhead of the attack against existing evils and play [their] full part in winning Canada for Christ.'[18]

Some of the recruitment material patronized women by implying that the qualities of loyalty and hard work needed now were rarely displayed in females and were available to them only in emergencies and extremely rare circumstances. Little doubt was left in the mind of the reader that what was being asked of women in wartime was considered unique. The recruitment folder *A Full-Time Vocation for Christian Women* stated that 'many of these women [are in] difficult and responsible positions which offer inducements, not of high salaries or easy hours, but of opportunity to do real work, interesting and worthwhile, with scope for vision and initiative ... The present war emergency accentuates the need for a rigorous and courageous faith and offers unusual opportunities for leadership.'[19]

Other new areas of work were created for deaconesses and other women workers. Early in 1942 the United Church set up a committee on camp and war production communities to establish and direct the religious programs in new camp and war industrial areas. The committee began its work in the midst of the migration and uprooting of families as people moved into factory and production jobs and into training centres for the armed forces. It was estimated that over 750,000 young people had moved from their homes to new forms of employment, and an additional 600,000 had joined the forces and were moved to training camps across the country.[20] The result was a chaotic concentration of people in previously small places. By 1942 the request for workers in these areas had come from all of the new war production centres across the country.

The majority of people hired by the United Church to work in these centres were women, many of them deaconesses. Seven women were hired initially in 1942, with an additional five in the first months of 1943. Their salaries were paid by the Woman's Missionary Society and, by late 1943, there were ninety women at work in such communities across Canada. At first their work was investigative and involved surveys of newcomers through house-to-house visiting programs.[21] Later, as it became obvious that such communities would be in existence for a considerable length of time, the work took on a more educational and recreational focus, and included the establishment of Sunday schools, church vacation schools, fresh air camps, boys' groups, girls' programs, and leadership of women's groups, as well as cooperation in such community projects as wartime day nurseries, day care for school children, home hospitality for men and women in the forces, and recreation for young people in war industries.[22]

In 1944 the committee also began to anticipate the need for work among 'war brides' and initiated welcoming programs, social groups, and cultural events for the thousands of women who would come to Canada with their new Canadian soldier husbands. In 1944 the committee also reported to general council that there were 'approximately 40,000 women in the armed forces' and that co-operation with the government was needed to appoint women as assistant chaplains, 'where there are large concentrations of women.'[23] In the summer of 1944 a request came from the federal government that the inter-church committee on the church's work among the women in the forces, of which the United Church was a member, name two women to take the training for chaplaincy work. In 1945 nine more women were appointed, including three from the United Church.[24]

As the need for skilled church workers increased, the committee on the deaconess order and women workers began to cooperate with other boards of the church to identify specific groups of women and to develop publicity materials that would appeal particularly to them. In 1943 women university graduates were inundated with promotion materials inviting them to give 'one year of war-time service to the work of the Church' and offering them a shortened training time, scholarship assistance, and an exciting year of professional work in the church.[25] This year of service included six weeks of training at the United Church Training School, three weeks of holidays, and ten months of work. Travelling expenses, a war allowance, and remuneration of not less than $800 were provided for all acceptable volunteers. Fifteen women were recruited, trained, and placed, many of them in new congested war communities.[26] A second and more extensive plan involved an offer of scholarships at the training school to short-term workers who pledged to give three years of service to the church. In 1944 seven such scholarships were awarded, and an additional six in 1945.[27]

These were the first of many appeals for short-term workers who would receive very specialized training to meet an emergency need for personnel in the church. While very effective in staffing urgent programs, such recruitment procedures also created problems for long-term women workers in the church, women such as deaconesses whose professional careers were dependent upon recognition and fair treatment by the church. The introduction of massive short-term programs for women tended, indirectly, to devalue the work of deaconesses and other long-term workers. The short-term training programs and the very specific work responsibilities of these specially recruited workers were soon seen as representing all women's professional work in the church. That work was perceived as secondary, short-term, and emergency-specific, with only a hasty educational program of preparation; women's contributions were framed in terms of meeting immediate needs in the church. Also, such special programs, while designed to meet very specific needs, became precedent setting. Often in the future, ministers would refer to them when they wished to secure short-term assistance for their congregations at minimal expense.

Though women's work in the church was in far greater demand than ever before, remuneration for such work was still very low. The problem of pensions was critical for those deaconesses who were now retired and looked after by the Methodist Rest and Relief fund. Even following an appeal for donations, this Fund did not have enough money to support the increasing number of deaconesses who were past retirement and living in poverty, and who had worked for the Methodist Church for a minimal income and the promise that their needs would be looked after in old age. Appeals went out, particularly soliciting donations from women's organizations and individuals who had benefited directly from the work of deaconesses over the years.

The fund, the committee soon discovered, was being subsidized by a number of retired deaconesses who took responsibility for the welfare of their sister workers by sharing their own limited financial resources. Several deaconesses who had married after retirement and were aware of the financial problems, refused their pensions and left the money in the fund for distribution to others. The minutes of the committee on the deaconess order and women workers contained several notations of this, such as the following: 'Mrs Mary Burwash has forgone her pension for the entire year and the amount credited to the Deaconess Rest and Relief Fund.'[28] In other cases single women returned their pensions for several years, only to find themselves in situations of desperate need when illness or accidents brought unexpected medical expenses requiring all of their meagre financial resources. Thus, almost twenty years after her retirement, the family of one deaconess was forced to write to the committee on her behalf, asking if she could begin to receive her pension.

The committee on the deaconess order and women workers continued to work on the rules of the deaconess order, to be published in a constitution in the *Manual of the United Church*. A large section entitled 'Work of a Deaconess' outlined in detail types of work performed by deaconesses both within Canada and around the world. The information was categorized not so much by the type of work done, as by the type of employer. There were sections on work in congregations, employment by boards of Christian education, work in social service institutions, and work under the WMS both within Canada and overseas. Local congregational work was given prominence and was the most detailed in its description of responsibilities and areas of activity. It stated the practice of many years: that the deaconess was to serve as the assistant to the minister. In practical terms this meant that 'she must share the viewpoint and aims of the minister and further them in every possible way.'[29]

As an assistant to the minister, the deaconess was to carry out any of a number of duties, many of them being Christian education functions. Religious education work had by this time become a dynamic and recognized area for women's leadership in Protestant churches. Deaconess work could include any of the following: development of programs of Christian education for all ages and days of the week, recruitment and training of all leaders, assistance with camps and vacation schools, supervision of junior congregations, assistance with the minister's visitation, welcoming of newcomers, organization and supervision of all welfare work of the church, assistance with all correspondence, records, and files for the church, and preparation of the Sunday worship bulletin. As the constitution and other materials were quick to add, such a position was new for many church committees and congregations. Many of the duties listed for deaconesses had previously been done by a host of volunteers; therefore churches unfamiliar with the work of deaconesses tended either to see the performance of these duties as of limited financial worth or, equally damaging, to see the deaconess as a person to whom all tasks could now be assigned, regardless of the amount of time required or the specific skills needed to perform them.

As pioneers, many deaconesses had to work hard at setting boundaries, defining what were to remain as tasks for volunteer workers and what could become part of deaconess responsibilities. They were compelled to promote themselves actively as valuable workers and 'worth the money' congregations were paying them. Some congregations deliberately chose a deaconess rather than a second ordained minister because they thought that, as a woman, she would be less competitive and dissatisfied with a secondary role than a man. Others had many questions about their value, questions that forced the deaconesses to justify and explain themselves constantly.

Work under the direction of the WMS continued to attract large numbers of deaconesses. In 1939, out of a total of sixty-nine employed deaconesses, twenty-nine worked for the WMS.[30] Five years later there were sixty-eight active deaconesses, thirty-one employed by the WMS.[31] The constitution of the deaconess order listed six possibilities for work with the Woman's Missionary Society: work with new Canadians in a downtown church or mining area; educational or worship work on a Native reserve; social work or teaching among 'orientals'; evangelism and Christian education in outlying areas and new communities; lay supply work on a pastoral charge without a minister; and superintendency or assistance in a social service institution.[32] With the exception of duties in a social service institution, most of this work was educational in focus; it included establishing children's groups, training and counselling leaders, leading Bible studies and adult education programs, visiting, and leading worship in groups.

Social service work, listed as another important area of work for deaconesses either within a congregation or on behalf of the Woman's Missionary Society, was described with words that contrasted the goodness and purity of the deaconess as 'faithful woman,' with the evil and suffering of her surroundings. She was portrayed in images that reinforced the understanding of her as an angel of mercy or handmaiden who brings comfort and help to those in need, and who somehow transforms both her surroundings and the people she helps.

'I never saw so many evil-looking faces in all my life' were the words of an authoress as she and the Deaconess were refused admission to one of the doubtful, cheap rooming-houses of the district. The family she was seeking had moved when a police raid had revealed the character of the house ... The Deaconess visits such rooming-houses – she goes down in the little basement rooms – she goes up to the attic rooms where the people freeze in the winter and swelter in the summer. She goes to the homes of dirt – physical, mental and moral ... She goes to the home where there is tragedy, sickness and death – always with a prayer in her heart and the knowledge that God will make her a channel of blessing and comfort and things will change.[33]

As well as visiting in homes, work in social service included interviewing and investigating calls that came into the office, distributing clothing, administering an employment service, developing mothers' clubs and teen programs and lunch and recreational events for unemployed women, collecting and distributing food, and organizing summer camps for women and children and one-day outings for those not able to go to camp.[34] The characteristics required for such work were spelled out in the publicity materials of the 1940s; they mixed a traditional view of woman as the 'natural' nurturer and relationship maintainer with an emerging awareness of the difficulty of doing this on a long-term basis. '[She] needs to be a woman of deep spiritual insight and experience, and one who, besides this, is trained to understand the forces that play upon human behaviour and that influence it ... The Deaconess needs insight, patience and experience, and skill in dealing with difficult situations, as well as character that will commend her faith to those under her care.'[35]

The constitution was finally completed, approved, and circulated in 1942. It spelled out in detail for the first time the conditions of employment of deaconesses and the tasks of the committee on the deaconess order and women workers. Women had no guarantee that once they were designated as deaconesses they would be employed. The only guarantee given to them was that the committee would assist them by seeking openings and recommending individual deaconesses for suitable positions. Employment, once found, was on a yearly basis and was to continue from year to year 'unless at two months prior to the expiration of any year of employment either party shall give notice to the other of intention to terminate the employment at the end of such year.'[36]

The committee continued to see the need to increase and standardize salaries, stating that '[there are] still great inconsistencies and disparities now obtaining and no rule endorsed by the Church. No provision is given for the retirement of women who have given all their years of service to the work of the Church. Such a situation seems unworthy of a great Church like ours.'[37] The situation, the committee concluded, was little better than it had been in 1928 when the first report of women workers in the church was presented to general council.

Salaries were far below men's, and they were also below those of women in comparable occupations of nursing and teaching. Well over half the women workers who were trained at the United Church Training School held university degrees. Many others had professional training and experience in nursing, teaching, or business.[38] Yet in 1944 the annual salary for women congregational workers was in the range of $1,000 for beginners to $1,500 for experienced workers.[39] Minimum salaries for single ordained ministers four years earlier, in 1940, had been $1,600.[40] The committee had constant discussions about the inadequacy of women's salaries. In 1945 committee members decided to contact all groups who employed deaconesses and inform them that salaries for deaconesses were too low and that a fair minimum salary for 1945 was $1,500. Wherever possible this should be increased, having 'due regard to years of service, experience and the cost of living,' to a maximum of $1,800.[41]

Through the discussions of deaconess work and salaries, deaconesses developed an awareness that they had much in common with other women workers, and that a major block to their fair treatment was their lack of unity with other women workers. Thus, in 1939 deaconesses and other women workers began to talk about the need for a new organization that would be national and separate from the official committees of the church, one that would enable them to share concerns, have fellowship together, and labour for better working conditions. They began to articulate questions of strategy, asking whether women were better off integrated into the official structures of the church or building up their own separate organization. Though deaconesses were by no means united in their estimate of the value of a separate organization, they greeted its formation with enthusiasm.

At the Winnipeg conference of the Deaconess Association in 1940 the constitution of the Fellowship of Professional Women Workers in the United Church was approved. The Deaconess Association and the new fellowship would have their biennial conferences together and would share information and tasks. The new organization would unite all women workers and its purpose would be fellowship, study of the field of women's work, promotion of the work of women, and critique of the church's policies and practices towards women. Membership was open to all trained women, including ordained women; organization and communication were through regional groups that met on a regular basis. At the national meetings, members would elect officers, receive reports from the national executive, and discuss employment and theological and social issues affecting women.

Following the war, the focus of deaconess work shifted from work in special short-term projects and jobs sponsored by the WMS to Christian education work within local congregations. The number of churches requesting women workers rose dramatically in the years between 1945 and 1960. The plethora of jobs available for women, particularly deaconesses, was caused by several factors. There continued to be a shortage of ordained men after the war, and trained women were hired by congregations who could not find ordained personnel. In addition, the United Church was entering a period of unprecedented growth. Early in 1947 it embarked on a church extension program referred to by historians as the 'building boom.' With the war over, immigration beginning to rise, and new housing developments starting to appear in most urban areas, the United Church appointed a staff person to supervise and promote its vast church-construction project. In the years between 1947 and 1962, two thousand new United churches were built, all requiring professional staff to provide programs for their members.[42]

Deaconesses moved into many of these newly created jobs and began to establish a reputation as experts in Christian education and church outreach. Their dedication and labour helped a church that was struggling to rebuild society and to recover from the horrors of war. As more deaconesses began to work in congregations and to develop exciting ministries in education and church outreach, they began to see the need for a voice in presbytery, the court of the church that made many of the decisions about ministry, finances, and programs that deeply affected their work. Thus, with the patience and the strength they had demonstrated in their earlier struggles, deaconesses began sustained and difficult political work towards this goal. Finally, in 1964, deaconesses were admitted to full membership in the courts of the United Church of Canada.[43]

ACKNOWLEDGMENT

This is from a much longer project, 'A Tale of Handmaidens: Deaconesses in the United Church of Canada 1925 to 1964,' completed in 1987. My appreciation goes to Sharon Rosenberg for her excellent advice and editorial assistance.

NOTES

1 For a comprehensive discussion of deaconess work during this earlier period, see John D. Thomas, 'Servants of the Church: Canadian Methodist Deaconess Work, 1890–1926,' *Canadian Historical Review* 65, 3 (Sept. 1984), and Diane Haglund, 'Sideroad on the Journey to Autonomy: The Diaconate Prior to Church Union,' in *Women, Work, and Worship*, Shirley Davy, ed. (Toronto: United Church of Canada [hereafter UCC], 1983). See also Mary Anne Mac-Farlane's chapter on deaconesses in her 'Gender, Doctrine, and Pedagogy: Women and "Womanhood" in Methodist Sunday Schools in English-Speaking Canada, 1880–1920' (Ph.D. dissertation, University of Toronto, 1992),

2 *Christian Guardian*, 29 Nov. 1911; *Agenda of the Ninth General Council* 1940, UCC, 298.

3 Descriptions of their work and employment conditions are available in *The Acts and Proceedings of the General Assembly of the Presbyterian Church in Canada, 1921–24.*

4 *Agenda of the Third General Council* 1928, UCC, 160.

5 *Forms of Service for the Offices of the Church* (Toronto: United Church Publishing House, 1926), 130–1.

6 'An Order for the Setting Apart of Deaconesses,' *The Book of Common Order* (Toronto: UCC, 1932).

7 *Agenda of the Third General Council* 1928, UCC, 160–72.

8 *Annual Reports, Woman's Missionary Society*, 1927. (Toronto: United Church Publishing House, 1927). By way of comparison, in 1929 the salaries for deaconesses were $1,000 to $1,200, whereas nurses in Ontario were paid $1,090 to $1,597. Salaries of women teachers in Toronto in 1930 were $1,000 to $2,400, whereas deaconesses were paid $1,100 to $1,300. Comparative statistics from nursing and teaching reported in Janice Acton et al., eds., *Women at Work: Ontario, 1850–1930* (Toronto: Women's Press, 1974), 147, 194.

9 'Report of the Committee on Employed Women Workers,' *Agenda of the Third General Council* 1928, 163, United Church Archives, Toronto (hereafter UCA).

10 Ibid., 165.

11 Ibid., 162–3, 167.

12 Personal files of Harriet Christie, letter from Mary Eadie to all deaconesses, Apr. 1931, seen by courtesy of Shelly Finson.

13 'Report of the Committee on Employed Women Workers,' *Agenda of the Third General Council* 1928, 166, UCA.

14 *Ready to Help Your Church* (Toronto: UCC, 1940), 14–15, Centre for Christian Studies (Toronto) Records (hereafter CCSR).

15 *The Manual of the Deaconess Order* (Toronto: UCC, 1940), 18–20.
16 Lydia Gruchy, 'Women and the Church,' *YWCA Notes* 21, 9 (Dec. 1939): 1.
17 *Agenda of the Tenth General Council* 1942, UCC, 87.
18 Association of Professional Church Workers Records, Transcript of a Radio Broadcast by Mrs W.J. Campion on CKCL, 27 Feb. 1944, 3, CCSR.
19 *A Full-Time Vocation for Christian Women* (Toronto: UCC, 1941), 3, CCSR.
20 *One Year of War-Time Service to the Work of the Church: June, 1943 – June, 1944* (Toronto: UCC, 1943), 2, CCSR.
21 *Eighteenth Annual Report of the Woman's Missionary Society*, 1942–3 (Toronto: United Church Publishing House, 1943), 13.
22 *One Year of War-Time Service to the Work of the Church: June, 1943 – June, 1944* (Toronto: UCC, 1943), 2, CCSR.
23 *Agenda of the Eleventh General Council*, 1944, UCC, 173.
24 *The First Fifty Years, 1895–1945: The Training and Work of Women Employed in the Service of the United Church of Canada* (Toronto: CDOWW, United Church Training School [hereafter UCTS] and Woman's Missionary Society [hereafter WMS], n.d.), 28.
25 *To University Women Graduating in 1945: Will You Give Three Years to Church Work?* (Toronto: UCC, 1945), CCSR.
26 *One Year of War-Time Service to the Work of the Church: June, 1943 – June, 1944* (Toronto: UCC, 1943), 2–3, CCSR.
27 *The First Fifty Years, 1895–1945: The Training and Work of Women Employed in the Service of the United Church of Canada* (Toronto: CDOWW, UCTS and WMS, n.d.), 28.
28 Minutes of the Committee on the Deaconess Order and Women Workers, 29 Nov. 1946, 2, CCSR.
29 *Ready to Help Your Church* (Toronto: UCC, 1940), 11, CCSR.
30 *Agenda of the Ninth General Council* 1940, UCC, 298.
31 Records of the Association of Professional Church Workers, 'Statistics of the Deaconess Order,' 15 Mar. 1944, CCSR.
32 *Handbook of the Deaconess Order of the United Church of Canada* (Toronto: CDOWW, 1944 ed.), 14–15.
33 *Ready to Help Your Church* (Toronto: UCC, 1940), 18–19, CCSR.
34 Ibid., 14–15.
35 Ibid., 16–17.
36 *Handbook of the Deaconess Order of the United Church of Canada* (Toronto: CDOWW, 1944 ed.), 12.
37 'Appraisal of the Work of the Committee on the Deaconess Order and Women Workers of the Church and Recommendations as to Future Policy,' 10 Apr. 1944, 2, Records of the Association of Professional Church Workers, CCSR.

38 'Interesting Facts for Reports to Conferences,' CDOWW, 27 Apr. 1950, Records of the Association of Professional Church Workers, CCSR.

39 *Women Serve the Church* (Toronto: UCC, 1944), 1, CCSR.

40 *Agenda of the Ninth General Council* 1940, UCC, 79.

41 'Recommendations for the Meeting of the General Committee of December 7th, 1945 to the Committee on the Deaconess Order and Women Workers,' 1, Records of the Association of Professional Church Workers, CCSR.

42 M.B. Pengelley, 'The Man Behind the Building Boom,' *United Church Observer*, 15 Apr. 1958, 10.

43 The remit which resulted in the admission of deaconesses as members of presbytery in 1964 included several proposed alterations in the procedures for administering the work of deaconesses, as well as a proposal that they become members of the courts of the church. Its passage gave them a substantial and mandatory salary raise. They became part of the general council salary scale for ministers, classified as 'unordained personnel.' This gave them a minimum salary of $4,500 for 1965.

From Christian Benevolence to Social Transformation: Religion as Catalyst

13

Women and Social Welfare in the Montreal Region, 1800–1833: Preliminary Findings

JAN NOEL

Some women found the expression of their Christian faith in working for the welfare of others in society. Especially during social crises there was room for innovative work. Because of a desperate need for social welfare in Montreal in the first two decades of the nineteenth century and in the cholera epidemic of 1832, their benevolent work was welcomed. Much of this relief work, medical service, and care for orphans was done by members of the established churches of Rome, England, and Scotland. Female evangelicals, many of whom had their roots in parts of the United States where revivals were common, also desired to reform society. They wanted to do so in order to put people 'in a suitable state to hear the Word of God,' and devoted themselves especially to literacy and temperance work. Yet the history of women's work in Montreal is not progressive; whereas in the early decades of the nineteenth century, women organized most of the social welfare available, only a few years later projects were initiated by male clergy, laymen, or male government officials instead.

Women provided most of the organized social welfare in Montreal and its environs in the first two decades of the nineteenth century. They founded and operated organized help for those unable to provide their own food, clothing, fuel, child care, housing, or health care. At that time there was a growing need for such efforts, and women were still initiating major projects as late as 1832 when cholera created an emergency in the town. After the early nineteenth-century period under review here, projects were increasingly initiated by male clergy, laymen, or government officials. Women would continue to supply much of the labour but were less apt to supply the direction.

Appreciation of this leadership of early efforts contributes to an understanding of the stages of the history of women – a history that has not always been progressive. Indeed, there seems to have been more independent action at the beginning of the nineteenth century than in subsequent decades. This was to some extent a post-conquest carry-over from the days of New France in which gender roles had been rather loosely defined.[1] Then, women not only bore children and kept house but often provided much of the family's livelihood; they also played an important part in shaping public endeavour, particularly in the welfare field.

The material here represents the first findings of a larger project to document the leadership of women in social welfare activity in the Montreal area in pre-industrial times, and particularly in the first third of the nineteenth century when both Catholic and Protestant women were active. It attempts to unearth this work and provide coherent categories for discussing it; in this case 'establishment' social service will be contrasted with the more radical 'evangelical' approach. Left for another day is a detailed analysis of why the independence of the early nineteenth century would later decline. This essay merely begins to reconstruct this neglected corner of our past.

The reconstruction itself is no simple task. Studying women's benevolence in early nineteenth-century Canada is similar to putting together a jigsaw puzzle that has many lost and warped pieces. Those 'lost' are the activities that went unrecorded because of their everyday character, or the modesty or haste of the actors, or records being discarded by those who came later and assumed that feminine philanthropy was trivial. Others are also 'lost' whose only trace is a sentence in a husband's biography describing the 'Mrs' as 'pious and devoted to the poor.' The 'warped' pieces are bits of evidence whose meaning is hard to discern because the context of women's work in 1815 differed from that of later times. The notion that women joined organizations because of their idleness or boredom rings particularly false for this period. Society still had many aspects of the *ancien régime* when both women and men produced and exchanged commodities. Farms could not function without women's dairying, poultry-keeping, and gardening. Households required the textiles, clothes, soap, and candles they made. In town, shops and workshops were often a family enterprise in a way that later waged work was not. This was no golden age – let the foolhardy declare tending cows in 1800 more worthy than tending children in 1880! There is, however, evidence to suggest a wider range of women's occupations at the beginning of the nineteenth century than at its end.

Women still had the skills, for example, to make the clothing and household items that fetched £700 at an 1831 charity bazaar in Montreal. To these events women also brought retailing experience, not a hobby but a livelihood for the thirteen female 'traders,' twelve grocers or drygoods dealers, seven tavernkeepers, and one auctioneer listed among about 1,500 occupations in the 1819 Montreal directory.[2] Throughout the century, women were grocers and tavernkeepers, boardinghouse keepers, dressmakers, and teachers; but the traders and a few skilled female artisans such as the tinplate manufacturer and tallow chandler hint at an earlier and wider pre-industrial range. Nuns who ran the hospital, assisted by the elderly women living there, made clothes and ornaments that the North West Company traded to the Indians; they also printed and bound books and worked in the fields of their seigneurie. The frequent use of women's own last names rather than that of their husbands during this period also suggests a certain independence.[3]

Compared with the later nineteenth century, this society placed more weight on social class and less on gender. Few men enjoyed a marked educational advantage over women. In government and the professions, career training was still somewhat rudimentary. Manners, names, and family ties opened doors. Social contacts were essential, and gentlewomen played a large part in cultivating them.[4] Until 1849 female property owners had the right to vote, and French civil law in the early nineteenth century entitled wives and widows to a more secure portion of family property than provided under British law.[5] Domestic service in 1820 also tended to be more a function of class than of gender[6]; it was with the subsequent identification of woman and home that the manservant would fall out of fashion. Child-rearing, too, was still an avocation rather than a destiny. Children were often raised by others: the Upper Canadian governor's wife, Elizabeth Simcoe, left four young daughters in England while she came to Canada for five years, and Canadian families of various classes sent young children away from home to schools or apprenticeships. Although British and American conduct literature preached 'separate spheres' to the elite by the late eighteenth century, the idea was still somewhat novel among the Canadian middle classes until the 1840s; then prosperity, the rapid growth of towns, occupational diversification, public schools, and better communications (which carried a rash of family newspapers and advice literature) would all work together to deal a decisive blow to the old family economy.[7] In the early nineteenth century, women tended to be somewhat at home in the public domain. They did not step into the street as timid amateurs when they undertook public relief work. Also, because of the less discriminatory property and civil laws, they had more discretionary spending power and more authority than would their daughters and granddaughters later in the century.

If pre-industrial Lower Canada was in some ways a highly traditional society, in others it was a raw 'frontier.' Institutional development, particularly in the recently arrived anglophone community, was rudimentary. Criminals and the mentally ill were locked up side by side in jails; they relied on private donors to bring them clothes. Although the town developed a number of private and charity schools by 1825,[8] neighbouring settlements were less fortunate, and some had no school at all; often one chapel was shared by several denominations. Outlying villages sometimes had to rely on none-too-sober itinerant preachers and physicians.[9] In these primitive conditions all able-bodied people laboured, and any available hands were apt to be recruited to cook, clean, doctor, stump, or sow.

Whereas in traditional systems people were defined more by class than by gender, on frontiers necessity increased the likelihood that tasks would be based on abilities rather than gender stereotypes. Experiencing aspects of both these systems, early nineteenth-century women were less constrained than later Victorian Canadians who had gender distinctions drummed into them and fortified by an array of gender-based regulations and institutions. These more fluid circumstances help explain women's energetic public welfare activity.

As seen in so many cases of social work discussed in this volume, most of this activity was religiously motivated or church-related. Yet often such work crossed denominational lines. These activities might be placed in two categories: 'establishment' relief work and 'evangelical' attempts to reform society. 'Establishment' work emanated from the three churches established in Canada in the seventeenth and eighteenth centuries, the Churches of Rome, England, and Scotland, all receiving state support for some or all of the period under review. By 1800 all three groups were firmly rooted in Canadian soil and had experience with its multicultural, multidenominational reality. Fittingly, they shared church buildings: The Anglicans worshipped for some time at the Catholic Récollet Church, later sharing a building with the Scots. They had also learned to live not only with the religious beliefs of others but also with their moral failings. The St Gabriel Street Presbyterian Church, for example, tolerated the indiscretions of a minister who drank too much, and quietly baptized fur magnates' children conceived in various beds.[10] Similarly the Catholics took in foundlings without asking about their origins, one Mother Superior noting that 'prudence and delicacy forbids us to put any question on that score.'[11] 'Established' efforts tended to draw on the resources of Montreal's elite: private bequests, fund-raising efforts such as bazaars, church or neighbourhood collections, and government subsidies. In contrast to American evangelical denominations, these churches derived from countries with fairly rigid class systems, pre-Revolutionary France and anti-Revolutionary Britain (with an added conservative injection of American Loyalists). Lower Canada's elite generally belonged to these churches, as did the majority of its poor.

The established tradition produced most of the recorded female benevolence in this early period. This is seen both in the work of the Catholic nuns and the primarily Protestant Female Benevolent Society. Springing from the traditional order, these groups embodied classic Canadian virtues of conciliation and compromise. They had learned to cooperate with various denominational and ethnic groups. Their ability to work with powerful men was also important to their success. If these virtues had a corresponding vice, it was perhaps a proclivity to bend too much to the prevailing winds, be they the windy advice of ambitious clergymen, or the tendency to place increasing burdens of self-sacrifice on overworked members when a change of system might have better served both donors and recipients of aid.

ESTABLISHMENT SOCIAL WELFARE: THE NUNS

Catholic nuns continued to carry the major burden of social welfare in Montreal for at least a half-century after the British conquest of 1760. From the seventeenth century, Congregational nuns had provided schooling to working class children; they added two new Montreal locations to their Notre Dame motherhouse in the early 1830s.[12] Other groups of nuns had cared for the orphaned, indigent, aged, and ill. Beginning as a dedicated group of missionaries funded by government, private donors, and their own lands and labours, the nuns had long provided services that had compared favourably with hospital care and female education in France.[13] After the conquest, despite financial difficulties, their role was enhanced. Having cared for British as well as French cases during and after the Seven Years War (a blend of charity and *politique*), the nuns were permitted to remain and to recruit in Canada at a time when the Jesuit and Récollet orders were forbidden to do so and vocations to the parish priesthood were not keeping pace with population growth.

The nuns were sufficiently flexible to survive the Conquest and to evolve with the times. Besides extending their services to non-Catholics, they learned to work with non-Catholic physicians. Conciliation and diplomacy helped win the regard of British governing families, who began sending their Protestant daughters to Catholic schools. Convents were open to curious British visitors. Lady Aylmer, the governor's wife, described in 1831 being treated by the Congregational nuns to a picnic on their island farm. The nuns ran about in the long grass swatting flies and mosquitoes lest they reach madame's cheek.[14] Such exercises apparently bore fruit. From the beginning of the nineteenth century the government was regularly funding the work of the nuns in Lower Canada's three urban centres. The sum of £17,103 was forwarded to Montreal nunneries between 1800 and 1823 to help pay for the care of growing numbers of sick and homeless in the expanding town.

The Hôtel Dieu, for example, between 1800 and 1823 received £4,740 in government money to care for the ill and infirm. Located on the bustling business street of St Paul, this thirty-bed hospital consisted of two wards until its expansion in the late 1820s. The Hôtel Dieu benefited from the gratuitous services of Dr William Selby and of nuns working as administrators, apothecaries, nurses, and ward supervisors.

The Hôpital Général, run since 1737 by Madame Youville's Grey Nuns, was a larger establishment with about eighty sickbeds. Unlike the Hôtel Dieu (which turned away children, maternity cases, communicable diseases, and several other kinds of cases), the Hôpital had an open door. It nursed a number of indigent invalids along with wealthier pensioners. By sheltering a number of Irish orphans and other victims of a typhus outbreak in 1822–3, the Hôpital received legislative commendation for preserving the town's 'uncommon degree of health at that time.' In 1823 it treated 485 Protestant and 367 Catholic patients, of whom apparently only 41 died.[15]

This large and useful establishment owed its prosperous condition to capable superiors such as Thérèse-Geneviève Coutlée, its director from 1792 to 1821. The daughter of a day labourer, Coutlée had entered the convent in 1762 and was early singled out for her intelligence and judgment. When appointed superior, Coutlée had wept at the responsibility. However, she soon displayed the business acumen not unusual in eighteenth-century women. The Hôpital was in financial difficulty because of the French government's failure to pay certain annuities. Coutlée did her best to restore sound footing: She rented out part of the land and developed workshops where the nuns made candles and vestments, embroidered cloth, and bound books, exercising a range of craft skills typical of the ancien régime. For part of Thérèse-Geneviève Coutlée's tenure the sisters also still toiled in the fields to feed their community; but the premature death of several nuns apparently persuaded the superior their overtaxed energies were better used indoors. Doctors, legislative councillors, and all parties involved in the 1824 Legislative Council Enquiry on the Insane, Foundlings, and the Sick and Infirm Poor spoke with respect of the dedication of the religious women and their 'great and unremitting exertion' to feed, clothe, and care for all those in their charge.

The Hôpital Général's Foundling Street location bespoke its other major function: to receive abandoned infants. The nuns sent these out to wet-nurses, paying the nurses, providing them with baby clothes, and visiting to check up on their small charges. At age two the babies were brought back to the Grey Nuns and sent out for adoption or contractual placement with 'respectable families.'

This infant care, which might have been one of the nuns' more cheerful tasks, was in fact the grimmest. As Montreal developed into a major port, military centre, and reception point for immigrants and displaced habitants, increasing numbers of children were abandoned. The nuns received seventeen infants in 1760, thirty-nine in 1800, and eighty-six in 1823.[16]

Many arrived at the Grey Nuns' door nearly dead, some brought in carts from considerable distances. Between 1800 and 1823 more than three-quarters of the foundlings received by the nuns – 841 of 1207 – died after being sent out to nurse, most of them in the first month of life. This contrasted with a 25 per cent infant mortality rate in Montreal generally. Questioned about this by the Legislative Council Committee in 1824, the Grey Nuns' Superior, Marguerite Lemaire St Germain (who succeeded Coutlée in 1822), attributed it to 'the bad state in which we receive them, which proceeds from that shame which induces the mothers to resort to the utmost means of concealing the offspring of their crime from the eyes of the world.'[17]

Concerned by the death rate and also by the expense of caring for the growing numbers of foundlings, the government committee expressed the opinion that the system itself was defective. Their research indicated that high mortality rates characterized foundling hospitals everywhere. They felt that the moral effect of these institutions was pernicious: Giving unwed mothers a place to send their infants was 'calculated to weaken that mainspring of a healthy population, matrimony, and to blunt or destroy ... parental affection by encouraging mothers to abandon their offspring.' Besides being an 'incitement to vice and licentiousness,' foundling hospitals swallowed up public money. As a result the 1824 committee recommended phasing out the system as soon as possible. The gulf between their scientific aspirations and Mother St Germain's charitable realism appears in the proceedings:

Query: What is the System in respect to them?

Answer: Not understanding completely the object of the query I am not able to answer it in a satisfactory manner: all that I have the honor to say to you, is, that we attend to all the details, and we bestow all the care that forsaken, unsupported and unprotected children can inspire.

Despite the council's laudable concern for systemic change, Mother St Germain may have understood the situation better: Given Montreal's large military and transient population, closing the foundling hospital would probably have increased infanticide rather than lowering illegitimacy.[18] Indeed the committee had no alternative forms of prevention or care to suggest, and the foundling work would continue for decades to come. Yet laywomen soon began to take steps to help women in childbirth, relieving at least some of the desperation that led to abandonment of infants.

At the same time that the numbers of foundlings increased, the Grey

Nuns also accepted the burden of housing insane patients. The situation was Dickensian. The afflicted lived in six-by-eight-foot cells with grated windows. The nuns eschewed corporal punishment and, according to their physician, fed the patients 'if anything too well.' Although the sisters cleaned and cleaned, a noxious smell arose from the cells. The building's riverside location added winter damp to the pungent atmosphere. There was no exercise yard and no room for one. The situation, the Hôpital's physician asserted, was 'more likely to ... increase insanity than to cure it.'[19] Remarkably, forty-nine of the eighty-four mental cases the nuns received between 1800 and 1823 had been discharged as 'cured or relieved.' Here too was a system recognized as obsolete; but in this case the Legislative Council was able to propose an alternative, a government asylum based on the famous mental asylum in Glasgow with facilities for classification, treatment, and exercise. Such an institution would eventually be built at Beauport in 1845. In the meantime, however, the nuns cared for up to eight patients, while that many again overflowed into the town jail. In 1818 the Grey Nuns made an unwonted refusal of a £2000 government grant allocated for building more cells for the insane, 'as it would increase what is in itself bad and inadequate to the object' of helping the mental cases.

The nuns had successfully made the transition to a new regime by diplomacy with their British rulers and by the continuing tradition of dedicated care, broadened now to include non-Catholics. Above all, they survived and grew because they filled a vital need, to which the large grant from a parsimonious government stands testimony. There were no other hospitals available until 1816 and no sizeable Protestant institution until 1822, despite the preponderance of Protestant patients. Both the Hôpital Général and the Hôtel Dieu continued to provide services for decades, the latter functioning to this day as a teaching hospital in connection with the Université de Montréal. One cannot contemplate with satisfaction the primitive treatment the nuns' charges received and the seemingly calm acceptance of appalling conditions. Without the nuns, however, such cases would have marched more surely and swiftly to the alternate destinations of jailhouse and grave.

ESTABLISHMENT SOCIAL WELFARE: LAYWOMEN

So important was the nuns' contribution to early nineteenth century welfare that Protestant benevolence to some extent simply picked up the pieces that fell outside the nuns' wide net. The founders of the Female Benevolent Society (FBS) were struck by the plight of immigrants arriving after the

Napoleonic wars ended in 1815. The FBS's approach to poverty displayed much of the same religious tolerance and female initiative seen in the work of the nuns. Apparently the first permanent English-language voluntary relief association in Montreal, it filled a major gap in the city's welfare services.[20] Like the convents, it looked to the powers of the land for support and worked within the established order. The women who were most active in initiating the Female Benevolent Society, Eleanor Gibb, H.W. Barrett, and the widow Janet Finlay Aird, worshipped at the St Gabriel Street Church connected with the Church of Scotland.[21]

This trio and a handful of their friends placed a notice in Montreal newspapers and bookstores shortly before Christmas in 1815 that 'a number of Ladies, deeply impressed with the destitute situation of the poor, wish to form a society to relieve indigent women and small children, the sick, the aged and the infirm poor of the city.'[22] To achieve their aim they fashioned a structure that involved a directress and a board of twelve managers. They sought donations and began by helping about fifty people in distress. To support their work they persuaded the Reverend Robert Easton, pastor of the St Peter Street Scottish Secession congregation, to preach a charity sermon, which he did on a Sunday night in September 1816.

The sermon was no revolutionary manifesto. Easton accepted the class system; he counselled his hearers to be prudent in their giving, retaining whatever was necessary for the support of their 'rank and credit in the world.' Yet he acknowledged the common humanity of the poor: 'Whoever wears the human form challenges our respect, and, being found in a state of wretchedness, is entitled to relief.'[23] Most notable is what the sermon did *not* do. Scarcely any mention was made of benevolent activity as a womanly or motherly endeavour. Easton dwelt instead on compassion as 'one of our natural endowments ... a sentiment of nature ... a maxim of true religion.' He appears to have been aware of the upsurge of such benevolence in Britain and the United States, and towards the end of his sermon he did mention this work as highly becoming to members of the female sex and a good example to their daughters. In contrast to later nineteenth-century ministerial counsels, however, there was a refreshing emphasis on the common humanity of givers and recipients of aid. Charitable workers were generic good Samaritans, rather than gendered nurturers.

In the Female Benevolent Society's first year the members used their £190 treasury to give food, firewood, clothes, and medicine to about sixty adults and forty-five children, mostly drawn from the several thousand immigrants who began annually to inundate a town then numbering about nine thousand. Some of this group were unfit to go on to the usual immigrant destination of Upper Canada, so FBS members rented a small house in the Récollet suburb which they named the House of Recovery. They hired several housekeepers, while the twelve managers took turns supplying and visiting the house. By 1817–18 the society was helping some 370 people a year including twenty 'permanent charges,' and the annual treasury had grown to £1,200. Supplementing their efforts from 1818 was another voluntary society for the relief of emigrants, which included Catholic, Presbyterian, and Anglican ministers, formed to arrange westward passage for destitute but able-bodied immigrants. By 1820 the FBS was sending five hundred people a year by this agency, agreeing in return to open a soup kitchen for hungry immigrants in one of its houses.[24]

Alongside this emigrant work, the society cared for a number of women in childbirth as well as some forty invalids unable to gain admission to the Hôtel Dieu. Securing discarded bedding from the military barracks, they moved their sick patients into a larger house on Craig Street that had three wards and could hold twenty-four patients. When this experiment proved viable, doctors and businessmen such as John Richardson and William McGillivray began plans to give the city a permanent general hospital. The Female Benevolent Society's historian in 1920 reported that 'the large Craig Street house to which the patients from the House of Recovery were moved was the first General Hospital, the direct result of the efforts of the Ladies' Benevolent Society on behalf of the sick poor.'[25] Doige's *Montreal Directory* of 1819 corroborates the claim: 'the bright example of superior benevolence evinced by the female sex in this institution has at length aroused the energies of the gentlemen, who have lately caused a public dispensary to be established, which, with the increase of the population and the difficulties of the times ... has made necessary.'

With the hospital passing into the hands of a male committee and the clergy beginning to address itself to immigrant aid, the women expanded another arm of their work. Increasingly the FBS turned to helping children, 'the prospect of training a rising generation to industry and sobriety being so much more promising than that of reforming those whose habits have become fixed.'[26] Several committee members worked to establish a national school while others formed a committee of the Society for Promoting Education and Industry.[27] In 1822 they opened the Protestant Orphan Asylum, directed by Janet Aird with H.W. Barrett as secretary. Many of the orphanage's twelve managers had previously served as managers of the FBS.

The charity flourished, growing in numbers and prestige. The seventy-three members of 1816 increased to eighty-one by 1819. The FBS appears to have been an upwardly mobile group. The founders were of the middle class; Eleanor Gibb belonged to a family of merchant-tailors who outfitted Montreal's elites, and Janet Aird and H.W. Barrett were also from mercantile families. By 1817, however, Mrs Ogden, wife of the Chief Justice, was the society's second directress. In 1819 there was an influx of 'several ladies of the first respectability ... who had not before honoured the meetings.'[28] The move towards exclusive work with children fit genteel conceptions of feminine duty better than did work with adult street people. A new sensibility is suggested, too, by the gradual replacement of the earthy 'Female' in the society's name with the more refined term 'Ladies,' made official in the society's reconstituted charter in 1832.

Ladies or not, the membership remained capable of taking to the streets in a crisis. A cholera epidemic reached Montreal with the arrival of the ship *Carricks* from Dublin on 8 June 1832. Within a week 261 people died in Montreal; 632 died the following week, and 166 the next; that year the city saw 2,500 cholera-related fatalities. Many citizens fled to the country in terror, and refugees huddled in the barns and granaries on the outskirts of town. The members of the Ladies' Benevolent Society (LBS) went out in pairs to canvass the town streets for donations to help the victims. They collected £500, to which was added £100 collected by a male citizens' committee. Again the society established a soup kitchen to feed the hungry, along with a house to receive destitute widows and children, and an employment office for domestics. With medical services volunteered by Dr John Stephenson, the women also ran a house for the homeless and for invalids released from the general hospital but still convalescing.

By 1833 the society had effectively demonstrated its usefulness. At its public general meeting a resolution was unanimously passed that they had 'as far as funds had permitted ... fulfilled their pledge to the public to relieve all those who were in real want and distress from the ravages of the cholera' and further resolved that the society should be permanent. The Montreal Sanitary Committee transferred its £50 balance to the LBS, and Stephenson offered his services and supplies for an indefinite period. Two prospective teachers for the orphanage were sent for training in the Lancastrian and Infant School methods. The financial future looked promising: along with £228 raised at a Government House Bazaar, the group also received £100 from the government, the first of a long series of such grants for the orphanage.[29]

The Ladies' Benevolent Society was an effective organization – so much so that it is still functioning in Montreal as a child-care organization after amalgamating with several other groups. Its longevity can be attributed to several factors. First, its members were dedicated: The same names recurred on the membership and managerial rolls year after year, some families serving for generations.[30] Second, its ecumenical membership made it acceptable in Montreal's multicultural setting. Third, the society showed a tendency to order and system as opposed to trends and enthusiasms. Early in its history, clear lines of responsibility and an endowment fund were both in place. This soundness, along with the status of its members, helped ensure success in securing government support as well as free care from physicians, charity sermons from clergy, and other important donations of goods and services. That in turn made possible the hiring of a small paid staff. Pioneering a Protestant orphanage, the LBS led the way for a number of such institutions founded in other colonial towns after 1850[31] in meeting the needs of children while addressing problems endemic to volunteer organizations.

The most notable aspect of Montreal Benevolent Society's welfare is the centrality of the work of women. They did not operate peripherally but initiated the response to a pressing public need – and sustained it. The society's 1919–20 historians wrote that 'the authority of older histories and statistics [established] the fact that this Society was the pioneer philanthropy of British Montreal, and that its work led directly to the founding of the Montreal General Hospital and the Protestant Orphan Asylum and to an organized assistance for that vast throng of immigrants continually progressing towards Upper Canada.'[32] As late as 1820 other groups were still so ephemeral that the Ladies' Benevolent Society was the only Protestant charity mentioned in the *Montreal Directory* of that year. A workhouse had a brief career from 1819 until it folded four years later. Apart from that, there appears to have been little besides a bread line at the Récollet Church to supplement the organized relief work of the nuns and laywomen. Until the opening of the commodious Montreal General Hospital in 1822, institutions for the ill in Montreal were also founded and administered by women.

The 1820s and 1830s would see an increase in benevolent activities. In contrast to the hope expressed in Doige's 1819 *Directory* that men would soon follow women's lead in the benevolent field, the writer of a directory published in 1839 boasted of Montreal's vigorous charitable activity relative to its size and wealth, and its successful projects for relief, reform, and immigrant aid.[33] Although they were no longer alone in the field, women did continue to direct several major efforts, as seen in the Benevolent Society's vigorous response to the cholera epidemic and consolidation of its orphanage.

After 1820 Catholic laywomen also became active. It is unclear to what degree groups such as the Ladies of Charity, founded by Angelique Blondeau, were initiated by activist priests such as Father Patrick Phelan or by the women themselves.[34] Hungry beggars going door to door were the immediate catalyst. The group was sufficiently large for diversification. Some members formed a society for education of the poor; others distributed piecework to needy women, paying them for the finished product with food. Some operated an employment bureau for domestics, while others helped unwed mothers, orphans, the aged, or the infirm. One of the most active members was Emilie Tavernier (Madame Gamelin), a young widow who noted that many of the recipients of aid were homeless. She took the initiative in requesting her parish priest to provide the St Catherine Street house in which she opened an Asile de la Providence in 1828 for sixteen infirm widows and several children, a work which soon expanded and long endured.[35]

In a number of respects the Catholic women's work resembled that of the Ladies' Benevolent Society. The originators were largely drawn from mercantile circles: Madame Blondeau, the wife of a Michilimakinac trader, contributed to the early work not only funds but personnel, since she also inspired in her three daughters a lifelong interest in the work with orphans. Marie-Amable Foretier, wife of politician Denis-Benjamin Viger, came from a wealthy and cultured business family. She brought to the Dames de Charité skills she used to manage their increasing properties, the most important being the Catholic Orphanage they opened in 1832 when their work outgrew its original three-storey house.[36] Like the Protestants, the Dames de Charité expanded rapidly, soon recruited the elite, and used the familiar tactic of going door to door to assess needs and solicit funds.

In the 1830s these lay groups continued the ecumenical tradition established by the nuns. Some women joined both Catholic and Protestant groups. Marie C.-J. LeMoyne, owner of the seigneurie of Longueuil and widow of Captain David Grant, served as the first president of the Catholic Orphanage and second president of the Protestant one.[37] Other French-English liaisons produced individuals such as Marie McCord who had connections with both groups. In 1831 Catholic and Protestant women co-sponsored a notable bazaar that netted £710, which appears to have been divided with the best of will on all sides: one-third to the Ladies of the Roman Catholic Church, £237; Montreal General Hospital, £175; Orphan Asylum, £108; National School, £40; British and Canadian School, £40; Infant School, £30; eight Protestant Clergy for the poor, £10 each.

The Catholic ladies reciprocated in the same spirit by promptly donating £50 to the Montreal General Hospital from their share of the proceeds.[38]

EVANGELICAL INNOVATIONS

In contrast with these societies that were rooted in the established churches, the evangelicals were more disruptive. In the period under review they were only beginning the social crusading that became their trademark and would eventually spawn the Social Gospel movement discussed elsewhere in this volume. In Montreal they were drawn from various denominations outside the three established churches, such as Methodists, Congregationalists, and the group of American Presbyterians who had broken away from the Church of Scotland group in Montreal; later recruits came from the Free Kirk. A number of the evangelicals, including some 'American' Presbyterians, hailed from the British Isles; but more significant were the roots many others had in the 'Burnt Over Districts' of New York and New England, centres of the Second Great Awakening (a revival largely financed and attended by women). American origins were a liability in a town in which memories of the War of 1812 were still fresh; and the originally humble occupations of New England evangelical families such as the DeWitts, Hedges, Wadsworths, and Lymans who soiled their hands with hatmaking, hardware, and pharmaceuticals, further blocked entry into Montreal's first circles.

The evangelicals' root conviction was that all human beings must subscribe to a pure biblical faith and a single standard of morality. Moreover, this daunting goal had an imminent deadline. Montreal evangelicals shared the widespread millennial expectations of Awakened America and post-Wesleyan Britain. Tending to discern the Second Coming of Christ in passing storm clouds, they hastened to save the world before it was too late. They saw the anti-Christ in churches accommodating double or multiple standards or corrupted by accretions of non-biblical ritual or dogma. To their credit the evangelicals – who were not uninterested in upward mobility – were brave about attacking harmful customs, no matter how long established or well entrenched. They were ready to bear rebuff or ridicule for what they thought right; this remained true even of many of them who ascended to Montreal's higher social circles (surprising the governor, for example, by lecturing him on teetotalism at his own banquet).[39]

What is more, dedicated evangelicals believed that the most lowly scrap of humanity deserved sustained attention (though not all the lowly welcomed the zealot's penetrating gaze). They accepted the need to feed and clothe beggars to put them in suitable state to hear the word of God. They also went deeper, recognizing the more lasting effect of touching hearts and changing minds. Their belief in the redeemability of the inner person caused them to protest a whole range of brutal practices that ignored the existence of conscience by assuming desirable conduct must be forced rather than taught or inspired. Evangelicals fought slavery and the use of the lash on sailors and soldiers and on the young. They believed that the consciences of children and others must be awakened and trained to do what was right so that external constraints could be removed. To the extent that society made immoral demands on its weaker members, society itself must be changed.[40]

In the early nineteenth century the evangelical sense of urgency and its mission to teach opened a door for female endeavour. Indeed, it is among the evangelicals that one catches flickers of rebellion against the established order that seem altogether lacking in established churchwomen with their cordial relationship with the powers of the land. At a time when Sunday schools often provided the only literacy working class children received, Lucy Hedge established one in Montreal; founded in 1817, it was claimed to be the first such institution in the city. Hedge, one of the founding members of Montreal's American Presbyterian congregation, had been educated in Litchfield, Connecticut; her pastor there had been the renowned American evangelist and reformer Lyman Beecher. Apparently the school she founded ossified and fell into other hands. This elicited a seeming *coup d'état* meeting held at Hedge's house in 1826 in which she, her sister, and fifteen other women and men signed a manifesto declaring the school's constitution totally inadequate and insisting on a new one directed to the religious and moral improvement of the young of all classes without distinction. The staff, they demanded, was to consist of 'persons of both sexes, all of whom shall be actively employed in the school.'[41] This work soon led to outreach to children in other parts of the city. Hedge worked with a committee to form the British and Canadian School for educating children of the labouring classes which opened in 1821 in the Craig Street house where the Benevolent Society had earlier operated the general hospital.[42] In the 1830s the church itself had five hundred children enrolled in several Sunday schools as well as a Free School giving gratuitous instruction to a large number of children.[43] It was by that date considered sufficiently useful to warrant government support.[44]

Most of the evangelical women's public activity, however, was in more controversial realms than teaching the poor the three R's. Women in Laprairie encountered priestly opposition to their distribution of French-language Bibles, which was under way by 1826. Evangelical women in Montreal followed suit, and they were in possession of sufficient funds to hire a city missionary in 1830.[45] These women were more interested in spreading the gospel than in doing social welfare work. This caused a reaction in the Roman Catholic community, with the priests forbidding their parishioners to accept the Bibles or attend the Sunday schools.

Equally unpopular, but of much greater significance for social welfare, was temperance work. Well into the 1840s in Canada some zealous temperance advocates suffered dismissal from jobs and regiments and censure by church congregations for 'speaking out too frankly on certain points.' Nevertheless, temperance work in that hard-drinking society was, as scholars have begun to recognize, a humanitarian endeavour. Historians of women have long treated temperance with respect, as a politicizing agent in the suffrage campaigns. Partly because of the excesses of the post-1850 prohibition movement, even those who appreciate this benefit have tended to analyse the attack on alcohol as melodrama, as middle class status-seeking, or as social control: in all events a distraction from the deeper problems that drove people to drink. The movement did contain all these elements; but recent research tends to confirm early temperance workers' claims that heavy drinking was a severe social problem in its own right, causing or exacerbating violence, family abuse or neglect, accidents, and many alcohol-related health problems.[46]

Evangelical women in the Canadas supported this important reform from its inception. Indeed their participation predates the years of 1826 to 1828 that historians have identified as its start.[47] G.W. Perkins, a Presbyterian missionary who later served as pastor of Montreal's American Presbyterian Church, wrote in 1822 of an earlier society. The family of Mrs John Forbes ran the local store in the little logging settlement of Russelltown, about forty kilometres south of Montreal. Energetic and resourceful, Mrs Forbes was concerned about conditions in her neighbourhood, which had no minister and was by several accounts 'fearfully intemperate.'[48] American-born, she may have been influenced by the Second Great Awakening and the temperance work accompanying religious revivals in the United States after 1815. She undertook to have a church built by raising subscriptions on both sides of the border and organizing a local dressmaking operation to bring in additional funds. Perhaps in reaction to the succession of dissolute doctors, teachers, and even preachers who passed through the village, Forbes also 'commenced ... the formation of a temperance society ... The proposal at first met with universal neglect and even derision. Still she persisted through private conversation, and the distribution of tracts and papers, she endeavoured to disarm prejudice. Her efforts were so far successful that she ventured at length to request a meeting of a few of the neighbours at her own house for the purpose of forming a temperance society ... She conversed with them individually, and a society was formed.'[49] The minister's comments reflect both the evangelical openness to action by people from outside the establishment and the apocalyptic expectations of the era. Forbes's efforts to transform Russelltown's 'moral desert' would, the young missionary wrote, 'bless the present generation and affect the temporal and eternal interests of the place as long as the world stands ... How was this accomplished? – By someone of great talent, wealth and influence? No, the piety, zeal and prayers of one female accomplished this ... Soon would the millennium come, were each Christian in his place, as efficient as this devoted female.'

Evangelical women in the Montreal Temperance Society would continue this tradition in 1840 by sending the first of a series of temperance circuit riders out to preach the cause across the Canadas in 1840, a crusade that would soon be expanded by the wealthy businessmen of that society. Thus, beginning in 1822, temperance leadership by evangelical women appeared in Canada a half-century earlier than is generally recognized. As outsiders, the evangelicals were willing to attack a social custom entrenched at all levels of society – in a way that nuns and other 'established' churchwomen with their gentlemen supporters and government funds were not likely to venture.

Female activists were overshadowed during the 1840s. Montreal's merchant princes would then begin to incorporate zealous reformers in their ranks, born-again, evangelical businessmen, ardent Presbyterians such as John Redpath with his sugar empire, the Lyman pharmaceutical magnates, and the Mackay brothers who made a fortune in drygoods. These men turned the women's wooden hospices and rented houses into the great pillared and iron-railed institutions of Victorian Canada. While philanthropic laymen replaced the hard-living fur traders at Montreal's social summit, the powerful Bishop Bourget created and controlled a new network of Catholic welfare institutions, and the paeans praising woman's place in the home grew deafening. Thereafter, men would tend to supply the direction to major welfare efforts, while women continued to supply much of the labour.

At the beginning of the century, things had been different. The field was dominated by women. In the first decade the nuns worked virtually alone in social welfare. In the second and third decades, a number of laywomen, mostly in connection with the established churches, took charge of social cases falling outside the nuns' network. The older benevolence associated with the established churches acted to relieve the growing numbers of urban poor. It did so without enquiring too closely into either the lifestyle of those who begged or the shortcomings of society. Yet these church-women alleviated human suffering in a time when little other relief was available; they left a legacy of interdenominational cooperation rather than bitterness. Clearly the work was solid, for the nuns and the Ladies' Benevolent Society built institutions that continued to evolve and endure to this day.

The evangelicals, beginning as outsiders because of American origins or lower status, dispensed a critique along with their charity. Their dogmatism and proselytization fostered decades of ill will. Yet in refusing to accept the maxim 'the poor we have always with us' and preferring to 'go teach all nations,' they determined to go beyond relieving distress to rooting it out. In so doing they initiated in Canada one of the nineteenth-century's most important reforms, the temperance movement which addressed a serious problem for society in general and women in particular, and eventually mobilized the latter to reclaim their basic civil rights.

Together, established and evangelical forms of Christianity produced notable female activism in the Montreal vicinity in the early nineteenth century. A former Londoner then living in Montreal compared this activity favourably with that of British women, saying that 'Montreal, though not equal to London in the number of its females, far surpasses that metropolis in the activity, capability and independence of the female mind and spirit.'[50] With their hospitals, asylums, and dispensaries, Mother Coutlée, Eleanor Gibb, Madame Grant, and their associates shaped the first response to the problems of immigrants arriving in the port city in desperate need of help and of the growing numbers of indigenous poor. Evangelical women began to address the underlying ills of addiction, brutality, and ignorance. Many of these endeavours won the cooperation of clergymen, physicians, and politicians. The initiative, however, arose from the 'activity, capability and independence of the female mind and spirit.'

NOTES

1 Jan Noel, 'New France: Les Femmes favorisées,' *Atlantis* 6, 2 (Spring 1981), 81–2. For a discussion of changing attitudes in subsequent decades see Allan Greer, *The Patriots and the People* (Toronto: University of Toronto Press, 1993), chap. 7.

2 Thomas Doige, *An Alphabetical List of the Merchants, Traders, and Housekeepers Residing in Montreal* (Montreal: Lane, 1819), 48–183.

3 See, for example, the St Paul's Church, Montreal, baptismal records, where until the 1840s the child's parents are usually recorded as 'John Brown and his wife Mary Jones.' This usage was also found in the French Canadian community.

4 For a detailed study of this phenomenon see Katherine McKenna, *A Life of Propriety: Anne Murray Powell and Her Family, 1755–1849* (Montreal, 1994).

5 Clio Collective, *Histoire des femmes au Québec* (Montreal: Qunize, 1982), 82–5, 150–2.

6 Claudette Lacelle, *Urban Domestic Servants in 19th Century Canada* (Ottawa: Parks Canada, 1987), 31–2.

7 Jan Noel, 'Dry Millennium: Temperance and a New Social Order in Mid-19th Century Canada and Red River' (PhD dissertation, University of Toronto, 1987), 116–33.

8 Andrée Dufour, 'Diversité institutionelle et fréquentation scholaire dans l'Ile de Montréal in 1825 et en 1835,' *RHAF* 41, 4 (1988): 520–1.

9 These conditions occasioned the founding of the first known Canadian temperance society, discussed in what follows.

10 Robert Campbell, *History of the Scotch Presbyterian Church, St Gabriel Street, Montreal* (Montreal: Drysdale, 1887), 52, 262–3. Jennifer Brown, 'Children of the Early Fur Trades' in *Childhood and Family in Canadian History*, Joy Parr, ed. (Toronto: McClelland and Stewart, 1982), 52–3.

11 Legislative Council of Lower Canada, *Journal*, 1824, Appendix 1, 'Report from the Special Committee ... upon the Establishments in this Province, for the reception and cure of the Insane, for the reception and support of Foundlings, and for the ... sick and infirm Poor ...' (hereafter JLCLC 1824 appx.1).

12 Doige, 17 *Annuaire de Ville-Marie*, Premiere Année, 1863: Origins, Utilité et Progrès des Institutions Catholiques de Montréal (Montreal: Senecal, 1864), 144–5.

13 F. Rousseau, 'Hôpital et société en Nouvelle-France: l'Hôtel Dieu de Québec à la fin du XVIIe siecle,' *RHAF* 31 (June 1977): 47. Noel, 'Femmes favorisées,' 87–8. While eighteenth-century Canadian female literacy was not particularly high, the gap between the sexes was narrower than that in contemporary France, England, and New England. Allan Greer, 'The Pattern of Literacy in Quebec, 1745–1899,' *Histoire social / Social History* 11, 22 (Nov. 1978): 332.

14 Lady Aylmer, *Recollections of Canada, 1831*, MG 24, vol. A-43, Public Archives of Canada (hereafter PAC).

15 JLCLC 1824, Appendix 1; *Annuaire*, 1864, 70.

16 JLCLC 1824, Appendix 1.

17 This was asserted for a later time, in the 1860s. *Annuaire*, 1864, 63. By that time

babies were also sent by train, often in carpetbags, from as far away as Quebec City and Upper Canada. J.-C. Robert, 'The City of Wealth and Death, 1821–71' in W. Mitchinson and J. McGinnis, eds., *Essays in the History of Canadian Medicine* (Toronto: McClelland and Stewart, 1988), 31, and Peter Gossage, 'Les enfants abandonnéd à Montréal au 19ᵉ siècle: la crêche d'Youville des Soeurs Grises, 1820–1871,' *RHAF* 40, 4 (1987).

18 Despite changing judicial responses, the leading causes of infanticide remained the same in Quebec for three centuries: desperation of young unwed mothers with no resources to raise a child and fearful of disgrace, family disapproval, or dismissal from employment. Marie-Aimée Cliche, 'L'Infanticide dans la region de Québec (1660–1964), *RHAF* 44, 1 (Summer 1990).

19 JLCLC 1824, Appendix 1

20 'Until the founding of this society, the only sources of relief for the poor were the Hôtel Dieu, the convents, and the bread line.' PAC, MG 28, 1388, vol. I, 1933 typewritten history, Montreal Ladies' Benevolent Society.

21 Campbell, 114, 143.

22 Mrs C.A. Pearce, *A History of the Montreal Ladies' Benevolent Society* (Montreal: Lovell, 1920), 9.

23 Robert Easton, *A Sermon Delivered before the Members of the Female Benevolent Society in Montreal, Sept. 18, 1816* (Montreal: N. Mower, 1816), 4.

24 Alfred Sandham, *Ville-Marie* (Montreal: G. Bishop, 1870), 289; Pearce, 14–15.

25 Pearce, 18; Sandham, 290.

26 Pearce, 14.

27 *Montreal Almanack of Lower Canada Register for 1831* (Montreal: Rbt. Armour, 1831), 144–6.

28 Pearce, 15.

29 *Historical Sketch of the Montreal Protestant Orphan Asylum* (Montreal: 1860), 10.

30 PAC MG 28, 1388, vol. I, 1933 typewritten history, Montreal Ladies' Benevolent Society.

31 Patricia Rooke and R.L. Schnell, 'The Rise and Decline of British North American Protestant Orphans' Homes as Woman's Domain, 1850–1930,' *Atlantis* 7, 2 (Spring 1982), 22, situate the beginning of most Protestant orphanages after 1850. For the elaborate set of rules developed over time see Montreal Ladies' Benevolent Society, *Rules ... Confirmed at the Extraordinary General Meeting ... April 1874* (Montreal, 1874).

32 Pearce, 7.

33 N. Bosworth, ed., *Hochelaga Depicta* (Montreal: Wm. Grieg, 1839), 18, 80–93, 205, 210–1.

34 *Canadian Courant*, 5 Jan. 1828 attributes the idea of a soup kitchen run by the

ladies to Reverend Phelan; Marie-Claire Daveluy, *L'Orphelinat catholique de Montréal (1832–1932)* (Montreal: A. Levesque, 1933), 295ff, suggests Phelan's presence but not leadership; while Huguette Lapointe-Roy notes Sulpician interest in founding a Ladies of Charity organization from 1819 but attributes the actual founding to Madame Gabriel Cotté in 1827. Lapointe-Roy, *La Charité bien ordonée* (Montreal: Boréal, 1987) 82–3.

35 *Annuaire*, 1864, 77–8.

36 Daveluy, 310ff; *Dictionary of Canadian Biography*, IV, 172; VIII, 301.

37 She was also sister-in-law to the president of the Ladies' Benevolent Society, Mrs John Richards.

38 Figures have been rounded. Source: Lady Aylmer, *Recollections*, typescript, 73; also Develuy, 305.

39 Reverend J. Wood, *Memoir of Henry Wilkes* (Montreal: Grafton, 1887), 134.

40 For a Foucault-inspired interpretation of this internalization as a stage in state formation, see Jean-Marie Fecteau, *Un nouvel ordre des choses: La pauvreté, le crime, l'Etat au Québec de la fin du XIXe siecle à 1840* (Montreal, 1989).

41 American Presbyterian Church (Montreal), Sunday School Records, United Church Archives (hereafter UCA), Montreal.

42 *Montreal Almanack* 1831, 145; Sandham, 104.

43 *Hochelaga Depicta*, 114; American Presbyterian Church Records, A 523, 2 and 3, UCA, Montreal.

44 In Montreal's hinterland, evangelicals also organized to address poverty and illiteracy. A Baptist revival in Potton Township, Brome County, for example, led to the formation of a Female Benevolent Society in 1826. About fifty members made and sold cloth to help poorer neighbours in various ways, which included the purchasing of books for a Sabbath school. Reverend Ernest Taylor, *History of Brome County* (Montreal: Lovell, 1908 and 1937), vol. 1, 230–3; vol. 2, 112.

45 American Home Missionary Society Correspondence 1826–30, UCA, Toronto, esp. Reverend Purkis to Absolom Peters, May 1826, and S. Marsh to A. Peters, Oct. 1830; see also *Montreal Almanack*, 1831, which records a Montreal Ladies' Bible Association and a (female) Montreal Domestic Missionary Society.

46 See, for example, Ian Tyrell, *Sobering Up* (Westport, Conn.: Greenwood, 1979), and Ruth Bordin, *Woman and Temperance* (Philadelphia: Temple University Press, 1981) on the American movement; my own *Canada Dry: Temperance Crusades before Confederation* (University of Toronto Press, 1995) on Canadian temperance shares this basically favourable assessment, particularly of the early temperance movement.

47 The movement has been dated from the appearance of a group in Gloucester, New Brunswick, in 1826, and in Montreal, Brockville, Leeds County, the Niagara peninsula, and Beaver River, Nova Scotia, in 1827–8. Ruth Spence, *Prohibi-*

tion in Canada (Toronto: Dominion Alliance, 1919), 38–9; R.D. Wadsworth, *Temperance Manual* (Montreal, 1847), 4–5; F.L. Barron, 'The Genesis of Temperance in Ontario 1828–50' (PhD dissertation, University of Guelph, 1976), 36–7.

48 G.W. Perkins to Absolom Peters, American Home Missionary Society (AHMS) Correspondence, UCA, Toronto; Robert Sellars, *History of the County of Huntingdon and the Seigniories of Chateauguay and Beauharnois from the First Settlement to the Year 1838* (Huntingdon: Gleaner, 1888), 29, 462–71.

49 Perkins to Peters, AHMS correspondence, July 1822. The date on the inside of the letter is simply July '22 which leaves some ambiguity about whether 22 refers to the day or the year; but on the outside of the letter is written 'will Mr Judd take this to New York 1822.' While Perkins does not name the woman in question, her identity is supplied by E. McDougall in 'The Presbyterian Church in Western Lower Canada' (PhD dissertation, McGill University, 1969), 271. See also Sellars, 472.

50 Pearce, 23.

14

'The Union between Faith and Good Works': The Life of Harriet Dobbs Cartwright, 1808–1887

KATHERINE M.J. MCKENNA

The wife of an Anglican clergyman in Kingston, Ontario, Harriet Dobbs Cartwright expressed her spirituality through charitable and religious activities in church and community, as well as through writing hymns and religious poems. Filled with religious zeal, and discontented performing the duties and obligations of the wife of an Anglican pastor in Upper Canada, she was freed by her economic and social privilege to participate in work that interested her. An innovative and resourceful woman, she defied convention by spending much time away from her home and was thus subjected to criticism from members of her own family. In this she was typical of many women of her class throughout the nineteenth century, who used the new ideology of woman's role as moral guide of her family in order to justify entering the public sphere through charitable endeavours.

Oh that my soul were bound to Thee,
By more than mortal tie.
Oh that to thine own holy rest,
My wearied soul would fly.

And yet my earthly pilgrimage
Has scarcely well begun.
And shall I murmur at my lot
The appointed course to run?

Oh Lord forgive the restless thoughts
Of an immortal mind
That in earth's vain & low pursuits
No rest or peace can find.

Break Thou, the bonds of earthly sort
That bind my weak heart still
And give me strength of faith to walk
By thine own holy will.

Yet leave me not, Oh Lord my God
To vain pursuits of earth
But with my fainting spirit's power
To ends of nobler worth.[1]

Harriet Dobbs composed these verses around the time of her twenty-second birthday on 27 August 1830, in Dublin, Ireland. What they lacked in

poetic merit was amply compensated for by their heartfelt sincerity. Harriet's restlessness, her dissatisfaction with the 'vain pursuits of earth,' had tormented her throughout an emotionally turbulent adolescence. A consuming concern with religion and with the dubious state of her immortal soul was finally resolved by the conviction of the presence of God's salvation in her life and the further necessity of revealing this saving grace through good works. Thus, Harriet as a young woman, and later as a wife and mother, threw herself with enthusiasm into a wide variety of charitable and religious activities in the service of the Lord. She multiplied these useful endeavours during a long widowhood and died in Kingston, Ontario, on 14 May 1887, at the age of seventy-eight, in full assurance of entering heaven.

That, in brief, is the way Harriet herself would have told her life story. Even a superficial examination of her poem, however, reveals a subtext that she herself did not acknowledge. Why would a young woman who, as she put it, had 'scarcely well begun' her 'earthly pilgrimage' and 'appointed course' complain of a 'wearied soul' that 'no rest or peace can find'? Why did she suffer guilt and seek forgiveness for 'restless thoughts,' a 'weak heart,' and 'fainting spirit'? Why did she need the support of God to allow her to pursue 'ends of nobler worth'? The answer to these questions can tell us a great deal not only about Harriet's life, but more generally about the lives of women of her day. The dilemmas she faced and the solutions that she proposed to resolve them were not unique to her except perhaps in the fervour and intensity with which she embraced them.

The life of such a woman as Harriet Dobbs Cartwright does not fit easily with traditional notions about appropriate subjects for biography. Classical biography, as Phyllis Rose has observed, 'is a tool by which the dominant society reinforces its values.' Thus, it is the lives of exemplary individuals who have succeeded in very public ways that are generally written about. Politicians, royalty, heroes, and great artists are the characteristic subjects. Biography, Rose tells us, 'has ignored women; it ignores the poor and working class; it ignores the underprivileged; it ignores non-celebrities.'[2] To write about the life of a person who fits into one of these excluded categories, then, is to subvert the traditional purpose and meaning of biography.

Feminist scholars have been particularly interested in the revolutionary implications of women's biography. Writing about a woman's life makes a statement about its worth and importance. It reclaims women's lives and experience from obscurity, and even further than that, as Susan Mann Trofimenkoff has observed, 'when so much of our cultural heritage has stressed women's passivity, feminist biography allows us to see women as actors.'[3] All too often, however, this laudable aim results in searching for women who match up to the male standard of biography. Thus, only exceptional, atypical women who have succeeded on men's terms in the public world are examined. This is not to suggest that such studies should not be written. They make fascinating reading and are invaluable not only for the historical record but also as inspirational role models. But by this standard, a biography of a woman like Harriet Dobbs Cartwright could never be considered worthy of treatment: there is nothing particularly heroic about her life. She left behind no significant body of work or great achievement, she was no politician and obviously an indifferent poet. Her one claim to distinction might lie in the wealth of written sources that she has left behind her, now kept at the Public Archives of Ontario and the Queen's University Archives at Kingston. The early adult years of Harriet's life are particularly well documented with extensive correspondence covering the period from 1833 to 1845 and a remarkable religious autobiography written in 1833 following her marriage.[4] Such richness of sources certainly makes a biography of Harriet Dobbs Cartwright possible, but it does not necessarily mean that it deserves scholarly attention. How, then, can such a subject be justified?

Trofimenkoff considers the implications of such questions when she asks if women's biography ought to 'focus on explanation rather than on accomplishment? Standard biographies of men stress the latter; feminist biographies of men or women might have to stress the former.'[5] Joan Scott suggests the form for this explanation when she points out that historians need 'to examine the ways in which gendered identities are substantively constructed and relate their findings to a range of activities, social organizations and historically specific cultural representations. The best efforts in this area so far have been, not surprisingly, biographies.'[6] More recently, in her stimulating article on women's biography in history, Kathleen Barry has observed that 'by grounding history in the actual meanings interpreted in the situations of those engaged in that history, the subjects themselves, we are arriving at a new historical synthesis that will give us a grounding of women's subjectivity in its own history and begin to produce its own theories of history.'[7] My study of Harriet Dobbs Cartwright fits well within such an approach.

Specifically, Harriet's biography shows how one woman in the early nineteenth century dealt with the ideology of separate spheres, first called the 'Cult of True Womanhood' by historian Barbara Welter.[8] Women like Harriet were told that their proper place was in the home and that there they were to embody all that was good about domestic life. In particular, morality and religion became more and more the special province of women. Early Victorian women took their role as 'domestic angels' seriously, assuming a special responsibility in upholding Christian values in the face of the secular and corrupt new world of industrial capitalism. It was only a matter of time before women began to work to bring these higher values of womanhood into all aspects of life. The middle class woman who had time on her hands was not permitted to labour for pay in the public sphere, but might she not work for free, in the service not of capitalism but of the Lord? Many Victorian women with talent and enthusiasm adopted this line of reasoning and devoted their energies to good works. This new growth of women's charitable activity has been well documented on both sides of the Atlantic.[9] Eventually women's reforming power developed into what has been called 'maternal feminism' and increasingly throughout the nineteenth century served as a justification for such varied public political activity as temperance, female suffrage, and social reform. Thus, throughout the nineteenth century women embraced and then subverted the ideology of True Womanhood, using it to justify all sorts of occupations not originally envisioned. Harriet Dobbs Cartwright provides us with an early example of this tendency.[10]

The importance of religion in Harriet's life is underscored by her mother's idealized account of the beginnings of the lives of her three daughters. 'When your Grandmamma was very young, and that is a great many years ago,' Maria Dobbs wrote to her grandchildren, 'she had three beautiful girls, she was very proud of them, perhaps she was too proud of them. But these little girls were good as well as pretty and did whatever she bid them. I do not recollect that they ever told a lie.' Harriet and her sisters were also avid students and 'very anxious to inform themselves and took great pains to learn whatever was taught them.' These paragons, 'when they went to school ... used to get up at four O'Clock in the morning to learn their lessons ...' They were even prepared to sacrifice children's parties in order to keep up their studies, and so, Maria Dobbs admonished her grandchildren, 'whenever you are tempted to commit any fault, just say like your dear Mamma, it is not worthwhile displeasing God for all the pleasure this will give me.' This was a lesson well learned by her 'three dear little girls' who unsurprisingly, from their mother's point of view, 'grew up to be fine young women, everybody loved them because they were well-informed and modest.'[11]

Harriet's autobiography suggests that her younger years, particularly those of her adolescence, were much less idyllic than her mother's account implies. Where she went to school in Dublin and exactly what she learned there as a child is not clear, but her formal education came to an end when she reached her thirteenth year. At this time she 'began to consider myself almost a woman, now that I had entered my teens.' Harriet's father was a successful barrister, and she and her seven siblings lacked for nothing materially. Once the daughters left school, however, their time was filled by little else than socializing and practising the polite accomplishments that they had learned. Fortunately an indulgent male friend agreed to instruct them, and Harriet eagerly applied herself 'in some branches of knowledge not exactly belonging to young ladies' general routine of learning,' she wrote, 'but for that reason perhaps, possessing more zest.' However, this benefit was short-lived. The girls were forced to fall back on their own resources and develop their minds as best they could. At any rate, Harriet pointed out, 'if it did no more, it at least served to increase our eager desire after knowledge, to stimulate our exertions and to call forth and exercise our powers of reflection & comprehension.'[12]

Left without any serious occupation, Harriet cast around for something to give meaning to her life, and she soon found it. By chance she was invited to attend religious classes for young people at St Mary's Anglican Church where a charismatic and evangelical young pastor, Reverend Bardin, captivated her heart and soul.[13] Harriet explained her attraction with an innocent lack of self-awareness. The excitement she felt was to her purely religious: 'I was attracted at once by his manner of instructing in which the dignity of the Christian Pastor, was blended with the affection of the earthly parent. I soon learned to revere him as a zealous & devoted Minister of God, and to love him as a spiritual father and to every word he uttered, I listened with deep and fixed attention.'[14] Harriet's life became an agony of waiting from her Thursday class to Sunday service to Thursday again, full of anxiety and fear that some last minute problem would prevent her from going. Since she was not permitted to attend on her own, her sisters could force her to agree to anything simply by threatening not to accompany her. 'I was not independent of the wills of others,' Harriet complained, 'and often have I felt dejected & downcast & unable to refrain from tears, when prevented from enjoying the privilege of attending Mr Bardin's when I knew that many others were around him.' Harriet did recognize that 'in the study of the scriptures I had at first perhaps too much regard for the approval of our Pastor.'[15] Even if her motivations were less spiritual than she was prepared to acknowledge, Harriet was now hooked on an exciting evangelical style of religion, and, as she put it, 'The hungering & thirsting after spiritual things thus excited in my mind, was no transient feeling. I eagerly sought for & embraced every opportunity of receiving Scriptural instruction.'[16]

Harriet's obsessive concern with religion soon began to alarm her more conventionally pious mother. Her daughter would return from the classes and sermons she had so desperately wanted to attend, downcast and in agony over the state of her own sinfulness, and with a 'despairing heart.'[17] Scriptural study helped, 'but whatever thoughts of peace & consolation might dawn within, it was not in a moment that I could always resume the outward appearance of composure & cheerfulness and sometimes when deep convictions of sin & apprehensions of danger had laid me low before my Father's throne to supplicate with tears and earnest cries for pardon and peace & that when obliged to join the family circle, I still continued downcast and gloomy.' Such obvious depression and anxiety 'could not fail of attracting notice.' Her mother naturally 'did not understand the work-ings of my mind' and became 'apprehensive of the effects of too much reading of Scripture & attendance on preaching & lecturing & sometimes said if it tended to make me gloomy & unsocial, I should go no more.'[18] With her thoughts constantly on the eternal, Harriet had little interest in social life or, as she put it, 'but little relish for the gay and frivolous amuse-ments of worldly dissipation' which 'sometimes made me resist to the verge of disobedience the wishes of my mother on the subject.'[19] Thus, in her teens she established a pattern that was to continue throughout her life. Frustrated by her confinement at home, Harriet found a broader scope of activity and of intellectual and emotional engagement in religion. To her, religious involvement represented freedom and excitement, whereas domestic work and the social obligations of a middle class woman's sphere represented restriction and misery. Religion gave Harriet a sanction for doing what no well-brought-up young women could ever do – rebel against her role in family and social life.

Over the next five and a half years, from the age of eighteen to her mar-riage in 1832, Harriet struggled with the conviction of her own sinfulness, her desire for the assurance of salvation, and the demands of her family which pulled her away from religious concerns. When free of the pressures of other obligations, she read seriously and intensely in religious works. Two books that were particularly influential for Harriet's religious devel-opment were *A Practical View of the Prevailing Religious System of Pro-fessed Christians in the Higher and Middle Classes in this Country, Contrasted with Real Christianity* by the evangelical Anglican William Wilberforce, and *Death of Legal Hope, Life of Evangelical Obedience: An Essay on Galations ii* by Abraham Booth; both of these she read several

times.²⁰ Although Harriet found Booth too Calvinistic for her taste, he led
her to the serious contemplation of what became for her a central point of
spiritual contention – the conflict between her faith and her life, between
salvation by God's grace alone and the necessity of good works to earn that
salvation. Could the secular life that she was forced so unwillingly to lead
be combined with the care of her immortal soul? Harriet yearned to do
something active 'as though something of my own, must yet be added to
the perfect work of Christ, to fill up the measure of justification in the sight
of God.'²¹ Yet she knew that as a sinner she could never earn her own salvation, even if she worked to all eternity.

She struggled in despair and misery with this dilemma until finally the
light dawned: 'I saw then, and I rejoiced to see, that all was finished that
regards our justification before God – that the work of Christ for us was
full, free, perfect – that the justification of all who have or ever shall enter
into perfect life was completed when the redeemer exclaimed on Calvary
"It is finished!" ... proferred to all without money & without price, as the
free gift of God.' Harriet does not describe this realization as a conversion,
but her experience follows the classical pattern. With the recognition of
God's mercy, 'a weight seemed to rise from my heart & my spirit, light-
ened of the burthen of still remaining doubts & uncertainties ... rose up tri-
umphant from the pressure & ascended to the God of My Salvation, with
psalms & hymns of joy & praise, such as I had never joined in before, with
the same rejoicing spirit.' Harriet continued in this euphoric state for 'days
and weeks' praising the God of her redemption constantly in her heart.²²

The result of this dramatic conversion was not, however, a feeling of
contentment with her present life. On the contrary, it convinced her that
she owed something to God in return for his mercy. 'Though well may
shame & confusion, belong unto me, when I take a retrospect of the past,'
she avowed, 'yet I see & feel that every increase in the strength and firm-
ness of our faith, must *tend*, to urge us onward in the path of duty. So
inseparable is the union between faith & good works though so distinct in
their justifying power.'²³ Looking around her, Harriet found ample scope
for worthy endeavour. The conversion of her siblings was an obvious duty,
although one not always appreciated by them. She soon went to a Scripture
class on Sundays, expanded on this with more sabbath and weekday teaching, and later added visitation of the poor to her duties. Constantly seeking
to broaden her activities she found that 'these various engagements occupied much time and made many days almost like Sabbaths,' her favourite
day of the week. 'I met with occasional discouragements – but I have never
felt more happy.'²⁴ Harriet's conflicts were now resolved, and her course of

action was clear. Only by her absolute submission to the will of an all-powerful patriarchal God was she able to gain the happy assurance that she needed in order to chart her own course in life: It was not *her* will that she was asserting, but rather the Lord's. Harriet's autobiography reveals her conviction that God had a special plan for her and that all the events of her life should be viewed as evidence of God's workings.

It is not surprising, given Harriet's early attraction to Bardin, that she chose as her husband another Anglican clergyman, Robert Cartwright. That he was to take her far away from her family's restraining influence to a new country where she would find greater scope for religious activity was also an appealing prospect. Educated at Oxford, Robert was the son of a prosperous Upper Canadian merchant. The Cartwrights and the Dobbs were already connected through the marriage of Robert's older sister Mary to Harriet's uncle, who had served in Canada during the War of 1812. Robert did not earn much in his new position as minister at St George's Cathedral in Kingston, Upper Canada; he was, however, a man of independent means and Harriet was provided with a comfortable home and servants. This gave her more freedom from domestic cares than most women enjoyed, and thus she was able to pursue her interest in religious works.

Kingston society initially expected something different from the pastor's new wife. Following her arrival in the city she was subjected to all the social demands that she so much dreaded. All Kingston wanted to meet her; therefore she was 'obliged to sit up in state, to be introduced to, and receive congratulations.' According to the convention of the day, she was required to return all these compliments by calling at her visitors' homes, an onerous duty which took up the entire first month after her arrival. Harriet was much happier about her domestic arrangements. Robert's older sister Mary, now widowed, lived with them and managed most of the household chores for Harriet. 'I have been all this time leaving her to do various things I ought to have been arranging,' Harriet admitted. 'I have indeed much cause to feel indebted to her for all the trouble she has taken about our house.' Harriet jokingly referred to Mary as 'Robert's *first wife*. I intend only to be her deputy,' she declared, 'and leave her to be prime directress.' This left Harriet more time for other pursuits, and she was soon concerning herself about the poor attendance at the church school.[25] Within a very short time, she was teaching daily and contemplating forming a Scripture class for young ladies. Within two months of her arrival Harriet was gratified that Kingston society had accepted her dislike of socializing. She was no longer invited to any parties, her neighbours having been 'good in not obliging me, to make any false declarations of "regret," in declining invitations.'[26] Each day began early and in sober fashion with Robert delivering a short sermon to the assembled household.[27] This to Harriet was the ideal way to start a useful day of teaching. She later added hospital visiting to her duties, and she worked hard at renovating the school, engaging a full-time teacher to preside over the non-sectarian classroom. All in all, she was very happy in her new home.

Harriet's friends and relatives were far from happy, however, at the news of the many activities that her letters home described. A year following her arrival she became aware of 'apprehensions that seem to have arisen at home, that I may be doing too much and neglecting home duties.' Harriet conceded that the 'charge I acknowledge may be often true, through ignorance as well as carelessness.' However, in her own defence she pointed out that 'I am not at all disposed to deny the supremacy of those quiet duties connected with the right ordering of the family.' Harriet knew that the proper place for a woman was in the home. 'Nor am I in the least disposed,' she protested, 'to advocate the intrusion of females upon spheres of action, not belonging to their station.' Harriet was not prepared to acknowledge what others could see, that she was using her efforts in the service of her God as a means of escaping the usual domestic and social obligations of an early Victorian middle class woman. 'I know, that both by myself and by others, much time is squandered in frivolous & vain pursuits or in 'Shapeless Idleness,'' she responded tartly to her critics, 'that might well be redeemed for more useful occupations, without in the least infringing on home duties, and this I do earnestly desire, that I might be enabled to act more consistently in future, that the expectations & apprehensions of friends at home may not sound to me, so much like a bitter mockery of indolence and neglect.'[28] Harriet was fortunate to have such an understanding and wealthy husband who supported her in her endeavours, although even he at times was led to chide her 'for my being so long from Home.'[29]

Even the arrival of children did not stop, although they did interfere with, Harriet's extra-domestic pursuits. She gave birth to four boys and a girl between 1834 and 1841. A devoted mother, she nevertheless expressed frustration about the domestic demands on her time not six months after her firstborn's arrival. These became even more pressing following Mary Cartwright Dobbs's death in 1839. She complained that 'day after day glides by in the daily routine of occupation and wants with extra interruptions for every extra hour leaving little time for reading, writing or drawing or anything else, and what is worse, little prospect of amendments except it be by an increase in diligence, activity and regularity, on my own part, which I am afraid to promise, for I have so often determined in vain, and made resolutions only to be broken.'³⁰ Harriet's fondest dream was to do away with all domestic obligations, and at one point she even had hopes of combining her household with that of Sarah Cartwright, another sister-in-law. 'If such an arrangement should be made,' she wrote hopefully, 'I shall bargain with Sarah to give up the housekeeping department to her, and take to keeping school as more suited to my taste, as well as the other being in better hands with her.'³¹

Although she constantly complained about her lack of time, Harriet managed to juggle her various responsibilities so that she could undertake a multitude of good works. She continued to supervise both Sunday and day schools. Every Thursday afternoon she held sewing parties at her home where ladies made goods to donate to the poor or sell for charity while Harriet read to them from some edifying text. She also held singing meetings for the church choir.³² In 1839 she led the revival of the Kingston Female Benevolent Society. Through the society, she organized a regular program of distributing to the poor the raw materials with which they could make useful goods; these the ladies would then sell on behalf of the poor to provide them with income. This, however, was charity with a further purpose. 'The far more important part of the work to be done,' Harriet pointed out, 'is the visiting of families of the Poor and thus obtaining a general knowledge of their habits, wants, and attendance in religious ordinances.'³³ Harriet carefully planned her many activities to accomplish the organizational feat of discharging social obligations and doing good works all at once. 'In these various ways, we shall see a good deal of those we should otherwise be called on to visit from time to time, so that my circuit of visits will be still more confined than heretofore, and yet I hope to see more of the members of our congregation, and in a more profitable manner,' she explained.³⁴ Thus, unproductive socializing was kept to an absolute minimum.

Harriet's understanding of the causes of social distress was rudimentary and showed a strong class bias. In politics she was an instinctive conservative, observing that 'it is generally found that piety in religion & conservatism in politics, will form the same happy union that is almost universally found between liberalism and infidelity.'³⁵ Although she kept her school non-sectarian and supported Protestant unity, she was bigoted in her view of Catholicism. All Protestants should combine together, she felt, 'to forget our discussions & disputes and unite against the formidable and increasing power of popery & Infidelity.' Over time, however, Harriet did become somewhat more understanding of the plight of the poor. At first she was 'convinced that there is no poverty amongst us ... that might not be removed by a little attention in providing suitable employment, without any loss or expense to the community, but simply by directing industry into right channels.'[36] Later, after witnessing the misery and destitution of many of the Irish Catholic immigrants who arrived in Kingston impoverished and often very ill, she moderated this position somewhat. 'It is true that there are a great number of recently arrived destitute families of Emigrants, whose wants cannot at once be supplied,' she conceded. 'But even these, though they must endure hardship & privation for a season yet will gradually attain to comforts & independence.'[37]

Increasingly, Harriet came to blame chronic poverty on the problem of alcohol abuse, or intemperance. She did not, however, take an extreme stand by advocating prohibition, a position that became more common later in the century. The Female Benevolent Society pondered this problem with the result that they took some extraordinary action and 'ventured so far out of our place as quiet domestic Dames as to get up an humble Petition to the Magistrates to diminish the Licenses and look after the unlicensed drain shops abounding in every corner.' The society's appeal was successful: it resulted in the closure of several establishments and in a stricter control over the granting of new licences. Feeling the thrill of victory, Harriet hoped to press this advantage even further by working to 'stir up the minds of those possessed of authority to be more active in their exertions to repress an evil of so great & increasing an extent.'[38] Thus, we see a very early example of what was to occur on a larger scale all over Canada later in the century. Once a greater religious and moral sense was attributed to women, it was only logical that they would translate it into good works; then, inevitably, women extended their influence further into the public sphere to social and political reform. Ironically the ideology of True Womanhood held within it the seeds of its own destruction.

Harriet's happy marriage to her tolerant and beloved Robert was cut short by his early death from tuberculosis in 1843. Her family expected her to return with her children to Dublin, but instead she remained in Kingston. 'I sometimes fear I may seem ungrateful and wanting in natural affection in still clinging to a land from which all whom I most loved have been called away,' she admitted. 'Yet I feel that I could not be justified under present circumstances in removing from the spot where the providence of God has placed me.'[39] Harriet's excuses do not disguise what must have been her real reasons for remaining in Upper Canada. Returning to Ireland would mean going back to her old way of life with all its demands and restrictions. Not only had she a wider sphere of activity in Kingston, but she could now devote even more time to her true life's work: Harriet and Sarah, also recently widowed, had finally combined households.

Very sparse documentary evidence has survived from the last forty-two years of Harriet Dobbs Cartwright's life until her death in 1887. Widowed at the early age of thirty-six, she had more than half her life still ahead of her. Yet it is appropriate that so little can be found from this later period. As a financially independent woman with limited domestic, family, and social obligations, she was no longer disturbed by most of the conflicts that had marked her early life. Harriet chose not to remarry, although she must have been a very eligible widow. Instead she continued to pursue her life of charitable endeavour, not only working with the Female Benevolent Society, but from 1856 until her death serving on the executive of the Orphan's and Widow's Friend Society. She was also 'one of the first regular visitors to be concerned with the treatment of women prisoners in the penitentiary.'[40] Her obituary in the *British Whig* stated that 'she was a good old lady, full of piety and much given to good work, and her reward is certain. She was one of the founders of the Orphan's home, and held the position of corresponding secretary to the time of her death. For fifty years she had been active in good works, and the last thing she aimed at was the establishment of a Kindergarten school.'[41] As her brother noted following Harriet's death, 'Surely no one could be better prepared for the great change.'[42] If this indeed was true, then we must judge Harriet Dobbs Cartwright's life on her own terms to have been nothing short of a remarkable and unqualified success.

NOTES

1 Journal of Harriet Dobbs Cartwright, Cartwright Papers, Public Archives of Ontario (hereafter PAO), 57.
2 Phyllis Rose, 'Fact and Fiction in Biography,' in *Writing of Women: Essays in a Renaissance* (Middletown, Conn.: Wesleyan University Press, 1985), 68.
3 Susan Mann Trofimenkoff, 'Feminist Biography,' *Atlantis* 10, 2 (1985), 4. I would like to express my sincere thanks to Dr Trofimenkoff for her very helpful suggestions for revision of an earlier version of this paper prepared for the Canadian Historical Association meetings at Victoria in 1990.
4 Two works which specifically focus on women's spiritual autobiographical writings are Carol Edkins, 'Quest for Community: Spiritual Autobiographies of Eighteenth-Century Quaker and Puritan Women in America,' in *Women's Autobiography*, Jelinek, ed., 39–52; and Margaret Conrad, 'Mary Bradley's

Reminiscences: A Domestic Life in Colonial New Brunswick,' *Atlantis* 7 (1981): 92–101.

5 Trofimenkoff, 7.

6 Joan W. Scott, 'Gender: A Useful Category of Historical Analysis,' *American Historical Review* 91 (1986), 1068.

7 Kathleen Barry, 'The New Historical Synthesis: Women's Biography,' *Journal of Women's History* 1, 3 (1990), 91.

8 Barbara Welter, 'The Cult of True Womanhood,' *American Quarterly* 18 (1966), 151–74. Many subsequent historians have both enlarged on and refined this theme, most recently Leonore Davidoff and Catherine Hall, in *Family Fortunes: Men and Women of the English Middle Class, 1780–1850* (London: Hutchinson, 1987).

9 F.K. Prochaska examines the British context in *Women and Philanthropy* (Oxford: Clarendon Press, 1980). For the United States see Ruth Bloch, 'American Feminine Ideals in Transition: The Rise of the Moral Mother,' *Feminist Studies* 4 (1978), 101–26; Ann Boylan, 'Evangelical Womanhood in the Nineteenth Century: The Role of Women in Sunday Schools,' *Feminist Studies* 4 (1978); Nancy F. Cott, *The Bonds of Womanhood: Woman's Sphere in New England, 1780–1835* (New Haven: Yale University Press, 1977); Ann Douglas, *The Feminization of American Culture* (New York: Avon Books, 1977); Barbara Leslie Epstein, *The Politics of Domesticity: Women, Evangelism, and Temperance in Nineteenth-Century America* (Middletown, Conn.: Wesleyan University Press, 1981); Keith Melder, 'Ladies Bountiful: Organized Women's Benevolence in Early Nineteenth-Century America,' *New York History* 48 (1964), 231–54; Mary P. Ryan, *Cradle of the Middle Class: The Family in Oneida County New York, 1790–1860* (Cambridge: Cambridge University Press, 1981), 83–144; and Carol Smith-Rosenberg, 'Beauty, the Beast, and the Militant Woman: A Case Study in Sex Roles and Social Stress in Jacksonian America,' in *A Heritage of Her Own: Toward a New Social History of American Women*, Nancy F. Cott and Elizabeth H. Pleck, eds. (New York: Simon and Schuster, 1979), 197–211.

10 I am not the first to write about Harriet Dobbs Cartwright's life. Margaret Angus's article 'A Gentlewoman in Early Kingston' (*Historic Kingston* 24 [1976], 73–85) examines her life in the context of social life in Kingston.

11 Maria Dobbs to her grandchildren, Dublin, 18 July 1838, in 'Family Letters for My Grandchildren,' Cartwright Letterbook, Cartwright Papers, Queen's University Archives. Special thanks are due to Shirley Spragge and Anne MacDermaid of the Queen's University Archives for their extra efforts on my behalf which greatly facilitated my research on Harriet Dobbs Cartwright.

12 Journal of Harriet Dobbs Cartwright (hereafter Journal), Cartwright Papers, PAO, 4.
13 For the evangelical nature of the Church of Ireland in the early nineteenth century see Donald Harman Akenson, *The Church of Ireland: Ecclesiastical Reform and Revolution, 1880–1885* (New Haven: Yale University Press, 1971), 132–42.
14 Journal, 7.
15 Ibid., 19.
16 Ibid., 20.
17 Ibid., 9.
18 Ibid., 10–11.
19 Ibid., 16–17.
20 Ibid., 38.
21 Ibid., 39.
22 Ibid., 40–1.
23 Ibid., 45.
24 Ibid., 75–6.
25 Harriet Dobbs Cartwright to Maria Irwin, Kingston, 18 June 1833, Letterbook of Harriet Dobbs Cartwright, Cartwright Papers, PAO.
26 Ibid., to Marianne McNaughton, 14 Aug. 1833.
27 Ibid., to Marianne Martley (nee McNaughton), 24 July 1834.
28 Ibid., to Maria Dobbs, 26 Dec. 1839.
29 Ibid., to Marianne Martley, 26 Dec. 1834.
30 Ibid., 19 Dec. 1834.
31 Ibid., to Madeline Dobbs, 15 Feb. 1841.
32 Ibid., to Kate Dobbs, 8 Nov. 1838.
33 Ibid., to Maria Dobbs, 26 Dec. 1839.
34 Ibid., to Marianne Martley, 15 Dec. 1840.
35 Ibid., to Maria, Kate, and Madeline Dobbs, 10 Aug. 1841.
36 Ibid., to Maria Dobbs, 26 Dec. 1839.
37 Ibid., to Conway Dobbs, 14 Dec. 1840.
38 Ibid., to Conway Dobbs, 14 Dec. 1840.
39 Same to Mr and Mrs Conway Dobbs, Kingston, 24 Apr. 1845, Typescript of Harriet Dobbs Cartwright Correspondence, Cartwright Papers, Queen's University Archives.
40 Angus, 'A Gentlewoman in Early Kingston,' 85.
41 Kingston, *British Whig*, 16 May 1887.
42 Conway E. Dobbs to Richard Cartwright, Eglantine, 10 June 1887, Cartwright Papers, PAO.

15

The Ontario Young Woman's Christian Temperance Union: A Study in Female Evangelicalism, 1874–1930

SHARON ANNE COOK

The Young Woman's Christian Temperance Union was an organization of young Canadian women who took seriously the biblical injunction to go 'into all the world' with the gospel and bring 'souls out of darkness into light.' Its members carried on an extensive program combining evangelical proselytizing with social activism. They acted out of their Christian faith in a group that was founded by women with strongly held Christian beliefs, but that cut across denominational boundaries. Thus, the women operated outside the structures of the institutionalized church, but within a firm evangelical stance. They used many means to appeal to sinners, but gradually they turned away from individual rescue work and towards the preventive measures of social reform. In such projects as the Home for Friendless Women in Ottawa they worked tirelessly to offer new life to people on the fringes of Canadian society.

From about the middle of the nineteenth until the beginning of the twentieth centuries, the dominant form of religious expression in most Protestant
denominations in Britain, the United States, and Canada was evangelicalism.[1] Nineteenth-century evangelicals believed that the world could be
improved through the moral efforts of individuals to rise above personal
sin. 'The sinner stood alone before God,' suggests one scholar.[2] Having
faced this sinfulness, confessed sins completely and unreservedly, and
called on the Lord for forgiveness, often through the complex emotional
catharsis of revival, true believers could expect God to respond by
descending in the form of the Spirit into their being, releasing them from
anguish.[3] This personal salvation could be transformed into love for others.
'The divine method of human improvement begins in human hearts
through evangelical truth, and it spreads from within outwardly till all is
renewed.'[4] John Webster Grant reminds us that the community that had
experienced salvation could induce conversion in the sinful by disseminating literature, including Bibles, devotional manuals, and tracts, and staging
prayer meetings and rallies to awaken the sinner's hunger for salvation.[5]
Thus, it was assumed that a community of believers would help individuals
gain salvation: a community of the like-minded was central to Canadian
evangelicalism. As part of this spiritual renewal, evangelicals sought to create nurturant communities by upholding the primacy of the family and
sanctity of the home, while at the same time condemning all frivolous pas-
times, particularly dancing, gambling, and alcohol consumption. Canadian
and American evangelicalism also had a strong tradition of female piety[6]
that had its roots in American women's earlier activity in revivalism, aboli-
tionism, and the Women's Crusades against the liquor trade in 1873 and
1874.[7]

In the late nineteenth century, evangelicalism split into 'liberal' and 'conservative' camps. In general, the latter held that salvation was personal and experiential, rather than societal, and that society was composed, ideally, of sanctified, Christian family units in which moral leadership was exercised by the 'angel in the house,' the mother.[8] The former, liberal evangelicalism, took a more organic view of society, focusing on societal institutions and interactions as more worthy objects of Christian endeavour. Thus, women who combined evangelical religiosity with temperance reform and voluntarist social activism tended more to reflect conservative evangelicalism.

Yet conservative evangelicalism is virtually ignored by the two most celebrated scholars of the Social Gospel and its antecedents, Richard Allen and Ramsay Cook. Both assume that the most important roots of twentieth-century Protestantism reside in liberal evangelicalism which, when the inadequacy of its creed was revealed, sensibly melted into the more secularist social gospelism. This understanding of our religious history ignores those many Canadians who still held to a conservative evangelical creed well into the twentieth century; it misrepresents the motivation behind a good deal of the social activism carried out in this period; and it generally overlooks women entirely.

One group especially disadvantaged by Allen and Cook's widely accepted interpretation is the Woman's Christian Temperance Union (WCTU). This is no minor omission: the WCTU was the largest non-denominational women's organization of its time in the entire country, boasting over sixteen thousand members nationally by 1914, with over eight thousand in Ontario. It represented conservative evangelical women from all Protestant denominations – both married and single – who held tenaciously to their vision of a new social order.

To support the creation of the evangelical community of believers, the WCTU devoted its energies to the active recruitment of young people.[9] This, it was hoped, would comprise the supportive community of the future. The Ontario WCTU, like its counterparts in other provinces and at the Dominion level, organized several youth groups between 1874 and 1930. In addition to the Bands of Hope, which were weekly temperance clubs adopted from the British temperance movement,[10] these included the Little White Ribboners and the Loyal Temperance Legion. The WCTU also proselytized directly and extensively in public and Sunday schools.[11] The Young Woman's Christian Temperance Union, however, ranked above all these as the central focus of the nineteenth-century Ontario WCTU's youth campaign; not surprisingly, the YWCTU in turn became the most active and the most evangelical of all the WCTU's youth temperance organizations.

Originally intended for single women of about fifteen to thirty years of age, the Ontario YWCTU had a number of older single women in its ranks as well. Some unions also accepted a few married women into the young women's sector. Nevertheless, the YWCTU in Ontario's larger cities developed an identity that separated it from both the other youth groups and the mother organization and which often brought it into a close working relationship with YWCA women. This identity was based not on age or marital status, but on its evangelicalism, empowering the group to undertake a daunting program of social reform during the nineteenth century.[12] In 1886 Mary Scott, superintendent of young women's work for the WCTU, rhetorically asked: 'Do you ever think that if we were to stop the work of the young women in the world, at the present day, what a blank there would be? Take away the bright, earnest, young teachers out of the Sunday Schools, the teachers from the Day Schools, stop the Mission Bands, Sewing Societies, Church socials, everything in fact in which young women are concerned and just think what the world would be like.'[13] The rise of the YWCTU during the nineteenth century underscores the contribution made by single evangelical women to social reform; its collapse by 1930 illustrates the waning appeal of temperance and evangelical groups in the twentieth century among all classes, the decline of voluntarist measures with the growth of professionalism, and the process of marginalization successfully imposed by a threatened parent organization on its own creation.

The American WCTU – and the earlier Woman's Crusade – had drawn to its ranks single and married, young and middle-aged women who, in the words of the famous American WCTU president, Frances Willard, learned the 'power to transact business, to mould public opinion by public utterance ... and made them willing to take up for their homes and country's sake the burdens of that citizenship they would never have sought for their own.'[14] Single women who had been convinced to assert themselves during the crusade found a ready home in the WCTU from its start. The organization's early offices in both the United States and Canada and at all levels were occupied by single and married women. Thus, the important and equal role of the single woman within the WCTU was apparently widely accepted.

This early status, however, was not retained. By the late 1870s the American WCTU began noting the importance of self-renewal through training young and presumably single women in separate unions. In 1878 a national committee of young women's work was established, and this group was organized into a department of work in 1880 under the secretariat of

Frances J. Barnes.[15] In 1890 Barnes organized the World YWCTU. In Canada the first record at the Dominion level of a YWCTU appears in the minutes of the second convention, held in 1889, while provincially a department of young women's work in Ontario dates from at least 1885. It was headed by the remarkable Mary Scott who had helped to found the YWCTU in Ottawa and who would serve for many years as the editor of the official Canadian WCTU periodical, the *Woman's Journal*, and in other dominion superintendencies.[16]

As an offspring of the WCTU, the YWCTU shared many common ideas with the married women's group. There was also much common ground with the YWCA. The sanctity of the home was unquestioned. In 1898 one YWCTU spokeswoman described the members as 'home-loving women and no public work that will make the home of secondary importance should be favored at all by our bright, winsome Y's.'[17] Where the YWCTU could not sustain a separate organization, as in several Toronto unions, the remaining members apparently merged with little difficulty with the WCTU.[18]

Yet any separate structure encourages separate ideas, and this was true for the YWCTU. The chief difference between the WCTU and the YWCTU was the more powerful evangelical motive in the single women's social reform endeavours, particularly during the 1880s and 1890s. Before the turn of the century, the YWCTU adopted a pronounced, almost militant evangelicalism as the foundation of their activities. Many examples of this potent evangelicalism can be found in the YWCTU's efforts to explain its ideas and role differences, especially in contrast with the WCTU. 'Who but women have the power,' asked a speaker at the 1886 provincial convention, 'the mighty power of sympathy which alone can roll away the stones of prejudice so that the Master's life-giving words may penetrate into dead hearts! Who but women can perform the individual or personal heart-to-heart work which is so essential to the success of our object. "Go ye into all the world," meant the shop as well as the church, the kitchen as well as the hospital. It is in these neglected parts of our Lord's vineyard that we desire to extend the influence of our Young Woman's Christian Temperance Union.' The mission of acting as witness to Christ's salvation has frequently been seen by evangelical groups as the particular purview of young people, and especially young women. This has been found to have been true for both the English and American evangelical revivals.[19] A YWCTU woman considered the mission before her sisters and herself: 'Thinking it was a self-devised scheme (as opposed to a God-inspired one), she hesitated, was about to abandon the idea, but first laid it before the Lord and awaited His answer. A message from His own word came about immediately. "Arise, stand upon thy feet, for I have appeared unto thee for this purpose, to make thee a minister and a witness ..." This was our commission, here was our plan of work, the work of bringing souls out of darkness into light, from the power of Satan unto God, and all laid out by an unerring hand.'[20] Young women, then, were particularly fitted to 'roll away the stones of prejudice' by approaching sinners individually in the home and in the workplace to promote the creation of a community of believers. They could proclaim, in Christ's name, an 'eloquent ministry of loving deeds.'[21] Furthermore, 'women have the abandon of enthusiasm which shows an unselfish and lovelike spirit, they can give to a cause a love and loyalty and heart-force that is not found in man.'[22] Young women had the time to devote to the mission and the confidence arising from God's challenge. Further evidence of the evangelical ethic was the YWCTU proclivity to provide testimony of personal conversion long after the WCTU had ceased to entertain this practice.[23]

At the local level, too, the evangelical ethic is striking. The Toronto Central YWCTU explained their program to visit elderly women and invalids as springing from 'love and for Christ's sake ... We have striven to "do good as we had opportunity," remembering "that pure religion and undefiled before God and the Father is this, to visit the fatherless and widows in their affliction, and to keep ourselves unspotted from the world."[24] It seems, therefore, that while the YWCTU adopted the basic ideas of the senior organization, its members were more moved by evangelicalism as a primary motive force in their work during the late nineteenth century.

The greatest expansion and most significant work by the YWCTU in Ontario occurred during the 1880s and 1890s in several city unions. While various town or rural WCTUs established a YWCTU department, there is little evidence that any did so for long period.[25] For instance, the Newmarket YWCTU existed from December 1887 until it amalgamated with the WCTU in October 1888. A second Newmarket YWCTU was organized in early 1906 and survived until April of that year'[26] Furthermore, the few small town examples devoted themselves to helping the married women rather than taking on special projects, as occurred in the urban unions.

The nature and scope of young women's work in the Ontario WCTU can be understood by looking at the activities of the Ottawa YWCTU in the 1880s and in 1910. The date of the YWCTU's establishment in Ottawa is unclear, but by 1888 the local union had 119 members on its rolls,[27] and vice-presidents representing the Episcopalian, Reformed Episcopalian, Methodist, Presbyterian, Congregational, and Baptist Churches.[28] There were, however, far fewer active members. By 1888 only eighteen young women's names appear repeatedly in the minute book. This small group, all single women, took over and dramatically expanded the WCTU's evangelical department.

Some of the Ottawa YWCTU's works were of an educational nature. Between 1888 and 1890 it managed to offer a night school for working girls to improve literacy, serving about ten students each time. A second motive for the night school was to gain converts to evangelicalism: 'Lessons were simple, emotional and emphasized the need to have a religious experience by giving oneself up to Christ,'[29] reports the school superintendent. In both Upper and Lower Town the group maintained sewing schools where between sixty and eighty girls learned to make quilts and pinafores. It undertook a well-subscribed kitchen garden program where 'exercises were well performed' and prizes, a tea, and oranges were given to the girls at the end of the season when 'an exhibition of sweeping lesson in St George's Church' was staged.[30] The program was so popular that the evangelical superintendent, Bertha Wright, regularly bemoaned the lack of enough teachers to satisfy the demand. Calisthenics classes were also taught.

The YWCTU's provided temperance education through two Bands of Hope, one in Ottawa and the other in nearby Hintonburg, which children attended on Saturday afternoons. The YWCTU's appear to have been in competition with youth temperance instruction offered by the local temperance lodges.[31] A note in the minute book of April 1888 complains that many of the children had been 'taken away' by the lodge.

But the area where the YWCTU's made their greatest efforts was in evangelical proselytizing. A Flower Mission provided flowers and fruit weekly to Ottawa's Protestant Hospital. The hope was that after recovery the recipient of such gifts would remember the kindness and seek out the generous benefactors for religious advice. A Bible study class met regularly and formed itself into a choir that went weekly to the women's corridor of the county jail, on Sundays to the Protestant Hospital, and other times to the elderly women's Refuge Branch at the Orphan's Home. Apparently their enthusiasm outstripped their talent, since reports exist that some of the patients covered their heads with blankets to avoid the inspired young women![32] A 'training class' was held weekly, presumably for instruction in distributing tracts effectively; 724 tracts were delivered during the single month of April 1888. In November of the same year, the young women penned 109 'friendly letters' to the infirm and depressed, with the same motivation that they had for the Flower Mission.

The young women in the YWCTU persisted with their door-to-door visitations and became so keenly evangelical that they ran a series of gospel meetings in Anglesia Square, near the Fish Market. A report of the work at the Anglesia Square Mission was submitted to the Ontario convention in 1889. The YWCTU, in concert with the WCTU's Bible reader, started the mission,

with a view of reaching fallen men and women, many of whom we had met in the jail, and in house to house visitation. The meetings, which have been well attended, consist of a short open air song service, which generally attracts quite a number, who are afterwards invited to attend the meeting. In this way we have reached a large number of men and women under the influence of liquor, who have staggered out of the bar-rooms and other dens of iniquity to hear the singing. Several women have been brought from this meeting in an intoxicated state to the Home.[33]

The WCTU women declined to participate in the YWCTU-arranged evangelical gospel meetings, while the YWCTU's came to feel so proprietary about them that they moved at their March 1889 meeting that the project 'be under the auspices of the YWCTU.'[34] The gospel meetings were not always without incident. When the Ottawa YWCTU decided in 1890 to establish a mission in Hull, Quebec, a series of riots were sparked. In the most serious one, more than four hundred 'toughs and sluggers'[35] knocked down the 'gallant little band'[36] of YWCTU women and chased them across the bridge to Ottawa. The issue was debated on the floor of the House of Commons by John A. Macdonald and Wilfrid Laurier, both of whom denounced the 'brutal and cowardly' violence displayed by the attackers.'[37] By late 1889 the Ottawa YWCTU was attempting to reach 'students, society girls, young women in the Civil Service, girls in business and working girls.' The association reported proudly that the union supported eleven branches of preventive work and only four of rescue work.[38] Here, then, is demonstration of the changing evangelical ethic: Social activism was not discovered by evangelicals in the late nineteenth century as proto-Social Gospellers, but redefined, based on earlier and deeply held evangelical traditions.

As is true of the YWCA a few years later,[39] the YWCTU believed that individual rescue work among confirmed sinners had a more limited return in the war against sinful behaviour than preventive social measures. The most ambitious project undertaken by the Ottawa YWCTU demonstrates this gradual change in focus towards social reform, and away from moral rescue work, as the means to effect lasting changes. Ottawa's Home for

Friendless Women was a 'mission to the masses,' with emphasis on the 'fallen woman.' The idea for the home seems to have come from Mayor Howland of Toronto who addressed the Ottawa WCTU in 1885 on the 'advisability of having a home or refuge for female prisoners coming out of Jail. Also having a weekly Evangelistic Meeting so that that class and others addicted to drink might be drawn in.'⁴⁰ Eventually these two ideas were combined. Two months after Howland's visit, the question of 'providing a Temporary Home for female prisoners having then been discussed it was decided by a vote of 8 to 3 that the Union should take up work on behalf of discharged female prisoners.'⁴¹ It was not the WCTU that took on the project in the end, however, but the YWCTU.

The home was founded and managed for eight years by one of the Ottawa YWCTU's most capable and evangelical members, Bertha Wright, a descendent of Hull's founder, Philemon Wright. Explaining her entry into the field in her *Lights and Shades of Mission Work*, Wright (Carr-Harris) describes watching working class women on the street with their 'pale, careworn, unsatisfied faces' and notes her growing conviction, like that of Harriet Dobbs Cartwright described by Katherine M.J. McKenna in this volume, that God was pointing out the mission that she must follow: 'He had really chosen such an instrument to be used in the highest, the noblest, the grandest work in which mortal man can engage – the work of winning souls.'⁴² To this starkly evangelical end, Wright had organized the YWCTU's visits to female prisoners to try to offer them a new life. The YWCTU's limited successes here convinced her of the futility of such work, however, for the women seemed to be inexorably drawn back to the barroom because they saw themselves as outcasts without any hope of salvation. Wright concluded that there was a need 'where a helping hand and shelter could be offered to any sinful, friendless woman without regard to creed, nationality, age or condition, at any time, night or day, the only requisite being a desire to lead a better life.'⁴³ The Home for Friendless Women was to minister to the spiritual and physical needs of 'unfortunates,' that is, those women living by prostitution and those mothers abandoned by their husbands who required pre- and post-natal care, and who agreed to stay in the home for a full year so that a new way of life could be forged. Close attention to child care was regarded as essential to the regeneration of the mothers, for the presence of children pressed upon the women the recognition that they had sinned, and such recognition was the evangelical precondition of the conversion experience and eventual salvation. The home's rules ended with the stern statement that 'the board heartily disapproves of any arrangement or institution that provides for relieving the patients of the care of their offspring, thus rendering it easy for them to escape the full penalty of wrong-doing.'[44]

The YWCTU's work with friendless women was not undertaken without an expression of hostility from the community. It was argued that the home would become a 'hot bed of vice,' housing 'vicious creatures' who could not be managed by a troupe of delicate young women. The fever raging during the winter of 1887 was even used as a warning against the proposal.[45] In spite of Ottawa's anxiety about the home, the YWCTU forged on, canvassing the community for private donations. Neither the YWCTU nor the WCTU seems to have made formal financial contributions to the home; instead the YWCTU contribution was in the form of the initial inspiration and labour to make the idea reality.

In late December of 1887 the YWCTU Bible class cleaned a rented house from top to bottom in readiness for the first 'inmates.' Furnishings were made from inverted flour barrels with white marble oilcloth, and draped with cretonne. The work was finally finished on Christmas Eve with a view to opening the residence after the New Year. Solemnly, the YWCTU women held a prayer service in the new dining-room and departed for their homes. During the night a water-pipe burst in the upper storey and water flowed throughout the house all night. When the women returned the next day, they found six inches of cold water in the basement, whitewash coating everything, rugs soaked, and icicles hanging from the stoves. 'It seemed as though all the forces of evil combined had arrayed themselves against us in order to hinder the commencement of a work which had for its chief aim the glory of God in the salvation of the most degraded.'[46] Clearly the YWCTU saw its noble evangelical work pitted against evil in an almost physical contest.

Yet the home survived this early trial and soon flourished. It supported itself by opening a laundry: 'The Home is not a place for the maintenance of the idle.'[47] In September of 1888 the following notice appeared in the Ottawa papers: 'Washing and ironing done at the shortest possible notice at the Home for Friendless Women. Good satisfaction guaranteed. Terms cash on delivery.'[48] The conditions in which the laundry work was accomplished are reminiscent of a Dickens novel. The furnace and boiler were found in the basement through which the yard water ran so that the foundations of the engine were undermined. The ceiling was so low that a tall woman could not stand upright. A horizontal smoke pipe from the furnace ran so close to the beams that care was constantly needed to prevent a fire. The washing room itself was so laden with moisture that one could barely see the other figures in the room; the windows were so warped that none closed tightly; the floor was slippery, and the machinery was soon covered with rust from the condensation. All linen had to be carried from this basement room to the first floor where the wringer was kept, and from there to the dry closet on the second floor. The ironing room was also the nursery. 'From 15 to 20 babies are to be seen every day scattered on ironing tables, in clothes baskets, or creeping on the floor, while unceasing vigilance has to be exercised to keep them from the machinery.'[49]

In 1910 the home moved to larger quarters, and a new steam laundry was installed. But even with the improved quarters, the evangelical creed that one must work hard, shun the world, and adopt moral rigour was readily apparent. That the rehabilitation program was largely punitive was also clear. Judith Walkowitz has observed, 'Through laundry work, women could do penance for their past sins and purge themselves of their moral contagion. Clear starching, it would seem, cleanses all sin, and an expert ironer can cheerfully put her record behind her.'[50] In these circumstances laundry work appears to have had a symbolic function.

In addition to fallen women, the home accepted the children of mothers who, through love of hard drink or abandonment by their husbands, neglected them. A Mrs Nelson was found recovering from intoxication in a jail cell:

She was in a sad plight, poor thing, having slept part of the night in a coal bin, and lost her shawl, hat and shoes, and was evidently much concerned about her children, whom she had left alone in a house on Albert Street. As she was sent down for a month, we went in search of the neglected little ones, and found a beautiful curly haired boy of five, asleep on the broad windowsill, his pale, wan cheek resting against the pane, while his little sister had crept into a clothes basket on the floor which was half full of wet linen and she too, was fast asleep. They had evidently been waiting and watching for mother until at length they had cried themselves to sleep. We took them to the Home, which was only a short distance away and where they were kept until their unworthy mother's release.[51]

Finally, destitute old women who were not eligible for the Refuge Branch of the Orphans' Home were also accepted in the home: 'One cold January morning, an aged woman, clad in a thin calico dress, without a shawl, cloak or warm wrap of any kind, appeared at the gate. She was homeless and friendless, having been arrested the previous August for vagrancy, and so frail and feeble was she that it was with the greatest difficulty that she was led to the street cars, in which she was conveyed to the Home.'[52]

The Register of Inmates from 1888 to 1894 indicates the source of the women staying in the Home for Friendless Women. From January 1888 until September 1889 the majority of inmates came from the women's corridor of the local jail, from the street, and from the railway station, where 'vulnerable' young women were directed to the home. This is not surprising since the home, like the Anglesia Square Mission, had originated in jail visits. The home regarded itself as an extension of work carried out by the Ottawa superintendent of prison and public works for a number of years.[53] A few other inmates were referred by the police and by the local hospitals. The only period when women came in large numbers from the brothels was in late 1888 and in 1889, although a few continued to arrive from this source until 1894. As the home became more settled in its operating procedures, it accepted fewer cases from the jails, believing that such women were particularly hardened to the rough circumstances of life on the street and thus were not amenable to rehabilitation. A fairly steady clientele continued to be routed, however, from the street, railway station, and hospitals.[54]

The Register of Inmates also indicates the destination of women leaving the home. In 1888 and 1889 most women were transferred to some other facility, such as the hospital, back to their families, or into domestic service. From early 1889, however, increasing numbers of women fall into the 'removed' and 'left' categories, with fewer moving into other institutions or families. This suggests a general recognition that some women were beyond help and might be considered part of the Victorian 'social residuum.'[55] The record shows also that the home's numbers remained high throughout the period, indicating that there was a real need for the services provided. A rough classification for the inmates reveals that while almost an equal number were 'unfortunate' and 'abandoned,' the largest group by far were 'intemperates.' After the home became independent from the YWCTU in 1891, the 'intemperate' classification declined precipitously; this may have been because of a changed philosophy, although it is not possible to document this. In terms of nationality, Irish women far outnumbered the other groups that included English, Scots, French, American, German, and Canadian women. The Irish preponderance was likely a reflection of the endemic poverty of that community in Ottawa, as well as of the dominant size of the Irish group in Ottawa at the time.

The Home for Friendless Women was a bold experiment by the Ottawa YWCTU and one that required courage and entrepreneurial skills as well as deep faith. The YWCTU reported ongoing 'difficulties and discouragements' and concluded their report in 1890 by lamenting, 'God only knows what it has cost us to rise above all these trying circumstances. He only has seen the tears and heard the cries of distress that have gone up as we have waited at his feet, sometimes for whole nights, pleading for funds, for souls, for success.'[56]

The history of the home is consistent with the evangelical woman's refuge concept pioneered in the eastern United States during the period:

Not only as shelters, but also as retaining centers for fallen women, the homes catered to uniquely feminine needs. Through evangelical religion, education, and discipline, the matrons and managers offered courses to restore the womanhood of the residents, daily lessons in reading, writing, sewing and other feminine services, thus ensuring both domesticity and piety. Discipline included the banning of profanity, tobacco, alcohol, and coarse behaviour, plus a routine of early rising, regular work (sewing, laundry, cleaning) and habits of neatness and industry at all times.[57]

What is different from the American example was the failure to develop any apparent sense of 'sisterhood' between care-worker and inmate. One possible explanation for this relates to the change in administrative control. The Home for Friendless Women had its start with a group of dynamic single young women. In 1891, although 'all felt that the Home was doing a grand work ... if it were for the advantage of the Home to be independent of our Union it was certainly wiser to relinquish all claims.'[58] Once it became incorporated and established as a charitable institution under the review of the provincial government (and thus a recipient of the provincial grant), it lost most of its single women supporters other than Bertha Wright. The board of management came increasingly to reflect the middle class married woman club member associated not with the YWCTU, but the WCTU. Perhaps if the young single women had maintained control of the Home for Friendless Women, a climate of sisterhood would have developed.

Regardless of the apparent lack of female solidarity between classes, the YWCTU in Ottawa accomplished a significant amount in a relatively short time. A group of about twenty young women taught, evangelized, and attempted to reform a substantial group of troubled women in the Home for Friendless Women. During the same period the Ottawa WCTU remained active, distributing tracts at the railway and fire stations, monitoring the Scientific Temperance course in the city's public schools, and establishing a temperance coffee house. But the Ottawa WCTU never displayed the verve and evangelical energy that was the norm for the Ottawa YWCTU during this period. It took no hand in the energetic evangelism of gospel meetings or in its practical manifestation in female social reform.

Although tracking membership numbers is difficult, the YWCTU seems to have rivalled, and at times exceeded, the mother group in Ottawa. In 1886 and 1894 the figures show that in Ottawa the YWCTU was considerably stronger than the WCTU. Without doubt, the results of the YWCTU's efforts are far more impressive than those of the WCTU in that city during the same period.

By 1910, however, the YWCTUs were a mere shadow of their robustness of the 1880s and 1890s. At the international level, they were reduced to costume pageants: A suggestion was made that members dress in the costume of countries having YWCTUs. Each representative was to be introduced with a report of YWCTU activities in that country, while the hostess wound each representative with 'strands of broad white ribbon.'[59] Provincially, accounts of YWCTU activities virtually disappeared from the annual reports. The *Canadian White Ribbon Tidings* could only recommend the following 'hints' for surviving unions:

Always wear the white ribbon. Let at least 15 minutes be given to the devotional part of the program, have a regularly appointed organist if possible, and see that the leader of the devotions is appointed in advance. Begin each meeting on time. Give each member some definite work to do. Write to your provincial Y Secretary. Secure as many subscribers as possible to the National and Provincial Papers. Study carefully how to conduct all public meetings so that those not interested will be pleased and come again. Make it 'go' with a 'swing,' have a good program, good music, 'a presiding genius.'[60]

The evangelical zeal and extensive community involvement of earlier years was reduced almost pathetically to a procedure manual on protocol for running meetings!

In 1898 an ominous note was struck when YWCTU groups in various parts of the province began admitting men to full membership. Most of these groups soon thereafter called themselves young people's groups or Loyal Temperance Legions with women's special role being forgotten.[61] The Ottawa YWCTU had ceased to exist altogether. Conversely, by 1910, the Ottawa WCTU had 245 members and maintained twenty departments of work. Under its tutelage, the mixed-gender juvenile societies had 272 members, as well as two large anti-cigarette leagues.[62]

What had happened to the YWCTU organization in Ontario? How did the YWCTU work become so trivialized, irrelevant, and out of women's control? The YWCTU's demise was not caused by lack of effort in finding new members. There is a good deal of evidence to suggest that women in the YWCTU worked very hard recruiting new members, particularly from the late 1890s until about 1910. In fact, the Northern Toronto YWCTU was the first in Ontario to welcome young men at their meetings in 1901 in order to broaden its membership. One result of this extended membership was programming of a very different type than most YWCTU's had developed before, such as the establishment of a model parliament in which countries debated the wisdom of invoking prohibition.[63] This reorientation may have hastened the YWCTU's demise, since its female-oriented and female-controlled mandate was lost. By 1904 the union was left with no departments of work and only a skeletal executive.[64]

Doubtless, YWCTUs that devoted themselves primarily to social events succeeded in adding more women's names to the membership rolls. But these new members were a different sort of woman than had been attracted during the 1880s and 1890s. Minute books demonstrate that when local unions held more socials to attract outsiders, they attempted fewer evangelically inspired good works. There can be no doubt either that, as the nineteenth century drew to a close, it was increasingly unpopular to be a member of a young woman's evangelical temperance association such as the YWCTU. All the bluster of brave songs and membership drives could not dispel the fact that the YWCTU was designed to attract a particular type of serious and intensely religious young woman. By its very nature, it would not appeal to a mass audience in this era.[65] This is likely one of the strongest explanations for the organization's demise.

A third reason for the loss of the YWCTU's evangelical vision resides in the relationship that existed between the young women and the parent organization. Originally limited to a role encompassing only public relations, self-training, and work with children, the YWCTU obviously expanded its range far beyond those initial limits. By 1905 the YWCTU's were on record as supporting equal suffrage for men and women, social purity, a shorter work day, higher wages, and enlightened resolution of labour disputes.[66] That their ideas and actions were 'founded upon the Gospel of Christ' and the belief in 'the coming of His kingdom' gave these women the needed justification to 'seek the transforming power of divine grace for ourselves and all for whom we work.'[67] This was indeed a far-flung net, and Christian labour in defence of all the social injustices covered by it would have required extraordinary efforts by the YWCTU and the WCTU. In this context, there is evidence that the senior women were made uneasy by the sometimes unflattering comparison with their resourceful offspring.

While freely admitting the many advantages of organizing a young woman's sector, the WCTU was anxious almost from the beginning about having such a separate body. In 1886 the provincial president attempted to soothe the older women's concern in her address to the annual convention: 'Do not think that a "Y" in any place of considerable size will interfere with the work of the senior Union. The records all point the other way. Young ladies naturally feel more at home with a president and officers of their own, arranging and planning for their own work. Then their influence will be greater and more widespread when banded together as societies than as individuals, and they can reach and influence for good those whom the older ones among us cannot touch.'[68] Another speaker admitted, 'I know there is a feeling of opposition in some quarters from a fear of a division of interest in the work of the WCTU.'[69] And the opposition did not dissipate with the years. In 1892 a debate ensued in the *Woman's Journal* over whether or not the YWCTU should remain separate from the WCTU. One writer ('an old president') declared herself very much in favour of a continuing special sector for the young women because 'there was always too much work for too few in the days before the Y's.'[70] In 1897 the provincial YWCTU superintendent suggested 'that local presidents of the WCTU lay aside all personal objections to "Y" work and be willing to allow and assist the Superintendent to organize her territory.'[71]

Yet the fact that the issue was considered so often over the years suggests that many WCTU members never fully reconciled themselves to the YWCTU. That at least some of the criticism levelled at the YWCTUs was rooted in unkind comparisons is suggested by one writer in the *Woman's Journal*: 'I would be ashamed of any member of our Union, who would look upon this success [of the YWCTU] with any feeling of jealousy, or consider them rivals in any way ... Jealousies and rivalries are the death of many good societies and poison at the fountain head, the very waters of healing which we are trying to carry to the suffering.'[72] The situation may well have varied from region to region in Ontario, but it seems clear that at least some of the older women were ungrateful and perhaps threatened by the evangelical zeal and reforming competence of their young and single associates.

A fourth explanation for the YWCTU's failure to survive was rooted in its class identification. In the 1880s there was some support within the YWCTU to expand its membership into the respectable working classes. The establishment of Willard Home in Toronto and a similar residence in London for working girls had the potential to incorporate these women into the framework of the YWCTU on the model of the YWCA residence. A hopeful statement was also issued by the London YWCTU in 1886: 'Do not let us be content with looking forward to the reunion of our own family circles, much as we love them, but let us think of the many who have no homes and nothing to brighten their lives ... Some young women with just as refined tastes, and social natures as their more fortunate sisters are living in boarding houses.'[73] But the challenge was ignored, and the YWCTU remained determinedly middle class.

The Canadian YWCTU's class position was questioned by the Glasgow YWCTU in 1911 which welcomed working class women and had a stronger organization than its Canadian counterpart. 'We just go for everyone,' said the Scottish YWCTU organizer.[74] By this date in Canada, however, the YWCTU position on the young working class woman had hardened to revulsion. One report of the British Factory Girls' Drinking Club portrayed the women as participating in 'wanton orgies' with their hard-earned salaries. It concluded, 'Drunkenness saps a woman's moral fibre more quickly than it does a man's, yet these misguided factory girls are the potential mothers of a future generation.'[75] The YWCTU women in Canada saw the working class as the target of their efforts, not as allies in the cause.

If they were not prepared to be identified with even the respectable working classes, the YWCTU members could not hope to be considered part of the 'smart' upper middle classes either. In a lament on the WCTU's class position, a correspondent to the *Woman's Journal* in 1892 begs the YWCTU not to separate from the main organization because it is so badly needed. She says, 'We learned that not many rich or influential women will join, that we cannot expect to be popular or numerous ... most of us keeping no servants.'[76] The YWCTU must have assumed the same class profile as the WCTU; by rejecting the possibility of expanding their organization into the working classes, they may have further assured their demise, while at the same time not achieving the upward class mobility some members clearly sought.

A final factor in explaining the YWCTU's decline involves the ideas held by the organization in the twentieth century. The YWCTU experienced a lessening of that sense of evangelical mission that had been so obvious in the earlier period. Here again the records do not pinpoint the exact date when the vision began to fade. Because by 1910 the YWCTU's activities suggest a religious social club lost in self-absorption, the erosion was probably well under way by that time. By 1931 the official ideals of the YWCTU were contained in the *Manual of the Young People's Branch*. The prospective member was told that, although she could expect to study 'Christian citizenship' and 'social welfare,' there also awaited her a verita-

316 From Christian Benevolence to Social Transformation

ble 'University of Reforms,' 'delightful entertainment,' and a 'community of pleasure and interest.' YWCTU organizers were directed in the *Manual* to run meetings with lots of YWCTU songs and to provide some temperance information: 'bright, pithy news items from latest Press reports ... All meetings should bristle with brightness and song and good cheer.'[77] The evangelical nightmare of inward-looking selfishness to the exclusion of external societal needs seems to have become reality for the YWCTUs sometime prior to the First World War. Before long all YWCTUs were absorbed into the omnibus 'Young People's Branch,' with young men part of the membership.

Thus, the YWCTU disappeared for a number of reasons: As a 'farm team' for the WCTU, it lacked authority in the wider organization and suffered from the WCTU's jealousy. By 1930 both evangelical and temperance organizations had lost their social cachet. While evangelicalism had in the nineteenth century been in the vanguard of women's social reform in Ontario, in the early twentieth century its confidence and sense of mission was dulled. Ontario temperance organizations of all kinds were increasingly marginalized after the passage of the Ontario Temperance Act in 1916. Finally, the YWCTU failed to court working women, a group that held the potential for sustained growth through a broadly based program, as the YWCA was to prove. At the same time, the professionalization of social work reduced the role of the well-meaning but untrained middle class single woman. The result for the organization was a gradual slide into a new role as a rather pathetic cheer-leader for an increasingly unpopular cause. This decline into social irrelevance seems to have been mourned by few in the WCTU.

Yet at their height in the nineteenth century, evangelical urban single women in the YWCTU had initiated an impressive program of social reform activism, through 'the transforming power of divine grace for ourselves and all for whom we work.'[78] The most fortifying ingredient of the YWCTU – and of the WCTU to a lesser degree – was evangelicalism. Without its strengthening influence, the many disappointments faced by Ontario's YWCTU and WCTU would have dulled the edge of their optimism and resolve.

NOTES

1 See D.W. Bebbington, *Evangelicalism in Modern Britain: A History from the 1730's to the 1980's* (London: Unwin Hyman, 1989); George Marsden, *Funda-*

mentalism and American Culture: The Shaping of Twentieth Century Evangeli-calism, 1870–1925 (Oxford: Oxford University Press, 1980); William Westfall, *Two Worlds: The Protestant Culture of Nineteenth-Century Ontario* (Kingston: McGill-Queen's University Press, 1989); and A.B. McKillop, *Matters of Mind: The University in Ontario, 1791–1951* (Toronto: University of Toronto Press, 1994).

2 Marsden, *Fundamentalism*, 34.

3 Westfall, *Two Worlds*, 55–6.

4 Ibid., 12.

5 John Webster Grant, *A Profusion of Spires: Religion in Nineteenth-Century Ontario* (Toronto: University of Toronto Press, 1988), 103–5.

6 See Westfall, *Two Worlds*, and Grant, *A Profusion of Spires*.

7 It is important to distinguish evangelicalism, whatever the denominational con-text, from evangelism. The latter derives from the Greek work for 'gospel' (evan-gelion) and refers to the enthusiastic spreading of the 'good news.' However, it ignores the system of thought being transmitted to others. Thus, while most evangelicals were also evangelists of their faith, by no means were all evangelists evangelicals. See Nancy Hardesty, *Women Called to Witness: Evangelical Femi-nism in the 19th Century* (Nashville: Abingdon Press, 1984), 9–10, on this issue.

8 Hardesty, *Women Called to Witness*.

9 Jack S. Blocker, Jr., *American Temperance Movements: Cycles of Reform* (Bos-ton: Twayne Publishers, 1989), 82.

10 See Sharon Anne Cook, 'Educating for Temperance: The Woman's Christian Temperance Union and Ontario Children, 1880–1916,' *Historical Studies in Education / Revue d'histoire de l'éducation* 5, 2 (1993), 251–77.

11 See Sharon Anne Cook, '"Continued and Persevering Combat": The Ontario Woman's Christian Temperance Union, Evangelicalism, and Social Reform, 1874–1916' (PhD thesis, Carleton University, 1990).

12 In spite of a proud record of public achievement, the YWCTU has been consis-tently underestimated, or ignored completely, in the relevant historiography. Ruth Bordin in her account of the American WCTU provides one of the few scholarly assessments of the impact of the YWCTU: 'The exciting, innovative Union projects were not the work of the Y's but of the older women ...' (*Woman and Temperance: The Quest for Power and Liberty, 1873–1900* [Phila-delphia: Temple University Press, 1981], 151). Similarly, Nancy Sheehan inaccu-rately identifies the YWCTU as one of the three 'informal' youth departments, with the YWCTU trailing as 'probably the least successful of the three' ('The WCTU and Educational Strategies on the Canadian Prairie,' *History of Educa-tion Quarterly* 24 [1984], 112). The history of the Ontario YWCTU reveals that Bordin's conclusions do not hold for the Canadian case and that Sheehan's

assessment is incorrect. This is largely because both are based on sources post-dating 1918. And the Y's are not mentioned at all in Wendy Mitchinson's study of the Dominion WCTU ('Aspects of Reform: Four Women's Organizations in Nineteenth-Century Canada' [PhD thesis, York University, 1977]).

13 *Annual Report of the Ontario WCTU*, 1886, MU 8406, WCTU Collection. Note: Unless otherwise stated, all primary documents cited in this chapter are located in the WCTU Collection of the Public Archives of Ontario (AO) in Toronto.

14 Frances Willard, 'Introduction' to Annie Wittenmyer, *History of the Woman's Temperance Crusade* (Chicago: University of Chicago Press, 1882), 15–21.

15 Manual: Young People's Branch of the Canadian Woman's Christian Temperance Union, [n.d., ca. 1931] 4–5, MU 8288, WCTU Collection.

16 Surviving documents make it difficult to specify exact dates. The first report for a dominion convention is in 1889, the second to be held, and by this time a YWCTU had been organized. The first provincial records in the AO date from 1886, by which time figures were being collected for YWCTU groups around the province.

17 *Woman's Journal*, Oct. 1898, MU 8455, WCTU Collection.

18 For example, the Newmarket YWCTU seems to have existed from at least December, 1887, until it amalgamated with the WCTU in Oct., 1888. During that brief period it organized a Flower Mission and supported the WCTU in its many endeavours. A second YWCTU was organized sometime in early 1906 when its only activity seems to have been a social staged by the members in the Temperance Hall, followed by refreshments, in April, 1906. Minute Book of the Newmarket WCTU, 1885–1913, MU 8422, WCTU Collection.

19 See Hardesty, *Women Called to Witness*; Martha Tomhave Blauvelt, 'Women and Revivalism,' in *Women and Religion in America*, vol. 1, Rosemary Radford Ruether and Rosemary Skinner Keller, eds. (San Francisco: Harper and Row, 1981); D.W. Bebbington, *Evangelicalism in Modern Britain*; and Brian Heeney, *The Women's Movement in the Church of England, 1850–1930* (Oxford: Oxford University Press, 1988).

20 *Annual Report of the Ontario WCTU*, 1886, MU 8406, WCTU Collection.

21 Principal Austin, 'What Christ Has Done for Woman,' *The Friend of the Friendless* (Oct. 1892), Ottawa YWCA, City of Ottawa YWCA Records.

22 World's Y Hand-Book, 1906, MU 8471, WCTU Collection.

23 *Woman's Journal*, June 1892.

24 Records of the Toronto Union WCTU, 1904–5, MU 8432, WCTU Collection.

25 See note 13. The Mizpah Union was unable to sustain its own YWCTU, but a 'coloured' WCTU and YWCTU operated for a time in 1917 under its direction. Minute Book of the Mizpah WCTU, 1916–18, MU 8422, WCTU Collection.

The Peterborough Union established a Y in Nov., 1915, which survived until May, 1916. Minute Book of the Peterborough WCTU, 1914–22, MU 8284, WCTU Collection. It is clear that more YWCTUs existed than can now be traced, however. Lynne Marks has found that a YWCTU existed in both Campbellford and Thorold in the 1890s, neither of which were reported to the YWCTU provincial superintendent. Lynne Marks, 'Ladies, Loafers, Knights and "Lasses": The Social Dimension of Religion and Leisure in Late Nineteenth-Century Small Town Ontario.' (PhD thesis, York University, 1992), 226–30.

26 Minutebook of the Newmarket WCTU, 1885–1913, MU 8422, WCTU Collection.

27 Minute Book of the Ottawa YWCTU, 1888, Ottawa YWCA Records.

28 Ibid., 20 Sept. 1889.

29 Bertha (Wright) Carr-Harris, *Lights and Shades of Mission Work or Leaves from a Worker's Note Book; Being Reminiscences of Seven Years Service at the Capital, 1885–1892* (Ottawa, 1892), 36.

30 Untitled newspaper clipping, 14 Feb. 1890, assorted papers of Bertha Wright Carr-Harris, Carr-Harris Private Collection, Oakville.

31 Sharon Anne Cook, 'Letitia Youmans: Ontario's Nineteenth-Century Temperance Educator,' *Ontario History* 84, 4 (Dec. 1992), 329–42.

32 Carr-Harris, *Lights and Shades of Mission Work*, 24.

33 Eleventh Annual Report of the Ontario WCTU, 1889, MU 8406, WCTU Collection.

34 Ibid.

35 *Daily Citizen*, 13 Feb. 1890.

36 Ibid., 8 Feb. 1890.

37 *Evening Journal*, 10 Feb. 1890.

38 *Annual Report of the Ontario WCTU*, 1889.

39 Diana Pedersen, 'The Young Woman's Christian Association in Canada, 1870–1920: A Movement to Meet a Spiritual, Civic, and National Need' (PhD thesis, Carleton University, 1987), 3.

40 Minute Book of the Ottawa WCTU, 17 Feb. 1885, MU 8425, WCTU Collection.

41 Ibid., 20 Apr. 1885.

42 Carr-Harris, *Lights and Shades of Mission Work*, 11.

43 Ibid., 38.

44 Ibid., 55–6.

45 Ibid., 39.

46 Ibid., 41.

47 Ibid., 36.

48 Untitled newspaper clipping, Sept. 1888, Carr-Harris Collection.

49 *Home for Friendless Women Annual Report*, 1931–2, Ottawa YWCA Records.
50 Judith Walkowitz, *Prostitution and Victorian Society* (Cambridge: Cambridge University Press, 1980), 221.
51 Carr-Harris, *Lights and Shades of Mission Work*, 52.
52 Ibid., 53.
53 *Eleventh Annual Report of the Ontario WCTU*, 1888.
54 Register of Inmates for Home for Friendless Women, 1888–94, Ottawa YWCA Records. A fuller analysis can be found in Sharon Anne Cook, '"A Helping Hand and Shelter": Anglo-Protestant Social Service Agencies in Ottawa, 1880–1910' (MA thesis, Carleton University, 1987), chap. 4, appendices 2–6.
55 Gareth Stedman Jones, *Outcast London: A Study in the Relationship Between Classes in Victorian Society* (London: Penguin, 1971).
56 *Thirteenth Annual Report of the Ontario WCTU*, 1890.
57 Estelle Freedman, *Their Sisters' Keepers: Women's Prison Reform in America, 1830–1930* (Ann Arbor: University of Michigan Press, 1984), 55.
58 Minute Book of the Ottawa YWCTU, 9 Feb. 1891.
59 'A World's Y Demonstration,' *World's Y Hand-Book*, 1906, MU 8471, WCTU Collection.
60 *Canadian White Ribbon Tidings*, Mar. 1910, MU 8456, WCTU Collection.
61 *Annual Reports of the Ontario WCTU*, 1886–1907.
62 Minutes of the Ontario WCTU Convention, 1910.
63 Ibid., Feb. 1901.
64 Toronto District Report and Directory of the WCTU, 1889–1918.
65 See A.B. McKillop, *A Disciplined Intelligence: Critical Inquiry and Canadian Thought in the Victorian Era* (Montreal: McGill-Queen's University Press, 1979).
66 Cook, 'Continued and Persevering Combat,' chap. 5.
67 *Canadian White Ribbon Tidings*, 1 Apr. 1905, MU 8455, WCTU Collection.
68 Minutes of the Ontario WCTU Convention, 1886.
69 Ibid.
70 *Woman's Journal*, June 1892.
71 *Annual Report of the Ontario WCTU*, 1897.
72 *Woman's Journal*, June 1892.
73 Ibid, Dec. 1886.
74 *Canadian White Ribbon Tidings*, Dec. 1911.
75 Ibid., Aug. 1910.
76 *Woman's Journal*, June 1892.
77 *Manual of the Young People's Branch* of the Canadian Woman's Christian Temperance Union, [n.d., c. 1931], MU 8288, WCTU Collection.
78 *Canadian White Ribbon Tidings*, 1 Apr. 1905.

16

'The Power of True Christian Women': The YWCA and Evangelical Womanhood in the Late Nineteenth Century

DIANA PEDERSEN

The YWCA was a strong group of Christian women from different Protestant denominations who banded together to work in accordance with their shared Christian faith. They hoped to win the cities to Christ by reaching Canada's young women, and towards this end they used a variety of creative strategies. The Canadian members were inspired by the work of Y's in major American cities, and they gained new ideas for their own institutions by inviting speakers from the United States, and by travelling to American cities to visit Y's there. Through participating in meetings and through circulating written reports, the women built up a strong network of support that was invaluable to a young, developing organization. Volunteers were able to hire professional staff as the work grew. Although some men failed to understand the work and trivialized it, many men supported it. The women sought and made use of this support, but at the same time they created their own space in which they could express their own form of social religion.

During the decades of the 1870s and 1880s, an important transitional period that remains relatively neglected by historians of Canadian feminism, the Victorian cult of domesticity was increasingly challenged by the phenomenon of organized womanhood. Women's organizations were not, of course, unprecedented by this time: a tradition of women's benevolent and charitable societies dedicated to the care of the destitute, the sick, and the orphaned was already well established.[1] Although the nineteenth-century doctrine of separate spheres assigned to women responsibility for domestic and family life, the care of the helpless and disadvantaged in the local community was seen as a natural extension of the work of mothers. The role of Lady Bountiful provided one of the few socially sanctioned avenues for middle-class women who were attracted by the prospect of activity in the public realm, a role that was also compatible with the tradition of Christian stewardship.

Throughout the nineteenth century the religious impulse was fundamental to the appearance of women's organizations in Canadian communities, with church groups, and especially missionary societies, becoming the largest laywomen's organizations in the country.[2] Evangelical Protestant women, who felt a special obligation to take responsibility for their own souls, to demonstrate their faith by doing good works, and to spread the gospel of salvation to others, in both the home and foreign mission fields, were prominent among the founders of nineteenth-century North American women's organizations.[3] They consciously promoted what American historian Anne Boylan has aptly characterized as an ideal model of evangelical womanhood, representing both a rejection of the frivolous, gay, and useless life of the lady and an attempt to create an alternative ideal of womanhood that combined the traditional Protestant ideal of the 'vertuous woman' with a new evangelical stress on action.[4]

One of the most important and influential organizations of evangelical women in late nineteenth-century Canadian cities was the Young Women's Christian Association (YWCA). Originating in Britain in 1855 and spreading rapidly to the United States and throughout the British Empire, YWCAs first appeared in Canadian cities in the early 1870s. They were organized in each community by a committee of women drawn from the major Protestant churches and from the families of leading businessmen and prominent professionals. Sharing the conviction of Protestant clergymen that the evangelical crusade required a sustained attack on Canada's growing cities as centres of godlessness, immorality, and organized vice, YWCA women promoted what they believed would be the most effective strategy for winning the cities to Christ. Arguing that young women, as the mothers of the future generations, constituted the cornerstone of the Christian family home and hence the moral and spiritual foundation of the urban community, they insisted that what they identified as a growing 'girl problem' required the immediate attention of the churches and their congregations. In particular they targeted the increasing numbers of young single women migrating to Canadian cities in search of employment or educational opportunities, many of whom lived in unsupervised boarding-houses where they appeared to enjoy a degree of financial and sexual autonomy unknown to their mothers and grandmothers. YWCAs argued that these young women, without Christian influences and maternal supervision, stood in danger of losing their traditional ties to family, home, and church.[5] By insisting that Canada's girl problem should be addressed by the churches and that its resolution should be accomplished by women, the YWCA attempted to make women central both to the evangelical attack on the cities and, ultimately, to the churches' struggle to effect the coming of the kingdom by remaking Canadian society according to the teachings of Jesus Christ.

The appearance of the first YWCAs in the 1870s heralded the beginning of a new phase in the history of Protestant women's organizations in Canadian cities. Previously the work of churchwomen had been organized on a denominational basis, but YWCAs were among the pioneers of interdenominational cooperation. This strategy greatly increased the resources available to the Protestant churches but also provided women with an unprecedented degree of autonomy, as they found themselves no longer directly answerable to individual clergymen and their congregations. The founders of the first Canadian YWCAs were able to draw upon a tradition of lay evangelical organization that was well established in North America by the end of the nineteenth century, and their shared commitment to the tenets of evangelicalism helped to overcome divisive doctrinal differences.[6]

Early YWCAs were representative of all the major Protestant denominations, and they depended to a considerable extent upon the funds solicited from church congregations, but control of the organization was completely vested in the hands of the female board of managers. The advisory boards composed of three or four prominent businessmen seem to have functioned in a purely advisory capacity, generally with respect to the purchase of property, and they probably served primarily to reassure financial supporters. Volunteer service on a YWCA board provided churchwomen with opportunities to greatly expand the range and scope of their activities. Beginning with a leased or rented house on a residential street, most YWCAs came into being as a boarding-home for young working women, but the rental of additional rooms in the downtown business district made possible the opening of a public department. Pioneering programs and services such as employment bureaux, schools of domestic science, classes in stenography and physical culture, and noon rest facilities for office and retail sales workers all increased the administrative demands of the work and led to the hiring of professional staff by the 1890s. By the end of the century Canadian YWCAs, beginning with Toronto in 1894, were financing the construction of buildings especially designed to meet the requirements of a YWCA.[7]

In late nineteenth-century Canada, many factors, including improved transportation, the rise of nationalism, immigration, and the spread of the factory system, were encouraging women's organizations to broaden the scale of their operations beyond the purely local.[8] From the inception of the YWCA, churchwomen realized that the dimensions of the girl problem extended far beyond their own communities and required new solutions, broader and more imaginative than anything conceived by their earlier counterparts of the ladies' aid societies and Dorcas sewing circles. In 1891 the Toronto YWCA reported that 'Christian Association boarding houses are now like a network all over Great Britain, Ireland, the United States and Canada. Any young woman can go directly from one to the other.'[9] As this observation suggests, cooperation between branches quickly led to calls for systemization and standardization of services and methods. The administration of YWCAs frequently required new kinds of expertise that exceeded the demands of women's traditional charitable work, leading to calls for the training of both staff and volunteer board members. The organizers of early YWCAs found themselves required to conduct business meetings and master the principles of committee work, hire and supervise staff, develop and administer programs, purchase and manage property, oversee the construction and furnishing of buildings, and engage in substantial fund-raising and publicity work. The enormity of their task was compounded by the fact that the very concept of a public institution for 'respectable' women aroused considerable scepticism and opposition in late nineteenth-century Canadian cities. Within the churches and the business sector, doubts were frequently expressed about the objectives of the YWCA and the ability of churchwomen to manage such a facility along sound business lines.[10]

In meeting these new challenges and defining the parameters of what was to become known as YWCA work, the early YWCAs greatly benefitted from the example and assistance of the Young Men's Christian Associations (YMCAs), whose appearance in Canadian cities invariably preceded that of the women's organization.[11] YMCAs offered advice and assistance with fund-raising and the purchase of property, sent their staff of trained secretaries to lecture YWCA board members on the principles of scientific philanthropy, and, in communities where the YWCA did not yet have its own building, lent or rented their facilities for the holding of public meetings. Suggestive of the close ties between the two organizations is the fact that in many communities, members of the same prominent families, frequently husbands and wives, served on the two boards of managers, and YMCAs were frequently among the women's most vocal supporters during organizational and building campaigns. The relationship was, nonetheless, an ambiguous one. The YMCA's support for the women's organization was extremely self-interested, for it was rooted in the conviction that its own work for young men would be undermined without a similar work for the uplift of the young women of the community. In order to increase public support for their undertakings, YWCAs adapted and modified the YMCA's argument that young men were the future leaders and builders of the community by emphasizing the importance of young women as the future generation of mothers. Canadian churches and communities, however, were simply not prepared to give to the YWCA the same kind of support that was forthcoming for efforts on behalf of young men; in any case, the women's organization insisted that its work for women was a distinct one to which the YMCA's experience was not necessarily applicable.[12]

Nineteenth-century YWCAs developed in a context that was truly international, an aspect of the history of Canadian feminism that remains largely unexplored by historians.[13] Almost from its inception, the British founders conceived of the YWCA as a global evangelical enterprise, intended both to supervise young British women travelling throughout the Empire and to evangelize the women of 'heathen' populations. This vision achieved institutional expression with the establishment of the World's YWCA in 1894.[14] During the formative decades of the 1870s and 1880s, however, the Canadian YWCAs developed as part of a North American network, affiliating with two coordinating bodies based in New York and Chicago. During this critical period YWCAs recognized the value of sharing their experiences with like-minded women who faced similar difficulties in cities across North America. Canadian evangelical women, in particular, were inspired by the activities of their counterparts in major American centres such as Boston, New York, and Seattle, assuming, as Canadian social reformers were wont to do, that American cities and their problems portended the future for Canada. Quickly coming to the realization that they would benefit by comparing methods and programs and by sharing information and solutions to common problems, many YWCA executives initiated mutual contacts through correspondence and the exchange of annual reports. Visiting speakers from the United States frequently provided Canadian YWCAs with useful information about Christian women's work in American cities and with valuable publicity as they attracted large crowds to public meetings; likewise, Canadian YWCA board members travelling outside the country made a point of visiting the local YWCA, returning to share their experiences and insights with churchwomen in their own communities.

Even before the appearance of the first YWCAs in Canada, branches in several American cities had begun to share information by exchanging annual reports through the mail, a development that quickly led to informal meetings of representatives from the various branches.[15] This resulted, by the 1870s, in the holding of the first formal YWCA conferences, a novel and frequently unprecedented phenomenon in many North American cities. The first such gathering was held in Hartford, Connecticut, in 1871, as delegates from Boston, Providence, Lowell, Buffalo, Washington, Cincinnati, and Philadelphia arrived to gather for prayer and discussion of questions of common concern to those engaged in 'striving to protect and to benefit in every way their young sisters, who are toiling for their own and others' support, with many trials and temptations.'[16] A model for those of successive conferences, the Hartford program consisted of reports on the work of the eight associations represented and in thirteen other cities unable to send delegates. From their inception YWCAs emphasized their commitment to a practical or applied Christianity, an approach reflected in the emphasis placed at Hartford on developing concrete solutions to common problems such as securing funds, organizing efficient committees, and improving the teaching of Bible or sewing classes for young women. Although there is no record that any Canadian delegates attended the gathering at Hartford, this conference was to have a direct bearing on the formation of the first permanently organized YWCA in Canada.[17] Among the delegates at Hartford was H. Thane Miller, one of the leading laymen of the American YMCA, who was the principal guest speaker at the ceremonies dedicating the new building of the Toronto YMCA two years later, in 1873. During his stay in Toronto, Miller addressed a public meeting attended by over three hundred women who were anxious to learn about the work of the YWCA in Boston, Philadelphia, and Cincinnati. With encouragement from some of the city's leading clergy and representatives of the local YMCA, the Toronto women responded unanimously to Miller's appeal for a similar work on behalf of their own young women, immediately forming a committee composed of two representatives from each Protestant church in the city. Borrowing from the constitution of the Boston YWCA, they dedicated their fledgling organization to 'the temporal, moral and religious welfare of young women who are dependent upon their own exertions for support.'[18]

The delegates at the Hartford conference passed a resolution providing for similar meetings to be held at intervals of not more than two years. These national conferences for consultative purposes soon became the major vehicle for the standardization of American YWCA work in the nineteenth century. In 1873 forty-eight delegates from seventeen cities met in Philadelphia where they were pleased to learn that YWCA work was being undertaken by Christian women in thirty-six American cities. The greetings received from Italy and word of new associations in Canada led to the first international YWCA conference in Pittsburgh in 1875. There reports and letters were received from England, France, Holland, and Switzerland, and from Canadian branches in Quebec City and Belleville, Ontario.

Until the formation of a national Canadian organization in 1895 these early American conferences, dubbed international in deference to the small number of foreign delegates, remained the most effective means by which isolated Canadian locals learned from one another's experiences and gained a sense of their common objectives. Delegates from the Quebec WCA who attended the Seventh Biennial Conference of Women's Christian Associations in Boston in 1883 reported, 'While all the Associations have different branches of work to suit the exigencies of their surroundings, uniformity of construction is the prevailing characteristic. All have the same end in view, many of the same difficulties to overcome.' Even more important than the practical insights into the problems and possibilities of the work, however, was the opportunity to associate with like-minded Christian women and to gain a larger perspective of YWCA work. The Quebec delegates commented: 'It was indeed a glorious privilege to meet those noble women whose names had so long been familiar to us, and to feel that our Association, feeble and insignificant though it is, does not stand alone, but is an integral part of a great whole.'[19]

During the 1870s and 1880s these YWCA conferences were important community events that helped to increase the visibility of the organization and generate public support for the work of the local branch. The unusual spectacle of Christian women meeting in conference inevitably attracted the attention of the press, resulting in valuable publicity and, more significantly for the historian, generating what is in many cases the only surviving record of the conference proceedings. As the press reports indicate, the conference sessions and public meetings not only provided the delegates with opportunities to share experiences and learn from one another; they also provided a unique opportunity for Christian women to explain and justify their work to a larger public.

When the Montreal YWCA hosted the Fourth International Conference of Women's Christian Associations in 1877, such a gathering was unprecedented in the history of the city and, at first, 'the citizens did not seem to understand why ladies should meet in this way.'[20] The fledgling local branch was only three years old at the time; it had been organized in 1874 on the initiative of a Miss Hervey 'who urged a number of ladies to organise themselves for the purpose of attending to the temporal, moral, and religious welfare of the many young women who are attracted from different parts of the country to Montreal.'[21] The 1877 conference was a coup of major proportions for which the members of the Montreal YWCA were much indebted to their president, Mrs P.D. Browne, who had travelled as a delegate to Pittsburgh in 1875 and had persuaded the largely American gathering to hold its next meeting in Montreal. Fifty-two delegates arrived for the conference, representing fifteen American cities, England, Quebec City, and Brockville, Ontario, and reports and greetings were sent from many other branches. The arrival of so many prominent Christian women was, as the *Montreal Daily Witness* observed, 'an event of no small importance' in that community, and, after the initial misgivings had passed, 'the interest was so great that many who had no delegates allotted to them felt quite neglected, and begged the privilege of entertaining for part of the time at least.'[22] The delegates were welcomed at an elaborate reception held in the Congregational Church of the Emmanuel where some four hundred ladies and gentlemen spent the evening in 'social intercourse' accompanied by music and refreshments. Among their numbers members of the press noted 'many of our most prominent and benevolent citizens and a number of the city clergy.'[23]

YWCA conferences provided churchwomen in Canadian cities with an education in the methods and principles of evangelical social reform and aimed to mobilize evangelical women as a force in the community. The reports of the Montreal conference sessions reveal the wide range of programs and services being offered by Women's and Young Women's Christian Associations in the 1870s, including boarding-houses, employment bureaux, industrial schools, reading rooms, dispensaries, flower missions, hospital and prison visitation programs, Magdalen Asylums, homes for aged women, and experimental projects such as a cooking school and a seaside home for working women. At the opening of the 1877 conference, the retiring president, Mrs Lamson of Boston, greeted the delegates with the declaration that since her arrival in Montreal, and particularly in view of the accomplishments of the host association in three short years of existence, her thoughts had been filled with the growth of women's work. 'Not only in Christian Associations are women called to work now; the wise men in many of our States are calling us to help them on all their various boards which have the care of women and children. In the workhouses, the reformatory schools and the prisons for women our counsel is sought. The power of women has been felt throughout the land in the temperance work of the past two years. Ladies, we must meet these demands upon us. Can we not as Christians hear the voice of our Heavenly Father in the call, and see His hand is opening all these doors of usefulness to us?'[24] Christian work represented new and unprecedented opportunities for women, and, exhorting the delegates to 'prepare to meet the demands of the nineteenth century by training ourselves,' Mrs Lamson declared that 'there is no better school than the Christian associations, and ... no better college than these conferences.'[25] Montreal women eagerly followed her advice, with between two and three hundred women attending each session of the conference.

The sessions at the 1877 conference included detailed reports of the work being undertaken in each city represented, including a short history and statement of the objectives of the work, a description of the programs and religious services offered, and a report on the status of the mortgage and condition of the treasury. In addition, lengthy papers were read on important topics of general interest such as 'Employment for Women,' 'Boarding

Homes,' and 'The Rescue of Fallen Women,' substantial extracts of which appeared in the Montreal English press. One Montreal delegate, a Miss Mackin, lady superintendent of the Montreal General Hospital, contributed a paper on the training of nurses. In addresses such as that of Mrs A.B. Leslie of Cleveland, who spoke on 'The Rescue of Fallen Women,' the delegates were educated in the principles of evangelical social reform, being advised, in this case, that 'in overcoming the evil of prostitution, as that of its sister evil, intemperance, they must get to the very root of the matter – in the heart. New motives, new principles must be supplied.'[26] The conference sessions also provided valuable opportunities to discuss the practical details of organizing and managing a YWCA. The following exchange, for example, was prompted by the paper on boarding-homes presented by Miss Drinkwater of Boston:

Q. Has any difficulty arisen from receiving young men as visitors?
A. No.
Q. Have you ever had any trouble as to time for family worship?
A. Yes. The hour was nine and afterwards changed to 7, i.e. immediately after tea.
Q. Do you compel your boarders to go to church?
A. Yes, as a rule, it is expected.
Q. Would you tell us something about your socials?
A. The young ladies invite their own friends and that works well.
Q. Do you limit the age of those you admit?
A. Yes, since we have been crowded we admit none over forty years old.[27]

For many churchwomen these sessions must have provided valuable lessons in organization and proper business procedures, as well as exposure to role models whose competence, expertise, and religious convictions were beyond question.

The reports of the Montreal conference reveal that the founders of the YWCA were among those nineteenth-century women who developed and promoted a maternal feminism that loosened the constraints of the cult of domesticity while not directly challenging traditional gender roles.[28] Maternalist arguments could be used to justify women's involvement in the public sphere, but they also soothed the apprehension aroused in some quarters by the still novel spectacle of organized Christian womanhood. In her opening address to the conference, Mrs Lamson spoke of the duty of women to train their daughters for Christian work, 'but never should they have cause to doubt that we believe our duties as wives and mothers are paramount to all others, and that, however good the work we may be doing, it had better be left undone if we must neglect our home duties.' Lamson's message simultaneously stressed the strength of women while reassuring those who viewed women as usurpers in the domain of men. 'That woman is to be an increasing power in America, I may say in the world, no one doubts. Let us see to it that it is the power of true Christian women. Bear with me in one warning word: that influence is not to be exerted by unsexing ourselves. Why is it that gentlemen ask our aid in their public work? Is it because we are like themselves? No, but because we are women, and have women's hearts, and women's heads, and women's instincts.'[29]

While obviously taking care to woo male support and undercut potential opposition, the organizers of the Montreal conference were adamant that Christian women's work should remain under female control. Following the initial public meeting, the women insisted on their right to conduct their own proceedings, and their bemused gentlemen supporters found themselves excluded from the conference sessions. That not all accepted their fate with good grace was evident in the irritated comment of the reporter from the *Daily Witness*. He noted that the conference deliberations had been 'of an able, interesting and important character,' as could be judged 'from the broken and somewhat confused reports of their proceedings which have appeared in our columns – and which have been obtained second-hand and with some difficulty, in consequence of the ladies excluding newspaper reporters (and all others of the sterner sex) from their sessions and attempting to report themselves.'[30]

The delegates' decision to exclude men from their sessions reflected the YWCA's commitment to training women for Christian work and to promoting its vision of an active and competent evangelical womanhood. In late nineteenth-century Canada it remained socially unacceptable for a middle-class woman to address a mixed audience from a public platform, and even during YWCA conferences, the large public meetings were conducted entirely by men. If Christian women were to acquire experience in leading public prayer and conducting business meetings, and have the opportunity to be exposed to capable female role models, the exclusion of men was essential. YWCA conference organizers could not help but be aware that even the most sympathetic gentlemen supporters could be patronizing and often seemingly unable to grasp the significance to the women of what the latter stressed was a Christian work 'for women and by women.' During the public meeting held as part of the 1877 conference, such attitudes were clearly in evidence when some of the clergy appeared to have difficulty in treating a conference of Christian women as a serious event.

The Reverend A.J. Bray observed in addressing the mixed gathering that he was glad the ladies 'had found something to do.' Bray's mirthful remarks barely concealed his contempt for the conference delegates and their undertaking, evident even to the reporter from the *Daily Witness*.

He said he did not know much what to say; did not know much about the object of the meeting. Two of the ladies had called on him, and suggested a subject on which he should speak; but, about ten minutes before leaving home, he had tried to think what it was, and for the life of him could not. The speaker proceeded in this strain, and in the course of further remarks said he presumed a portion of their work was to educate young women in domestic duties, for which there was need. So far as his acquaintance went, the ladies did not know much about work(!); they did not know when a potato was cooked. There were many unhappy marriages of young women, who when you heard them giggle, you heard all there was of them; when you saw them smile you saw all there was of them; they possessed no ideas. He was glad the Convention had come to Montreal, and he was sure it would result in good.[31]

These remarks were apparently greeted with polite silence by the visiting delegates and the undoubtedly mortified members of the host association, but the chairman, Reverend G.H. Wells, publicly rebuked the speaker, remarking that 'if Mr Bray had taken the trouble to make himself acquainted with the ladies who had been meeting in Convention, he would have had a more favorable opinion of women.'[32] Other speakers, including Reverend L. Gaetz, Reverend J.F. Stevenson, and Principal Dawson of McGill University, rallied to the women's defence, comparing them to Mary Magdalene and Naomi, and praising effusively 'their ability and tact – which the men could not aspire to.' Yet the support given by these men was clearly contingent upon an understanding that an expanded role for churchwomen would not in any way challenge their own monopoly of doctrinal matters. While acknowledging that 'it would belong to women to stay the approaching tide of opposition to Christianity,' the women's defenders pointedly noted that because of the 'higher ministry' that God had given them, 'women could afford to put aside all the controversies about creeds, &c., which occupy men's minds.'[33]

At female gatherings like these early YWCA conferences, evangelical women created both female spaces allowing women to speak and act independently of men and 'alternative institutions through which the evangelical ideal of woman could be developed, taught, and promulgated.'[34] Perhaps most valued was the opportunity to share religious fellowship with like-minded women. An enthusiastic observance of evangelical forms such as public prayer and the singing of gospel hymns reflected the YWCA's commitment to evangelical Christianity as a form of social religion that created emotional bonds among the delegates and affirmed their membership in a community of female believers.[35] The sessions at the Montreal conference, which were held in the city's leading Protestant churches, were opened and closed with audible prayer, and the presentations of reports and papers were punctuated by the reading of psalms and the singing of favourite gospel hymns. Telegrams received from supporters elsewhere, including the ladies of the Zenana Mission meeting concurrently in Pittsburgh, contained greetings and messages in the form of biblical verses. Even during their final expedition to shoot the Lachine Rapids on the steamer *Empress* before leaving Montreal, the delegates, overcome by the excitement, could not refrain from bursting into exuberant choruses of 'Shall We Gather at the River?' and 'Hold the Fort.' The Montreal YWCA later reported that 'not a single unpleasantness occurred to mar the wonderful unanimity of feeling that rested upon the assembly.' When at last the delegates departed after 'the warmest expressions of good will,' the members of the host association were left deeply affected and profoundly grateful for their experience. 'The many lessons learned; the useful hints obtained by hearing of the management of the different Associations; the excellent papers read and remarks made by ladies whose whole-heartedness was manifest, could not fail to produce lasting benefit.'[36]

While Canadian historians have carefully documented the use of maternalist arguments to justify the expansion of the activities of Victorian middle-class women beyond the confines of the private and the purely domestic, less attention has been paid to women's conscious use of religious arguments to accomplish a similar effect. The press reports of the Montreal conference demonstrate that organized evangelical women repeatedly explained and justified their activities with reference to women's 'special ministry' and their unique relationship with Jesus. The YWCA shared the view, widely held among liberal evangelicals, that Christianity valued women more highly than any other religion and that Jesus Christ was the first major religious leader to embody the particular virtues of women, such as gentleness, meekness, patience, and self-denial. Not surprisingly, in view of their debt to Christ who conferred a special honour on womanhood, women were largely represented among his followers and were among those most anxious to spread the news of his salvation.[37] An obvious favourite with the founders of the YWCA was the argument that

Jesus had demonstrated his commitment to women, and had endorsed their role in the spreading of the gospel, by entrusting the news of the resurrection to Mary Magdalene, rather than to any of the disciples. In laying claim to this special ministry that Christ himself had been the first to recognize, evangelical women countered Pauline arguments that women's place in the church was to remain quiet and subordinate to men, a view that devalued women's abilities and their potential contribution to the church. While not asserting their right to serve the church as preachers and ministers, the founders of the YWCA consciously employed the example of Christ's life and teachings to justify an increasingly public role for organized church-women.

An examination of the YWCA in the late nineteenth century clearly demonstrates the extent to which the horizons of evangelical church-women had broadened since the organization of the first denominational ladies' aid and missionary societies earlier in the century. The formation of YWCAs beginning in the 1870s illustrates the importance of the evangelical commitment to good works as a factor in the appearance of the phenomenon of organized womanhood in Canadian cities, and it serves as a reminder of the role played by churchwomen, seeking greater autonomy outside male-controlled institutional structures, in pioneering new models of interdenominational cooperation. The administration of a YWCA entailed operations on a scale considerably surpassing that of earlier local activities and required new kinds of expertise that far exceeded the demands of women's traditional charitable work. Early YWCA conferences illustrate the process by which evangelical churchwomen consciously set about acquiring the requisite new skills and educating themselves in business methods and the principles of social reform. In so doing they consciously promoted a model of evangelical womanhood that served both to justify their expanded endeavours and to provide emotional and spiritual support in the face of scepticism or hostility. Unprecedented gatherings such as the YWCA conference held in Montreal in 1877 also clearly demonstrate that Canadian churchwomen functioned in a larger context and were conscious participants in a global enterprise and an international network of Christian women. Although limited by an ultimate dependence on male support, which was forthcoming only so long as women agreed not to challenge male institutional control or doctrinal hegemony, 'the power of true Christian women' resulted in the creation of a relatively autonomous and supportive female-controlled and church-sanctioned space and the promotion of a new model of an active evangelical womanhood increasingly engaged with the world outside the home and the church.

NOTES

1 See Patricia T. Rooke and R.L. Schnell, 'The Rise and Decline of British North
   American Protestant Orphans' Homes as Woman's Domain, 1850–1930,'
   Atlantis 7, 2 (1982), 21–35; Gail Cuthbert Brandt, 'Organizations in Canada:
   The English Protestant Tradition,' *Women's Paid and Unpaid Work: Historical
   and Contemporary Perspectives*, Paula Bourne, ed. (Toronto: New Hogtown
   Press, 1985), 79–87; and Wendy Mitchinson, 'Early Women's Organizations
   and Social Reform: Prelude to the Welfare State,' *The 'Benevolent' State: The
   Growth of Welfare in Canada*, Allan Moscovitch and Jim Albert, eds. (Toronto:
   Garamond Press, 1987), 77–92.
2 Wendy Mitchinson, 'Canadian Women and Church Missionary Societies in the
   Nineteenth Century: A Step Towards Independence,' *Atlantis* 2, 2 (Spring
   1977), 57–75.
3 Diana Pedersen, 'The Young Women's Christian Association in Canada, 1870–
   1920: "A Movement to Meet a Spiritual, Civic, and National Need" (PhD thesis, Carleton University, 1987), chap. 1.
4 Anne M. Boylan, 'Evangelical Womanhood in the Nineteenth Century: The
   Role of Women in Sunday Schools,' *Feminist Studies* 4, 3 (1978), 62–80.
5 Diana Pedersen, '"Keeping Our Good Girls Good": The YWCA and the "Girl
   Problem," 1870–1930,' *Canadian Woman's Studies / les cahiers de la femme* 7, 4
   (Winter 1986), 20–4; and Wendy Mitchinson, 'The YWCA and Reform in the
   Nineteenth Century,' *Histoire sociale/Social History* 12, 24 (Nov. 1979),
   368–84.
6 On lay evangelical organizations, see Robert T. Handy, *A History of the
   Churches in the United States and Canada* (New York: Oxford University
   Press, 1976), 171–5. YWCA constitutions appended the following definition of
   an evangelical church: 'We hold those churches to be evangelical which, maintaining the Holy Scriptures to be the only infallible rule of faith and practice, do
   believe in the Lord Jesus Christ, the only begotten Son of the Father, King of
   Kings, Lord of Lords, in whom dwelleth the fullness of the godhead bodily, and
   who was made sin for us, though knowing no sin, bearing our sins in His own
   body on the tree, as the only name under heaven given among men whereby we
   must be saved from everlasting punishment.'
7 Pedersen, 'The Young Women's Christian Association,' chap. 3; and '"Building
   Today for the Womanhood of Tomorrow": Businessmen, Boosters, and the
   YWCA, 1890–1930,' *Urban History Review/Revue d'histoire urbaine* 15, 3
   (1987), 225–42.
8 Veronica Strong-Boag, '"Setting the Stage": National Organization and the
   Women's Movement in the Late 19th Century,' in *The Neglected Majority:*

Essays in Canadian Women's History, Susan Mann Trofimenkoff and Alison Prentice, eds. (Toronto: McClelland and Stewart, 1977), 87–103.

9 *Annual Report*, 1891, 15, Toronto YWCA Records, Public Archives of Ontario (hereafter PAO).

10 Pedersen, 'The Young Women's Christian Association,' chap. 3.

11 The best source on early Canadian YMCAs remains Murray G. Ross, *The YMCA in Canada: The Chronicle of a Century* (Toronto: Ryerson Press, 1951).

12 Pedersen, 'The Young Women's Christian Association,' chaps. 3 and 4. It is important to remember that, despite the contacts between the boards, Canadian YWCAs and YMCAs were entirely separate organizations, each with its own national and international coordinating bodies. The practice of sharing facilities in smaller communities for administrative and financial reasons did not begin until the opening of the Windsor YM–YWCA in 1927.

13 This observation was first made by Deborah Gorham in 'English Militancy and the Canadian Suffrage Movement,' *Atlantis* 1, 1 (1975), 83.

14 See Anna V. Rice, *A History of the World's Young Women's Christian Association* (New York: Woman's Press, 1947).

15 This account of early WCA and YWCA conferences in the United States is drawn largely from Elizabeth Wilson, *Fifty Years of Association Work among Young Women, 1866–1916: A History of the Young Women's Christian Associations of the United States of America* (New York: National Board of the Young Women's Christian Associations of the United States of America, 1916), chap. 13.

16 Quoted in ibid., 160.

17 YWCA historians have designated as the first Canadian YWCA a short-lived effort in Saint John, NB, that collapsed after only a few years under circumstances suggesting that conditions were not ripe for the formation of a YWCA. See Mary Quayle Innis, *Unfold the Years: A History of the Young Women's Christian Association in Canada* (Toronto: McClelland and Stewart, 1949), 9; and Josephine Perfect Harshaw, *When Women Work Together: A History of the Young Women's Christian Association in Canada* (Toronto: Ryerson Press, 1966), 11. YWCA accounts written in the late nineteenth and early twentieth centuries all identify the Toronto branch as the first Canadian YWCA.

18 *Annual Report*, 1874, 1886, Toronto YWCA Records; Toronto *Daily Mail*, 20 Feb. 1873, 4; 21 Feb. 1873, 4.

19 *Annual Report*, 1884, 15, Women's Christian Association of Quebec, National Library of Canada, K-63-4. Because not all nineteenth-century branches focused solely on young single women, as in the case of Quebec City where the population of young Protestant women was very small, many were known as WCAs rather than YWCAs.

20 *Annual Report*, 1878, 15, v. 38, Montreal YWCA Records, MG 28 I 240, National Archives of Canada.

21 *Montreal Herald*, 25 May 1874, 4; *Montreal Gazette*, 25 May 1874, 2; *Montreal Star*, 26 May 1874, 3; *Montreal Daily Witness*, 26 May 1874, 2.

22 6 June 1877, 4; *Annual Report*, 1878, 15, v. 38, Montreal YWCA Records.

23 *Montreal Herald and Daily Commercial Gazette*, 6 June 1877, 4. See also *Montreal Daily Witness*, 6 June 1877, 4; *Gazette*, 6 June 1877, 4; *Montreal Daily Star*, 6 June 1877, 2.

24 *Montreal Daily Witness*, 6 June 1877, 4.

25 *Gazette*, 6 June 1877, 4.

26 Ibid., 7 June 1877, 8.

27 Ibid., 4.

28 Linda Kealey, ed., *A Not Unreasonable Claim: Women and Reform in Canada, 1880s–1920s* (Toronto: Women's Press, 1979).

29 *Gazette*, 6 June 1877, 4.

30 *Daily Witness*, 8 June 1877, 4.

31 Ibid.

32 Ibid.

33 *Montreal Daily Star*, 8 June 1877, 2.

34 Boylan, 76. See also Estelle Freedman's influential article, 'Separatism as Strategy: Female Institution Building and American Feminism, 1870–1930,' *Feminist Studies* 5, 3 (Fall 1979), 512–29.

35 See Sandra Sizer, *Gospel Hymns and Social Religion: The Rhetoric of Nineteenth-Century Revivalism* (Philadelphia: Temple University Press, 1978).

36 *Annual Report*, 1878, 15, vol. 38, Montreal YWCA Records.

37 One of the most articulate exponents of this view was the Reverend Benjamin Fish Austin, Methodist principal of Alma Ladies' College in St Thomas, Ontario and editor of *Woman: Her Character, Culture, and Calling* (Brantford, 1890). The YWCA heartily endorsed the views of Principal Austin (this of course was some years before his expulsion from the Methodist Church for his heretical views on spiritualism), the Ottawa branch seeing fit to reproduce his short essay, 'What Christ Has Done for Woman,' in its own publication. See Ottawa YWCA Records, the *Friend of the Friendless* 4, 6 (Oct. 1892). On Austin's career, see Ramsay Cook, *The Regenerators: Social Criticism in Late Victorian English Canada* (Toronto: University of Toronto Press, 1985), 69–78.

17

Nellie McClung's Social Gospel

RANDI R. WARNE

By the early twentieth century many women were vocal in their criticism of church and society, demanding radical change. Yet they chose different ways of working towards this transformation. Some worked within religious organizations for personal or social reform. For others religion might be the catalyst that would motivate them to work independently, outside strictly religious structures. For the social activist Nellie McClung, the biblical imperative to do God's will meant to fight 'for a fair chance for everyone, even women!' There was no question in her mind that it was a religious responsibility to change social conditions. McClung devoted herself to this task through her fiction and her political writings, and as she did so, she worked to put the condition of women on the agenda of the Social Gospel.

The early years of this century saw the rise of a new spirit in Christianity. Far from the 'opium of the masses' which Karl Marx decried, the Social Gospel[1] swept the North American continent with its fervid and unshakeable conviction that Christianity was a 'social religion' whose prime purpose was 'building God's Kingdom here on earth.' How that lofty goal was to be achieved was the subject of some dispute. Historian Richard Allen identifies three main groups within the Canadian Social Gospel movement whose different definitions of the problem led to significantly disparate strategies for social transformation.[2] These positions were united, however, in their overall agreement that the core of the Social Gospel was the need to regenerate 'right relationship between man and man.' One of the major obstacles to this new social harmony was the exploitative economic system of unfettered capitalism which fostered competitiveness and individualism rather than Christian cooperation. Winnipeg's radical professor and activist Salem Bland was not alone in his call for a new social order where the 'I-consciousness' of existing society would be replaced by the 'we-consciousness' of the 'sacred cause of Labor.'[3] 'Every man and woman a worker' was Bland's rallying cry.[4]

Historians in the United States and Canada have generally concurred with this reading of the Social Gospel, seeing 'the building of the Kingdom' primarily played out in resolving tensions of labour and capital.[5] Their focus, therefore, has tended to be on the fight to establish workers' (usually working men's) rights in the public sphere. In contrast, relatively little attention has been paid to what the Social Gospel might have meant to the majority of those who inhabited the pews, not the pulpits, of Protestant Christendom. An important question has not been asked: 'What did the Social Gospel mean for women?'

Ronald Huff has explored the understanding that male Social Gospel leaders in the United States held of women's place in the 'new Kingdom.' Huff concludes that these clergymen were decidedly ambivalent towards the advancement of women: The most active support for or opposition to women was 'sometimes taken back by the undertow of the perhaps unstated contradiction, even within a sentence or phrase. The incongruities were between the ideals inherent within the 'new social theology,' which in theory wholeheartedly supported women's gains towards equality, and the innate proclivities of the writer's heart.'[6] Huff's work highlights the importance of using gender as an interpretive category when considering so-called universal movements in human history. Despite their theological openness, male practitioners of the American Social Gospel apparently found themselves more conventionally positioned around issues of women's rights.

Gender could likewise prove a useful category in reconsidering the Canadian Social Gospel. As it stands, women's religious social reform activities have tended to be considered as subordinate, or subsequent to mainstream Social Gospel activism. Nor have the agendas of religious feminist social activism figured in generating interpretive categories for understanding the Social Gospel movement as a whole.[7] It is necessary to redress the imbalance by asking what the Social Gospel might look like from a woman's perspective. This question can be explored through examining the life and work of Canada's famous Christian feminist social activist, Nellie L. McClung. McClung has repeatedly, if superficially, been linked with the Social Gospel.[8] Her reform activities and Christian commitment are well documented, as are her pronouncements on a range of social issues. Until further studies are done that seriously consider women as potentially equal actors in the Social Gospel movement, it would be both futile and misleading to attempt to state whether McClung was idiosyncratic in her understanding or representative of some larger 'woman's perspective.' It is possible now, however, to gain some understanding of at least one woman's reading of Christianity as a social religion and to broaden the interpretive base available for scholars of the Social Gospel by lifting up aspects of women's experience which may have slipped notice in the past.

Nellie McClung was born Nellie Mooney on 29 October 1873, in a small farmhouse near Owen Sound, Ontario. She was the youngest child of six born to immigrant parents who had come to Canada seeking a better life. John Mooney had arrived in Canada in 1830, working first as a logger in the Ottawa area, moving west to Grey County, Ontario, to farm. Letitia

McCurdy arrived with her mother and sister from Dundee, Scotland, after her father died in a cholera epidemic. She married John Mooney, thirty years her senior, in 1858 at the age of sixteen.[9] Farm life on the rocky Bruce Peninsula soil proved hard and unrewarding, and hearing glowing tales of the bounty awaiting in the west, the Mooneys resolved to begin life anew on the prairie plains. In 1880 they set out to homestead, travelling by steamship, foot, and oxcart to the Tiger Hills of southwest Manitoba.

These early years of struggle to build a new life on the prairie marked McClung deeply. The lessons McClung thus learned emerge repeatedly in both her fiction and her political writings. Her respect for her parents' labour is evident in the following passage, in which her fictional alter-ego, Pearlie Watson, reflects on the place of such labour in the current social order:

She began to wonder now if Mr Donald had been right in his idealistic way of looking at life and labor. She had always thought so until this minute, and many a thrill of pride had she experienced in thinking of her parents and their days of struggling. They had been and were, the real Empire-builders who subdued the soil and made it serve human needs, enduring hardships and hunger and cold and bitter discouragements, always with heroism and patience. The farm on which they now lived had been abandoned, deserted, given up for a bad job, and her people had redeemed it, and were making it one of the best in the country! Every farm in the community was made more valuable because of their efforts ... But since she had been away, she had learned to her surprise that the world does not give its crowns to those who serve it best – but to those who can make the most people serve them.[10]

This disparity between hard, creative labour and worldly reward would continue to trouble McClung throughout her life.[11]

McClung's rural experience led her to be particularly sensitive to the importance of non-waged labour, whether on the farm or within the domestic sphere. She did not like 'the term "working people" applied exclusively to those who work for wages,' and objected to 'the way we draw lines between different kinds of work, counting some higher than others in the social scale.'[12] She was also keenly aware of the interrelation of individual effort and community support. Just as one family's farming success could improve land values for the whole community, or one woman's achievements could open possibilities for all women,[13] so too the community had to embody justice so that individuals could have an equal chance to demonstrate their own unique character and reach their own self-determined limits. McClung's vision was both individual and social: 'We know there is no such thing as equality of achievement, but what we plead for is equality of chance, equality of opportunity. We know that equality of opportunity is hardly possible, but we can make it more nearly possible by the removal of all movable handicaps from the human race.'[14] As she succinctly states, 'To bring this about – the even chance for everyone – is the plain and simple meaning of life.'[15]

While 'the even chance' might be God's intention for Creation, it is not won without a struggle. As Pearl observed, 'hoggish ones' are likely to take more than their share, leaving the rest of us to '[travel] below our privileges.'[16] Furthermore, the very nature of Creation requires striving towards a more beneficent state of affairs. The influence of McClung's rural upbringing pervades in her discussion of this point, which concludes with the following rousing passage:

There is no resignation in Nature, no quiet folding of the hands, no hypocritical saying, 'Thy will be done!' and giving in without a struggle. Countless millions of seeds and plants are doomed each year to death and failure, but all honor to them – they put up a fight to the very end! Resignation is a cheap and indolent human virtue, which has served as an excuse for much spiritual slothfulness. It is still highly revered and commended. It is so much easier sometimes to sit down and be resigned rather than to rise up and be indignant.

Years ago people broke every law of sanitation and when plagues came they were resigned and piously looked heavenward, and blamed God for the whole thing. 'Thy will be done,' they said, and now we know it was not God's will at all. It is never God's will that any should perish! 'Thy will be done!' should ever be the prayer of our hearts, but it does not let us out of any responsibility. It is not a weak acceptance of misfortune, or sickness, or injustice, or wrong, for these things are not God's will.

'Thy will be done' is a call to fight – to fight for better conditions, for moral and physical health, for sweeter manners, cleaner laws, for a fair chance for everyone, even women![17]

McClung shared the generally liberal, progressivist theology that marked the Protestant Social Gospel at the turn of the century. She rejected the notion of Hell and, in a touching story called 'Bells at Evening,' pictured Heaven as the place where people of faith, who have reaped the rewards of living a religious life, help 'the people who come over unprepared, and who have terrible remorse over their wasted lives, and all sorts of bad habits to overcome.'[18] Sin is a waste of God's gift of Creation, while a life of faith is its own reward.

The task of the religious person, then, is to help those who are broken to heal. In addition to the work of evangelization and education, which were women's traditional tasks, for McClung this also included changing social conditions that led people into temptation or forced them into a less than savoury life. Like J.S. Woodsworth, whose father subscribed to the belief that children were born sinless, McClung was convinced that poor social conditions were the cause of many human transgressions. Once these were remedied, she felt, most people would naturally work towards making the best life possible for all. She was particularly critical of 'charity work' which temporarily alleviated the symptoms of social injustice, but which left the basic structures of injustice untouched. It was this belief that underscored her support for Woodsworth's All People's Mission. As she stated in her submission to the *All People's Mission Annual Report* of 1914, 'All People's Mission is not a charity – it is an institution which aims to making charity unnecessary, it teaches the people to help and respect themselves.'[19]

For women to do God's work, social convention that relegated women to the so-called private sphere of the home had to change. McClung spells out women's obligation to political action in the following:

If women would only be content to snip away at the symptoms of poverty and distress, feeding the hungry and clothing the naked, all would be well and they would be much commended for their kindness of heart; but when they begin to inquire into causes, they find themselves in the sacred realm of politics where prejudice says no women must enter.

A woman may take an interest in factory girls, and hold meetings for them, and encourage them to walk in virtue's way all she likes, but if she begins to advocate more sanitary surroundings for them, with some respect for the common decencies of life, she will find herself again in the sacred realm of politics – confronted by a factory act, on which no profane female hand must be laid.

Now politics simply means public affairs – yours and mine, everybody's – and to say that politics are too corrupt for women is a weak and foolish statement for any man to make. Any man who is actively engaged in politics, and declares that politics are too corrupt for women, admits one of two things, either that he is a party to this corruption, or that he is unable to prevent it – and in either case something should be done.[20]

McClung's understanding of her Christian duty to help bring about 'the even chance for everyone' led inescapably to the conclusion that the 'separate spheres' ordained by Victorian convention and sanctioned by traditional religion violated God's will. Women were obliged by their faith to engage the political order so as to change it. McClung's claim that 'the demand for votes is a spiritual movement' was not mere rhetoric.[21]

Nellie McClung's focus on women's experience and social reality led her in a different direction from most male Social Gospellers. Her rural upbringing ensured a definition of labour that was not limited to 'work for wages.' She likewise saw firsthand the realities of the 'prairie partnership' in which women and men worked equally to build a new life on the frontier. There are additional influences that shaped her thought.

Among the key factors engendering reform movements of the late nineteenth and early twentieth centuries were the social consequences of industrial capitalism. Even in the Canadian west, cities like Winnipeg saw a rapid growth of slums and all the social problems attendant thereto, as workers crammed into the urban core to take whatever wages they could in the factories.[22] Additionally, many of those so employed were immigrants, often foreign-speaking and poorly educated, whose way of life in the 'old country' left them ill-prepared to combat the abuses they faced. Having moved to Winnipeg in 1911, McClung was well aware of these conditions, as her graphic description of taking Conservative Premier Sir Rodmond Roblin on a tour of a sweatshop well attests.[23] Social historians have generally faulted McClung for not directing more of her energies towards analysing such conditions along conventional socialist lines, seeing her equal concern for women's traditional experience as evidence of bourgeois sympathies. New developments in social history that take women's experience seriously and centrally offer a different explanation. As Dolores Hayden points out in her ground-breaking work, *The Grand Domestic Revolution*, failure to understand the material realities of women's experience 'has led scholars to misunderstand feminist ideology as a whole.' Rather than being 'limited' in its concern for domestic space and labour, 'the overarching theme of the late nineteenth and early twentieth century feminist movement was to overcome the split between domestic life and public life created by industrial capitalism, as it affected women.'[24]

Scholars have tended to distinguish too sharply between 'types' of feminists, separating what was in fact a very interrelated agenda covering a range of issues, both 'private' and public. As Hayden notes, 'Whether feminists sought control over property, child custody, divorce, 'voluntary motherhood,' temperance, prostitution, housing, refuse disposal, water supplies, schools, or workplaces, their aims were summarized by the historian Aileen Kraditor: "Women's sphere must be defined by women."'[25]

The era produced a number of important and influential feminist theorists who addressed these questions, central among whom was Charlotte

Perkins Gilman.[26] McClung was deeply familiar with Gilman's work, as is evident in her many allusions to Gilman's classic text, *The Man-Made World* in McClung's *In Times Like These*.[27] She also drew from South African feminist Olive Schreiner, whose lengthy excoriation of 'sex-parasitism' is echoed in McClung's treatment of the 'Gentle Lady.'[28] Probably then, as today, feminist texts were more likely to be read by feminists than by the male mainstream. Thus, it would not be surprising if McClung brought to her understanding of the desired shape of the new Kingdom a different set of assumptions, indeed a different analytical tradition and body of literature, from her male contemporaries. Her primary focus on women's experience would seem in itself to be distinctive. Even when an issue such as worker's rights and privileges in the public workforce was equally problematic for women and men, women faced the additional problem of sex-prejudice, thus necessitating McClung's call for 'equal pay for equal work.'[29]

A central issue for women reformers of this period was women's status within marriage, and McClung was no exception. Drawing heavily from both Gilman and Schreiner, McClung decried the economic dependence of women upon men and argued for a new relationship of interdependent equality:

The time will come, we hope, when women will be economically free, and mentally and spiritually independent enough to refuse to have their food paid for by men; when women will receive equal pay for equal work, and have all avenues of activity open to them; and will be free to choose their own mates, without shame, or indelicacy; when men will not be afraid of marriage because of the financial burden, but free men and free women will marry for love, and together work for the sustenance of their families. It is not too ideal a thought. It is coming about, and the new movement among women who are crying out for a larger humanity, is going to bring it about.[30]

McClung did not believe that every woman needed to be employed in the public sphere, although she advocated women's full access to every field of activity.[31] Like many of her Christian contemporaries, she valued women's traditional vocation in the home, but she also felt that it should be more genuinely respected – evidenced in laws ensuring married women's property rights, access to adequate health care, good schools for women's children, the abolition of prostitution, and other material concerns. She also recognized that women in the home traditionally worked very hard, as her opening salvo to the Fifth Ecumenical Conference, confirms:

'The Awakening of Women' is a rather misleading title. Women have always been awake. The woman of fifty years ago who carded the wool, spun it, wove the cloth to clothe her family, made the clothes without any help from Mr Butterick or the *Ladies Pictorial*, brewed her own cordials, baked her own bread, washed, ironed, scrubbed, without any labour-saving devices, and besides this always had the meals on time, and incidentally raised a family, and a few chickens and vegetables in her spare time, may be excused if she did not take much interest in politics, or even know who was likely to be the next Prime Minister. But her lack of interest was not any proof that she was asleep – she was only busy![32]

McClung reserved her scorn for indolent characters like Eva St John, the bridge-playing, heroin-addicted doctor's wife of *Painted Fires*,[33] and the 'gentle ladies' of *In Times Like These* who used 'feminine frailty' as an excuse for self-indulgence and laziness.

McClung also valued motherhood, although this has sometimes been misread as a claim that all women *must* be mothers. In the passage that is usually cited as proof of her 'maternalism,' McClung states, 'Deeply rooted in almost every woman's heart is the love of home and children ...' She continues, however, 'but independence is sweet, and when marriage means the loss of independence, there are women brave enough and strong enough to turn away from it.'[34] Neither did she sentimentalize motherhood, or feel that it should fulfil a woman's every aspiration. As she points out, 'Children do not need a mother's care always, and the mother who has given up every hope and ambition in the care of her children will find herself all alone – a woman without a job.'[35] Her short stories in particular focus upon single, independent women making their way in the world.[36]

This being said, McClung's concern for children's well-being was undeniable. One of the ways many reformers felt that both women and children's lives could be bettered was through family planning. Responsible parents would then be able to have only the number of children they could afford, and women's health could be spared.[37] While McClung does not openly use the words 'birth control' in her writings, her lengthy discussion of children and marriage in 'The Sore Thought' suggests her support for limiting family size.[38] She also speaks positively of 'Better Babies' campaigns in which women 'disseminat[ed] information' – 'Better Babies' being a well-known code phrase for birth control advocacy: 'Women in several states have instituted campaigns for "Better Babies," and by offering prizes and disseminating information, they have given a better chance to many a little traveler on life's highway. But all who have endeavoured in any way to secure legislation or government grants for the protection of children, have found that legislators are more willing to pass laws for the protection of cattle than the protection of children, for cattle have a real value and children have only a sentimental value.'[39] So-called private functions such as childbearing have for McClung important public, social implications. Bringing about the 'even chance for everyone' that was God's intention for Creation therefore involves remedying conditions in the domestic, 'natural' sphere as well. Women's experience will likewise improve conditions in the social order overall. Again echoing Gilman, McClung writes: 'No doubt, it is because all our statecraft has been one-sided that we find human welfare has lagged far behind material welfare. We have made wonderful strides in convenience and comfort, but have not yet solved the problems of poverty, crime or insanity. Perhaps they, too, will yield to treatment when they are better understood, and men and women are both on the job.'[40] Clearly for McClung, women's experience was an important and unique vantage point from which to assess, and then transform, the social order.

Being grounded in women's experience, and strongly influenced by her rural upbringing, McClung brought a different agenda to the question of labour activism from male Social Gospellers. McClung supported women's entry into whatever professions they chose, and she continually urged women to set a high value on their labour.[41] She also recognized that unchecked capitalism was a destructive force in society. In an unpublished article on the Winnipeg General Strike of 1919, for example, she observes:

What, then, is the remedy? Certainly not a return to the old system whereby a firm of textile manufacturers may make 72% on their capital (as announced in today's paper) and quite frankly rejoice over their handsome profits and disclaim all responsibility of the high price of clothing, which now prevents many a man and woman from clothing themselves in decency and comfort. There is no doubt that the high cost of living has driven the working man to desperation, and the Government can no longer ignore the conditions which have brought this to pass.[42]

Her remedy to these conditions was to increase the role of government in economic life, and she outlined the 'many things that the Government can do to relieve the situation.'[43] Alone, however, this would be insufficient: 'Legislation is not enough – it is not new laws that we need, it is a new spirit in our people ... No law or set of laws can bring peace to a world of grabbers.'[44] Much of the divisive and ideologically confrontational stance of Winnipeg's labour scene before 1920 seemed to McClung as specifically designed to benefit 'grabbers,' a reality that offended both her Christian commitment to cooperation and her deep respect for individual effort and hard work.[45] She envisioned a 'land of the Fair Deal, where every race, color, and creed will be given exactly the same chance; where no person can "exert influence" to bring about his personal ends; where no man or woman's past can ever rise up to defeat them; where every debt is paid; where no prejudice is allowed to masquerade as a reason; where honest toil will insure an honest living; where the man who works receives the reward of his labour.' McClung's vision was much more richly textured than the rigidly oppositional politics of capital and labour would allow.[46]

This eschewing of narrowly drawn labour politics, combined with an analytical base grounded primarily in women's experience rather than men's, would seem to place Nellie McClung outside of the Social Gospel movement, at least as it is currently construed by historians. It is significant, therefore, to note that she was apparently viewed quite differently by her contemporaries. It has already been noted that she was considered to be an authoritative spokesperson for J.S. Woodsworth's All People's Mission. Her personal papers provide further confirmation of her connection. One telling piece of evidence is a church bulletin announcing a Sunday evening lecture series on 'The Church and the New Social Reformation.'[47] The list of participants reads like a virtual 'Who's Who' of Winnipeg social activists, including J.S. Woodsworth on 'The Ethical and Religious Aspects of Social Reform,' Alderman R.A. Rigg of the Trades and Labor Council on 'The Problem of Unemployment,' and Salem Bland on 'The Church and Social Reform.' McClung's 'The New Chivalry,' given on 15 February 1914 and later published in *In Times Like These*, is a forthright challenge to end sexual discrimination and advance the vote to women. The importance of the topic for the series is emphasized by the fact that McClung's speech is the only one advertised in boldface. Such evidence suggests strongly that McClung was considered to be a figure of some stature in the area of 'The Church and the New Social Reformation.' It further suggests that the role of women in the new Kingdom was neither an afterthought nor a subordinate issue.

As urbanization and industrial capitalism changed the face of the nation, women's traditional labour in the home and on the farm likewise changed. Far more slowly transformed were people's attitudes towards women and their convictions about the roles appropriate to women and men. As a religious feminist, Nellie McClung felt called to challenge those who believed that women's lives ought to be circumscribed by male self-interest, and she did so on the basis that God intended that everyone be given a 'fair deal.' Grounding her thought in women's experience, and speaking from a woman's perspective, she addressed issues that were problematic in women's lives, such as women's status in marriage, in addition to concerns like conditions in the public workforce, which were problematic to both women and men. By putting women first, Nellie McClung challenged structures in both the private and public spheres. Arguably, her contemporaries were aware of the importance of that challenge. How historians of the Social Gospel in Canada will re-engage the issue remains to be seen.

NOTES

1 Known variously as Social Christianity, the gospel of the kingdom, and Christian Sociology, the Social Gospel movement took its name from the journal published by the short-lived Christian Commonwealth Colony of Georgia. In 1898 the journal opened by defining the Social Gospel as follows: 'The social gospel is the brotherhood of man and the fatherhood of God. It is the old gospel of peace on earth among men of good will. It is the proclamation of the kingdom of heaven, a divinely ordered society, to be realized on earth. It is the application of Christ's Golden Rule and Law of Love to all the business and affairs of life. It is the glad tidings of peace and purity and plenty.' Charles H. Lippy, 'Social Christianity,' *Encyclopedia of the American Religious Experience*, vol. 2, Charles H. Lippy and Peter W. Williams, eds. (New York: Scribners', 1988), 917.

2 Allen names these conservative, progressive, and radical: 'The conservatives were the closest to traditional evangelicalism, emphasizing personal-ethical issues, tending to identify sin with individual acts, and taking as their social strategy legislative reform of the environment. The radicals viewed society in more organic terms. Evil was so endemic and pervasive in the social order that they concluded that there could be no personal salvation without social salvation, [through] an immanent god working in the social process to bring his [*sic*] kingdom to birth. Between the conservatives and the radicals was a broad centre party of progressives, holding the tension between the two extremes, endorsing in considerable measure the platforms of the other two, but transmuting them somewhat in a broad ameliorative programme of reform.' Richard Allen, *The Social Passion: Religion and Social Reform in Canada, 1914–28* (Toronto: University of Toronto Press, 1973), 17.

3 Salem Bland, *The New Christianity: Or, the Religion of the New Age* (Toronto: University of Toronto Press, 1973), 53 (Reprint of 1920 ed.).

4 Ibid.

5 Classic American texts include Robert T. Handy, *A Christian America: Protes-*

tant Hopes and Historical Realities (1971) and as ed., *The Social Gospel in America, 1870–1920: Gladden, Ely, Rauschenbusch* (1966); C. Howard Hopkins, *The Rise of the Social Gospel in American Protestantism, 1865–1915* (1940); Ronald C. White, Jr, and C. Howard Hopkins, *The Social Gospel: Religion and Reform in Changing America* (1976). More recent works like Janet Forsythe Fishburn's *Fatherhood of God and the Victorian Family: The Social Gospel in America* (1981) move beyond analysis of economic and labour relations to consider more 'woman-centred' issues of family structure and personal relations. Ramsay Cook's *The Regenerators: Social Criticism in Late Victorian English Canada* (Toronto: University of Toronto Press, 1985) has recently joined Richard Allen's *The Social Passion* (cited above) as the main references for the Social Gospel movement in Canada.

6 Ronald P. Huff, 'Social Christian Clergymen and Feminism During the Progressive Era, 1890–1920' (PhD thesis, Union Theological Seminary, 1978), 193–4.

7 Richard Allen discusses prohibition and briefly considers the Woman's Christian Temperance Union in that connection, but he makes no mention of feminism or the battle for woman suffrage. Ramsay Cook spends several pages on Social Gospel novelist Agnes Maule Machar and does treat woman suffrage briefly, but his 'cast of characters' is overwhelmingly male. The famous reformer Nellie McClung is mentioned by name three times by Allen, and once by Cook, in relation to the Single Tax. Neither Allen nor Cook locates women's social reform agenda centrally with men's.

8 For example, Thomas Socknat remarks, 'At the core of McClung's feminism, a product of the Social Gospel, was the faith in women as redeeming agents in a militaristic civilization.' Socknat, *Witness against War: Pacifism in Canada, 1900–1945* (Toronto: University of Toronto Press, 1987), 34. Feminist historian Carol Bacchi works from the opposite assumption, that McClung's faith was an impediment to her feminism, rather than the cause of it. Bacchi, *Liberation Deferred? The Ideas of the English-Canadian Suffragists, 1877–1918* (Toronto: University of Toronto Press, 1983), 58–68. Lloyd Clifton's unpublished MA thesis (University of Toronto, 1979), 'Nellie McClung: A Representative of the Canadian Social Gospel Movement,' assumes throughout that McClung is at the centre of the Social Gospel movement. Though well documented, the work is analytically thin, making no attempt to explore the implications of locating McClung's feminist agenda within the Social Gospel movement as a whole.

9 (Mooney's wife, Jane Shouldice, had died some time prior after just over a year of marriage.) See Nellie L. McClung, *Clearing in the West* (Toronto: Thomas Allen, 1935), 12–15; in this, the first volume of her autobiography, McClung also describes her early years on the prairie.

10 Nellie L. McClung, *Purple Springs* (Toronto: University of Toronto, 1992), 71–2. Reprint of 1921 ed.

11 McClung concludes Pearl's reflections with a flash of insight that resolves to a prophetic vision for social action: 'Something in Pearl's heart cried out at the injustice of this. It was not fair! All at once she wanted to talk about it to – some one, to everybody. It was a mistaken way of looking at life, she thought; the world, as God made it, was a great, beautiful place, with enough of everything to go around. There is enough land – enough coal – enough oil. Enough pleasure and beauty, enough music and fun and good times! What had happened was that some had taken more than their share, and that was why others had to go short, and the strange part of it all was that the hoggish ones were the exalted ones, to whom many bowed, and they – some of them – were scornful of the people who were still working – though if every one stopped working, the world would soon be starving' (ibid., 73–4.) McClung also addresses the problem of the 'hoggish ones' in *In Times Like These* (Toronto: University of Toronto Press, 1972), 10–11.

12 'No Classes on a Lifeboat,' McClung papers, Add MSS 10, vol. 52, Provincial Archives of British Columbia. McClung goes on to cite domestic labour as one example of disparaged work.

13 This issue is played out fictionally in the second volume of the Pearlie Watson trilogy, *The Second Chance* (Toronto: Ryerson Press, 1910). Martha Perkins, a hard-working, self-abnegating farmer's daughter, wishes to use the money she has earned selling eggs from her own chickens to buy a magazine subscription from Mrs Cavers, the drunkard's wife, to help Mrs Cavers earn enough money to take her daughter to visit her own mother in Ontario. Martha's father objects, so the subscription is never bought. McClung devotes much of the remainder of the novel to having Pearlie build up Martha's sense of self-confidence so that she might be able to assert her rightful claims in future. In order to help others, it seems, women must first help themselves.

14 *In Times Like These*, 100.

15 Ibid., 11.

16 Ibid., 10.

17 Ibid., 9.

18 Nellie L. McClung, 'Bells At Evening,' in *All We Like Sheep* (Toronto: Thomas Allen, 1926), 259.

19 Nellie L. McClung, cited in James Woodsworth, *Thirty Years in the Canadian Northwest* (Toronto: McClelland and Stewart, 1917), 259.

20 *In Times Like These*, 48. Elsewhere in the text McClung revises the story of the Good Samaritan to make her point: 'The road from Jerusalem to Jericho is here, and now. Women have played the good Samaritan for a long time, and they have

found many a one beaten and robbed on the road of life. They are still doing it, but the conviction is growing on them that it would be much better to go out and clean up the road!' Ibid., 79.

21 Ibid., 78.

22 See, for example, J.S. Woodsworth, *My Neighbor: A Study of City Conditions / A Plea for Social Service* (Toronto: University of Toronto Press, 1972) (Reprint of 1911 ed.).

23 Nellie L. McClung, *The Stream Runs Fast* (Toronto: Thomas Allen, 1945), 102–6.

24 Dolores Hayden, *The Grand Domestic Revolution: A History of Feminist Designs for American Homes, Neighborhoods, and Cities* (Cambridge: MIT Press, 1981), 4.

25 Ibid., 5.

26 See Hayden, chap. 9, 'Domestic Evolution or Domestic Revolution?'; also, Polly Wynn Allen, *Building Domestic Liberty: Charlotte Perkins Gilman's Architectural Feminism* (Amherst: University of Massachusetts Press, 1988).

27 For example, see the following (first page reference is to Charlotte Perkins Gilman, *The Man-Made World: or Our Androcentric Culture* [New York: Source Book Press, 1970; (reprint of 1911 ed.]; the second to McClung, *In Times Like These*): on the effect of proprietary ownership of women in marriage, 42, 75; on men and history, 90ff, 15ff; on Christianity's opposition to brute force, 138, 68; on growth as the major process in life, 139, 8ff; on women and work, 148, 82; on male statecraft vs. human statecraft, 189, 89; on 'crimes with no name,' i.e., economic crimes against humanity, 204, 90; on 'new histories,' 213, 16; on 'the God of Battles' vs. 'the God of Workshops,' 213, 15. Other themes that are pursued throughout both texts include the debilitating effects of women's economic dependence upon men and a concern for the underlying causes of poverty and crime.

28 Olive Schreiner, *Woman and Labour* (London: Virago, 1978) (Reprint of 1911 ed.), 31–150. McClung discusses the 'Gentle Lady' in chap. 7 of *In Times Like These*, 59–66.

29 *In Times Like These*, 85. The chapter by Mary Anne MacFarlane in this volume illustrates how pressing this issue was for church workers as well.

30 Ibid., 85–6.

31 McClung recognized that employment in the public sphere was not a guarantee of immediate emancipation and contained its own drawbacks and constraints. In *Sowing Seeds in Danny*, for example, she has one of her more attractive characters remark in her diary: 'It is nearly six months since I came to live with Mrs Francis, and I like housework so well and am so happy at it, that it shows I am not a disguised heiress. My proud spirit does not chafe a bit ... I have n't [*sic*] got

the fear on my heart all day that I will make a mistake in a figure that will rise up and condemn me at the end of the month as I used to be when I was book-keeping on a high stool, for the Western Hail and Fire Insurance Company (peace to its ashes!) ... Farewell, oh Soulless Corporation! A long, last, lingering farewell, for Camilla E. Rose, who used to sit upon the high stool and add figures for you at ten dollars a week, is far away making toast for two kindly souls, one of whom tells her she has brains and virtue and the other one who opens his mouth to speak, and then pushes fifty cents at her instead.' Nellie L. McClung, *Sowing Seeds in Danny* (Toronto: Thomas Allen, 1965), 140–1 (Reprint of 1908 ed.).

32 Nellie McClung, 'The Awakening of Women,' Address to the Fifth Ecumenical Conference, *Proceedings, Fifth Ecumenical Conference, London, England, September 6–16, 1921* (Toronto, Methodist Book and Publishing House, n.d.), 257.

33 Nellie L. McClung, *Painted Fires* (Toronto: Thomas Allen, 1925).

34 *In Times Like These*, 86.

35 Ibid., 75.

36 See esp. Nellie L. McClung, *Be Good to Yourself* (Toronto: Thomas Allen, 1930) and *Flowers for the Living* (Toronto: Thomas Allen, 1931). As the titles suggest, McClung advocates women's self-care throughout.

37 See McClung's scathing criticism of 'Brother Bones' in *In Times Like These*, 117–18.

38 *In Times Like These*, 85–8. Social historians Angus and Arlene McLaren make the contrary claim that 'birth control was ... considered ideologically dangerous by that generation of Canadian feminists, including Nellie McClung and Emily Murphy, who regarded motherhood as woman's highest calling,' giving McClung's articles in *Maclean's*, in May of 1916 (pp. 25–6) and June 1926 (p. 28) as references. Angus McLaren and Arlene Tiger McLaren, *The Bedroom and the State: The Changing Practices and Politics of Contraception and Abortion in Canada, 1880–1980* (Toronto: McClelland and Stewart, 1986), 68. Entitled 'Speaking of Women,' the 1916 article was written by McClung on request, as a response to Stephen Leacock's antifeminist 'The Woman Question,' published by *Maclean's* the previous year. Throughout, McClung provides a defence against Leacock's charges of women's inherent incompetence, responding particularly to his desire to have women return solely to their roles as mothers. In contrast to the McLarens' analysis, McClung explicitly rejects the position of exclusive maternalism. 'But when all other arguments fail, the antisuffragist can always go back to the "saintly motherhood one," and "the hand that rocks." There is the perennial bloom that flourishes in all climates. Women are the mothers of the race – therefore they can be nothing else ... Children have been blamed for many things very unjustly, and one of the most outstanding of these is that they take up all their mother's time ... and that no one can do anything for

the child but the mother.' Nellie McClung, 'Speaking of Women,' *Maclean's*,
May, 1916, 26. She further points out 'Children do grow up. And when they
have gone from their mother, she still has her life to live.' Ibid. As to the second
reference, neither p. 28 of either the 1 June or 15 June 1926 issue of *Maclean's*
appears to contain material written by Nellie McClung.
39 Ibid., 88.
40 Ibid., 89.
41 'It shows where women have made their mistake. They have been too patient
and unassertive – they have not set a high enough value on themselves, and it is
pathetically true that the world values you at the value you place on yourself.'
Ibid., 92.
42 'The Winnipeg General Strike,' McClung Papers, Add MSS 10, vol. 12, 196.
43 'There is the taxation of profits, the fixing of all prices, supervision of crops, so
that there may not be overproduction of some things and underproduction of
others. Better and cheaper housing, State care of the sick, so that a family who
are so unfortunate as to have sickness will not be further penalized by having to
pay for it, old age pensions to relieve the minds of our people from the fear of
want.' Ibid., 196–7.
44 Ibid., 197.
45 McClung addresses this issue in chap. 2 of *Painted Fires* through the character
of Anna Milander, a young Finnish immigrant girl who has become seduced by
the promised of constant leisure and wealth once the 'capit-alists' [*sic*] are over-
thrown. Anna eventually is arrested for throwing a stone at a policeman, and
McClung's description leaves no doubt as to her view of Anna's actions: 'It was
all rather vague in Anna's mind. She was rather favorably disposed to policemen
as a class, but having joined the Union she was determined to become "class
conscious." Policemen were enemies; so were employers; every one was an
enemy except members of the Union. So Anna, having a clear program in her
mind, sat on her narrow bed in a warm cell, well content. Her picture would be·
in the paper; she would be praised by the speakers. She had risen from the dull,
gray, dusty depths of obscurity, which the speaker called the base of the economic pyramid, and in the interests of her comrades in the submerged strata had
heaved an honest rock ... So Anna sat on her narrow bed, a prisoner before the
law, but not cast-down or desolate. She, too, had her own little painted fire, and
she had not yet found out that there was no heat in it' (21–2).
46 *In Times Like These*, 97.
47 McClung Papers, Add MSS 10, n.v.

Bibliography

COMPILED BY MARILYN FÄRDIG WHITELEY

BOOKS

Allard, Michel, ed. *L'Hôtel-Dieu du Montréal: 1642–1973*. Montreal: Hurtubise HMH, 1973.

Bélanger, Diane, and Lucie Rozon. *Les religieuses au Québec*. Montreal: Éditions Libre Expression, 1982.

Boucher, Ghislaine. *Dieu et Satan dans la vie de Catherine de Saint-Augustin 1632–1668*. Montreal: Bellarmin, 1979.

– *Du Centre à La Croix: Marie de l'Incarnation, 1599–1672: Symbolique Spirituelle*. Sillery: Les Religieuses de Jésus-Marie, 1976.

Brouwer, Ruth Compton. *New Women for God: Canadian Presbyterian Women and India Missions, 1876–1914*. Toronto: University of Toronto Press, 1990.

Caron, Anita, ed. *Femmes et pouvoir dans l'Eglise*. Montreal: VLB éditeur, 1991.

Casgrain, Henri-Raymond. *Histoire de la Mère Marie de l'Incarnation, première Superieure des Ursulines*. Montreal [n.p.], 1964.

Chabot, Emmanuelle. *Elles ont tout donné: Les Ursulines de Stanstead de 1884 à 1934*. Quebec: Anne Sigier, 1983.

Charbonneau, Fernande. *Marguerite Bourgeoys: Traits Spirituels et Mystiques*. Montreal: Éditions Paulines, 1983.

Charles, Aline. *Travail d'Ombre et de Lumière: Le bénévolat féminin à l'Hôpital Sainte-Justine 1907–1960*. Quebec: Institut québecois de recherche, 1990.

Chicoine, Emilia. *La Métaire de Marguerite Bourgeoys à la Pointe-Saint-Charles*. Montreal: Fides, 1986.

Chown, Alice A. *The Stairway*. Introduction by Diana Chown. Toronto: University of Toronto Press, 1988.

Cimichella, André-M. *Marguerite Bourgeoys, lumière sur notre ville*. Montreal: Éditions Jésus-Marie et notre temps, 1974.

d'Allaire, Micheline. *Les dots des religieuses au Canada français, 1639–1800: Étude économique et sociale.* Montreal: Hurtubise HMH, 1986.
- *L'Hôpital Général de Québec, 1692–1764.* Montreal: Fides, 1971.
- *Vingt ans de crise chez les religieuses du Québec, 1960–1980.* Montreal: Éditions Bergeron, 1984.
Danylewycz, Marta. *Profession: religieuse; Un choix pour les Québecoises, 1840–1920,* trans. Gérard Boulard. Montreal: Les Éditions du Boréal, 1988.
- *Taking the Veil: An Alternative to Marriage, Motherhood, and Spinsterhood in Quebec, 1840–1902.* Toronto: McClelland and Stewart, 1987.
Daveluy, Marie-Claire. *La Société de Notre-Dame de Montréal 1639–1663: Son Histoire, Ses Membres, Son Manifeste.* Montreal and Paris: Fides, 1965.
Davison, James Doyle. *Alice of Grand Pré: Alice T. Shaw and Her Grand Pre seminary; Female Education in Nova Scotia and New Brunswick.* Wolfville, NS: James Doyle Davison, 1981.
Davy, Shirley, coordinator. *Women, Work, and Worship in the United Church of Canada.* Toronto: United Church of Canada, 1983.
Deroy-Pineau, Françoise. *Marie de l'Incarnation: Marie Guyart, femme d'affaires, mystique, mère de la Novelle France, 1599–1672.* Paris: Éditions Robert Laffont, 1989.
Dickson, Irene, and Margaret Webster. *To Keep the Memory Green: A History of Ewart College, 1897–1987.* Toronto: Ewart College, 1986.
Donnelly, Mary Rose, and Heather Dau. *Katharine.* Toronto: Wood Lake Press, 1992.
Dumont, Micheline. *Girls' Schooling in Quebec, 1639–1960,* trans. Carol Élise Cochrane. Ottawa: Canadian Historical Association, 1990.
- and Nadia Fahmy-Eid. *Les Couventines: L'éducation des filles au Québec dans les congrégations religieuses enseignantes, 1840–1960.* Montreal: Boréal Express, 1986.
Femmes et pouvoir dans l'Église. Collectif sous la direction d'Anita Caron. Montreal: VLB éditeur, 1991.
Gagan, Rosemary R. *A Sensitive Independence: Canadian Methodist Women Missionaries in Canada and the Orient, 1881–1925.* Kingston and Montreal: McGill-Queen's University Press, 1992.
Gough, Lyn. *As Wise as Serpents: Five Women and an Organization that Changed British Columbia, 1883–1939.* Victoria: Swan Lake Publishing, 1988.
Hall, Alfreda. *A Baptist Minister: A Woman; The Story of the Reverend Mae Benedict Field, Canadian Baptist Missionary and Minister.* Toronto: published privately by Alfreda Hall, Yorkminster Park Baptist Church, 1983.
Hancock, Carol L. *No Small Legacy: Canada's Nellie McClung.* Toronto: Wood Lake Books, 1986.

Huot, Giselle. *Une femme au séminaire: Marie de la Charité, 1852–1920, fondatrice de la première communauté dominicaine du Canada, 1887*. Montreal: Bellarmin, 1987.

Jean, Marguerite. *Évolution des communautés religieuses de femmes au Canada de 1639 à nos jours*. Montreal: Fides, 1977.

Lacelle, Élisabeth J., ed. *La femme et la religion au Canada français*. Montreal: Bellarmin, 1977.

Lambert, Thérèse. *Marguerite Bourgeoys, éducatrice, 1620–1700: Mère d'un pays et d'une église*. Montreal: Bellarmin, 1978.

Lapointe-Roy, Huguette. *Charité Bien Ordonnée: Le premier réseau de lutte contre la pauvreté à Montréal au 19e siècle*. Montreal: Boréal Express, 1987.

Laurin, Nicole, Danielle Juteau, and Lorraine Duchesne. *A la recherche d'un monde oublie: Les communautés religieuses des femmes au Québec de 1900 à 1970*. Montreal: Édition de Jour, 1991.

McClung, Nellie L. *Purple Springs*. Introduction by Randi R. Warne. Toronto: University of Toronto Press, 1992.

MacEwan, Grant. *And Mighty Women Too*. Saskatoon: Western Producer Prairie Books, 1975.

Malouin, Marie-Paule. *Que sont devenues les soeurs de nos écoles? Recherche sur les orientations actuelles des religieuses enseignantes du Québec*. Quebec: AREQ, 1989.

– *Ma soeur, à quelle école allez-vous? Deux écoles de filles à la fin du XIXe siècle*. Montreal: Fides, 1985.

Merrick, E.C. *These Impossible Women: The Story of the United Baptist Woman's Missionary Union of the Maritime Provinces*. Fredericton: Brunswick Press, 1970.

Mitchell, Estelle, and Antoine Hacault. *Les Soeurs Grises de Montréal à la Rivière-Rouge, 1844–1984*. Montreal: Éditions du Méridien, 1987.

Morton, W.L., with Vera Fast, ed. *God's Galloping Girl: The Peace River Diaries of Monica Storrs, 1929–1931*. Vancouver: University of British Columbia Press, 1979.

Muir, Elizabeth Gillan. *Petticoats in the Pulpit: The Story of Early Nineteenth-Century Methodist Women Preachers in Upper Canada*. Toronto: United Church Publishing House, 1991.

Oury, Guy Marie. *Marie de l'Incarnation, 1599–1672*, 2 vol. Quebec: Presses de l'Université Laval, 1973.

Pelletier-Baillargeon, Hélène. *Marie Gérin-Lajoie: De mère en fille, la cause des femmes*. Montreal: Boréal Express, 1985.

Perron, Normand. *Un siècle de vie hospitalière au Québec: Les Augustines et l'Hôtel-Dieu de Chicoutimi, 1884–1984*. Sillery: Presses de l'Université de Québec; Chicoutoumi: Augustines de la Misericorde de Jésus, 1984.

Pichette, Robert. *Les Religieuses, pionniers en Acadie*. Montmagny, PQ: Marquis, 1990.

Robertson, Allen, and E.B. Carolene, eds. *Memoir of Mrs Eliza Ann Chipman: Wife of the Rev. William Chipman, of Pleasant Valley, Cornwallis*. Hantsport, NS: Lancelot Press, 1989.

Robillard, Denise. *Emilie Tevernier-Gamelin*. Montreal: Éditions du Méridien, 1988.

Roth, Lorraine. *Willing Service: Stories of Ontario Mennonite Women*. Waterloo: Mennonite Historical Society of Ontario, 1992.

Rousseau, François. *La croix et le scalpel: Histoire des Augustines et de l'Hôtel-Dieu de Québec*. Vol. 1, *1639–1892*. Quebec: Septentrion, 1989.

Savard-Bonin, Jeanne. *Une Stigmatisée: Marie-Rose Ferron, 1902–1936*. Montreal: Éditions Paulines, 1987.

Sinclair, Donna. *Crossing Worlds: The Story of the Woman's Missionary Society of the United Church of Canada*. Toronto: United Church Publishing House, 1992.

Sisters of Mercy. *Sisters of Mercy of Newfoundland 150th Anniversary, 1842–1992*. St John's: Sisters of Mercy of Newfoundland, 1992.

Sylvestre, Paul-Françios. *Les communautés religieuses en Ontario français: Sur les traces de Joseph Le Caron*. Montreal: Éditions Bellarmin, 1984.

Tremblay, Fleurette. *Voici que je viens ...: biographie de soeur Rose-Yvonne Tremblay, a.s.a., 1916–1985*. Montreal: Éditions Paulines, 1989.

Valverde, Mariana. *The Age of Light, Soap, and Water: Moral Reform in English Canada, 1885–1925*. Toronto: McClelland and Stewart, 1991.

Warne, Randi R. *Literature as Pulpit: The Christian Social Activism of Nellie L. McClung*. Waterloo: Wilfrid Laurier University Press, 1993.

CHAPTERS IN COLLECTIONS

Ainsley, Claire. 'Les communautés religieuses féminines du diocèse de Montréal de 1650 à 1986.' In *L'Église de Montréal, aperçus d'hier et d'aujourd'hui, 1836–1986*. Montreal: Fides, 1986, 198–235.

Allen, Christine. 'Women in Colonial French America.' In *Women and Religion in America. vol. 2, The Colonial and Revolutionary Period: A Documentary History*, edited by Rosemary Radford Ruether and Rosemary Skinner Keller. San Francisco: Harper and Row, 1983, 79–131.

Barber, Marilyn. 'The Fellowship of the Maple Leaf Teachers.' In *The Anglican Church and the World of Western Canada, 1820–1970*, edited by Barry Ferguson. Regina: Canadian Plains Research Center, 1991, 154–66.

Barnett-Cowan, Alyson. 'The Bishop's Messengers: Women in Ministry in North-western Manitoba, 1928–79.' In *The Anglican Church and the World of Western*

Canada, 1820–1970, edited by Barry Ferguson. Regina: Canadian Plains Research Center, 1991, 176–87.

Bennett, Ethel M.G. 'Madame de La Tour.' In *The Clear Spirit*, edited by Mary Quayle Innis. Toronto: University of Toronto Press, 1966, 3–24.

Bentall, Shirley. 'Lucy Lowe Bagnall – Missionary Pioneer and Distinguished Educator.' In *Costly Vision: The Baptist Pilgrimage in Canada*, edited by Jarold Knox Zeman. Burlington, Ont.: Welch, 1988, 59–67.

Bouchard, Mary Alban, CSJ. 'Pioneers Forever: The Community of St Joseph in Toronto and Their Ventures in Social Welfare and Health Care.' In *Catholics at the 'Gathering Place': Historical Essays in the Archdiocese of Toronto, 1841–1991*, edited by Mark McGowan and Brian Clarke. Hamilton: Dundurn Press, 1993, 105–18.

Brandt, Gail Cuthbert. 'Organizations in Canada: The English Protestant Tradition.' In *Women's Paid and Unpaid Work: Historical and Contemporary Perspectives*, edited by Paula Bourne. Toronto: New Hogtown Press, 1985, 79–90.

Brouwer, Ruth Compton. '"Far Indeed from the Meekest of Women": Marion Fairweather and the Canadian Presbyterian Mission in Central India, 1873–1880.' In *Canadian Protestant and Catholic Missions, 1920s–1960s*, edited by John S. Moir and C.T. McIntire. New York: Peter Lang, 1988, 121–49.

– 'Opening Doors through Social Service: Aspects of Women's Work in the Canadian Presbyterian Mission in Central India, 1877–1914.' In *Women's Work for Women: Missionaries and Social Change in Asia*, edited by Leslie A. Flemming. Boulder, Col.: Westview Press, 1989, 11–34; reprinted in *Prophets, Priests, and Prodigals: Readings in Canadian Religious History, 1608 to Present*, edited by Mark G. McGowan and David B. Marshall. Toronto: McGraw-Hill Ryerson, 1992, 241–61.

Brown, Jennifer S.H. 'A Cree Nurse in the Cradle of Methodism: Little Mary and the Egerton R. Young Family at Norway House and Berens River.' In *First Days, Fighting Days: Women in Manitoba History*, edited by Mary Kinnear. Regina: Canadian Plains Research Center, 1987, 19–40.

Chabot, Marie-Emmanuel. 'Marie Guyart de l'Incarnation.' In *The Clear Spirit*, edited by Mary Quayle Innis. Toronto: University of Toronto Press, 1966, 25–41.

Chalmers, J.W. 'Marguerite Bourgeoys, Preceptress of New France.' In *Profiles of Canadian Educators*, edited by Robert S. Patterson, John W. Chalmers, and John W. Friesen. Toronto: D.C. Heath, 1974, 4–20.

Clarke, Brian. 'The Parish and the Hearth: Women's Confraternities and the Devotional Revolution among the Irish Catholics of Toronto, 1850–85.' In *Creed and Culture: The Place of English-Speaking Catholics in Canadian Society*, edited by Terrence Murphy and Gerald Stortz. Montreal and Kingston: McGill-Queen's University Press, 1993, 185–203.

Colwell, Judith. 'The Fitch Twins: Poets and Social Workers.' In *Costly Vision: The Baptist Pilgrimage in Canada*, edited by Jarold Knox Zeman. Burlington: Welch, 1988, 43–58.

Cook, Ramsay. 'Francis Marion Beynon and the Crisis of Christian Reformism.' In *The West and the Nation*, edited by Carl Berger and Ramsay Cook. Toronto: McClelland and Stewart, 1976, 187–208.

Cooper, Barbara J. 'A Re-examination of the Early Years of the Institute of the Blessed Virgin Mary (Loretto Sisters) in Toronto.' In *Catholics at the 'Gathering Place': Historical Essays in the Archdiocese of Toronto, 1841–1991*, edited by Mark McGowan and Brian Clark. Hamilton: Dundurn Press, 1993, 89–104.

d'Allaire, Micheline. 'Conditions matérielles requises pour devenir religieuse au XVIIIe siècle.' In *L'Hôtel-Dieu du Montréal, 1642–1973*, edited by Michel Allard. Montreal: Hurtubise HMH, 1973, 183–208.

Danylewycz, Marta. 'In Their Own Right: Convents, An Organized Espression of Women's Aspirations.' In *Rethinking Canada: The Promise of Women's History*, edited by Veronica Strong-Boag and Anita Clair Fellman. Toronto: Copp Clark Pitman, 2nd ed., 1991, 161–81.

– 'Une novelle complicité: Féministes et religieuses à Montréal, 1890–1925.' In *Travailleuses et féministes: Les femmes dans la société québécoise*, edited by Marie Lavigne and Yolande Pinard. Montreal: Boréal Express, 1983, 245–69.

Davies, Gwendolyn. '"In the Garden of Christ": Methodist Literary Women in Nineteenth-Century Maritime Canada.' In *The Contribution of Methodism to Atlantic Canada*, edited by Charles H.H. Scobie and John Webster Grant. Montreal and Kingston: McGill-Queen's University Press, 1992, 205–17.

Davison, James D. 'Alice Shaw and Her Grand Pré Seminary: A Story of Female Education.' In *Repent and Believe: The Baptist Experience in Maritime Canada*, edited by Barry M. Moody. Hantsport, NS: Lancelot Press, 1980, 124–37.

Dekar, Paul R. 'Canadian Baptist Women Missionaries as Peacemakers.' In *Costly Vision: The Baptist Pilgrimage in Canada*, edited by Jarold Knox Zeman. Burlington: Welch, 1988, 85–99.

Denault, Bernard. 'Sociographie générale des communautés religieuses au Québec (1837–1990).' In *Élements pour une sociologie des communautés religieuses au Québec*, edited by Bernard Denault and Benoit Lévesque. Montreal and Sherbrooke: Les Presses de l'Université de Montréal et Les Presses de l'Université de Sherbrooke, 1975, 15–117.

Dumont, Micheline. 'Des garderies au 19e siècle: Les salles d'asile des soeur Grises de Montréal.' In *Maîtresses de maison, maîtresses d'école: Femmes, famille, et éducation dans l'histoire du Québec*, edited by Nadia Fahmy-Eid and Micheline Dumont. Montreal: Boréal Express, 1983, 261–85.

– 'Vocation religieuse et condition féminine.' In *Travailleuses et féministes: Les femmes dans la société québécoise*, edited by Marie Lavigne and Yolande Pinard. Montreal: Boréal Express, 1983, 272–92.

Epp, Frank H., and Marlene G. Epp. 'The Diverse Roles of Ontario Mennonite Women.' In *Looking into My Sister's Eyes: An Exploration in Women's History*, edited by Jean Burnet. Toronto: Multicultural Society of Ontario, 1986, 223–42.

Fahmy-Eid, Nadia. 'L'éducation des filles chez les Ursulines de Québec sous le régime français.' In *Maîtresses de maison, maîtresses d'école: femmes, famille, et éducation dans l'histoire du Québec*, edited by Nadia Fahmy-Eid and Micheline Dumont. Montreal: Boréal Express, 1983, 49–76.

Fast, Vera K. 'Eva Hasell and the Caravan Mission.' In *The Anglican Church and the World of Western Canada, 1820–1970*, edited by Barry Ferguson. Regina: Canadian Plains Research Center, 1991, 167–76.

Haglund, Diane. 'Side Road on the Journey to Autonomy: The Diaconate Prior to Church Union.' In *Women, Work, and Worship in the United Church of Canada*, edited by Shirley Davy. Toronto: United Church of Canada, 1983, 206–27.

Hall, Nancy. 'The Professionalisation of Women Workers in the Methodist, Presbyterian, and United Churches of Canada.' In *First Days, Fighting Days: Women in Manitoba History*, edited by Mary Kinnear. Regina: Canadian Plains Research Center, 1987, 120–33.

Hancock, Carol L. 'Nellie McClung: A Part of a Pattern.' In *Prairie Spirit: Perspectives on the Heritage of the United Church of Canada in the West*, edited by Dennis L. Butcher, Catherine Macdonald, Margaret E. McPherson, Raymond R. Smith, and A. McKibbon Watts. University of Manitoba Press, 1985, 203–15.

Jean, Michèle. 'Féminisme et religion au Québec, 1900–1978.' In *La femme et la religion au Canada français*, edited by Élisabeth J. Lacelle. Montreal: Bellarmin, 1979, 33–42.

Johnston, Geoffrey. 'The Road to Winsome Womanhood: Presbyterian Mission among East Indian Woman and Girls in Trinidad, 1868–1939.' In *Canadian Protestant and Catholic Missions, 1820s–1960s*, edited by John S. Moir and C.T. McIntire. New York: Peter Lang, 1988, 103–19.

Kemper, Alison. 'Deaconess as Urban Missionary and Ideal Woman: Church of England Initiatives in Toronto, 1890–1895.' In *Canadian Protestant and Catholic Missions, 1820s–1960s*, edited by John S. Moir and C.T. McIntire. New York: Peter Lang, 1988, 171–90.

Lapointe-Roy, Huguette. 'Les religieuses hospitalières de saint-Joseph: 329 ans de présence à Montréal.' In *L'Histoire des Croyants: Mémoire vivante des hommes*. Vol. 2, *Mélanges Charles Moletter*, edited by Brigitte Waché et al. Abbeville: Imprimerie F. Paillart, 1959, 650–9.

Leacock, Eleanor. 'Montagnais Women and the Jesuit Program for Colonization.' In *Rethinking Canada: The Promise of Women's History*, edited by Veronica

Strong-Boag and Anita Clair Fellman. Toronto: Copp Clark Pitman, 1986, 7–22.

Marks, Lynne. 'The "Hallelujah Lasses": Working-Class Women in the Salvation Army in English Canada, 1882–1892.' In *Gender Conflicts: New Essays in Women's History*, edited by Franca Iacovetta and Mariana Valverde. Toronto: University of Toronto Press, 1992, 67–117. Revised and abridged in *Rethinking Canada: The Promise of Women's History*, edited by Veronica Strong-Boag and Anita Clair Fellman. Toronto: Copp Clark Pitman, 2nd. ed., 1991, 182–205.

McPherson, Margaret E. 'Head, Heart, and Purse: The Presbyterian Women's Missionary Society in Canada, 1876–1925.' In *Prairie Spirit: Perspectives on the Heritage of the United Church of Canada in the West*, edited by Dennis L. Butcher, Catherine Macdonald, Margaret E. McPherson, Raymond R. Smith, and A. McKibbin Watts, University of Manitoba Press, 1985, 147–70.

Mitchinson, Wendy. 'Early Women's Organization and Social Reform: Prelude to Welfare State.' In *The Benevolent State: The Growth of Welfare in Canada*, edited by Allan Moscovitch and Jim Albert. Toronto: Garamond Press, 1987, 77–92.

– 'The WCTU: "For God, Home, and Native Land": A Study in Nineteenth-Century Feminism.' In *A Not Unreasonable Claim: Women and Reform in Canada, 1880s–1920s*, edited by Linda Kealey. Toronto: Women's Educational Press, 1979, 151–67.

Muir, Elizabeth. 'The Bark School House: Methodist Episcopal Missionary Women in Upper Canada, 1827–1833.' In *Canadian Protestant and Catholic Missions, 1820s–1960s*, edited by John S. Moir and C.T. McIntire. New York: Peter Lang, 1988, 23–47.

Owen, Michael. '"Keeping Canada God's Country": Presbyterian school-homes for Ruthenian children.' In *Prairie Spirit: Perspectives on the Heritage of the United Church of Canada in the West*, edited by Dennis L. Butcher, Catherine Macdonald, Margaret E. McPherson, Raymond R. Smith, and A. McKibbin Watts. University of Manitoba Press, 1985, 184–201.

Parsons, Shelagh. 'Women and Power in the United Church of Canada.' In *Women, Work, and Worship in the United Church of Canada*, edited by Shirley Davy. Toronto: United Church of Canada, 1983, 170–88.

Pedersen, Diana. '"The Call to Service": The YWCA and the Canadian College Woman, 1886–1921.' In *Youth, University, and Canadian Society: Essays in the Social History of Higher Education*, edited by Paul Axelrod and John Reid. Montreal and Kingston: McGill-Queen's University Press, 1989, 187–215.

Plante, Lucienne. 'Marguerite Bourgeoys, fille de France, missionaire in Nouvelle-France.' In *L'Histoire des Croyants: Mémoire vivante des hommes*. Vol. 2, *Mélanges Charles Moletter*, edited by Brigitte Waché *et al*. Abbeville: Imprimerie F. Paillart, 1959, 643–50.

Ross, H. Miriam. '"Sisters" in the Homeland: Vision for Mission among Maritime

Baptist Women, 1867–1920.' In *A Fragile Stability: Definition and Redefinition of Maritime Baptist Identity*, edited by David T. Priestley. Hantsport, NS: Lancelot Press, 1995.
– 'Shaping a Vision of Mission: Early Influences on the United Baptist Woman's Missionary Union.' In *An Abiding Conviction: Maritime Baptists and Their World*, edited by Robert S. Wilson. Hantsport, NS: Lancelot Press, 1988, 83–107.
Selles-Roney, Johanna. '"Manners or Morals"? OR "Men in Petticoats"? Education at Alma College, 1871–1898.' In *Gender and Education in Ontario*, edited by Ruby Heap and Alison Prentice. Toronto: Canadian Scholars' Press, 1991, 249–72.
Smyth, Elizabeth. 'Educating Girls and Young Women in a Nineteenth Century Convent School.' In *Dimensions of Childhood: Esssays on the History of Children and Youth in Canada*, edited by G. Dodds, A. Esau, and R. Smandych. Winnipeg: Legal Research Institute, University of Manitoba, 1991, 85–105.
– '"A Noble Proof of Excellence": The Culture and Curriculum of a Nineteenth Century Ontario Convent Academy.' In *Gender and Education in Ontario*, edited by Ruby Heap and Alison Prentice. Toronto: Canadian Scholars' Press, 1991, 273–94.
Van Dieren, Karen. 'The Response of the WMS to the Immigration of Asian Women, 1888–1942.' In *Not Just Pin Money: Selected Essays on the History of Women's Work in British Columbia*, edited by Barbara K. Latham and Roberta J. Pazdro. Victoria: Camosun College, 1984, 79–97.
Veer, Joanne. 'The Attack of the Maternal Feminists of the Maritime Woman's Christian Temperance Union on the Victorian Double Sexual Standard, 1875–1900.' In *The More We Get Together: Woman and Dis/Ability*, edited by Houston Stewart, Beth Percival, and Elizabeth R. Epperly. Charlottetown: Gynergy Books, 1992, 113–24.
Warne, Randi R. 'Nellie McClung and Peace.' In *Up and Doing: Canadian Women and Peace*, edited by Deborah Gorham and Janice Williamson. Toronto: Women's Press, 1989, 35–47.
– 'Christian Feminism in the United Church of Canada: Resources in Culture and Tradition.' In *Women, Work, and Worship in the United Church of Canada*, edited by Shirley Davy. Toronto: United Church of Canada, 1983, 189–205.
Whelen, Gloria. 'Maria Grant, 1854–1937: The Life and Times of an Early Twentieth Century Christian.' In *In Her Own Right: Selected Essays on Women's History in B.C.*, edited by Barbara Latham and Cathy Kess. Victoria: Camosun College, 1980, 125–46.

JOURNAL ARTICLES

Airhart, Phyllis D. '"Sweeter Manners, Purer Laws": Women as Temperance Reformers in Late-Victorian Canada.' *Touchstone* 9, 3 (Sept. 1991): 21–31.

Allen, Prudence, RSM. 'Six Canadian Women: Their Call, Their Witness, Their Legacy.' *Canadian Catholic Review* 5, 7 (July-Aug. 1987): 246–58.

Anderson, Cora. 'Shall Women Preach? Principles and Practices in the Salvation Army and in the Methodist Church in Ontario 1882–1900.' *Conrad Grebel Review* 8, 3 (Fall 1990): 275–88.

Arcand, R. 'Expansion et déclin d'une communauté religieuse au Québec, le Soeurs de Sainte Anne (1928–1969).' *Cahiers d'histoire* 9, 3 (Spring 1989): 41–64.

Ballstadt, Carl, Michael Peterman, and Elizabeth Hopkins. '"A Glorious Madness": Susanna Moodie and the Spiritualist Movement.' *Journal of Canadian Studies* 17, 4 (Winter 1982–3): 88–101.

Barnett-Cowan, Alyson. 'The Bishop's Messengers: Harbingers of the Ordination of Women.' *Journal of the Canadian Church Historical Society* 28, 2 (Oct. 1986): 75–91.

Begnal, Reverend Sister Calista. 'The Sisters of the Congregation of Notre-Dame, Nineteenth Century Kingston.' *Canadian Catholic Historical Association Study Sessions* 40 (1973): 27–33.

Belanger, Anne. 'Une éducatrice d'hier pour aujourd'hui: Marie Guyart de l'Incarnation.' *La société canadienne d'histoire de l'Église catholique Sessions d'étude* 39 (1972): 55–64.

Bergeron, Angèle. 'Les Augustines en terre québecoise.' *Église canadienne* 23, 3 (Feb. 1990): 82–4.

Bocking, D.H. 'The First Mission of the Sisters Faithful Companions of Jesus in the North-West Territories, 1883.' *Saskatchewan History* 36, 2 (Spring 1983): 70–7.

Bonin, Sr Marie. 'The Grey Nuns and the Red River Settlement.' *Manitoba History* 11 (Spring 1986): 12–14.

Bradbrook, Pauline. 'A Brief Account of the Church of England Women's Association in Newfoundland.' *Journal of the Canadian Church Historical Society* 28, 2 (Oct. 1986): 92–105.

Brouwer, Ruth Compton. 'Transcending the "Unacknowledged Quarantine": Putting Religion into English-Canadian Women's History.' *Journal of Canadian Studies* 27, 3 (Fall 1992): 47–61.

– 'Moral Nationalism in Victorian Canada: The Case of Agnes Machar.' *Journal of Canadian Studies* 20 (Spring 1985): 90–108.

– 'The "Between-Age" Christianity of Agnes Machar.' *Canadian Historical Review* 65, 3 (Sept. 1984): 347–70.

Caron, Anita, *et al.* 'Femmes dans l'Église catholique: Statut et pouvoir (1945–1985).' *Annales de l'ACFAS* 58 (1990): 399.

Chabot, Marie-Emmanuel. 'Les Ursulines de Québec en 1850.' *La société d'histoire de l'Église catholique Sessions d'étude* 36 (1969): 75–92.

Cliche, Marie-Aimée. 'Droits égaux ou influence accrue? Nature et rôle de la

femme d'après les féministes chrétiennes and les antiféministes au Québec, 1896–
1930.' *Recherches féministes* 2, 2 (1989): 101–20.

Cook, Sharon Anne. 'Educating for Temperance: The Woman's Christian Temperance Union and Ontario Children 1880–1916.' *Historical Studies in Education /
Revue d'histoire de l'éducation* 5, 2 (1993): 251–77.

– 'Letitia Youmans: Ontario's Nineteenth-Century Temperance Educator.'
Ontario History 84, 4 (Dec. 1992): 329–42.

Cooper, Barbara J. 'The Convent: An Option for Quebecoises, 1930–1950.' *Canadian Woman Studies / Les cahiers de la femme* 7, 4 (Winter 1986): 31–5.

Côté, Sylvie. 'Les orphelinats catholiques au Québec de 1900 à 1945.' *Canadian
Woman Studies / Les cahiers de la femme* 7, 4 (winter 1986): 36–8.

d'Allaire, Micheline. 'Jeanne Mance à Montréal en 1642: Une femme d'action qui
force les événements.' *Forces* 23 (1973): 39–46.

– 'Origine sociale des religieuses de l'Hôpital-Général de Québec.' *Revue d'histoire de l'Amérique française* 33, 4 (March 1970): 559–82.

– 'Les prétentions des religieuses de l'Hôpital-Général de Québec.' *Revue d'histoire de l'Amérique française* 33, 1 (June 1969): 53–67.

Danylewycz, Marta. 'Changing Relationships: Nuns and Feminists in Montreal,
1890–1925.' *Social History / Histoire sociale* 14 (Nov. 1981): 413–34; reprinted in
*Prophets, Priests, and Prodigals: Readings in Canadian Religious History, 1608 to
Present*, edited by Mark G. McGowan and David B. Marshall. Toronto:
McGraw-Hill Ryerson, 1992, 191–212.

Davy, Shirley. 'Why Church Women's Organizations Thrived.' *Canadian Woman
Studies* 5, 2 (Winter 1983): 50–61.

de Moissac, Elisabeth. 'Les Soeurs Grises et les événements de 1869–1870.' *La
société canadienne d'histoire de l'Église catholique Sessions d'étude* 37 (1970):
215–28.

Désilets, Andrée. 'Un élan missionaire à Gaspé: Les Soeurs Missionaires du Christ-
Roy (1928–1972). *La société canadienne d'histoire de l'Église catholique Sessions
d'étude* 46 (1979): 65–85.

Dumais, Monique. 'L'originalité de l'oeuvre sociale des congrégations religieuses de
Montréal aux XIXᵉ et XXᵉ siècles.' *Études d'histoire religieuses* 59 (1993): 25–41.

– 'L'autre salut: femmes et religions.' *Recherehes féministes* 3, 2 (1990): 1–11.

– 'Les Religieuses, leur contribution à la societé québécoise.' *Canadian Women's
Studies / Les cahiers de la femme* 3, 1 (1981): 18–20.

Dumont-Johnson, Micheline. 'Les communautés religieuses et la condition féminine.' *Recherches sociographique* 19, 1 (Jan.-Apr. 1978): 79–102.

Dumont, Micheline, and Marie-Paule Malouin. 'Évolution et rôle des congrégations religieuses enseignantes féminines du Québec, 1840–1960.' *La société canadienne d'histoire de l'Église catholique Sessions d'étude* 50, (1983): 201–30.

Epp, Marlene. 'Carrying the Banner of Nonconformity: Ontario Mennonite Women and the Dress Question.' *Conrad Grebel Review* 8, 3 (Fall 1990): 237–58.
- 'The Mennonite Girls' Homes of Winnipeg: A Home Away from Home.' *Journal of Mennonite Studies* 6 (1988): 100–14.
- 'Women in Canadian Mennonite History: Uncovering the "Underside."' *Journal of Mennonite Studies* 5 (1987): 90–107.
Foley, Mary Ann. 'Uncloistered Apostolic Life for Women: Marguerite Bourgeoys' Experiment in Ville-Marie.' *U.S. Catholic Historian* 10, 1 and 2 (1992): 37–44.
Gagan, Rosemary. 'More than "A Lure to the Gilded Bower of Matrimony": The Education of Methodist Women Missionaries, 1881–1925.' *Historical Studies in Education / Revue d'histoire de l'éducation* 1, 2 (Fall 1989): 239–59.
Gagnon, Hervé. 'Les Hospitalières de Saint-Joseph et les premiers pas de Montréal: Vie quotidienne et soins des malades au XVIIe siècle.' *Cahiers d'histoire* 10, 3 (Spring 1990): 5–47.
Graham, Ferne. 'Katharine Hockin: A Woman in Mission.' *Touchstone* 10, 2 (May 1992): 11–19.
Guay, Hélène. 'L'établissement des études classique chez les religieuses de Jésus-Marie à Sillery, d'après un texte de soeur Léa Drolet.' *Recherches féministes* 3, 2 (1990): 179–194.
Hallett, Mary. 'Ladies – We Give You the Pulpit!' *Touchstone* 4, 1 (Jan. 1986): 6–17.
- 'Lydia Gruchy – The First Woman Ordained in the United Church of Canada.' *Touchstone* 4, 1 (Jan. 1986): 18–23.
- 'Nellie McClung and the Fight for the Ordination of Women in the United Church of Canada.' *Atlantis* 4, 2, part 1 (Spring 1979): 2–16.
Hancock, Carol L. 'Nellie L. McClung.' *Touchstone* 1, 1 (Jan. 1983): 31–5.
Headon, Christopher. 'Women and Organized Religion in Mid and Late Nineteenth Century Canada.' *Journal of the Canadian Church Historical Society* 20, 1–2 (1978): 3–18.
Heap, Ruby. 'Les femmes laïques au service de l'enseignement primaire publique catholique à Montréal: les écoles des "dames et demoiselles."' *Canadian Woman Studies / Les cahiers de la femme* 7, 3 (Fall 1986): 55–60.
Henneguin, Jacques. 'Marie de l'Incarnation (l'Ursuline Canadienne) et la Pauvreté.' *XVIIe Siecle* 89 (1970): 3–22.
Hill, Meredith. 'The Women Workers of the Diocese of Athabasca, 1830–70.' *Journal of the Canadian Church Historical Society* 28, 2 (Oct. 1986): 63–74.
Hodder, Morley F. 'Stella Annie Burry: Dedicated Deaconess and Pioneer Community Worker.' *Touchstone* 3, 3 (Oct. 1985): 24–33.
Hooke, Katharine N. 'Women's Teaching and Service: An Anglican Perspective in Ontario, 1867–1930.' *Journal of the Canadian Church Historical Society* 33, 2 (Oct. 1990): 3–23.

Jean, Marguerite. 'L'État et les communautés réligieuses féminines au Québec, 1839–1840. *Studia Canonica* 6, 1 (1972): 163–79.

Juteau, Danielle, and Nicole Laurin. 'From Nuns to Surrogate Mothers: Evolution of the Forms of the Appropriation of Women.' *Feminist Issues* 9, 1 (Spring 1989): 13–40.

- 'Nuns in the Labour Force: A Neglected Contribution.' *Feminist Issues* 6 (Fall 1986): 75–87.

Korinek, Valerie J. 'No Women Need Apply: The Ordination of Women in the United Church, 1918–65.' *Canadian Historical Review* 74, 4 (Dec. 1993): 473–509.

La Palm, Loretta. 'The Hotel-Dieu of Quebec: The First Hospital North of the Rio Grande under Its First Two Superiors.' *Canadian Catholic Historical Association Study Sessions* 41 (1974): 53–64.

La Serre, Claudette. 'L'église et l'éducation des filles au Québec de 1850 à 1950.' *Canadian Woman Studies / Les cahiers de la femme* 5, 2 (Winter 1983): 21–3.

Lauer, Bernarda. 'Russian Germans and the Ursulines of Prelate, Sask., 1919–1934.' *Canadian Catholic Historical Association Study Sessions* 46 (1979): 83–98.

Laurin, Nicole. 'Le travail des religieuses au Québec, de 1901 à 1971.' *Annales de l'ACFAS* 58 (1990): 401.

Lee, Danielle Juteau. 'Les religieuses du Québec: Leur influence sur la vie professionelle des femmes, 1908–1954.' *Atlantis* 5, 2 (Spring 1980): 22–33.

'Les Ursulines de Gaspé: Une demi-siècle de présence, 1924–1974.' *Revue d'histoire de la Gaspésie* (April/June 1974): 76–189.

Loewen, Royden K. '"The Children, the Cows, My Dear Man, and My Sister": The Transplanted Lives of Mennonite Farm Women, 1874–1900.' *Canadian Historical Review* 78, 3 (Sept. 1992): 344–73.

McFarlane, John. 'Dr Jessie Saulteaux: The Faith Goes On.' *Touchstone* 9, 1 (Jan. 1991): 41–6.

McGuire, Rita. 'The Grey Sisters in the Red River Settlement, 1844–1870.' *Canadian Catholic Historical Association Historical Studies* 53 (1986): 21–37.

McKeen, R. Catherine. 'Harriet Christie: The People-Maker Lady.' *Touchstone* 8, 2 (May 1990): 20–34.

Macleod, G. Enid, and Irene M.J. Szuler. 'Medical Missionaries of the Early Female Medical Graduates, 1894–1929.' *Nova Scotia Medical Journal* 69, 1 (Feb. 1990): 7–14, 30.

McMahon, Nancy. 'Les Religieuses Hospitalières de Saint Joseph and the Typhus Epidemic, Kingston, 1847–1848.' *Canadian Catholic Historical Association Historical Studies* (1991) 41–55.

McMullen, Lorraine. 'Lily Dougall: The Religious Vision of a Canadian Novelist.' *Studies in Religion / Sciences religieuses* 16, 1 (1987): 79–90.

McPherson, Margaret E. '"From Caretakers to Participants": Amanda Norris MacKay and the Presbyterian Women's Missionary Society, 1876–1925.' *Touchstone* 9, 3 (Sept. 1991): 32–44.

Macpherson, Sarah. 'Religious Women in Nova Scotia: A Struggle for Autonomy: A Sketch of the Sisters of St Martha of Antigonish, Nova Scotia, 1900–1960.' *Canadian Catholic Historical Association Historical Studies* 51 (1984): 89–106.

Marr, Lucille. 'Church Teen Clubs, Feminized Organizations? Tuxis Boys, Trail Rangers, and Canadian Girls in Training, 1919–1939.' *Historical Studies in Education / Revue d'histoire de l'éducation* 3, 2 (Fall 1991): 249–314.

– 'Hierarchy, Gender and the Goals of the Religious Educators in the Canadian Presbyterian, Methodist, and United Churches, 1919–1939.' *Studies in Religion / Sciences Religieuses* 20, 1 (Autumn 1991): 65–74.

– 'Anabaptist Women of the North: Peers in the Faith, Subordinates in Marriage.' *Mennonite Quarterly Review* 61 (Oct. 1987): 347–62.

Mitchinson, Wendy. 'The Woman's Christian Temperance Union: A Study in Organization.' *International Journal of Women's Studies* 4, 2 (1981): 143–56.

– 'The YWCA and Reform in the Nineteenth Century.' *Histoire sociale / Social History* 12 (Nov. 1979): 368–84.

– 'Canadian Women and Church Missionary Societies in the Nineteenth Century: A Step Towards Independence.' *Atlantis* 2, 2, part 2 (Spring 1977): 57–75.

Morgan, Cecilia. 'Gender, Religion, and Rural Society: Quaker Women in Norwich, Ontario, 1820–1880.' *Ontario History* 82, 4 (Dec. 1990): 273–87.

Morrison, George M. 'Emma Douse Crosby "Mother of The Tsimpsheans."' *Touchstone* 4, 3 (Oct. 1986): 38–45.

Nicholson, Murray W. 'Women in the Irish-Canadian Catholic Family.' *Polyphony* 8, 1–2 (1986): 9–12.

O'Gallagher, Marianna. 'The Sisters of Charity of Halifax – the Early and Middle Years.' *Canadian Catholic Historical Association Study Sessions* 47 (1980): 57–68.

Pedersen, Diana. '"Building Today for the Womanhood of Tomorrow": Businessmen, Boosters, and the YWCA, 1890–1930.' *Urban History Review* 15, 3 (Feb. 1987): 225–42.

– '"Keeping Our Good Girls Good": The YWCA and the "Girl Problem," 1870–1930.' *Canadian Woman Studies / Les cahiers de la femme* 7, 4 (Winter 1986): 20–4.

Pelletier-Baillargeon, Hélène. 'La Québécoise d'hier.' *Canadian Woman Studies / Les cahiers de la femme* 5, 2 (Winter 1983): 42–4.

Prang, Margaret. 'Caroline Macdonald of Japan.' *Touchstone* 6, 1 (Jan. 1988): 33–42.

– '"The Girl God Would Have Me Be": The Canadian Girls in Training, 1915–39.' *Canadian Historical Review* 66, 2 (1985): 154–84.

Reid, Elspeth M. 'Women's Missionary Records in the Presbyterian Archives.'
Archivaria 30 (Summer 1990): 171–9.

Ridout, Katherine. 'A Woman of Mission: The Religious and Cultural Odyssey of
Agnes Wintemute Coates.' *Canadian Historical Review* 71, 2 (June 1990): 208–
44.

Roberts, Barbara. 'Sex, Politics, and Religion: Controversies in French Immigration
Reform Work in Montreal, 1881–1919.' *Atlantis* 6, 1 (Fall 1980): 25–38.

Rooke, Patricia T., and R.L. Schnell. 'The Rise and Decline of British North American Protestant Orphans' Homes as Women's Domain, 1850–1930.' *Atlantis* 7, 2
(Spring 1982): 21–35.

Rousseau, François. 'Hôpital et société en Nouvelle-France: L'Hôtel Dieu de
Québec à la fin du XVIIe siècle.' *Revue d'histoire de l'Amérique française* 31, 1
(June 1977): 29–48.

Royce, Marion V. 'Education for Girls in Quaker Schools in Ontario.' *Atlantis* 3, 1
(Fall 1977): 181–92.

– 'Methodism and the Education of Women in Nineteenth Century Ontario.'
Atlantis 3, 2, part 1 (Spring 1978): 131–43.

Selles-Roney, Johanna. 'A Canadian Girl at Cheltenham: The Diary as an Historical Source.' *Historical Studies in Education / Revue d'histoire de l'éducation* 3, 1
(Spring 1991): 93–104.

Sheehan, Nancy M. 'The WCTU and Educational Strategies on the Canadian Prairie.' *History of Education Quarterly* (1984): 101–19.

– '"Women Helping Women": The WCTU and the Foreign Population in the
West, 1905–1930.' *Prairie Forum* 6, 5 (Nov./Dec. 1983): 395–411.

– 'The WCTU on the Prairies, 1886–1930: An Alberta-Saskatchewan Comparison.' *Prairie Forum* 6, 1 (Spring 1981): 17–33.

– 'Temperance, Education, and the WCTU in Alberta, 1905–1910.' *Journal of Educational Thought* 14 (1980): 108–24.

Simmons, Christina. '"Helping the Poorer Sisters": The Women of the Jost Mission, Halifax, 1905–1945.' *Acadiensis* 14 (Autumn 1984): 3–27. Reprinted in
Rethinking Canada: The Promise of Women's History, edited by Veronica
Strong-Boag and Anita Clair Fellman. Toronto: Copp Clark Pitman, 1986, 157–
77; also in 2nd ed., 1991, 286–307.

Sinclair, Donna. 'Victoria Cheung.' *Touchstone* 11, 3 (Sept. 1993): 37–43.

Sinclair-Faulkner, Tom. 'One Size Fits All: Marie de l'Incarnation.' *Touchstone* 10,
1 (Jan. 1992): 40–5.

Smyth, Elizabeth. '*Congregavit nos in unum Christi amor*: The Congregation of the
Sisters of St Joseph, in the Archdiocese of Toronto, 1851–1920.' *Ontario History*
84, 3 (Sept., 1992): 225–40.

– '"Developing the Powers of the Youthful Mind": The Evolution of Education for Young Women at St Joseph's Academy, Toronto, 1845–1911.' *Canadian Catholic Historical Studies* 690 (1993–4), 103–25.

Stackhouse, John G. 'Women in Public Ministry in 20th-Century Canadian and American Evangelicalism: 5 Models.' *Studies in Religion / Sciences religieuses* 17, 4 (1988): 471–85.

Thomas, John D. 'Servants of the Church: Canadian Methodist Deaconess Work, 1890–1926.' *Canadian Historical Review* 65, 3 (September 1984): 371–95.

Thompson, Arthur N. 'The Wife of the Missionary.' *Journal of the Canadian Church Historical Society* 15, 2 (June 1973): 35–44.

Verdun, Christyl. 'La religion dans le journal d'Henriette Fadette.' *Atlantis* 8, 2 (Spring 1983): 45–50.

Whitehead, Margaret. 'A Useful Christian Woman: First Nations Women and Protestant Missionary Work in British Columbia.' *Atlantis* 18, 1 and 2 (Fall-Summer 1992–93): 142–66.

– 'Women Were Made for Such Things: Women Missionaries in British Columbia, 1850s–1940s.' *Atlantis* 14, 1 (Fall 1988): 141–50.

Whiteley, Marilyn. '"Allee Samee Melican Lady": Imperialism and Negotiation at the Chinese Rescue Home.' *Resources for Feminist Research / Documentation sur la recherche féministe* 22 (1993), 45–50.

– '"Doing Just About What They Please": Ladies' Aids in Ontario Methodism.' *Ontario History* 82, 4 (Dec. 1990): 289–304.

– 'Elizabeth Dimsdale Aikenhead: "Lady Evangelist."' *Touchstone* 7, 1 (Jan. 1989): 35–41.

Zink, Sister Ella. 'Immigrants and the Church: The Sisters of Service – 1920–1930.' *Canadian Catholic Historical Association Study Sessions* 43 (1976): 23–38.

PRINTED PAPERS

Airhart, Phyllis. 'Sobriety, Sentimentality and Science: The WCTU and the Reconstruction of Christian Womanhood.' In *Papers of the Canadian Methodist Historical Society* (1990), 117–36.

Brouwer, Ruth Compton. 'The Canadian Methodist Church and Ecclesiastical Suffrage for Women, 1902–1914.' In *Papers of the Canadian Methodist Historical Society*, vol. 2 [n.d.], 1–27.

– '"New Women" for God: Marion Fairweather and the Founding of the Canadian Presbyterian Mission in Central India, 1873–80.' In *Papers of the Canadian Historical Association* (1984).

– 'Presbyterian Women and the Foreign Missionary Movement, 1876–1914: The Context of a Calling.' In *Papers of the Canadian Society of Presbyterian History* (1985), 1–24.

- 'Wooing "the Heathen" and the Raj: Aspects of Women's Work in the Canadian Presbyterian Mission, in Central India, 1877–1914.' In *Papers of the Canadian Society of Church History* (1987), 17–32.

Colwell, Judith. 'The Role of Women in the Nineteenth Century Baptist Church of Ontario.' In *Papers of the Canadian Society of Church History* (1985), 31–57.

Gagan, Rosemary. 'The Methodist Background of Canadian WMS Missionaries.' In *Papers of the Canadian Methodist Historical Society* (1989), 115–36.

Gossage, Peter. 'Foundlings and the Institution: The Case of the Grey Nuns of Montreal.' In *Canadian Historical Association Historical Papers* (1986).

Grant, John Webster. 'Presbyterian Women and the Indians.' In *Papers of the Canadian Society of Presbyterian History* (1978), 21–36.

Ivison, Stuart. 'The Activities of Margaret Edwards Cole (1853–1929): As a Baptist Church Member, Journalist, Temperance Worker, and Advocate of Women's Suffrage in Canada.' In *Papers of the Canadian Society of Church History* (1984), 140–55.

Marr, Lucille. 'Hierarchy, Gender, and the Goals of Religious Educators in the Canadian Presbyterian, Methodist and United Churches.' In *Papers of the Canadian Society of Church History* (1990), 1–28.

- 'Sunday School Teaching: A Women's Enterprise.' In *Papers of the Canadian Historical Association* (1991).

Muir, Elizabeth. 'Methodist Women Preachers: An Overview.' In *Papers of the Canadian Methodist Historical Society* (1987), 46–57.

- 'Petticoats in the Pulpit: Three Early Canadian Methodist Women.' In *Papers of the Canadian Society of Church History* (1984), 26–49.

- 'Woman As Preacher: Early 19th Century Canadians.' In *Women: Images, Role-Models*, CRIAW Conference Proceedings (1984), 195–201.

Prang, Margaret. 'Caroline Macdonald and Prison Work in Japan.' In *University of Toronto-York University Joint Centre for Asia Pacific Studies, Working Paper Series* (March 1988), 1–34.

Ross, H. Miriam. 'Women's Strategies for Mission: Hannah Maria Norris Blazes the Trail in 1870.' In *Papers of the Canadian Society of Church History* (1992), 5–23.

Whiteley, Marilyn Färdig. '"My Highest Motive in Writing": Evangelical Empowerment in the Autobiography of Annie Leake Tuttle.' In *Papers of the Canadian Society of Church History* (1992), 25–38.

- 'Conversion and Corrective Domesticity: The Mission of the Chinese Rescue Home.' In *Papers of the Canadian Methodist Historical Society* (1990), 158–173.

- 'Called to a More Suitable Mission: Conversion in the Life of Annie Leake Tuttle.' In *Papers of the Canadian Methodist Historical Society* (1988), 34–47.

- 'Women Learning to Work for Women: The Chinese Rescue Home in Victoria, B.C.' In *Papers of the Canadian Society of Church History* (1988), 87–96.

– 'Modest, Unaffected and Fully Consecrated: Lady Evangelists in Canadian Methodism, 1884–1900.' In *Papers of the Canadian Methodist Historical Society* (1987), 18–31.

THESES AND DISSERTATIONS

Blais, Gabrielle. 'The Complete Feminine Personality: Female Adolescence in the Canadian Girls in Training (CGIT) 1915–1955.' MA dissertation, University of Ottawa, 1986.
Boivin, Denis J.A. 'Marie de l'Incarnation: Catéchète.' MA thesis, Université Laval, 1986.
Brouwer, Ruth. 'Canadian Women and the Foreign Missionary Movement: A Case Study of Presbyterian Women's Involvement at the Home Base and in Central India, 1876–1914.' PhD dissertation, York University, 1987.
Clifton, Lloyd M. 'Nellie McClung: A Representative of the Canadian Social Gospel Movement.' ThM thesis, Knox College, 1979.
Cook, Sharon Anne. '"Continued and Persevering Combat": The Ontario Woman's Christian Temperance Union, Evangelicalism, and Social Reform, 1874–1916.' PhD dissertation, Carleton University, 1990.
Cooper, Barbara J. 'In the Spirit: Entrants to a Religious Community of Women in Quebec, 1930–1939.' MA thesis, McGill University, 1983.
– '"That We May Attain to the End We Propose to Ourselves …": The North American Institute of the Blessed Virgin Mary, 1921–1961.' PhD dissertation, York University, 1989.
Coops, P. Lorraine. 'Not a Romantic Notion: Single Women Missionaries from the Maritime Baptist Convention Who Served in the Telugu Fields in India, 1880–1912,' MA thesis, Queen's University, 1992.
Dufresne, Yolande. 'Reconnaissance ecclésiale des premières constitutions: Soeurs des Saints-Noms de Jésus et de Marie, 1843–1887.' MA thesis, University of Ottawa, 1985.
Eaton, Linda M. 'The Issue of Female Ordination in the Maritime Baptist Convention, 1929–1954.' BA (Hon) thesis, Mount Allison University, 1989.
Gagan, Rosemary. 'A Sensitive Independence: The Personnel of the Women's Missionary Society of the Methodist Church of Canada, 1881–1925.' PhD dissertation, McMaster University, 1987.
Hall, Nancy. '"Not by Might, Nor by Power, But by My Spirit": Women Workers in the United Church of Canada, 1890–1940.' MA thesis, University of Manitoba, 1986.
Hansen, Denise Mary. 'Sisters Unite – The Maritime Baptist Woman's Missionary Movement, 1867–1914.' BA (Hon) thesis, Acadia University, 1979.

Heap, Ruby. 'L'Église, l'État et l'éducation au Québec, 1875–1898.' MA thesis, McGill University, 1978.

Langlois, Marielle. 'Le développement de la pédagogie chez les Filles de la Charité du Sacré-Coeur de Jésus, 1911–1969.' MA thesis, Université de Sherbrooke, 1987.

Legendre, Anne Carmelle. 'The Baptist Contribution to 19th Century Education for Women: An Examination of Moulton College and McMaster University.' MA thesis, McMaster University, 1981.

Louagie, Kimberly. 'Women's Groups in Two Ottawa Churches: Glebe United and St Giles Presbyterian Church, 1925–1950.' MA thesis, University of Ottawa, 1992.

MacFarlane, Mary Anne. 'Gender, Doctrine, and Pedagogy: Women and "Womanhood" in Methodist Sunday Schools in English-Speaking Canada, 1880 to 1920. PhD dissertation, University of Toronto, 1992.

– 'A Tale of Handmaidens: Deaconesses in the United Church of Canada, 1925–1964.' MA thesis, University of Toronto, 1987.

Marr, Lucille. 'Church Hierarchy and Christian Nurture: The Significance of Gender in Religious Education in the Methodist, Presbyterian, and United Churches of Canada, 1919–1939.' PhD dissertation, University of Waterloo, 1990.

Mitchinson, Wendy. 'Aspects of Reform: Four Women's Organizations in Nineteenth Century Canada.' PhD dissertation, York University, 1977.

Muir, Elizabeth. 'Petticoats in the Pulpit: Early Nineteenth Century Methodist Women Preachers in Upper Canada.' PhD dissertation, McGill University, 1990.

Pedersen, Diana. 'The Young Women's Christian Association in Canada, 1870–1920: "A Movement to Meet a Spiritual, Civic and National Need."' PhD dissertation, Carleton University, 1987.

Plante, Lucienne. 'L'enseignement classique chez les soeurs de la Congrégation de Notre Dame, 1908–1971.' PhD thesis, Université Laval, 1971.

Profit, Elizabeth L. 'Education for Women in the Baptist Tradition: An Examination of the Work of the Canadian Literary Institute, Moulton Ladies' College and McMaster Divinity College.' MTS thesis, McMaster Divinity College, 1987.

Proulx, Marcienne. 'L'action sociale de Marie Gérin-Lajoie, 1910–1925.' MA thesis, Université de Sherbrooke, 1976.

Redekop, Gloria L. Neufeld. 'Mennonite Women's Societies in Canada: A Historical Case Study.' PhD Thesis, University of Ottawa, 1993.

Smyth, Elizabeth. 'The Lessons of Religion and Science: The Congregation of the Sisters of St Joseph and St Joseph's Academy Toronto, 1854–1911.' EdD dissertation, University of Toronto, 1990.

Warne, R.R. 'Literature as Pulpit: Narrative as a Vehicle for the Transmission and Transformation of Values in the Christian Social Action of Nellie McClung.' PhD dissertation, University of Toronto, 1988.

Index

opportunities for women in, 10–11, 177; Social Gospel in, 340

Van Cott, Margaret Newton, 176
Vancouver, United Church of Canada women employed in, 242
Veazey, Abby, 143
Viger, Amanda. *See* St Jean de Goto, Sister
Village Island, 123, 125
volunteer work: by Anglican women, 220–37; and employed church workers, 11; by leisure class women, 228–9; by married women, 11; by middle class women, 288

Waldron, Susannah Farley, 167–8
Walkowitz, Judith, 309
Webb, Mary, 79
Weber, Urias K., 61
Wells, Rev. G.H., 332
Welter, Barbara, 287
Wesley, John, 151, 163, 166–7, 186, 196, 202, 204, 209–10
Wilberforce, William, 290–1
Wilcox, Herb, 205
Willard, Frances, 120–1, 198n7, 302
Willard Home (Toronto), 314
Williams, Mrs, 85
Williams, Sadie, 188–9, 191, 193–4
Wilson, Isaac, 170
Wilson, Jane Woodill, 170
Winnipeg, United Church of Canada women employed in, 242
Winnipeg General Strike (1919), 347
Wintemute, Agnes, 149
Woman's Auxiliary (Anglican), 221, 233
Woman's Baptist Missionary Union, 3, 83–9; friction with Foreign Mission

Board, 83–5; leadership of, 88–9; and mission education, 85–8
Woman's Foreign Missionary Society (Presbyterian) 100–16; control over candidature by, 112–13; and control of Native work, 112; expansion of, 104; financial power of, 100, 104, 113, 113–14n2; and Foreign Mission Committee, 103–4, 110–13; founding of, 100, 111; in India and Taiwan, 101; later Native work of, 110; missionaries of, background, 106–7; organization of, 110–11; responsibility for work with women, 101, 105; and 'special objects,' 106; start of work with Natives by, 102–3; work of Lucy Baker for, 107–8; work of Catherine Gillespie for, 108–10
Woman's Journal, 303, 314–15
Woman's Mission Aid Societies (Baptist), 81–4
Woman's Missionary Society (Methodist), 111, 137–57; conflict with General Board of Missions, 147–8; as employer of deaconesses, 252; and evolution of missionary work, 138; independence of, 185; inquiry of, into controversy, 149; origin, 140; at Presbyterian meeting, 102; and women's right to preach, 120–2
Woman's Missionary Society (Methodist) Japan mission: administration of, 144; age of missionaries at, 152; and challenge to patriarchal authority, 151; conflict with General Board missionaries in, 138–9, 143–6; consequences of gender controversies of, 139, 151; and 'cult of true womanhood,' 141–2; defence of Eliza Large, 148; educational work of, 140–1; fol-